The Divided Path

The Divided Path

*The German Influence
on Social Reform in France
after 1870*

by Allan Mitchell

The University of North Carolina Press / Chapel Hill and London

95   94   93   92   91   5   4   3   2   1

Library of Congress Cataloging-in-Publication Data
Mitchell, Allan.
   The divided path : the German influence on social reform in France
after 1870 / by Allan Mitchell.
      p.   cm.
   Includes bibliographical references and index.
   ISBN 0-8078-1964-6 (cloth : alk. paper)
   1. Public welfare—France—History—19th century.   2. Public welfare—
France—History—20th century.   3. France—Relations—Germany.   4. Germany—
Relations—France.   5. France—Social conditions—19th century.   6. France—
Social conditions—20th century.   7. France—Politics and government—1870–
1940.   I. Title.
HV265.M58   1991
361.944—dc20   90-23845
                                                                      CIP

Contents

Tables

Preface

This book completes a trilogy that has occupied me for the better part of two decades. When I began the first volume, of course, I already had some notion of the third and was certain that it would treat "the social question." Yet I cannot now claim much clairvoyance about the actual contents. One needs only to scan the bibliography of scholarly publications to see how much progress has occurred in social history during recent years: over half of the titles listed have appeared since 1980. Before then, that is, many aspects of this study were literally inconceivable. There is thus good reason for me to be grateful to many colleagues who have labored mightily in the archives and whose findings have been indispensable for my own work. I hope that they, in turn, will view with some indulgence my efforts to gain footing in their areas of specialization.

A preface is hardly the place for true confessions, but the reader should realize that I was born in the United States as a son of immigrant parents (from Scotland) and as an offspring of the Depression and the New Deal. These circumstances help to explain a certain passion that I have brought to my research and writing. Not only do I hold that a society is obligated to offer equality of opportunity to citizens of every origin; I am also persuaded that politics should serve to promote that ideal, however unattainable it may be in practice. I therefore believe in the necessity of state intervention to deal with social problems. It is this premise, and not a preference for Germany over France, that has colored my judgment about events in Europe. Surely no American in my lifetime has any reason to observe with smugness the difficulties of late nineteenth-century France. Insofar as social policy is concerned, the parallels between the French republic then and the American republic now are impossible to ignore. It affords little comfort to conclude that, a full century later, the United States has barely attained the level of the early Third Republic in crucial matters of public health and welfare.

With respect to scholarship, fortunately, the situation is less bleak, to which I can testify as the recipient of senior research grants from the Fulbright Commission and the National Endowment for the Humanities. Their assistance made possible two long periods of investigation in France. For shorter research trips to Germany I am also indebted to the Deutscher Akademischer Austauschdienst and to the Fritz-Thyssen-Stiftung. Two generous colleagues were instrumental in arranging pleasant surroundings for reflection and discussion: Jürgen Kocka at the Zentrum für Interdisziplinäre Forschung in Bielefeld and Stefi Jersch-Wenzel at the Historische Kommission zu Berlin.

In such an extensive undertaking as this, the expert advice of others has been essential. For their combination of personal encouragement and professional criticism, I want to thank Marilyn Boxer, Patrick Fridenson, Peter Hennock, Martha Hildreth, Bennetta Jules-Rosette, Annemarie Kleinert-Ludwig, Gabriel Motzkin, Christoph Sachsse, Johanna Schmid, and Hannes Siegrist. Likewise, the *conservateur* of the Musée Social in Paris, Mme. Colette Chambelland, was an amiable source of bibliographical information. No less important in that regard was the help offered by the staff of the Assistance Publique de Paris in the Service de la Documentation et des Archives at 7 rue des Minimes, a "good address" for every scholar of French social history.

In the preparation of the manuscript I received aid from Donna Andrews, who introduced me to the mysteries of word processing and provided a prompt *service de dépannage*. Helene Carol Brown was a peerless research assistant, who tracked down a thousand details and saved me from unspeakable embarrassments. Above all, I owe gratitude to Lewis Bateman, executive editor of the University of North Carolina Press, who believed in this project from the beginning and who has supported it throughout.

Finally, I want to mention the late Yigal Shiloh. During one long, hot summer in Jerusalem he taught me the difference between the nineteenth century B.C. and A.D. Then, far too soon, he was cut down. He never finished his book, but to him this one is gratefully dedicated.

La Jolla, California
October 1990

Introduction

The history of the French Third Republic between the wars of
1870 and 1914 was crossed by three major waves of reform. The first
appeared during the initial decade after the military disaster at Sedan, which ended the reign of Bonapartism and brought its liberal
opposition to power. Out of the confused and unstable circumstances
of those early years emerged a certain kind of republic whose middling orientation in politics and economics has left deep traces ever
since.[1] Meanwhile, a second wave began almost at once after 1870,
although it did not crest until two decades later. One of its aspects
was military reform, which was inaugurated by a recruitment law in
1872 that established the principle of universal conscription. But in
reality it was not until the end of the 1880s that provision was made
for a system of three-year service that finally set France on the way to
a citizen army. At the same time controversy over religious issues
grew increasingly rancorous, especially in regard to educational reforms. Once more, the principle of universal primary schooling was
quickly accepted, but its full implications remained problematical.
Not only did anticlerical pressure to enforce secularization produce
endless friction, but structural and curricular disputes also delayed
implementation of reform legislation. Hence, a critical revision of
secondary education—the establishment of a "modern" track to parallel the classical French *lycée*—was not adopted before the 1890s.[2]

By then a third wave of reform was manifest, a movement for the
improvement of public health and welfare, which is the subject of
this book. It is my intention in treating "the social question" (as it was
commonly called at the time) to present both a thesis and a synthesis.

The thesis has been sufficiently explained in the preceding two volumes of this trilogy: that the public life of republican France after 1870 was heavily influenced in all of its major facets by imperial Germany. As I began my research into the social history of the period, this premise naturally guided my approach to the archives. Yet it would have been unconscionably reductionist to seek nothing more than direct references to Germany and to ignore the broader context of France's social problems. Accordingly, I have tried to conduct my investigation with as wide a lens as possible, hoping thereby to bring a balanced synthesis of French social history into focus. This dual objective seems all the more appropriate given my assumption that a full appreciation of the special relationship between France and Germany is crucial to our understanding of the development of modern Europe.

In attempting to define the social question and to evaluate the extent of German influence in France, my thinking was initially guided by three earlier studies that were quite diverse in their nature. The first was René Rémond's lucid three-volume survey of the European experience since the Old Regime.[3] As Professor Rémond had been my teacher at the Institut d'Etudes Politiques in Paris, his work provided a familiar orientation. I was able to renew my admiration for the keenness and clarity of his analysis, which is a model of what a textbook should be. Moreover, it has the virtue of calling specific attention to the expanding role of the state everywhere in Europe during the nineteenth century: "It is henceforth called upon to correct social inequities, to regulate exchanges, to stimulate activities. . . . The extension of its attributes is marked by a change of kind in the notion of responsibility."[4] Persuasively as this central theme is presented, nonetheless, for my purposes it suffered from two deficiencies. First, Rémond displays no special knowledge of German historiography (as he does of French, English, and American) and he cannot therefore summon all the accumulated research *outre Rhin* that might have furnished his account. Furthermore, and more fundamentally, Rémond's entire conception of modern Europe posits that the impulse for social reform invariably passed from West to East. Accordingly, he is bound to regard the introduction of welfare measures in republican France strictly as "extensions of the [Western] democratic idea" rather than as responses to the example of an autocratic Eastern neighbor. As a consequence, neither in his discussion of obligatory military conscription nor of compulsory primary education does Rémond acknowledge that these reforms had already been implemented to good effect by the Germans. The same oversight recurs in reference to social reform, for which he omits any mention of Germany's pathbreaking legislation or its influence on France.[5] The reader of my work will readily understand why it was unavoidable for me, after all, to abandon this view and to revise some of its primary tenets.

That enterprise was greatly assisted by Henri Hatzfeld's brilliant 1971 dissertation on the evolution of French social security in the century after 1850.[6] Heretofore this book has constituted the only major synthetic treatment of French welfare in the late nineteenth century. Invaluable to any researcher of that era, Professor Hatzfeld's account is sinuous and probing, particularly in its portrayal of those elements in French society that applied (as he says) either an accelerator or a brake to state intervention in the area of public health and hygiene. Two limitations of his technique are conceded by Hatzfeld himself: his study is that of a sociologist who is more concerned to derive analytic categories than to observe chronology; and it deliberately eschews international comparisons. The first of these is bound to befuddle historians, who might wish for a more consecutive and uncluttered presentation, but they will nevertheless find his random *aperçus* intelligent and insightful. And the second is perhaps only sensible, given the intrinsic complexity of Hatzfeld's topic and the paucity of competent secondary literature at his disposal two decades ago. Besides, Hatzfeld demonstrates a complete awareness that the German model was carefully weighed by French reformers, even when it was rejected by them. These self-criticisms may thus be waived as relatively inconsequential. The principal shortcoming of Hatzfeld's contribution actually lies elsewhere, and it can be simply put: he never entered an archive. His explication of social problems and welfare legislation is derived exclusively from printed parliamentary proceedings. He has, in other words, accepted the public record of debate as a valid basis of research. For reasons that should become clear, I could not do likewise. In a sense, I have attempted to continue Hatzfeld's journey by delving into such unpublished sources as the minutes of parliamentary committees, ministerial papers, and private correspondence. These, I believe, provide us with a far more revealing and complete picture of reform motives than the rhetorical duels of French politicians. Future historians are certain to find Hatzfeld a reliable guide, but only for the opening phases of their inquiry. Like me, they must regret that he has taken leave from us at the threshold of the archives.

Especially challenging for me was a third book, edited by Peter Flora and Arnold J. Heidenheimer, that compares different forms of welfare in Europe and America.[7] The various authors in this collection of essays are concerned to question the concept of "diffusion" (which I have termed "influence") among modern nations. There exists an obvious consensus among them that Germany assumed a pioneering role in welfare reform, but they express doubts about the process whereby other states were affected—or not—by the German precedent. Social insurance schemes, they conjecture, might have developed independently: "The mere fact that the other countries followed chronologically is not sufficient proof that these countries were decisively influenced by the German example." In order to establish such proof, "we would have to know whether the German institutions were really viewed as a model by the public, the legislators, and administrators in other countries."[8] Unfortunately, as the editors note, it was impossible for them to offer an analysis for all Western nations, and among those missing was France. It is precisely this conspicuous lacuna that I have undertaken to fill. Whether Flora and Heidenheimer will entirely agree with my conclusions is moot, but I trust that they will recognize this volume as an effort to address the fundamental questions posed in their anthology.

None of the foregoing three titles is mentioned here merely to point out imperfections. All have caused me to examine my methods and preconceptions, and each has helped me to locate my work amid the overabundance of monographs and documents with which every historian of modern Europe must ultimately contend.

A few peculiarities of the present volume should be indicated. One of them is sure to cause the reader some difficulty: the unusually large cast of supporting actors and spear carriers. Political and military historians can ordinarily assume a reasonable familiarity with the names of prime ministers, party bosses, marshals, and generals. But the subject of social reform is less customary and many of the minor personalities may appear obscure. Perhaps one should distinguish among three levels. At the top were those political leaders with established national reputations: Léon Bourgeois, Jules Simon, Alexandre Millerand, Jean Jaurès, and Georges Clemenceau. Behind them came a second cluster whose contribution was hardly less essential but whose public activity was more directly attached to the implementation of social reform: Henri Monod, Émile Cheysson, Paul Strauss, Jules Siegfried, Paul Guieysse, Paul Brouardel, and Jacques Bertillon. Finally there followed a considerable number of little-known individuals who played less prominent roles but who provided significant support on certain occasions: A.-J. Martin, Lucien Dreyfus-Brisac, Henri-Alfred Henrot, Émile Rey, Jean Cruppi, Albert Bluzet, Henry Fleury-Ravarin, Pierre Paplier, Henri Schmidt, and many others. Whenever we speak of "the reformers" in France, such names also deserve to be remembered, and they have found a place here.

A similar problem was created by the proliferation of welfare organizations, bureaucratic agencies, and pressure groups during the Belle Epoque. The result was a lively trade in administrative titles that has generated confusion then and now. Some of the appellations were cited irregularly; several changed in form over time; and many were barely distinguishable from one another. I have attempted to sort out these ambiguities, and in a few instances I have supplied an abbreviation or acronym to aid in the identification of the Conseil Supérieur de l'Assistance Publique (CSAP), the Commission d'Assurance et Prévoyance Sociales (CAPS), the Comité Consultatif de l'Hygiène Publique (CCHP), and so forth. I hope that these mnemonic devices will relieve rather than compound the reader's inevitable trouble in identifying the different forums of reform activity.

At the end of this concluding volume I have appended a general summary of the entire trilogy. Drafting that brief essay proved to be fiendishly difficult. To compress is to simplify, and to narrate is to omit analytic subtleties. Yet I felt that it was important to integrate my findings into a concise overview that would recall the main themes announced in the introduction of my first volume: political innovation, economic adjustment, military reorganization, religious controversy, and social transition. "My purpose will be served," I wrote then, "if these volumes add to a comprehensive understanding of the early years of the Third Republic and also provide a basis for further studies of the Franco-German confrontation that has dominated western Europe ever since." I can only repeat that aspiration now and hope that my contract has been, however imperfectly, fulfilled.

Part One

Private Charity and Public Health

Chapter 1

The Aegis of Liberalism

The middle of the nineteenth century is commonly recognized as the liberal era of European history. Yet specialists of that period readily concede the extreme difficulty of deriving a coherent definition of liberalism. The complexities and disparities of liberal theory defy any neat analytic structure; and the multiplicity of liberal practice tends to defeat even the most ingenious schemes of classification.[1]

Disagreement therefore persists about the most appropriate grouping of the three major west European nations—not to mention the smaller ones. One view stresses the vigorous and pervasive liberal dynamic of English tradition, contrasting that with a more cautious and contested liberalism on the Continent.[2] Another regards the German variant as unique because of its unbroken attachment to the authority of the state, unlike the more democratically oriented liberalism of "the West."[3] A third school dwells on the pivotal role of Gallic liberalism, granting scant attention to the rest and implicitly according a special status to French experience as the bellwether of political thought before and after the Great Revolution.[4]

In the face of such daunting theoretical perplexities, it is well to begin with a few elementary assumptions. First, we may suppose that every one of the principal European countries boasted a form of liberalism that was distinctive. There exists, after all, no absolute criterion by which to determine what was normative and what was not. The distribution of ideal liberal types actually reveals little more than the predilection of certain scholars. Second, there is ample reason to posit that European liberalism, although fragmented, nevertheless possessed an identifiable core of shared intellectual premises. If a political and social terminology retains any claim at all to descriptive force, it must finally be definable as an analytical category that has an irreducible number of basic postulates. Hence liberalism, to put it succinctly, may be fairly characterized as an ideology that stressed individualism, limitations of governmental intervention, and allowance for the free enterprise of commercial interests.[5] Third, however, we cannot be content to leave this matter at rest in the realm of theory. Liberalism was above all a historical phenomenon that was transmuted over time. Any analysis of a great nation like France must therefore be willing to enter the arena of everyday existence and to inquire about the practical implications for the many ordinary people whose lives were affected by liberal creed.

The Problem of Pauperism

In the beginning was poverty. It had always existed, and only an eccentric utopian could imagine that it would ever cease to exist. Yet social perceptions of the problem altered noticeably over time. In the seventeenth century, it has been plausibly argued, the poor were largely ignored. If so, that was certainly not true in the eighteenth. The reasons for such a marked change in attitude have been intensively studied, without attaining unimpeachable clarity. To say that the increased concern for misery was a product of the Enlightenment is to commit the fallacy of misplaced concreteness. Surely it is more sensible to reverse the proposition and to conclude that an incrementally heightened awareness of poverty gradually created a new philanthropic spirit.[6]

Yet such large generalizations risk missing the essence of eighteenth-century welfare. Charity had long been an apanage of the church. Aid to the poor was mostly voluntary and usually confessional, an arrangement that was reinforced as the century proceeded. But that development—a reaffirmation of religion's claim to dispense alms in the name of all humanity—was overtly challenged by those for whom a transition from private charity to public assistance was preferable. This secular vision was enhanced by the sheer magnitude of the problem (as much as one-third of the population could be counted as poor in the late eighteenth century) and by the fact that many charitable institutions were already beginning to falter before the French Revolution began. The political events of 1789 therefore revealed, and did not create, a social crisis already at hand.[7]

The most obvious symptom of change was a growth of vagrancy. Profoundly troubling and sometimes dangerous for the more affluent portion of the population, beggars abounded in France. They roamed the countryside and infested the cities. It was altogether fitting that the principal agency created by the revolutionary government to deal with the problem should be called the Comité de Mendicité. Its main activities, under the leadership of the Comte de Rochefoucauld-Liancourt, were twofold: to propagandize in favor of a more active role by the state in dispensing welfare assistance and to gather statistics to prove the necessity of such a policy. If results of the latter effort were imprecise, they demonstrated beyond reasonable doubt that poverty was indeed spreading and that a fresh impetus to deal with it was imperative. For this undertaking, however, the Revolution allowed neither time nor circumstance. Instead, the attitudes and institutions of the Old Regime were soon retrenched: the Directory restored to their former status both general hospitals and *dépôts de mendicité*, hostels that habitually treated the poor like criminals and that were frequently indistinguishable from penitentiaries or workhouses.[8]

This repressive tone was all the more marked under Napoleon Bonaparte, who was inclined to care for indigents by conscripting them into his armies. Poverty in the imperial conception was mainly a problem for the police, whose task it was to rid society of vagabonds and beggars, not to attack the roots of their deprivation. Nothing was substantially altered in this respect by the creation in 1808 of *bureaux de bienfaisance*, state welfare organizations that were to be attached to the prefecture of each French department. Even apart from the incomplete realization of this intention, these new agencies represented only a minimal acceptance of the still-controversial principle that the state should share responsibility in the realm of public health and welfare. Nor did they precisely set forth what should be the actual extent of the state's participation. That was the unavoidable issue with which the nineteenth century began.[9]

The Restoration meant a revitalization of voluntary confessional organizations. Of these the most important was the Société de Morale Chrétienne, founded in 1821, which included Orleanist family scions and several of the glittering names of early-century liberalism: Guizot, Broglie, Dufaure, Constant, Lamartine, and Tocqueville. This group embodied an amalgamation of Roman Catholicism and political reformism that was a chief beneficiary of the revolution of 1830.[10] The ensuing decade was anything but a period of intense social progress. Yet in all fairness one must mention a few innovations or extensions of welfare under the July Monarchy: a reform of the penal system and of public education, savings banks (*caisses d'épargne*), pawn shops (*monts de piété*), nurseries, and *crèches*. A pair of negative observations is nonetheless relevant: one, that these arrangements were quite inadequate to alleviate pauperism; and another, that they stood roughly in the same relationship to the more radical proposals of 1848 as did the lame efforts of the Old Regime to those of 1789.[11]

During the 1840s the social question centered on a proposal to create a national pension plan. The Guizot government was less than enthusiastic and pointed out that, although the objective of "ameliorating the condition of the workers" might be laudable, many "difficulties of implementation" remained to be resolved.[12] Ironically, it was the prefect of police who made the best case for such a program. Not only would it bring direct benefits in the form of assistance to the aged and infirm, he explained to the cabinet, but it would also reap indirect advantages through a strengthening of popular morality and social order, "conditions indispensable to [public] security."[13] In a similar vein, official interest began to stir in favor of promoting an expansion of mutual aid societies (in effect, private insurance groups) in order to encourage "habits of order and temperance" among the laboring population.[14] In sum, such reformism as existed in the time of Louis Philippe was inextricable from a concern of the government to counter mounting public discontent, which was being exacerbated by economic crisis and unemployment.

This discussion of social betterment was suddenly dislocated by the swift sequence of events in 1848. These need not be recounted here, except to underscore the enduring significance of Louis Blanc's Luxembourg Commission and its demand for "the right to work," which brought the specter of "state socialism" to the front and center of the political scene. Although this eruption proved to be only brief, it left an indelible impression on the then youthful generation that was later to provide the principal actors of French public life until the end of the nineteenth century.[15]

Like July 1830, the initial insurrection of February 1848 was an apparent step forward for French liberalism. Its more conservative elements, such as Guizot, were now jettisoned and the heretofore flagging spirit of social reform was resuscitated. The tragedy of the June Days and the election of Louis Bonaparte to the presidency, however, left the Second Republic in no condition to sponsor bold innovations, even though the urgency of the social question could no longer be in doubt. At least the solicitousness of the new government for the problems of the poor was evident in the renewed effort to create a pension plan, which culminated in 1850 as the Caisse Nationale des Retraites pour la Vieillesse. For future reference, it is important to specify the premises upon which this institution was based. They were explained by the current minister of agriculture and commerce, Jean-Baptiste Dumas, who presented a reform bill to the republican parliament in November 1849. The essential purpose of the proposed legislation, he began, was "to come to the aid of the laboring population," who must understand that the surest way to eliminate social misery was through "work and savings." The government wished to foster a spirit of "prudence" (*prévoyance*) in place of the "dangerous illusions" of the recent past. No Frenchman could mistake this allusion to Louis Blanc's workshop scheme and its advocacy of a minimum existence for every citizen. The proposal for universal participation in an obligatory national pension program had received wide attention and significant intellectual support, Dumas acknowledged, but the government favored a voluntary plan that would serve to stimulate self-help, rather than to allow a dependency on public assistance and thereby to perpetuate "the inertia of the workers." The state would be willing to participate to a limited extent in the pension plan and to accept some "sacrifice" for the benefit of the laboring poor. But there was to be a clear quid pro quo: the workers would be expected to maintain "certain conditions of order, economy, and regularity in the conduct of their lives."[16]

Rendered here in a somewhat cryptic form, this rationale of the Second Republic's pension bill was an epitome of French liberalism in the realm of public welfare. The state would accept some political responsibility and financial liability, but only to a very moderate degree. The plan would be voluntary, not obligatory, and thus an incarnation of the principle of self-help. Public morality and therewith public security would be strengthened through the harmonious reconciliation of social classes. The new law would promote both individualism and national solidarity. It would thus reassure persons of property, restore commerce, and regain the allegiance of the laboring masses. Manifestly, good intentions were not lacking as France reached midcentury.

From the Second Republic to the Third

Although his liberal convictions were always clouded by personal ambition, Adolphe Thiers was clearly the pivotal political figure of nineteenth-century France. Indefatigable, blessed with extraordinary intellectual and rhetorical talents, convivial to a fault, he was destined for eminence and very early in his long career achieved it. His well-publicized efforts on behalf of Louis Philippe in 1830 and 1848 justifiably earned him the reputation of an Orleanist, but he was one of a pliable sort who readily adapted to a republican form of government once the monarchy was gone. Thiers's main consideration, it is only accurate to say, was his own prominence in public affairs—and that he would retain, one way or another, until the day of his death in 1877.[7]

After a brief hiatus in 1848, Thiers returned to the political arena under the Second Republic as a member of parliament. As such, he was soon named to a committee on public welfare, and in 1850 he drafted for that body an extensive report on the status of the social question in France. In many regards this document restated the principles already enunciated in the preamble of the government's pension plan. But it had two additional characteristics that gave it particular significance: the Thiers report offered a far broader and more detailed analysis of French poverty and its possible remedies; and it was written by a man whose opinions would weigh heavily in the formation of the Third Republic after 1870. Still, we should remain aware that the report ostensibly expressed the collective ideas of a committee of thirty, which included such outstanding personalities of the time as Montalembert, Melun, Buffet, Arago, Rémusat, and Beaumont. It is impossible to separate distinctly Thiers's own conceptions from those of his colleagues. We must therefore evaluate the document cautiously as a kind of midcentury liberal consensus on the topic of welfare, albeit one that bears the stamp of a singular personality.

Repeating a rhetorical formula of years past, the Thiers report began by reaffirming that the state's primary objective was "to ameliorate the condition of the laboring classes." Thiers elaborated on the government's intention "to come to the aid of the poor classes, to facilitate their work, to alleviate their suffering, [and] finally to achieve that fraternity so often proclaimed but [seldom] practiced." These irreproachable aspirations were immediately qualified, however, because "the state has precisely defined limits" founded in "the principles of justice and reason." Lest that seem too elusive, Thiers amplified: "The fundamental principle of every society is that each man is himself obligated to provide for his needs and those of his family." In states that tolerated an excess of charity (Spain, for example), the result had been to encourage mendicity. After all, it is God who has divided humanity into the strong and the weak, the young and the old, the healthy and the sick, the male and the female. It is assuredly the role of private charity and public assistance to aid the feeble. But for such help to be "virtuous," it must be voluntary and spontaneous. Welfare efforts would suffer from "a disastrous restraint" if they were made obligatory. "Were an entire class to demand rather than to receive, it would assume the role of a beggar who asks with a weapon in his hand." Charity would then become self-defeating and indeed corrupting.[18]

No attentive reader should have difficulty in extrapolating from these characteristic phrases the main elements of orthodox liberal ideology. Concern about poverty is affirmed but restricted. The social order is a given, and it is not the function of the state to alter it. Public assistance should augment Christian charity, yet the voluntarist principle must remain inviolate. The state has a duty to contribute to welfare programs, but that contribution is necessarily delimited—not only to retain a policy of moderate taxation but to avoid the encouragement of sloth, which would inevitably result from excessive social assistance by undercutting any incentive to individual self-help. Thus liberal precepts emerged in Thiers's unctuous prose with a moral glow of prudence, economy, and virtue.

The longer second part of the Thiers report was devoted to a survey of France's existing welfare agencies. Least contestable in principle were those that aided the young and the old. The advance of French civilization was confirmed by the multifarious care of infants: nurseries, *crèches*, homes for foundlings, a placement service for wet nurses, agricultural colonies, maternal societies, reform schools, institutions for the deaf and the blind. France's elderly citizens likewise benefited from the ministrations of private and public groups that provided hospital or home care. To these institutions had been added savings banks and the newly legislated national pension plan. Thiers praised these efforts but was careful to stress that they conformed to a voluntarist ethic and that participation in them was not mandatory. Were the state to impose an obligation on every individual to join, "this new communism" would generate social confusion (an unsubtle reference to 1848) and thus vitiate "the liberty of man." Especially problematic, in Thiers's judgment, was the question of welfare assistance for adults. Some persons in this intermediate age group had recently indulged in "the most extravagant utopias" and "the most foolhardy passions." Obviously implied once more were the right-to-work campaign and the national workshops of 1848, which Thiers explicitly dismissed as "mad schemes." With varying degrees of approval he could mention credit banks, workers' associations, and mutual societies as examples of government-accredited assistance to the laboring population. But it was faint praise indeed, never far removed from an insistence (curiously formulated for effect) that the participation of the state must remain "infinitely limited." This condition was coupled in turn with a moralistic diatribe against indolence "often encouraged by welfare assistance itself." Thiers then ventured a distinction between the genuinely poor, on one hand, and those shiftless professional vagabonds "whom the police of course have the right to repress." He neglected to explain the criteria by which the law was to distinguish between the two categories, and his lone suggestion for coping with vagrancy was to create bigger and better poorhouses (*dépôts de mendicité*), despite their deserved reputation for appalling filth and neglect.[19]

Perhaps it would not be unfair to reduce the entire Thiers report to a single citation from its conclusion: the activities of the state must always remain "constrained within the strict limits of the possible."[20] Yet it is worthwhile to contemplate this text at length, and to quote some of its more striking locutions, because no other document so thoroughly portrayed the liberal view of welfare as the latter half of the nineteenth century began. Nor was any other single statement to reverberate for so long in public discourse concerning the social question. The Thiers report of 1850 provided the most conspicuous bridge between liberal theory and political practice for decades to follow.

Although it may be true, as one historian has suggested, that liberalism was "the great loser" of the Bonapartist coup d'état in December 1851, this observation was primarily valid in politics and must otherwise be qualified. There is no doubt about the authoritarian pretentions of the early Second Empire, for which Thiers's arrest and temporary banishment from public life represented only one instance of a more extensive net of illiberal repression.[21] But in its social and economic policy the regime of Napoleon III did not dramatically depart from liberal precepts. Free thought was out but free trade was in. Like his more famous uncle, Louis Bonaparte bore an ideological trademark of ambiguity, proving that it is quite possible to be selectively liberal—or inconsistently autocratic—in practice. His earlier essay on the eradication of pauperism was no fluke. Yet the means he chose to address the social question were not strikingly etatist. A telling example was the treatment of mutual aid societies, which will at a later point in this account require more detailed consideration. Here we may simply record the emperor's personally expressed desire to bring the societies under tighter state supervision and to promote their expansion. Still, that ambition did not alter the basic principle of voluntary enrollment. Such private agencies hence remained impervious to random proposals for mandatory insurance coverage directly controlled and financed by the state.[22]

The grip of Napoleon III began to loosen perceptibly as his political woes mounted. The emperor's absolutist airs had never been entirely convincing and they were already badly compromised by 1866. His hesitations during the civil war in Germany and his awkwardness in the Luxembourg crisis thereafter permitted the harsh critique by his liberal opponents, notably including Thiers, to revive. Bonaparte's foolish decision to risk everything in a showdown with Prussia in 1870 was doubtless a consequence of his weakness vis-à-vis the renewed liberal opposition and of a desire somehow to play out his political trump. These familiar events do not demand recapitulation.[23] We need only underscore the generalization that, insofar as public welfare policy was concerned, the Second Empire was without lasting effect. The liberal consensus, incarnated by Thiers and incorporated in his 1850 report, survived two decades of eclipse and regained status as the official social dogma of the French state. In regard to welfare, then, the Third Republic began as the Second Republic had ended. Thiers's part as the first chief of state after 1870 was altogether appropriate. For the time being, at least, other opinions were crowded out, and liberal orthodoxy enjoyed its place in the shade of military defeat.

Liberalism and Socialism

The Paris Commune was primarily a product of the lost war of 1870. But it was by no means anomalous to the general social development of the late 1860s. Those years had been marked by a gathering discontent among the laboring population, which erupted in a wave of strikes. The most publicized of these occurred at Le Creusot in early 1870; but that was, as Charles de Mazade commented in the *Revue des deux mondes*, "only the manifest expression of a more general movement." Another contributor to the journal added that "these subversive ideas and these frequent material disorders" must be attributed to a "spirit of radical hostility against the existing order." Thus socialism, moribund in the two decades after 1848, was once again in the streets.[24]

The waning regime of Napoleon III, well aware of this agitation, was willing to meet it with dispatch. A directive from the Ministry of the Interior admonished in January 1870 that "the government will not tolerate any attempted disorder" and that it would "repress every arbitrary act, every excess of force, no matter who the perpetrator may be." The government's firm determination was one part of the story. Another was contained in the same instructions to the prefects of France, who were to implement "the liberal transformation proclaimed by the emperor and awaited by the nation."[25] Bonaparte's belated concessions to his liberal critics were thereby closely linked to control of public agitation. As usual, liberalism found itself somewhere between carrot and stick. It was Napoleon's intention to keep French liberals within the imperial camp by appealing to their innate sense of law and order. But once his regime was swept away and replaced by a republic, this entire equation necessarily had to be recalculated. Now the former liberal opposition itself held positions of authority and was forced to decide what measures of repression were justifiable to quell the incipient spirit of insurrection. We know with what alacrity and ruthlessness the Thierist regime moved to acquit—and hence to define—its duty as the guardian of domestic tranquility. The Paris Commune, it must be kept in mind, was crushed by the liberals.[26]

In the most drastic manner imaginable, the Third Republic thereby began with an irrepressible question: what would be the relationship between a liberal republican state and the large mass of its underprivileged citizenry? The political aspects of this issue have been often examined in the many competent studies of the French left.[27] Yet social history should presumably be something more than the history of socialism, and far less attention has been devoted to the concomitant phenomena of public health and welfare. In fact, we know intellectual efforts to grapple with the social question preceded the formation of French socialism as an organized faction. Long before there was a political party by that name, in other words, socialism was an idea that posed fundamental problems for the leadership of the new republic.

Of the many essays and books written after 1870 that expounded liberal theory, one stands out for its centrality and lucidity. Originally published in 1880, and appearing thereafter in several revised editions, Paul Leroy-Beaulieu's treatise on the distribution of wealth was a key work of the time. As a member of the Institut de France, lecturer on political economy at the École Libre des Sciences Politiques, regular contributor to the *Revue des deux mondes*, and sometime editor of both the *Journal des débats* and *L'économiste français*, Leroy-Beaulieu was extraordinarily well situated to serve as an ideologue of late-century liberalism. Although no single author could articulate every conceivable theme of such a complex tradition, a study of his writings affords our most direct approach to orthodox liberal attitudes toward socialism and social assistance in the period between the wars of 1870 and 1914.[28]

Leroy-Beaulieu began by describing socialism as a form of "economic pessimism," because it assumed that a necessary corollary of the accumulation of capital was an increment of social inequality. Advocates of this view held that a widening of the gap between rich and poor would require, in turn, an increasing intervention of the state in order to counteract "tendencies that would [otherwise] be fatal to the social body."[29] Those who accepted such logic—socialists like Lassalle, Marx, and Proudhon as well as certain liberals—were charged by Leroy-Beaulieu with "sysiphism," because they projected a further expansion of pauperism with every advance of industry. He, to the contrary, wished to challenge the initial premise of this transparent excuse for state interventionism. The truth of the matter, according to Leroy-Beaulieu, was that the lower classes were reaping more rapid and tangible benefits from industrialization than the upper. Falling prices, rising wages, better working conditions, improved housing, better nutrition, and more leisure were the salutary effects of economic growth that was tending in reality to reduce social inequality. The socialist supposition of a steady immiseration of the laboring population was without foundation. "No fact, no statistic, supports that prejudice."[30]

In certain instances, Leroy-Beaulieu granted, the intervention of the state could be legitimate. Just as it took some measures to regulate schools, churches, theaters, hotels, restaurants, and cafés, the state might also mandate some provisions for factories. But it must always be cautious, and above all it must not interfere in the employment of adult males (with the notable exception of miners), a matter better left to settlement between them and their employers. Similar limitations applied to mutual societies, which were acknowledged by Leroy-Beaulieu to be "a great progress," because they addressed the problem of general welfare and yet did so while preserving private initiative.[31] He likewise recognized the need for better public hygiene as well as for insurance against accidents and illness. But these measures were sure to develop in any event "with the simple collaboration of time, capital, education, liberty, philanthropy, and also charity." Indeed, he claimed, "liberty and time are sufficient to resolve all social difficulties." As a consequence, "the expansion of any state administration is suspect."[32]

It would be difficult to compose a more rhapsodic paean to rugged individualism and free enterprise. Leroy-Beaulieu's formulation of liberalism was appropriate to the second half of the nineteenth century, because its self-definition derived not from a defense against monarchist or Bonapartist autocracy but in contrast to what had become categorized as "state socialism." He faced squarely forward, not backward, simultaneously accepting the republican form of government and setting strict boundaries for its operation. He specifically stressed his opposition to a progressive income tax, which he considered an artificial and arbitrary redistribution of wealth. Neither a utilitarian nor a socialist slogan of the greatest good for the greatest number should guide France's legislators, in his opinion, but a sense of social justice for all—"even," as Léon Say added with emphatic support, "the rich." An excessive intervention by the state would not only be contrary to the natural order of things, concluded Leroy-Beaulieu, it would also be useless, for "the great general economic causes [are] infinitely more powerful than all human laws." In the end, he believed, harmony among the classes and progress of the nation would be realized through an inexorable dialectic of increasing public wealth and lessening social inequality.[33]

Leroy-Beaulieu's critique of socialism did not remain without a reply, although—in the wake of legal repression that followed the Paris Commune—criticism arose less decisively from the dislocated political left than from within liberalism itself. The most conspicuous example was the Comte d'Haussonville, who rejected the hypothesis that pauperism evolved in inverse proportion to industrialization. Instead, he indicated, the concentration of labor in the French capital had created "a belt of misery." Haussonville made special reference to the wretched plight of women, who were often alone and always ill paid. "In effect," he asked, "what is the inevitable consequence of liberty?" Answer: it is to allow the natural laws of society to pit the powerful against the weak, with the invariable outcome that the latter are forever undone and poverty is ceaselessly increased. To this point Haussonville's critique cut straight across the grain of Leroy-Beaulieu's optimism. But his own liberalism became apparent as soon as he contemplated a remedy for France's social problems: "Is this to say that the role of the state should be to intervene constantly in this struggle to reestablish equilibrium? No, because the state . . . would produce a disarray worse than the severe consequences of the natural order." Haussonville's solution to the social question, in sum, was to offer greater encouragement to private initiative and to temper the precept of laissez faire with the "superior principle" of charity.[34]

This final assertion by Haussonville brings into sight an additional factor. Although he wrote as a liberal and may fairly be classified as such, Haussonville was also a Roman Catholic. Because no sharp division separated Catholic liberalism from liberal Catholicism in France, it is indispensable to take note here of these intellectually and politically overlapping viewpoints. The origins of liberal Catholicism can be traced back at least to Lamennais, who shared with early nineteenth-century liberals a desire to balance authority and liberty.

The difference was an emphasis by Lamennais on the proposition that social harmony could exist solely within a genuinely Catholic context. The resulting internal controversies of the church and the eventual ostracization of Lamennais under the papacy of Pius IX do not concern us here.[35] But the evolution of Catholic social thought thereafter is directly germane. It may be described in general terms as a movement toward a more active concern by the church for public welfare and a greater acceptance of state participation in the heretofore largely confessional domain of charity. These trends were noticeably accelerated after 1878 during the pontificate of Leo XIII, whose conscious reorientation of Catholic social doctrine would culminate in 1891 with the remarkable encyclical *Rerum Novarum*, in which Leo openly acknowledged the persistent blight of poverty and the consequent necessity for public welfare: "The richer class have many ways of shielding themselves, and stand less in need of help from the state; whereas the mass of the poor have no resources of their own to fall back upon, and must chiefly depend upon the assistance of the state." In effect, these words admitted the inadequacy of charitable efforts alone to assuage pauperism, yet they stopped short of assigning an exclusive patronage of the poor to the secular state.[36] One commentator in the *Revue des deux mondes*, Anatole Leroy-Beaulieu (the brother of Paul), hastened to reassure his readers that *Rerum Novarum* in no sense presaged an abdication by the church from its traditional role. Still, he conceded, "the intervention of the state is the central point around which the entire social question turns." Leo intended to admit the utility of governmental action against pauperism, but only within limits necessary to preserve the rights of the individual, of the family, and of religious societies. The pope remained fully aware that the state was capable of being "violent, hectoring, arbitrary, tyrannical, . . . presumptuous, and expensive." Surely Leo wished to restrict the state's competence and, as before, to encourage the development of private associations and corporations.[37]

French liberalism and Roman Catholicism thereby searched toward the common ground of an implicit theory of *juste milieu*. They met on the proposition that, in treating the social question, the state could go thus far but no farther. It might initiate some steps to feed, clothe, and heal the poor. Yet it must always and by all means avoid opening the gates of welfare to socialism.

Liberalism and Centralism

This brief survey of French liberalism requires attention to another theoretical issue. What was the relationship of liberal ideology and practice to the republican state? Thanks to Alexis de Tocqueville, we are quite aware of the paradox that the First Republic in the 1790s had actually enhanced the centralism of French government, thereby sealing a victory of sorts for the Old Regime.[38] Napoleon's creation of the prefectoral corps then became centralism incarnate. And we know how each successive regime thereafter sought to model the administration in its own image, thus further emphasizing the importance of an etatist tradition that was justly thought to be characteristically if not uniquely French. The Third Republic was no exception. Elsewhere we have considered how the extraordinarily rapid turnover of prefects in the 1870s was symptomatic of a struggle to control the administrative apparatus of the state. When that contest was finally resolved in favor of the Gambettist republicans in 1877, France emerged as centralized as ever.[39]

But what does that term imply? Not, it would seem, that the new republic was therefore an immensely powerful state. Perhaps Tocqueville is partly to blame for the spurious assumption that centralized states are necessarily "strong" and federal states are "weak." Any comparison of imperial Germany with republican France in the late nineteenth century should dispel that notion. A recent commentary has put the matter in a better perspective: "Centralization concentrates jurisdictions. It does not concentrate effective power."[40] What was centralized in France was the *competence* to formulate policy and the *potential* to implement it. If the state decided on a specific course of action and wished to move decisively in that direction, the instruments of enforcement were not wanting. But if not, little might be accomplished precisely because most of the levers of power were located within a single administrative structure. It was axiomatic that initiative lay with the centralized state.

An obvious corollary was the significance of clientism. Centralism meant that private interest groups could weigh heavily in public affairs whenever they had access to the inner sanctum of government. Far from being harmful to private interests, a centralized state might enhance their impact if they could but prevail with state officials *not* to exercise some possible administrative functions. Such was, in the early Third Republic, the habitual role of French lobbies and pressure groups, which sometimes favored governmental action but more frequently attempted to discourage it. The typical private interest groups of this time could properly be called liberal insofar as they militated against state initiatives that interfered with the private sector. In one fashion or another, as we shall observe, public power might thereby be harnessed to protect special interests rather than to promote the general weal.

The French began in the late nineteenth century to refer to an undue extension of the government's role as "the providential state" (*l'état-providence*). For liberal publicists this expression was clearly pejorative. It implied what the state should *not* be.[41] To be sure, there were many legitimate functions of government. They included above all the police and the army, without which the maintenance of domestic order and national security would be impossible. Outside these narrow bounds, in the liberal view, a few grey areas existed, such as public education (orthodox liberals received the Ferry reforms with some anxiety). But beyond the pale were public health and welfare, and the liberals aimed to keep them there. In a centralized state like France, their effort to do so was actually facilitated because the potential to act, when unexpended at its center, existed virtually nowhere else in the country.[42] Thus, whenever constrained by liberal precepts and societal connections among influential vested interests, the central state was marked by an absence of authority. Under these circumstances a failure to decide usually resulted in an inability to act. Deprived by tradition of much political responsibility or bureaucratic competence, local and regional officials were often inclined to await an initiative from above. When there was no state policy in public welfare, they were politically constrained because they lacked either the requisite funds or, no less crucial, a suitable precedent for independent action.[43]

A comparison with Germany, although very concise here, offers a striking contrast. No doubt the delay of nationhood until 1871 created certain handicaps for the imperial regime in Berlin. Yet we should recall the commonplace that political retardation—in the sense of a restricted centralism at the national level—had its advantages for Germany. In regard to welfare reform, the innovative role of Bismarckian social legislation has been often and appropriately praised. But surely no less important were the many local and regional initiatives that preceded or extended national legislation.[44] It was just such impulses that, in many respects, the Reich often attempted to coordinate rather than to create. From an administrative standpoint the traditional French provinces—Normandy, Brittany, Anjou, Poitou, Burgundy, Franche-Comté, and so on—were merely fabled names throughout the nineteenth century. Not so in Germany, where such territories as Bavaria, Saxony, Baden, Württemberg, and foremost Prussia were thriving bureaucratic and political entities. Moreover, the German lands still retained an impressive tradition of municipal autonomy for which France had preserved few if any counterparts. These are vastly complex propositions, of course, but they may at least hint that a federal structure like Germany's could be a source of strength for the social policy of a modern nation-state. We need not glorify the otherwise troubled German circumstance to conclude that it was a country in which local and regional authorities, measured against those in France, were less prone to wait for the rulers of the centralized state to act.

It is also true, and telling, that liberalism was a waning force in Germany after the mid-1870s. There the ideological battle of the century was quickly decided at the national level and the imperial government was better able than the successive republican cabinets of France to determine a coherent course of action. Again, we cannot assume a priori that a high degree of administrative centralism necessarily connotes a government consensus—least of all in a republican form of state where pluralistic social interests are represented and might readily enter into conflict. The Third Republic provided a manifest example of the observation that centralism can aid the implementation of policy but may complicate its formulation.[45] In this instance, we may surely add, there is no chicken-and-egg dilemma: formulation must come first. Hence any study of the social question in republican France must explore the complicated process by which policy was either derived or left inchoate. Republican France, to repeat, was no less centralized than previous imperial and monarchical regimes in the nineteenth century, but it was less decisive. After 1870, therefore, the French government frequently found it appropriate not to exercise the prerogatives of political power. In that fact we find the full implication of laissez-faire liberalism.

Liberal Theory and Political Practice

"Theory is grey," so runs one of Goethe's most quoted aphorisms, "but green is the tree of life." The intrinsically unstable and often rancorous history of the French Third Republic provided a case in point. It was one thing to proclaim a moderate and enlightened liberalism in some sophisticated journal or ideological tract, another to implement it amid the constant turmoil of politics. We may therefore close out this preliminary discussion by sampling a few of the practical issues whose outcome was to define the real character of the social question in France. Three examples should suffice.

One was a prolonged debate over the conditions of labor. In a general fashion this question was repeated throughout the nineteenth century, having already reached an acute stage in the insurrections of 1848 and 1871. But not until after the Franco-Prussian war was a serious investigation for the first time conducted by a French parliamentary committee into the daily functioning of factory life. In the initial decades of the republic, as we shall later examine, the fulcrum of inquiry was the issue of working hours—including, of course, the ancillary problem of night labor by children and women. During these years, in the absence of a reliable statistical base, such discussions usually proceeded deductively from political principles. Debate within a committee on labor practices in the Chamber of Deputies in 1887 is illustrative. Members could agree on the need for binding regulations, because French trade unions were too ineffectual to extract uniform concessions from their more powerful and better-organized employers (*patrons*). Some deputies wished to legislate an eleven-hour day. A minority even favored a further reduction to ten. But there was also opposition to any state intervention whatever into working conditions other than those involving children. As one speaker stated: "Liberty alone should regulate contracts among adults." A consensus thus emerged in favor of regulating child labor; but the rest was more complex. The committee finally decided against implementing any specific restrictions for the employment of men. This result led Senator Charles Ferry to summarize the entire altercation: "The majority of the panel decided for the liberal solution [and] against the authoritarian solution."[46] Such a judgment both stylized the basic ideological dichotomy of the period and suggested its practical implication for millions of workers. A theoretical spectrum stretched from the extremes of an absolute freedom in the marketplace to its total regulation—that is, from strict laissez-faire to state interventionism. It is important to note, even at this early stage, that the former pole was customarily identified in French parlance with England, whereas the opposite approach to the solution of social problems was ordinarily associated with Germany. Even though the simplistic nature of this binary conception was frequently to result in contradictions and confusions, because neither of those foreign nations quite conformed to the French stereotype, its enduring power of suggestion should not be underestimated.

A second example was workers' insurance. The creation of a national pension plan, as noted, had been the chief institutional gain of the Second Republic in the field of public welfare. Yet this program was voluntary and required regular contributions by its members over many years before any benefits could be realized. An estimate presented by Fernand de Ramel to the Chamber of Deputies in 1890 placed at 4 percent the number of French workers, employees, and domestic servants who were actually covered by the plan. "No doubt," commented Ramel, "we should like an organization completely independent of the state," but the concrete results after forty years were undeniably disappointing.[47] Meanwhile, illness and accident insurance also came under preliminary consideration. The pragmatic issue hinged on the concept of "obligation," which had in the French context at least two possible connotations: either that communes, departments, and the central state administration would be mutually bound to guarantee a minimum of medical care; or that individual workers and employees would be automatically enrolled in insurance plans that were partially underwritten by the state and presumably financed to some extent by mandatory contributions from employers. These were complex proposals, and their ramifications were by no means certain when a parliamentary committee in the summer of 1890 passed a resolution favoring "the principle of obligatory assistance."[48] But total unanimity was lacking among French deputies. For the opposition spoke the Comte Lemercier, who found it "regrettable that the republic tends to place individual liberty in the hands of a collectivity that is the state. We are sliding toward state socialism." When others objected that no practical reform of public health care was possible without the participation of the state, Lemercier reiterated his support for "the liberal doctrine stipulating that each citizen conserves the most complete freedom of his person and his activities. The state has no reason to intervene in questions of insurance."[49] Despite this classical defense of liberalism, the Chamber's labor committee voted in November 1890 to support obligatory accident insurance of workers by their employers. Still, there was much more confusion than such a ballot indicated; and it was evident that the members were still scattered along a broad range of opinion. In reality the debate was only beginning.[50]

A third and somewhat less specific issue was the state's role in the construction and operation of physical facilities such as hospitals and hospices, asylums, maternity wards, and sanitation units. Once more, the facts of life and death seemed to undercut an extreme liberal position. French law placed responsibility for implementing sanitary regulations on the mayor of each commune. Indispensable as it might be on a local scale, as Édouard Lockroy pointed out in urging reform, this stipulation was completely ineffective in dealing with infectious diseases: "The government alone possesses the right, by its intervention, to prevent the contamination of the communes by one another." Furthermore, most smaller towns and cities lacked the financial means to create adequate medical facilities. Did it make sense, then, for the state to offer substantial monetary subsidies and still not to mandate compliance by the communes with minimal standards of professional care and public hygiene? Put in these terms, the welfare issue did not allow an intransigeantly dogmatic refusal to recognize the state's prerogative to intercede.[51] Yet it was precisely when liberal principles were apparently compromised that they were most stoutly defended. Witness this statement by an outspoken member of the Conseil Supérieur de l'Assistance Publique, Loys Brueyre: "I confess that I belong absolutely to the liberal school and that for me each person, each being, each citizen is responsible in principle for his own destiny. . . . Therefore the state should not come to his aid except when he has fallen into misery through no fault of his own and when it would be impossible for him to recover by his own force." This rendition of liberal orthodoxy was unsurprisingly accompanied by a dire warning against "the colossal danger" of state socialism. And the prompt rebuttal by reformers was by now equally predictable: the French state could not remain passive in the face of poverty when it became obvious that private charity was inadequate to cope with it.[52]

Undoubtedly liberalism had been more comfortable with its anti-autocratic posture before 1870 than it was with a prodemocratic stance thereafter. To advocate constitutional restrictions on royal or imperial authority was relatively unproblematical. Far more perplexing was the task of devising and implementing a conception of liberty within the framework of a republic. The intractable problems of public health and welfare did not permit tidy or timid answers. Suddenly the world seemed more crowded and more complex. If so, it was unlikely that a liberal consensus could long remain intact.

Chapter 2

The Demographic Imperative

Long after its prime, liberalism is likely to strike the impartial observer in retrospect as an exercise in rhetoric. And for explicable reasons, so it was. Every knowledgeable European of the mid-nineteenth century was somehow aware that society was undergoing a fitful and permanent transition through industrial expansion. One needed only to ride a train, pass by a factory, or walk a city street to witness the more obvious effects. Yet exceptional was the person who possessed any coherent notion of the dimensions of that change. It is in fact remarkable how little most people knew about their own collective experience. Partly that ignorance was a function of illiteracy. But even the wealthy and educated portions of the populace did not travel widely beyond their country estate or favorite spa. What they knew of the world outside their circle came from a few exotic novels, from reports of foreign correspondents in daily newspapers, or perhaps from the pages of a fashion magazine that reported the latest trends in etiquette and style.[1]

Two ingredients were lacking that we, a century or so later, virtually take for granted: an international perspective and an accumulation of precise data. Absence of the former is hardly surprising, and we cannot wonder that the average Frenchman had only the vaguest conception of whom he was fighting in the war of 1870, or why. On the other side were "les boches"—enough said, so it was thought. The absence of exact numbers through much of the nineteenth century was a no less significant, if less durable, factor of the national mentality. Regular census reports had existed in France since the Restoration; and the *Statistique générale de France* was available through governmental agencies. Yet these tabulations, even when carefully studied, yielded at most a crude and unreliable picture of French public life. Above all, they were incomplete. If reporting was regularized by late century in some of the major cities, it was altogether absent in hamlets and rural communes. In the majority of instances, truth to tell, French statisticians were helpless to estimate with assurance the national aggregate or average of anything.[2]

Such incapacity was especially critical in the sector of public health. Communicable diseases could not be controlled if they were not counted. Without numerical precision and rapid notification procedures, epidemics could flair before they could be contained. Numbers might be a matter of life or death. The lack of them left society at the mercy of alarms and rumors. One must always bear in mind this irrational component, which was further magnified by the social stigma attached to certain maladies: leprosy, syphilis, and even tuberculosis. In general, the total mortality rates of the late nineteenth century were probably reliable, but we shall never be certain of just how many French citizens died of various identifiable causes, both because they were incorrectly or incompletely recorded and because the reality was in many cases deliberately dissimulated.

Under these circumstances a political philosophy like liberalism was literally a *Weltanschauung*. It expressed a vague and generalized conception of society, not an exact analysis of it, for which sufficient data were unavailable. Liberal ideology was therefore vulnerable to attack from two different quarters. One was from those, like the socialists, who opposed one set of lofty principles with another. The other, more insidious, came from statisticians who challenged the very bases of liberal thought by bringing a greater numerical exactitude to bear. Better data might thereby undermine established doctrines by demonstrating unacceptable errors of fact or judgment. Maybe, in short, the unexamined life of the liberal mind was not worth leading.

The Puzzles of Poverty

For nearly two decades after the revolution of 1848 the French economy had flourished. Prosperity was evident throughout the land. Commerce and industry expanded, aided by a vastly enlarged railway network and an increased fluidity of finance capital. Until about 1865 the sustained annual rate of economic growth was respectably elevated, and real wages (although not exactly measurable) were correspondingly on the rise.[3] Strangely, however, it seemed that the motley army of beggars, clochards, and vagabonds did not disappear. Their number, if anything, increased. How many vagrants there actually were, no one could really say—not even the public health administration of Paris, whose direct responsibility it was to distribute welfare funds through *bureaux de bienfaisance* in the twenty arrondissements of the capital. If any agency had a chance to grasp the problem, this was it; and statistics on the city's indigent population had a gratifying look of precision. By the end of December 1864, they disclosed, there were exactly 45,679 families on the Paris relief roles, comprising a total of 117,740 individuals.[4] Yet the social reality was far different, less pedantic, and more troubling. To count the number of officially registered paupers in Paris failed to indicate how many of them the city actually contained, not to mention the suburbs, the surrounding Department of the Seine, the other cities of France, or the outlying regions. As always, prosperity and poverty coexisted in indeterminate proportions.

A broader view was afforded by a presentation of the 1864 national census, published in the official *Moniteur Universel* three years later. From this source it could be established that the entire French population was expanding rather gradually: births in 1864 exceeded deaths by 145,550, that is, at a rate of 3.8 per 1,000. The birth rate in the countryside was somewhat higher than in the cities, but internal migration toward urban areas more than offset the difference. Surely, if slowly, France was becoming urbanized—no place more so, of course, than Paris, even though many recently arrived paupers did not appear on the municipal role of welfare recipients. One disturbing note was a steady decline of marriages: from a total of over 305,000 in 1861 the national statistic fell for the first time below 300,000 four years later. But more encouraging was the simultaneous decline of illiteracy, particularly around Paris and in areas adjacent to Germany. Still, it was dismaying to learn that fully one-third of the French were unable to sign their own name on a marriage certificate. And it remained true that men were far less likely to be illiterate than women (27.88 percent versus 41.45 percent).[5]

Such numbers were typical of what could and what could not be counted. They told nothing of the health and happiness of the

French population. Moreover, they left full range for subjective interpretation. By certain criteria the French nation was doing splendidly. The combination of a low birth rate and a rising literacy rate might well indicate that the quality of life was improving. This was the conclusion of a famous physician, Dr. Paul Broca, who was the first to comment extensively on the recent demographic survey before the Academy of Medicine in March 1867. Placed into an international context, Broca claimed with comparative statistics at hand, France was the leader among western European states in the number of productive citizens in adulthood (see Table 1).

One of Broca's auditors—then a journalist and himself later a distinguished member of the Academy—was Léon Lefort, who saw a different and less flattering meaning in this population profile. The French citizenry, he pointed out, was aging more rapidly than those with a higher birth rate. When Lefort attempted to bring his view to the attention of the president of the Academy, Dr. Ambroise Tardieu, he was cut off with the rebuff: "Broca is well acquainted with these questions, of which you are ignorant."[6] Undeterred, Lefort proceeded to publish an account of his own in the *Revue des deux mondes*, where he was certain to receive the attention of a sophisticated readership. True, he wrote, the French populace was still increasing in absolute numbers, but an international comparison disclosed a "fatal lethargy" in France's demographic growth, whereas "that of the great neighboring states is expanding with a rapidity . . . altogether disquieting for the future of French power." The overriding reality, Lefort argued, was the nation's slow relative decline. In an era of large standing armies, that drift could only lead "directly to the ruin of France." At the current rates of growth England would double its population in 52 years, Prussia in 54, France only in 198. All the while, moreover, the French population would continue to age more rapidly than the others. Already the average age was 25 in Prussia, 26 in Austria and England, 29 in Belgium, and 31 in France. Lefort blamed this development on antiquated religious and military institutions that annually deprived over 200,000 celibate Frenchmen of their most fertile years. The continued proliferation of monasteries and barracks was characteristic of a social inadaptation that was leading "little by little to the degeneracy of the race." France stood in need of reform, for "the nation is in danger."[7]

The conclusion reached by Léon Lefort was not uniquely his.

Table 1 / Age Categories in Western Europe (per 10,000),
ca. 1865

Nation	Children (under 20)	Adults (20–60)	Aged (over 60)
France	3,612	5,373	1,015
Belgium	4,132	4,973	895
Britain	4,534	4,732	734
Prussia	4,740	4,683	577

Source: Bulletin de l'Académie de Médecine, 29 Mar. 1867.

Indeed, the explicit advocacy of a reduction in military service for conscripts from seven to four or three years placed him within a French reformist current following the Prusso-Austrian war of 1866.[8] Yet his remarks are of interest here for another reason, because Lefort's essay was typical of a time when France's demographic reality was just beginning to gain more widespread public attention. This new awareness had two conspicuous aspects, the relationship of which was still unclear. One was a persistent pauperism throughout France, in the cities as well as in the countryside. The other was a sagging birth rate, with its inexorable gerontological corollary. Both of these factors—more poor and more aged—suggested that the quality of French public life was perhaps not so admirable as some believed. The future of the nation might be in jeopardy. These dark thoughts could not fail to be confirmed when France stumbled foolishly into the war of 1870, only to be vanquished by a younger and demographically more vigorous Germany.

The Depopulation Crisis

The easiest and least disturbing explanation of the disaster of 1870 was that France had been outmanned. The Germans were victorious because they had fielded a numerically superior force. This plausible assertion, often repeated, suggested an obvious conclusion: France must adopt a citizen army.[9] Yet a small nation in arms could not confidently expect to compete with a large one, and a simple deduction thus dictated that France should maintain a population curve comparable to that of its closest neighbors. What, then, was the existing demographic pattern? It was impossible to know with certainty, because the regular sequence of the national census had been interrupted by the war. The first statistical survey under the republic was not conducted before 1873 and the results of it remained unknown to the public (given the usual time lag for tabulation) until three years later. The heyday of French liberalism thereby coincided with a long period of numerical blackout during which one might suppose that the Third Republic needed only to allow events to take their natural course. But no one had a way of knowing exactly what was the natural course.

In this initial phase the republican parliament adopted one important piece of social legislation: the so-called Loi Roussel of 1874. It should be recalled that public aid for the very old and the very young had long appeared less problematical in France than welfare for the adult laboring population. In that sense, this measure to organize assistance for foundling infants and their mothers was well within the established tradition. It was also, of course, in partial response to the perceived manpower deficit of the war and was thereby a complement to the military recruitment bill adopted the year before.[10] Whereas the impulse for this legislation came from the central government, the new law did not depart from liberal principles insofar as its application was not compulsory for the departments and communes of France. The role of the central state, in other words, would be to urge and to guide the nation toward implementing voluntary regulations rather than to mandate compliance with them.[11]

In 1876 the awaited census results were finally published. The indisputable facts were that France's rate of demographic growth was declining. The sudden boom of marriages right after the war of 1870 was not being sustained, and the annual number was threatening to sink again below the threshold of 300,000. Meanwhile, if the mortality rate was fairly steady, the birth rate had resumed its erratic downward pitch.[12] With only a brief statistical series of the early 1870s at hand, it was admittedly impossible to pronounce definitively on these trends. But in years following they were to be confirmed. France's negative spiral, which had already caused some concern in the decade before 1870, became an ever more compelling source of alarm.[13]

For two reasons this broad backdrop must be kept constantly in view. First, it loomed behind every one of the specific social questions that faced France before 1914: vagabondage and vagrancy, epidemic disease and alcoholism, prostitution, slums, overcrowded hospitals, and the rest. The suspicion unavoidably grew that the nation was demographically enfeebled, vulnerable, and therefore incapable of solving its most elemental problems—incapable, that is, if events were allowed to take their (now exposed) natural course. Second, with more time and a longer statistical perspective, the "depopulation crisis" was to become deeply pervasive in the French national mentality, contributing importantly to a mood of cultural decadence that, rightly or wrongly, colored the Belle Epoque.[14]

To comprehend that crisis requires attention to its mundane details as well as its ultimate implications. We have direct access to both, fortunately, through the minutes of the French Academy of Medicine in the year 1885. By that time a full decade had passed since the initial postwar census was released. On 20 January of that year, in a report about the emerging statistical pattern, Dr. Gustave Lagneau presented a paper soberly entitled: "The Demographic Situation of France: Decline of the Population in Certain Departments." Few of Lagneau's remarks could have astonished his fellow physicians. Twenty-six French departments had suffered an absolute loss of inhabitants in the half century since the mid-1830s. They were grouped in four large clusters on the Spanish, Italian, and German borders, plus the Normandy coastal region in the northwest. Lagneau reiterated what had long been common knowledge: France was slowly becoming urbanized. He estimated that, whereas only one-quarter of the French populace had been urban about 1850, that proportion by 1880 was one-third. This shift was numerically much more significant than France's colonial expansion. Barely 15,000 French citizens were departing each year to take up residence abroad, whereas the annual movement from countryside to city (defined as a municipality over 2,000) exceeded 200,000. The main recipient of this inner migration was of course Paris. Indeed, were it not for the arrival of provincials, the population of the capital would also be in decline. On the average, Parisians married later and less often than other French men and women (annually 59 per 1,000 against 69 per 1,000 of single persons between the ages of eighteen and sixty). Fecundity was also lower in Paris (the birth rate for women between fifteen and fifty was only 89 per 1,000 in the capital but 102 per 1,000 elsewhere in France). But, predictably, the illegitimacy rate in the capital was far higher than in the rest of France (47.4 versus 18 per 1,000 births). This latter estimate had disturbing implications, because the rate of mortality among illegitimate infants was at least twice that of legitimate children. Moreover, figures gathered from records of military recruitment establish that this phenomenon was persistent: of every 1,000 males born legitimately, about 660 were still alive by the age of twenty-one, whereas for illegitimate males the survival expectancy was no more than 260. The inference was unmistakable that a direct line could be drawn from cradle to military cadre, and that France could not afford such heavy losses.[15]

Lagneau's report preoccupied the Academy of Medicine for nearly two months and was extensively discussed in the newspaper press. This publicity briefly made him a minor celebrity and, more important, focused unaccustomed attention for a time on the proceedings of the Academy. Of subsequent speakers there, the most incisive was Dr. Jules Rochard, who characterized the nation's demographic devolution as "a real social peril." Even the most encouraging development—an increase since 1800 of the average life expectancy from twenty-eight to thirty-seven years—was vitiated by the declining birth rate, because France's relatively low infant mortality among European nations was partly a function of its more aged general population. Where fewer infants were born, fewer would die; and the French birth rate had become the lowest in western Europe, dropping by 1890 even below that of Ireland. Why this fateful infertility? Rochard offered an explanation in terms of five basic factors, the combination of which he believed to be distinctive for France:

1. *Family structure*: A constraining and oppressive upbringing stifled the young, who were still required by law to obtain parental approval for marriage until the age of twenty-five.

2. *Social convention*: Ritualized courtship was often culminated by expensive and wearisome weddings, which discouraged spontaneous early marital alliances.

3. *Military legislation*: Conscription laws retained young men in social quarantine during their most fertile years, as a result of France's excessive five-year recruitment system.

4. *Inheritance practices*: Restrictive primogeniture rules limited nuclear families or led younger progenies to abandon even the most prosperous regions.

5. *Urban life*: Cities fostered cramped and unhealthy quarters for the poor and indolent luxury for the rich, neither of which sustained an urge for reproduction.[16]

Dr. Joseph Lunier corroborated this cryptic agenda of social constraints and echoed what he called Rochard's "cry of alarm." The French family, he noted, had produced an average of 4.24 children at the beginning of the nineteenth century. By 1850 that figure had dropped to 3.45, and by 1880 it was down to 3.10. The reasons for this alarming decline were to be found in widely practiced methods of voluntary birth control or, that failing, in abortion, infanticide, and the abandonment of children. Lunier contended that the only sure remedy lay in stricter enforcement of the Loi Roussel throughout France, which he believed could save as many as 80,000 infants annually and double the yearly excess of births over deaths. But such an increment was only possible through an active effort by the central government. Otherwise essential matters of public health would continue to be neglected by local officials. "When it is a matter of general interest," Lunier told his medical colleagues, "the state alone has the capacity to ordain and to act. In this regard, for very good reason, it should be armed with absolute power when it concerns a question that touches the very existence of the country [and] the national security." This assertion, one among many in a similar vein by members of the Academy, demonstrated how the demographic crisis could be construed as inimical to the prevailing political assumptions of laissez-faire liberalism.[17]

The fashion in which statistical precision could affect a rhetorical debate was well illustrated by an unfortunate venture of Léon Lefort, who charged Rochard and Lunier with undue pessimism. Lefort contended that the French demographic growth rate was actually higher than usually supposed, that an upward trend had been partially hidden by the "military period" around 1870, and that the French population would double in only 165 years, not 198 as he himself had earlier assumed. But within a week Lunier was able to expose the error of Lefort's calculations and to prove that France's current population growth would not in fact permit a doubling of the nation in less than 300 years.[18] At the next session of the Academy of Medicine, Lefort had to concede his mathematical mistake. When he attempted to cover the traces of his error with a few clever turns of phrase, his remarks fell lamentably flat.[19] The palpable lesson could not have been lost on a single member of the medical elite: henceforth rhetoric would not suffice. The verifiable data of France's decline were no longer to be denied.

A Matter of Survival

The worry about numbers, we know, had antedated the war of 1870; and it is demonstrable that, from that time, it was above all attached to competition with Prussia. The gathering sense of demographic crisis had not been engendered by absolute but by comparative statistics. Throughout the 1870s and 1880s France was not being literally depopulated. There was still some excess of births over deaths. But year by year the nation's relative position continued to worsen with regard to other European states, of which Germany was incontestably the most overbearing.

Prussia's demographic potency was a long-standing and well-known fact. In his 1867 article in the *Revue des deux mondes*, Léon Lefort had taken specific note of it: the Prussian birth rate in 1861 was 37.4 per 1,000, the French 26.8.[20] Thereafter, of course, it was the Franco-Prussian war and the German occupation that brought that statistical reality home to France, as nothing else could have done. One needs to recall that a substantial portion of the French populace, perhaps a quarter or more, had the unnerving experience in the early 1870s of witnessing a parade of large, strong, and superbly disciplined German troops. The famous procession of field grey uniforms down the Champs Élysées on the first day of March 1871 was but one of many such displays by German soldiers in the populous cities of northeastern France. Their closed ranks and regular stride could not fail to leave an abiding impression of shame on all those spectators who stood silently to the side. Unfortunately no photographers with flash cameras were present to record this emotion in the face of the French. But we can well imagine that it was no less anguishing then than it was later to be in 1940.[21] After the military occupation at last ended in 1873, the specter of German numerical superiority remained. Publication of the postwar census in 1876 was disturbing not only for what the statistics said about France but also because they revealed the depth of the French retardation when compared with the advance of Germany. In particular, Senator

Léonce de Lavergne stressed that Germany's annual margin of births over deaths was at least four times that of France. This initial fluster was brief, but coming as it did on the heels of a war scare in 1875, it could only reinforce apprehensions about the sheer size of the Teutonic masses.[22]

One of the first serious attempts to place France's performance into a comparative context was Émile Cheysson's treatise on the population question in France and abroad that appeared about 1880. Cheysson began by charting the drop of French population growth in the nineteenth century, calculating that it would require 271 years to double the total. He described the inherently baneful effects of this retardation on the French army, agriculture, industry, and commerce, adding that "such a result becomes especially ominous when compared with that of other peoples." In an international perspective, France's "relative stagnation" was tantamount to a "veritable decline." The slackening of the French growth rate "contrasted painfully" with the expanding population of the other powers, Cheysson said: "Our proportional influence continues to diminish, and within half a century our slump will result in a veritable decadence."[23]

The same theme was evident throughout the already examined depopulation debate of the Academy of Medicine. Gustave Lagneau buttressed his report on France's demographic lag by noting that the growth rate was "only" two and a half times weaker than that of Germany—and not four times, as Léonce de Lavergne had earlier contended.[24] As usual, Jules Rochard put the matter more dramatically. If present trends continued, he said, France would find itself in fifty years with the seventh largest population in Europe. It was hardly a time, when large standing armies were quartered everywhere on the Continent, for France to relax: "If we do not wish to be obliterated in the midst of conflicts that are to come, we must be prepared in the hour of peril to thrust a million men to the frontier."[25] Several other members of the Academy were more sanguine. Not that they could dispute the statistical tilt toward Germany. Yet there were two remaining lines of rhetorical defense. One held that the quality of a people is more determinant than the quantity: witness Germany's manifest superiority to Russia; or the worldwide importance of Great Britain, though it was less populous than France; or the significance of tiny Switzerland. Indeed, an excess of growth could only produce more social misery—a neo-Malthusian contention that was a favorite of the League for Depopulation, which was currently distributing printed posters with the uplifting message: "God blesses large families but does not feed them. Let's have fewer children."[26] Another contention was advanced by Théophile Roussel, author of the 1874 social law on child care, who approved of the new emphasis on comparative demography. He was convinced that France's circumstances were far from desperate. Basically, Roussel claimed, the nation needed but to enforce his legislation throughout the land and to restore faith in itself: "No, it is not true that our race, compared with its rivals in the world, is damned to infertility [and] consequently to inferiority." Roussel's optimism was greeted by salvos of enthusiastic applause in the Academy, which then voted—harmlessly—to support his stance.[27]

We shall observe how this already pronounced tendency of physicians, public health officials, and politicians to measure the French strength and statistics against those of Germany remained an intrinsic element not only of subsequent demographic analyses but also of related discussions about hygiene and welfare. The logic of social reform efforts in France cannot be comprehended apart from this comparative dimension. Repeated many times in the various forums that met to consider reformist principles and legislative proposals in the years before 1914, it was stated by no one more lucidly than the leading French demographer of the day, Jacques Bertillon: "France is on the verge of becoming a nation of the third rank, at the mercy of other peoples. Her economic force, her military prowess, her intellectual influence are threatened by a ceaselessly increasing danger. She owes it to herself to react."[28]

By 1890 nearly a quarter of a century had passed since Dr. Paul Broca first presented comparative statistics on France's demographic status. Commenting on the longer perspective now available, Léon Lefort acknowledged that the real danger had not been sufficiently recognized until "the disasters of 1870 brought us back to healthier ideas." Lefort traced the growing recognition of France's demographic inferiority from Léonce de Lavergne to Gustave Lagneau. There could be no more doubt that the republic faced a depopulation crisis of immense proportions. "What increases our alarm," he stated, "is the preoccupation of national defense. Our patriotism is agitated at the thought that a moment will come when, despite all our sacrifices, France will find it impossible to oppose the German army with an army [that is] numerically equal." Lefort believed that his nation still had time to reform. Awakened by the "thunderclap" of 1870, morally chastened and militarily reorganized, the French state should undertake measures to surmount the demographic deficit.[29] The only question was: how?

A Touch of Xenophobia

Before proceeding, it may be well to account for a factor too frequently ignored: the presence in late nineteenth-century France of more than a million foreigners. Between 1850 and 1890 their number tripled (see Table 2). It is difficult to say precisely when public concern became aroused about this development, although it is certain that the defeat of 1870 created a climate of suspicion about political spies and foreign agents that promoted a xenophobic strain later to erupt in the Dreyfus Affair.[30] As noted, one may find some scattered references by French writers before 1870 to the "degeneracy of the race," but there is no evidence that such remarks at first related this danger to the influx of foreigners, whose numbers were still scant.[31] By the 1880s, however, that association became established in the minds of many who commented on France's demographic crisis, a psychological phenomenon of the early Third Republic that is too characteristic to neglect.

Most of the newcomers to France were migrant laborers who infiltrated border areas and sought menial jobs in agriculture and industry, or in some cases as domestic servants. The two heaviest concentrations were Italians in the Marseille area and Belgians around Lille and in the mining regions of the north. Spaniards, in fewer numbers, remained mostly in the Midi; whereas the Germans, as Dr. Jules Rochard put it with a somewhat sinister twist, "slip in everywhere."[32] The latter were normally indistinguishable from the 100,000 or so Alsatians who had crossed the new national border immediately after 1870 to take up residence in France. By 1890 foreigners constituted virtually 3 percent of the French population, and they were reputed to be multiplying at a rate far exceeding that of the indigenous citizenry. This, too, had a comparative aspect: for every 1,000 residents, England had 5 aliens, Germany 6, and France 23. The first European people to face the modern social problem of *Gastarbeiter* in their midst were thus the French.[33]

Table 2 / Immigrants in France, 1850–1890

1851	379,289
1861	497,091
1866	635,495
1872	740,667
1876	801,754
1881	1,001,090
1886	1,115,214

Source: Gustave Lagneau, "Des mesures propres à rendre moins faible l'accroissement de la population de la France en restreignant ses fâcheuses conditions démographiques," Bulletin de l'Académie de Médecine, 22 July 1890.

Among those to express frank alarm at this development was Émile Cheysson, who projected that the steady rise of foreign population through immigration and reproduction would within fifty years reach a figure of 10 million. It required no statistical wizardry to calculate that such a number, given the nation's nearly stagnant demography, would in that event represent a quarter of the total French population. Besides, Cheysson commented, this huge alien work force might constitute a "hostile and dangerous element."[34] Before charging Cheysson with flagrant prejudice, it is proper to consider his purpose. A chief of the French temperance movement and an inveterate reformer associated with numerous worthy philanthropic causes, he apparently found the frightening prospect of a foreign inundation convenient as a warning to others about what could occur if moral regeneration and legislative action in France were not promptly forthcoming. A scare might be salutary.

Cheysson's views were soon repeated, however, by other members of the French medical community. Once again, the most strident of these was Jules Rochard, who wondered why France had three times as many alien residents as Germany and England combined. He placed blame on the moral sloth of the French worker, who "labors all the less the more he is paid" and who squanders half of his wages in drinking and whoring. Employers were consequently motivated to hire foreigners. But these outsiders, claimed Rochard before a plenary session of the Academy of Medicine, "do not have the same interests or the same feelings as we. They love their own country and do not respect ours. . . . In our foreign wars and in our domestic quarrels, we have never found among them but enemies."[35] If some plausible excuse may be advanced for Cheysson's statements, surely none can be made for Rochard's amplification of them, which manifestly exceeded the bounds of decency. His disparagement of immigrants also had a more reprehensible ring because it was noticeably tinged with anti-Semitism. When Dr. Louis Hardy praised French Jews as "diligent, intelligent, industrious, ambitious, . . . and prolific," in short as "good Frenchmen," Rochard retorted that "Israelites" living in France (including some of his colleagues in the Academy) might well justify Hardy's description of them, "but people who have known Jews elsewhere . . . do not share the same illusions."[36]

There is no way to measure the impact or extent of such innuendos. One can only record that racism was not entirely removed from the depopulation debate among the social and medical elite. It is relevant to observe, moreover, that this talk coincided with an increase of public discussion about the "three great scourges" of modern society: alcoholism, tuberculosis, and syphilis. These plagues were generally considered to be products of the "poisonous influence of urban life," as Gustave Lagneau said, but a supposition also survived that heredity remained a factor in their dissemination. Bad blood, especially lower-class blood, was thought to predispose an individual to dissipation, disease, and moral decadence—a leitmotiv in the popular novels of Émile Zola.[37] Thus a certain irrationality, on which xenophobia by definition thrives, surrounded the crowded and contaminated working quarters of Paris and other cities where foreigners gathered. Then as now, the social question of slums and their clearance held a racial as well as a class component.

In 1890 Lagneau, as one of the Academy's acknowledged experts on population growth, attempted to summarize the demographic situation. His lengthy report included several remarks about foreigners in France, whose presence had doubtless "frightened many of our compatriots." He did not neglect to praise the positive contribution of alien workers, who were helping in effect to offset the nation's insufficient birthrate. But his closing statement contained an apocalyptic vision of future French decadence: a people losing rank and respect, unable to defend itself, forever at the mercy of other nations. "Let us not forget," Lagneau wrote, "that 1,500 years ago a partially depopulated Roman Empire, although highly civilized, was helpless to resist the invasion of immigrant multitudes, who dismembered and destroyed it."[38] From this dubious analogy one might have surmised that Lagneau favored a proposal that France promptly close its borders. To the contrary, he advocated that naturalization procedures be simplified and financial assistance be extended by the republican government to hasten the integration of aliens. Yet, not surprisingly, Lagneau's generosity did not gain unanimous consent in the Academy of Medicine. Among his opponents it was, one more time, Jules Rochard who most forcefully restated the negative arguments and statistics of years past, thereby projecting a far less flattering image of France's immigrants: "It was they, during the Franco-Prussian war, who guided the enemy through our countryside and led their compatriots to farms where they were housed and fed. It is they whom we shall find, in a moment of rebellion, fanning the flames of discord in our workshops and factories." Such social elements were simply not to be trusted, Rochard insisted, and the republic must therefore act "to save our valiant race and to prevent the pollution of French blood."[39]

This narrow but sharp focus on French opinion within the medical community may suffice to document that a xenophobic tone was clearly detectable in the public discussion of demography. We now know that such latent racism was no isolated phenomenon. If France's dispersed resident aliens were statistically marginal in the early 1890s, their cumulative presence was psychologically more central than anyone as yet had reason to suspect. The full truth did not begin to emerge until that day, soon thereafter, when Alfred Dreyfus was falsely accused as a German collaborator.

The Search for Solutions

If an increase of state intervention was desirable to counteract France's relative demographic retardation, it was doubtful that much could be done to restore a higher birth rate. Instead, the initial priority of French social policy was to reduce the death rate, and in particular to minimize infant mortality. This had been the paramount objective of the Loi Roussel in 1874, just as it was the subject of a contest sponsored at the same time by the Academy of Medicine, which annually offered a prize of 2,000 francs for the best essay on "La mortalité du premier âge."[40] The republic thereby groped rather aimlessly for a remedy to social problems that would not be soon or easily solved.

As time passed, the conviction grew that a broad campaign would be required to cope with the questions of public health, hygiene, and housing. We have already located the more obvious irritants that roughed the surface of society: mendicants, alcoholics, prostitutes, the ill, the infirm, and the aged. Too numerous to be ignored, they somehow had to be controlled, cared for, and if possible cured, beyond the basic necessities of being fed and lodged. And they were all part of the depopulation crisis insofar as they represented unproductive elements of the population supported by the rest. Private charity had proved incapable of meeting their needs. More public assistance was consequently required. If so, the instigation of a greater role for the republican state was imperative. Such were the primary assumptions at which reformers arrived in the 1880s. "It is up to the government," exclaimed Dr. Paul Brouardel, dean of the faculty of medicine at the Sorbonne, as he threw his support to a mandatory vaccination program against smallpox.[41] This simple declarative sentence expressed the attitude of those who saw no other recourse if France hoped to remain competitive as a major European power and to retain stature in the vanguard of civilization.

But grand aspirations had first to be translated into legislative action. Here an initial glance at the housing question may serve to illuminate the problems and possibilities before 1890. The operative law concerning the construction and maintenance of private dwellings dated from April 1850. This was basically a sanitation measure passed by the Second Republic in the wake of cholera epidemics during the previous decade. Befitting the liberal ethos of that time, the adopted regulations urged—but did not mandate—the creation of communal sanitation committees to implement controls and fumigation procedures for homes and tenements. Yet by the end of the 1850s, of the approximately 35,000 communes of France, only about 500 had actually created such committees, mostly in the larger cities. Even these efforts, as Martin Nadaud noted in submitting a new bill to promote more sanitary housing in 1881, were "too timid." Placed under no obligation to comply, most landlords did nothing; and the intended reform languished. As a consequence, Nadaud charged, there were "millions of poor creatures lodged in ramshackle huts, exposed to every inclemency of the seasons." He estimated that there were 219,700 dwellings in France without a single window: "air and light enter these execrable hovels only through a door or through a hole in the door." The main culprit was an "odious" tax on doors and windows, borrowed from the English (who had meanwhile repealed it). Often with six persons confined to tiny enclosed living quarters, many families were forced to live in suffocating misery. Nadaud spoke of more than a million "martyrs" who existed in circumstances "completely identical to that of animals." His proposal was as simple as his portrayal was harsh: "Republican authorities must intervene."[42]

A parliamentary committee established to investigate Nadaud's bill bore out the accuracy of his description. In Paris alone, where more strenuous efforts to promote sanitation had been made than elsewhere, 6 percent of families still had no heat and 3 percent received air only from corridors. At least 25,000 Parisian families lived in one-room apartments, where "two, three, and four often sleep in the same bed." Such intolerable conditions were doubtless widespread in France, and the investigators accordingly recommended that the creation of sanitation committees be made obligatory in every commune.[43] A delegation of the Paris Municipal Council reached a similar conclusion. Despite Haussmann's construction of aqueducts and sewers before 1870, the city's water supply and drainage system were inadequate. A large percentage of apartments in the capital lacked running water or flushing toilets. These insalubrious conditions were bound to be reflected in the statistics of disease and death. "The truth is," read the committee's report, "that the evil is within our homes." It followed that new construction and sanitary regulations must be made obligatory.[44]

At the Academy of Medicine the diagnosis was identical. In January 1886 the retiring president, Jules Bergeron, commented on a study by Paul Brouardel of the recent cholera outbreaks in Marseille, where "the disastrous influence of insalubrity" had greatly aggravated the pestilence and revealed "monstrous abuses" permitted by existing legislation. Brouardel's resolution, also in favor of reforming the law of 1850, was unanimously adopted.[45]

Each of these three forums of reform—a parliamentary committee, the Municipal Council of Paris, and the Academy of Medicine—expressed mutual concern about the seriousness of social problems and a conviction that governmental intervention was essential to deal with them. These views were not deduced from ideological principles but derived from demographic facts. Nor did they fail to affect the highest levels of republican administration. In January 1887 Édouard Lockroy, an old ally of Léon Gambetta and currently minister of commerce and industry, introduced a legislative bill on "the sanitation of insalubrious lodgings and dwellings." This was to be part of a larger scheme to reorganize France's entire system of public hygienic services. Lockroy condemned the practices of the past, saying that roughly 29,000 of France's communes had neither a physician nor a health officer. Large areas lacked any possibility of ensuring the health of their population. The state should therefore attempt to establish communal health agencies, to implement uniform sanitary regulations, to provide inspection, and to enforce penalties in cases of noncompliance.[46] In essence, Lockroy's proposals were a logical sequel to adoption by the Third Republic of universal military conscription and compulsory primary education. His ambition to provide a minimum of health care for every French citizen was born of the same impetus and in much the same spirit. Yet it was unclear how far the movement for reform would carry.[47]

In the summer of 1890 a second major round of debate on the depopulation crisis was opened in the Academy of Medicine. We need not rehearse once more the statistical details, which only confirmed and extended those already recorded in 1885: marriages were fewer and later, the birthrate was down, illegitimacy was up, and so on. Gustave Lagneau could add but a few new numbers of consequence, explaining for instance that while an approximate average of 3 children were born into every French family, only 2.07 of them survived the ravages of infant mortality. Thus the French population was nearly stable, since the annual figures of births and deaths were in reality almost even. France was perilously close to an absolute demographic deficit (which would be reached by 1893 and attained irregularly in the decade thereafter). Some individuals might see the small family as a virtue, Lagneau observed, but "it is not the same from a collective point of view, from the standpoint of the nation."[48]

Although discussion of Lagneau's report filled dozens of pages of transcript, few of his medical colleagues found any reason to contest his general conclusion that "our demographic situation is far from brilliant." Nor was there much controversy over most of his specific suggestions for reform: to simplify marriage procedures, to discourage migration to Paris and to spur the growth of "secondary cities," to modify tax and inheritance laws, to foster colonial expansion, to aid pregnant women and unwed mothers. A minor disagreement erupted about reform of military recruitment: whether solely eldest sons should be drafted or whether conscription should be truly universal, as Lagneau himself advocated, "for against the armed nation of Germany we must be able to oppose the armed nation of France."[49] Even Lagneau's nemesis Jules Rochard was now willing to concede that France's demographic retardation was "a danger from every viewpoint." But his opinion was that the social issues raised in the depopulation debate should be left to the legislature. As for medical practice, Rochard unexceptionally advocated stricter enforcement of the Loi Roussel. More surprisingly, he also agreed with Paul Brouardel on the advisability of obligatory smallpox vaccination, even though that measure might be regrettable as an infraction of personal freedom. As Rochard now admitted: "The liberty of the individual has as its limit first the liberty of his neighbor and then the general interest."[50]

Therewith the depopulation controversy slackened in its intensity. The initially sharp differences had been somewhat eroded by a steady shower of statistics. The reality of France's demographic stagnation was established by irrefutable data, against which purely ideological arguments could no longer prevail. At the very least, some of the most fundamental assumptions of French liberalism had thus come under challenge. The traditional doctrines of individual freedom, limited government, and free enterprise were threatened by intractable numbers. Accordingly, the case for social reform through state intervention was henceforth on the national agenda.

Chapter 3

The German Model

Viewed in an international context, the social problems faced by France after 1870 were not untypical of late nineteenth-century Europe. Only their pace and pattern were peculiar. In the early phase of industrialization, of course, France had been a leader, along with Britain, at a time when artisanship was still a primary mode of production. But the passage to factory labor on a large scale was another matter, and it was one that the English and the Germans managed rather better than the French. Although Napoleon III presided over an expanding economy in the two decades after 1848, the rate of growth was already beginning to flag before 1870. The war was then a severe shock to an already weakened system, and three decades of relative economic lethargy followed.

Thus the French nation was slow to enter the later phase of industrialization and was handicapped when it did so. Among the obvious measurements of France's development was a persistently high percentage of rural population or, inversely, a consistent but slow pace of urbanization before 1900, which was thrown into especially sharp relief by the contrast with Germany.[1] Because the German industrial spurt of the late nineteenth century was unmatched by France, it is certainly logical—and perhaps accurate—to suppose that the attendant social problems were objectively more acute east of the Rhine. Poverty and pauperism, social dislocation and structural unemployment, rural misery and urban crowding: these are the general terms appropriate to describe the more pronounced effects engendered in Germany by a swift transition to modern industry based on concentrated factory production. France surely did not remain untouched. But meanwhile, by comparison with imperial Germany after 1870, the early Third Republic seemed to slumber.[2]

Urgent problems often require drastic solutions. Such may be in part the explanation of why Germany took the initiative in social welfare, whereas France moved more slowly and hesitantly. There is no doubt that Germany thereby assumed a pioneering role in regard to the social question in Europe. With a later start in this regard, like other nations on the Continent, France was forced to evaluate precedents already set. The German model could be accepted, modified, or rejected—but not ignored. It is therefore essential to take stock of the example that was to orient so much of reformist effort in France.

The Role of the State

Social reform in Germany was not solely a consequence of national unification. Yet the rapidity and comprehensiveness of legislative change would have been impossible without a coherent political framework. Long-standing German traditions of local and regional government provided the basis upon which a system of social welfare could be constructed, but they did not in themselves generate sufficient impetus for the quantum leap that occurred after 1870. For that remarkable transition only one explanation is finally adequate: the dynamism of the Bismarckian Reich.[3] Naturally it can be argued that a key lay in the unbroken continuity of Prussian etatism. Just as William added the title of Kaiser to that of king, one might say, so did the imperial state superimpose a new social program on a monarchical one. This assertion, however, understates the remarkable innovation of Germany's national welfare scheme and dismisses too lightly the obstacles to its realization. The manifest incapacity of older institutions to deal with the Reich's growing social difficulties was precisely the issue around which the German debate pivoted. Past initiatives had been too scattered and niggardly. To be successful, the theorists of reform contended, future legislation must be coherent in principle and broad in application. These were the conditions that the national state alone could assure. Within Prussia in the 1870s, the liberals still constituted the single most potent political faction, and elsewhere in Germany particularism continued to hold Berlin's aggrandizing proclivities in check. Much of the internal history of this period—such as Bismarck's woes over railways and taxes, for example—cannot otherwise be comprehended.[4] Yet a general dissipation of liberal and federal energies gradually became evident. Furthermore, the economic crisis after 1873 raised skepticism about the future of free trade. The dismissal in 1876 of Bismarck's chief economic advisor, Rudolf von Delbrück, was an unmistakable signal that a new policy of protectionist tariffs was in prospect. As the National Liberal party began to crumble, the chancellor was able to consolidate a more centralized authority through bureaucratic machinery in the nation's capital. This, rather than parliamentarization of the government, was the most characteristic political development of the Kaiserreich after the 1870s.[5]

Certain specific measures were already indicative of the regime's willingness to assume an active part in matters of health and welfare. The earliest and most striking of these was the *Reichsimpfgesetz* of 1874, which imposed a program of obligatory vaccination and revaccination against smallpox on all German citizens, thereby bringing large segments of the population for the first time into direct contact with state-sponsored medical care. The immediate salutary effect of this campaign went far to enhance Berlin's reputation as a patron of public hygiene.[6] Scarcely less significant was the creation in 1876 of a *Reichsgesundheitsamt*, which established its own laboratories and testing procedures intended to set national norms in the treatment of infectious diseases. The emergence of Robert Koch as a scientist of world rank was only the most notable aspect of this centrally subsidized research effort. At the same time, uniform entrance requirements and certification procedures were introduced for all German medical students, both as an encouragement and a control of what can fairly be described as a medical boom before the First World War. It is important to mention, finally, a law in April 1876 that regulated independent insurance companies and required all German industrial workers over sixteen years of age to enroll in an obligatory medical plan unless otherwise covered. This so-called *Zwangskasse* therewith became situated in the German landscape as an archtypical institution of the nation's welfare structure.[7]

Such was the background for the adoption of three major reform bills during the Reich's second decade: illness insurance (1883), accident insurance (1884), and disability insurance with retirement pensions (1889). Each of these will require closer examination as to content and impact. But first we should inquire about the surrounding circumstances and ask the obvious questions: why Germany, and why then? These queries unavoidably pose, in turn, one of the most frequently debated problems of modern European history concerning the innermost motivations of Bismarckian policy. No brief discussion can adequately summarize an already existing scholarly literature of immense proportions, but it is possible to distinguish three interpretive approaches by the specialists who have attempted to integrate biographical data with sociopolitical context.

The first is the most flattering for Bismarck. He is seen in this perspective as a progeny of old-fashioned patriarchalism and as an exponent of traditional Lutheran morality. Here one may properly stress Bismarck's origins within the petty nobility of east Prussia, his experience as a Junker landowner and manager of an estate, his benevolent lordly demeanor with peasants and rural laborers. It was therefore only natural that he should regard the social question in Germany in light of his manorial upbringing and respond to it with a benign spirit of Christian charity. The evident trace of hagiography in this version should not obliterate some larger realities that ring true: the highly stratified structure of Prussian society, the mixture of familiarity and apprehension (especially after 1848) with which patricians regarded their social inferiors, and the understandable wish to maintain a sturdy and devoted labor force in order to assure uninterrupted production. These seigneurial concerns could easily be transferred from feudal practice to national politics, and there is evidence that Bismarck was conscious of doing so. "If there is to be revolution," as he once observed, "it is better to make than to endure one."[8]

A second classic interpretation, far less personally obliging for Bismarck, is that he acted to undercut the appeal of German Social Democracy. His first and most fundamental impulse was always repressive, early expressed in the turmoil of 1848 and thirty years later through anti-Socialist legislation. But he needed to harness the labor force, not merely to throttle it, and hence he schemed to proffer generous welfare benefits to the German workers—all the better to keep them slogging along. Bismarck emerges as a cruel taskmaster whose rather small carrot seems altogether out of proportion to his huge stick. Historians who draw this image of the chancellor generally spice their story with ironical commentary on his devious character, although they may also concede that the new social legislation represented a considerable advance over the woefully inadequate poor relief measures (*Armenpflege*) of the prenational past. However hypocritical Bismarck's intentions may have been, the enduring results of his welfare bills were admittedly not deplorable. Such a concession comes all the easier in view of the Social Democratic party's success in rebounding after 1890 to become the largest single political formation in the country. Still, no special thanks for that advance need necessarily be wasted on Bismarck, who remains in this version a deceitful brute.[9]

Although the two foregoing scenarios appear at first blush to be totally incompatible, they in fact share a few common characteristics. Their complementarity was already suggested by the famous "imperial message" (*kaiserliche Botschaft*), written by Bismarck, which opened the Reichstag session in November 1881. This statement contained references to the "moral foundation of the Christian community" as well as to the need for a "repression of Social Democratic excesses." Both were somehow to contribute to the "well-being of the workers."[10] If Bismarck's biographers have tended to stress one or the other aspect of his policy, depending on the degree of their empathy for his efforts as a social reformer, we may safely assume that the chancellor himself saw no contradiction and claimed them both. His attitude reflected that of virtually all European statesmen of his time, particularly after the Paris Commune, when it was the presumed duty of every government to ensure the domestic tranquility of its citizenry by all appropriate means. Thus "repression" did not need to be a dirty word insofar as it implied a legitimate response to subversion.[11]

We may begin to trace a third scenario, then, by challenging the implicit premise of the first two that Bismarck must be understood as the Great Manipulator. Whether judged favorably or harshly, he has ordinarily been considered a consummate politician fully in charge of circumstances. He outmaneuvered friend and foe alike, we are led to believe, and had his way with them. But a closer look suggests that this assumption may be deficient by disregarding factors exceeding Bismarck's grasp. Arguably he is better depicted not as initiating change but as responding to conditions beyond his control. There was first of all the economy, which had spun out of its high orbit in 1873 and which left a trail of disastrous investments, bankruptcies, failed mergers, and disappointed speculators. The switch to protectionism was in actuality a slow process of political erosion rather than the shrewd calculation of an economic expert. The same was true of Bismarck's abandonment of the Kulturkampf, which had brought him only grief. The fortuitous death of Pius IX in 1878 gave him a chance to cut his losses, not to impose his will. Even the Dual Alliance with Austria-Hungary, concluded at the same time, may be properly perceived as the defensive measure of a statesman constantly worried about the *cauchemar des coalitions* and concerned to establish a tight island of security in the midst of diplomatic uncertainties. Nor were Germany's domestic politics in the 1870s more gratifying to Bismarck. The unruly bickering of parties and factions was an unending source of his dyspepsia. The chancellor found himself constrained to court the favor of liberals and progressives, and he was frequently rebuffed in his attempts to do so. Meanwhile, Catholics and Socialists reciprocated his mistrust of them. And the partisans of particularism remained hostile to his efforts to enhance the national regime at the expense of state's rights, as Bismarck's thwarted plans to consolidate the regional railways and to create a tobacco monopoly clearly revealed. Little wonder that he never literally resorted to a national plebiscite.[12]

To all these difficulties, which displayed anything but an indomitable captain firmly in command of his crew, another may be added that is of special concern here: the incapability of the central state before 1880 to regulate matters of public health. We have noted an exception confirming the rule: the implementation of a national smallpox vaccination program. Otherwise problems such as sanitation, water purification, assistance to the poor, hospices and hospitals, and the distribution of food, clothing, and medicine were largely under local or liberal auspices. The government of the Reich was as yet lacking the bureaucratic machinery, the cadre of public officials, and the extensive legal prerogatives necessary to conduct a coordinated campaign to improve public hygiene. Private and civic agencies functioned instead. They also proliferated. A significant facet of midcentury Germany had been the development of a network of independent organizations, collectively known as *Vereinswesen*, that attempted to aid the needy and to encourage them to self-help.[13] The liberals, too, came to be thought of as enemies of the Reich by Bismarck, because they were gradually consolidating their position as patrons of the poor and thereby, in their fashion, fostering estrangement from the national state. To rout the liberals and to repress the Socialists were thus two inextricable aspects of the same policy. Bismarck wanted to break the link between liberalism and socialism while capturing labor as a client of the state. Again, this motive can best be evaluated not as cool and skillful manipulation by a powerful impresario but as an improvised attempt to contend with disorder. Bismarck acted out of apprehension that events and institutions would stray irretrievably out of his control unless he somehow intervened.[14]

Speculative as it must remain, this third image of Bismarck is the one that best accords with his avowed objective in proposing welfare legislation: "I recommend the Reich itself as an entrepreneur."[15] That is, the chancellor hoped to have a highly centralized national insurance plan funded mostly through state subsidies and subjected to rigid state controls. But this ambition, initially attached to his accident insurance plan, was rejected by the Reichstag, and a series of compromises became unavoidable. In that sense it is a misnomer to speak of "Bismarckian social legislation," because the actual result failed to conform to the chancellor's intentions. Still, after 1880, the Reich moved farther and faster than any other European state to deal with the social question. By doing so, although imperfectly from Bismarck's point of view, Germany set a standard by which the other industrial nations must be measured.[16]

The Scope of Legislation

Because of its rejection by the Reichstag, Bismarck's initial draft of the accident insurance law had to be withdrawn for revision. Thus the first bill to pass in 1883 concerned sickness insurance, followed a year later by the chancellor's pet project after its modification. The two were meant to be complementary. They were then augmented in 1889 by legislation covering the disabled and the aged. Together, this trio of enactments constituted the first comprehensive program of social insurance in Europe. By any standards, not only Bismarck's, the outcome was only a rudimentary system, which at first affected barely 10 percent of the German population and which did so inadequately. But a fair evaluation should not stress unduly the early imperfections and limitations of this welfare concept without recog-

nizing the bold innovations that it embodied. Throughout, despite all
the original complexities and subsequent rectifications, the German
model of social reform steadfastly revolved on the principle of obligation: all workers were to be insured, and all insurance would ultimately be subject to state regulation. If certain voluntarist elements
were allowed to remain, and if administrative autonomy (*Selbstverwaltung*) was left to insurance agencies, the total plan was circum-
scribed within a set of mandatory provisions. In its central principle,
then, the German precedent was unequivocal.[17]

The 1883 law allowed for a variety of insurance groups. They
included the continued existence both of independent mutual funds
(*Hilfskassen*), in which membership was entirely voluntary, and of
agencies founded in individual enterprises (*Betriebskassen*). Also permitted were the special funds for miners (*Knappschaftskassen*), which
had long enjoyed a separate status. But the real novelty of the law
was to expand and strengthen the role of municipal insurance funds
(*Ortskrankenkassen*), which were charged with covering all those workers who were not included in some other plan. Thus the basic conception of obligatory insurance (*Kassenzwang*) was effectively combined with a latitude of free choice. The entire scheme was to be
under state supervision—presumably meaning that Berlin was the
final arbiter—but in keeping with the federalist spirit of the Reichstag, it was to be decentralized and corporative in administrative
structure. Accordingly, a central office was established in the nation's
capital (*Reichsversicherungsamt*), although the daily operations of the
program were handled through regional and professional groupings, not directly "from above" on a national basis.[18]

So much for the theory. In truth, as the most careful historians
of the subject have noted, a tendency toward consolidation and centralization was evident from the outset. Compulsory organizations
campaigned actively to absorb voluntary agencies. The advantages
of amalgamation were soon manifest: more members in a single insurance group meant more efficient and less costly administration,
broader coverage, higher allocations, and special services such as the
sponsorship of popular sanatoria for tuberculosis patients. The small
and scattered independent agencies were hard pressed to match such
benefits. Furthermore, they were more expensive for members. Employers were required to contribute one-third of the total income of
obligatory agencies but nothing for voluntary plans; the latter were

thus entirely dependent on the regular payment of premiums by workers. The law thereby created an uneven struggle, which could only tilt finally in one direction. Because the entire insurance system would function under state control, moreover, the intention of liberal parliamentarians to delimit government intervention favoring obligatory funds "revealed itself in reality as illusory."[19]

The 1883 plan provided coverage of sickness for a maximum of thirteen weeks (extended in 1903 to twenty-six), during which time the worker received compensation (*Krankengeld*): one-half of a man's wages, one-third of a woman's. Services included free medical care, free medication, and free hospitalization if necessary. A supplement was sometimes available for the worker's family, as well as a special bonus in case of death (*Sterbegeld*).[20] Even from this brief enumeration it is readily apparent that the adjustment of insurance claims was fraught with inequities and uncertainties. All disputes were to be settled by the agency's directorate (*Vorstand*), which also managed routine operations. The law stipulated that this executive body, in proportion to the monetary contributions over which it disposed, should be composed of two-thirds workers and one-third employers. At the time of the plan's inception the Social Democratic party was reluctant to participate in directorates, but it quickly became obvious that such recalcitrance was a foolish waste of opportunity, often to the detriment of individual claimants. A countertrend soon prevailed to encourage the active engagement by workers in insurance directorates, which they could often control, to the mutual discomfort of employers and medical personnel, who were thereby required by law to conform to orders from representatives of a lower class.[21]

In its structure and administrative procedures the 1884 bill on accident insurance was an extension of the previous law. Further details are therefore superfluous. The importance of this legislation lay not only in its broader and better coverage but also in a fundamental shift to the principle of no-fault accident insurance. Prior to the 1880s Germany had known a wide variety of accident plans, frequently founded by factory owners whose interest it was to rehabilitate skilled workers injured on the job. Yet what was common to such arrangements was a stipulation that, in order to collect benefits, the worker must first prove that an accident was caused by the neglect or mistake of an employer. In practice such irrefutable proof was possible only in about 20 percent of cases; and even in those instances an

adjudication was sometimes long, embarrassing, and financially ruinous for the individual laborer.[22] This cumbersome procedure, with
its intrinsic social injustice, was now terminated. Henceforth industrial accidents would be considered as an unfortunate consequence of
the workplace, in which management and labor were mutually engaged, and the sole criterion for insurance claims would be a medical
appraisal of injury. It is intriguing to note that, after adoption of the
1884 law, the number of reported industrial accidents increased,
whereas the percentage of deaths caused by them declined. This
phenomenon may seem ambiguous, but it suggests an atmosphere in
the factory that was at the same time less fearful and more safety
conscious.[23]

Innovative as these two earlier bills were, the most pioneering
law was potentially the third. It was also the most controversial,
barely passing through the Reichstag after an intensive debate in
1889. The arguments began with questions of administration. Financial support for disability and retirement pensions, certain to be extremely expensive, was to come equally from employers and workers.
This stipulation raised doubts about cost as well as distribution of
power in the directorate, which was likewise to be split fifty-fifty. The
possibilities for deadlock would be correspondingly greater, so it appeared, and as a consequence the importance of the Reich's central
insurance office as arbiter and enforcer of the law would be unavoidably enhanced. Although regional in principle, therefore, the plan
was sure to hasten centralization in practice. Insofar as disability insurance was concerned, such fears were perhaps exaggerated and
did not endure. By 1911 the number of those receiving invalidity
benefits surpassed a million, and the concrete advantages of a greater flexibility in insurance adjustments were apparent to all. A worker
who was incapacitated by illness or accident, and whose allocations
were about to lapse, could be simply reclassified as disabled and then
transferred to another category without interruption of benefits.
There is little doubt that this aspect of the 1889 legislation gained
rapid acceptance, not to say popularity, among the laboring population.[24]

More problematical, however, was the restrictive nature of retirement pensions. To be eligible a worker had to contribute regularly to
the plan for a period of thirty years (reduced in 1900 to twenty-four).
Benefits would not be returned to the worker until the age of seventy

(later set at sixty-five). No genius was necessary to calculate the infinitesimal chances for the average worker of living long enough to realize a secure retirement. Many employees plausibly saw this provision of the law merely as a de facto reduction of their wages, from which few would reap any ultimate reward. Accordingly, application of the pension program proved to be halting. Few lives were directly affected by it before 1914, by which time the number receiving benefits had barely reached 100,000 persons.[25]

The German welfare system, in sum, left much to be desired and criticized. As a safety net for the poor it remained skimpy and full of gaping holes. Even for those who benefited from the new programs, the result was often not what could literally be described as social security. Thousands of workers continued to live on the margin. Yet, that stated, it is distorting to dwell solely on the inadequacies of German social legislation. One must also underscore its pathbreaking precedents and its potential for improvement. The social question was far from resolved in Germany by 1889, but the design of a daring new structure was already discernible.

The Statistics of Expansion

Germany's extraordinary demographic surge in the nineteenth century, despite a slowly declining rate of birth after 1870, could not fail to have a severe impact on public health. The good news was a larger work force, hence greater productivity and an irregular but irrepressible rise in national wealth and real wages. The bad news was an urbanizing population containing more poor, more ill, and more aged persons than ever before. For better and worse, Germany was growing.

When moving beyond these imprecise generalities, one must proceed with caution. Reliable statistics for the period before 1870 are, with scattered exceptions, unavailable; and even for the decades following, there is always a danger of panning fool's gold. The best available source for the years from 1875 to 1892 is provided by the annual statistical reports of Prussia, and thereafter by those of the Reich. In 1913 a new method of calculation was introduced, which complicated comparisons.[26] These figures have been carefully studied by scholars of health and medicine, who have derived a fairly consistent numerical pattern, despite notable differences of interpretation. It is therefore on this uneven base of statistical consensus and ideological disagreement that any analysis must rest.

First the numbers. One simple arrangement of statistical curves is to sort out those that were falling from those that were rising. For instance—although the configuration is somewhat blurred by distinctions of age, gender, and region—the total mortality rate of Germany was unquestionably dropping between 1870 and 1914. This trend was especially marked for infants, notably after 1900; but it was also evident for young male urban workers.[27] One indication is provided by a decline in the rate of deaths from tuberculosis, still counted among the "big killers" of the time: in Prussia the mortality from consumption was recorded as 31.9 per 10,000 in 1875; 19.7 in 1903; and 13.7 in 1913. These sharply declining rates represented, respectively, 16.4 percent, 17.6 percent, and 16.5 percent of the nation's annual deaths. Because these percentages remained almost constant, the decrease in tuberculosis mortality manifestly mirrored a corresponding fall in the global death rate and contributed to it. When inverted, of course, these numbers reflected a rise in the average life expectancy of Germans, roughly from forty to fifty, in the years from 1870 to 1914.[28]

During the same period the number of licensed physicians in Germany nearly trebled: from about 12,000 in the early 1870s to 15,000 in 1886, then from 26,000 in 1901 to over 30,000 by 1911.[29] The growth of medical studies was more erratic. The quantity of students doubled in the early 1880s, leveled off for a time thereafter, then spurted once more in the years before 1914 (see Table 3). Medical facilities meanwhile expanded along with medical practice: 16.5 hospital beds per 10,000 in 1877, 31.0 in 1901, 41.5 in 1911, and 53.1 by 1921. In absolute terms this development meant that the number of patients who could be confined at any given moment tripled from 72,219 to 226,831—without counting specialized institutions such as sanatoria.[30] Naturally the distribution of available hospital space was unequal, favoring the larger cities. In Berlin over 60 beds per 10,000 were in service by 1913. Of those treated in these medical facilities, it should be added, about 90 percent were supported by public assistance funds or workers' insurance; the number of private patients was only a tenth of the total. Thus the general hospital remained primarily but not exclusively an urban institution for the poor, albeit one that was greatly expanded and diversified.[31]

Table 3 / Medical Students in German Universities, 1848–1912

1847–48	1,570
1859–60	2,025
1869–70	3,033
1879–80	3,760
1889–90	8,558
1899–1900	7,433
1909–10	9,274
1911–12	11,518

Source: Claudia Huerkamp, Der Aufstieg der Ärzte im 19. Jahrhundert
(Göttingen, 1985), p. 62.

The core of the German model of sickness insurance was the concept that all workers over sixteen years of age earning under 2,000 marks annually in mining, industry, and artisanal trades *must* be insured. Initially, as we saw, when the 1883 law was first implemented, this requirement included somewhat fewer than 5 million persons, or less than 10 percent of the entire German population. But as the years passed, the notion of "worker" was stretched to cover more and more occupational groups—farm and forestry laborers, for instance, and white-collar employees (*Angestellten*)—with the effect that by 1914 well over 15 million were directly insured against illness. Because the coverage was gradually extended to family members as well, it is permissible to conclude that half of the total German population was eligible for benefits before the First World War—and it was that half (as always, with exceptions) that needed social insurance the most.[32]

More clients meant more claims. It was inevitable that the number of local offices handling obligatory insurance would grow rapidly: from 754 in 1876 to over 23,000 by 1911. Meanwhile the quantity of voluntary agencies virtually stagnated.[33] Social insurance groups were not only more numerous, they became much more wealthy and were consequently able to distribute ever increasing sums to the ill: 47 million marks in 1885, 89 million in 1891, 163 million in 1901, and 358 million in 1911. These figures record a repeated doubling of volume.[34] Allocations for accident insurance likewise exploded: from 3.7 million marks in 1886 to 18 million already in 1891, that is, a leap of almost fourfold in the first half-decade of operations. Disability insurance and old-age pensions, as indicated, made much slower progress: from 11.5 million marks in 1891 to almost 14 million in 1905. By the eve of the First World War, all told, the amount of insurance funds flowing through publicly regulated agencies in Germany was approaching a half billion marks annually.[35] Furthermore, a matter insufficiently appreciated, insurance companies became major purveyors of development loans to German municipalities. By making massive credit available to cities and townships across the land, they contributed importantly to the creation of communal infrastructures, which were so crucial in the amelioration of public health and hygiene. Such municipal loans constituted less than 6 million marks in 1894 but exceeded a billion marks by 1912.[36]

The actual amount awarded by social insurance funds to an individual naturally depended on such variables as the type of medical problem, the technique of treatment, and the length of hospital care. Hence it is difficult to determine what impact such coverage had on the "average" patient. Yet we can gather an approximate sense from available statistics. They suggest, first of all, that claims were filed and honored in vastly increased numbers. The total days of sick leave covered rose from 25 million in 1885 to 40 million in 1891, to 66 million in 1901, and to 115 million in 1911. During that quarter of a century the average days of treatment per patient increased from 14 to 20, and the average sum allocated per illness climbed from 26 to 62 marks.[37] These figures give some concrete meaning to the otherwise vague notion of "medicalization." It seems that the Germans saw more opportunity to receive medical care, that they more frequently availed themselves of it, that they enjoyed longer periods of convalescence, and that their material needs as well as those of their families were better met during treatment. Such conclusions remain to some extent conjectural, to be sure, but they accord with a clear pattern of progression in public health.

More specific calculations for tuberculosis confirm the upward spiral both of total and of per capita allocations for health care. By 1897 disability insurance benefits administered through popular sanatoria barely reached a million marks per annum; but by 1901 it was over 5 million, by 1909 16 million, and by 1913 about 18 million. In that period the number of sanatorium patients covered by social insurance in a given year rose from circa 3,000 to 47,000. For a nation of 60 million, in which an estimated 100,000 died annually of tuberculosis and perhaps ten times that many were infected, the expansion of treatment facilities was far from meeting the global need. Yet the cumulative effect was not negligible. While the statistics of treatment were rising, mortality rates of consumption continued to decline.[38]

This observation raises a central question that must later be addressed: what was the correlation between the undeniable increase in medical practice and a presumed improvement in public health? Whatever stance we adopt on that controversial issue, we may safely close this brief statistical survey with the certain conclusion that the German social scene was characterized after 1880 by a sharp increase in state interventionism. That was the interior force as well as the foreign image of the German model. True, the potential—and to a certain extent the practice—already lay deep in a Prussian etatist tradition. Some local and regional efforts to purify water, improve sewage disposal, clear slums, and upgrade nutrition all preceded the founding of the Kaiserreich. Yet the quantitative acceleration of public health initiatives under the aegis of the new national government was truly remarkable, and this phenomenon cannot be separated from the social welfare laws of the 1880s, which provided an impetus for the spurt of activity that was so impressive for all contemporary observers in late nineteenth-century Europe.[39]

One final illustration may serve to clinch the point. Although Bismarck favored a national insurance program, he adopted a more conservative posture in his policy regarding the protection of labor (*Arbeiterschutzpolitik*). Specifically, he opposed the imposition of shorter working hours without the curtailment of wages; and he cared little about rigorous factory regulations. Yet a gradual shift from voluntary to mandatory inspection of industry was nonetheless discernible, and the number of the Reich's inspectors (not to count their staffs) rose from only 14 in 1875 to 46 in 1880, 71 in 1887, and then to 193 in 1905. Before 1914 this heavily augmented corps of government agents was capable of annually inspecting over 50 percent of German industrial firms that altogether employed more than 80 percent of the nation's labor force.[40] Thus, Bismarck or no, the long arm of the imperial state reached farther and farther into private enterprise, just as it extended ever deeper into local administration.

Social legislation was not only adopted, it was enforced. Regulations that had once been optional became obligatory. These were the operative attributes of the German model.

Public Health and Scientific Medicine

Localism was a bright spot of public health before 1870. Civic pride had long been a distinctive feature of German tradition. A relevant example was the so-called Elberfeld system, named after the Ruhr industrial center that innovated a municipal plan of public assistance. Founded in 1853, the health organization in Elberfeld was a typical product of midcentury liberalism, conceived on the premise that a substantial number of volunteers could be recruited from the town's wealthier burghers to staff a block-by-block network of social workers who monitored the needs of the laboring population and aided them to rehabilitation. This arrangement offered two significant advantages: first, the deprivation of the poor was carefully evaluated through frequent visitations and was thus more effectively diagnosed; and second, a more rational distribution of welfare funds combined with lower overhead costs (thanks to the volunteers) enabled the community to limit and even to lower the tax burden imposed on the rich. Such irresistible benefits were almost beyond belief and, understandably, the news of Elberfeld spread throughout Europe. Within Germany several cities implemented replications of the new method, often with salutary results.[41]

Yet one must guard against a mindless idealization of local welfare schemes, which were always limited, usually selective, and frequently nonexistent. Although the cheerful gospel of self-help undeniably succeeded for a time in Elberfeld, and with modification in some other municipalities, it did not prove to be a panacea for Germany's social problems. What was true of independent insurance funds usually obtained for voluntary welfare measures: they tended to reach only a narrow stratum of skilled and semiskilled laborers in certain urban areas. As a rule, they lacked the financial resources to cope with hard-core poverty and rural misery. Before 1870, it is fair to say, public health and hygiene for the poor in the countryside was terrible; and in the cities, if we are to judge by mortality statistics, it was often worse. Not until after 1870 did that circumstance decisively change for the better, and it did so generally where the national state took an active hand in prodding local administrations into action.[42] By 1914, as a consequence, public health measures in urban centers outstripped those of rural areas, and there occurred a shift in the relative balance of mortality rates that cannot be adequately explained apart from the expansion and application of hygienic regulations under state aegis.[43]

The impression should not thereby be created, to reiterate, that these developments were strictly the result of German political unification. Changes wrought by the rapid economic and demographic evolution of Germany were also favorable for the greater effectiveness of social insurance insofar as an industrialized urban labor force could more readily be counted and—from a medical standpoint—better controlled than a dispersed rural population. A comparison with France is again useful. Mandatory insurance could be imposed with relative efficiency in a land of large enterprise like Germany, where many employers already possessed an in-house bureaucracy and might absorb the extra cost and paperwork required by obligatory procedures. Industrial managers stood to gain an obvious advantage through the resulting stabilization of employment in an increasingly unionized and politicized labor market. In France, which was still a country of small entrepreneurs and weakly organized workers, the task of a government to impose a universal program of social security was infinitely more tedious. Farm or workshop inspection, so to speak, was far less feasible than factory inspection. Thus political unity, indispensable as it was to the German model, was not the sole variable.[44]

For clarity's sake it should be specified that, especially after 1890, a kind of bifurcation became evident in public health: while some traditional aspects of poor relief in Germany (notably aid to women and children) remained under local jurisdiction, the principal responsibility for other realms was progressively assumed by the central state through specialized social insurance coverage for the unemployed, the disabled, and the elderly. One should not imagine, therefore, that national unification swept aside all older forms of public assistance, many of which in reality expanded and reaffirmed their role in caring for the indigent.

On balance, Bismarck's fondest ambitions were thus largely realized. True, he did not immediately gain his intended objective of a highly centralized national insurance system in which the workers were directly beholden to the state. Nor, impressive statistics notwithstanding, was public health in Germany suddenly transformed to perfection. Financial and medical aid for the needy remained insufficient and partly incoherent. As late as 1905 Secretary of State Arthur von Posadowsky conceded that "it must be a project for the future to combine these three great insurance plans into one coordinated organization."[45] But as the Reich's health and hygiene capabilities multiplied, so did the participation of its populace, which enjoyed greater medical facilities, more capably trained physicians, and broader financial aid than ever before in history. These ameliorations did not remove the laboring classes from the jeopardy of personal catastrophe through illness or accident, but they did increase the possibility of medical recovery by individuals and families. If it is fanciful to posit a growing sense of gratitude among German workers before 1914, there is at least reason to question the notion that they were but "negatively" integrated into the nation-state.[46]

The totality of the German model has been evaluated by historians with varying degrees of enthusiasm. One writes confidently of "an increasingly favorable development" in public health; another describes "a qualitatively determinant progress in the improvement of the social situation" of the workers; and a third concludes that the welfare legislation of the 1880s placed Germany for decades "in an absolutely paramount position among industrial nations."[47] Even a severe critic of the Kaiserreich, who belittles the measures of the Bismarckian period as a mere palliative for the still-wretched conditions endured by the poor, concludes: "Nonetheless, compared to the nullity of preceding social protection, it was a significant progress, the benefit of which, despite often justified criticism, was embraced by those concerned and praised abroad."[48]

In view of such accolades it is especially instructive to regard the German model from the perspective of its harshest detractors. Their principal objections may be cogently summarized as four:

1. Available statistics are not only unreliable in many regards; they also concentrate unduly on the single question of mortality. A more nuanced picture of public health needs to be developed that will also take morbidity into account and more clearly reveal class distinctions.

2. When viewed more broadly, public health in imperial Germany created a "decidedly static impression."[49] It is therefore dubi-

ous to speak of a general improvement. Scourges of the past—communicable diseases like cholera, diphtheria, and typhus—were superseded by the characteristic ailments of modern civilization, such as heart disease and cancer, while new stress factors took their toll. Consequently, the poor continued to live with social inequality and personal insecurity.

3. Medical progress was for the most part an illusion. Scattered improvements that occurred in the nineteenth century had little to do with an alleged advance in scientific medicine. In fact, physicians were "absolutely marginal" to the falling death rate.[50] They were usually helpless to treat infectious disease, spent most of their time consulting with rich clients, resisted the socialization of medicine, and cared primarily to consolidate their own "dominance" over patients. Hence the trend toward hospital medicine was altogether welcome to doctors mostly concerned about improving their professional and social status.[51]

4. The rising life expectancy of the late century cannot be ascribed to an institutional amelioration of modern medical practice, whatever the inflated claims of its proponents. Nor can a satisfactory explanation reside in any other single cause: nutrition, housing and clothing, sewers and sanitation, or social insurance. Rather, one must recognize the emergence of an "infrastructure" and evaluate the entire "spectrum" of factors related to public health and hygiene.[52]

In this critique of the German model we cannot fail to detect some elements of caricature. The resulting portrait is marred by a skepticism that legitimately challenges some easy assumptions but that also collides at times with the available evidence. Reflecting their undisguised distaste for the pretensions of political and medical authority, the detractors of scientific progress too often resort to circumlocutions or tortuous interpretations to explain statistics that do not quite accord with their pessimistic convictions.[53] Surely, for example, it is absurd to suggest that the German medical scene was static. Nor is it convincing to juxtapose an inappropriate adverb with a dubious adjective so as to claim that German medicine was "absolutely marginal" to verifiable gains in public health. If official statistics were not ideal, they left no serious doubt about a remarkable achievement between 1870 and 1914 in the closely related realms of hygiene and welfare. The indisputable fact that the poor continued to fare less well than the rich does not alter the phenomenon that all benefited to some degree from improvements in medicine. In fact, it is plausible to argue that the poor had more to gain than the rich from social legislation and that they actually did so. A preoccupation with the undoubted efforts of physicians to solidify their social and professional status should not be allowed to obfuscate the vastly expanded availability of competent medical care for the poor. To see the hospital strictly in terms of a doctor's desire for power over his helpless patients is inadmissibly reductionist. Finally, it should be observed that there remains an almost mystical aura about such elusive terms as "infrastructure" and "spectrum," which conveniently appear like some *medicus ex machina* to solve nagging problems of historical analysis. Instead, we need to focus on the measurable advances of the welfare system in Germany; and, of course, we must wonder specifically why the German conception, despite its widely recognized advantages, was not always emulated by a neighboring country like France.[54]

Two provisional conclusions may be ventured here. The first, patently, is the conspicuous presence in post-1880 Germany of the interventionist state. By casting liberal inhibitions aside, the national government was able to sweep forward in an unprecedented fashion. Alternative explanations are finally unconvincing: the mere extension of traditional etatism, the cumulative effect of local initiatives, or some wondrous act of a beneficent nature. International contrasts bring the weakness of these propositions into focus. It is demonstrable through comparative mortality rates of tuberculosis, for instance, that Germany in 1880 had a considerable deficit compared with England. As late as 1905, according to one calculation, the English lead was still very substantial. Yet before 1930, despite a severe relapse in the war years, Germany had pulled even.[55] If so, a heavy burden of proof rests on those who denigrate the massive and purposeful effort of the imperial state to improve public health throughout the land. We must account, at the same time, for the fact that the French failed to match this performance and continued to allow their population to suffer an alarming rate of tuberculosis deaths. The relative inaction, not to say paralysis, of the liberal republican government in France before 1914 cannot be disregarded as an explanation of this striking difference.[56]

A second conclusion is closely related and no less compelling: the much higher degree of medical specialization in Germany. Later we shall examine this factor in detail from the French viewpoint. But let it already be stated here that the extraordinary expansion of German medical facilities after 1870 was accompanied by an increasing diversification of their function. In Germany, to a far greater extent than in France, it was not merely a question of adding more beds in general hospitals but of providing specialized care for separate ailments. This development was simultaneously evident in the education of German medical students, who were trained in a system that stressed scientific research over routine observation. The precondition in Germany was a successful transition from "clinical" to "laboratory" medicine, in which the Kaiserreich took a clear lead during the late nineteenth century.[57] Hence Germany began to produce an entire new generation of medical specialists whose diagnostic techniques and therapeutic apparatus were more effectively deployed than ever before. It is as part of this evolving pattern of scientific medicine that one must evaluate the movement for popular sanatoria (*Heilstättenbewegung*) in Germany. True, no wonder drug as yet existed to prevent tuberculous contagion or to cure afflicted individuals. But the long-standing practice of isolating patients with infectious symptoms could be greatly augmented in Germany, thereby at least checking the malady, removing the victim from dangerously close contact with others, and offering a kind of "hygienic drill" that might be shared later with family and friends once formal treatment was finished.[58] Thus, if the curative value of sanatorium care never quite matched the most optimistic claims for it, the total prophylactic effect probably helped to sustain a steadily declining mortality rate in Germany. Because the disease ravaged France at a much higher rate in the years before 1914, and beyond, there is indication enough that nothing was automatic about improvement in public health.[59] The twin engines of progress were state support and scientific medicine, which together constituted the quintessence of the German model.

The Model Perceived

A German model did not arrive in France at one time and in one piece. Rather, impressions of the German social insurance system were received fitfully over the years from the late 1880s until 1914. This long and irregular process of information thus constitutes a central theme of the entire investigation to follow. We may therefore usefully anticipate the remainder of this study by sketching those features of German public health and welfare that seemed most salient to the French. Necessarily stated here as a series of tentative postulates, these perceptions together form a working hypothesis about the French vision of Germany—a hypothesis that will need to be documented, refined, and elucidated as this account progresses.

No single description of a model, it goes without stressing, could have adequately reflected all the complex detail of the German development. Even if such a paradigm had existed, the reality of course exceeded the capacity of contemporaries to grasp it. Hence it was always on the basis of an incomplete and imprecise reading of the Reich that French debates about the social question were conducted. At least five characteristics of German welfare reform were commonly assumed in France.

1. *Obligatory.* Invariably this was seen as the fundamental premise of German social insurance. We saw that a "mandatory principle" (*Zwangsprinzip*) had slowly emerged as the victor over voluntary schemes in Prussia before 1870; and thereafter it was adopted by the Kaiserreich. The French well understood that in practice the Germans had by no means achieved universal coverage of their citizenry. Indeed, German imperfections were usually emphasized by French critics. But admirers of the Bismarckian social legislation could counter that the new compulsory laws had as a minimum established the basis for a future extension of benefits. Moreover, they could plausibly argue that large state-sponsored insurance organizations, like those encouraged in Germany, were more economical and more efficient than the smaller private funds in France.[60]

2. *Interventionist.* The imagination of most French observers was excited by Germany's impressive array of legal enactments in the 1880s. Little was known of the concurrent internal political complications or of Bismarck's frustrations in attempting to impose his will on a sometimes reluctant Reichstag. Nor did the French sufficiently appreciate the continuing importance of local and regional authorities in the administration of German social insurance and public sanitation. Instead, there was a tendency in France to view Bismarck as a bold innovator who had single-handedly fashioned a system in which the initiative flowed from a powerful source at the center. This perception was in particular corroborated by the international publicity that surrounded the achievements of Robert Koch and the *Reichs-*

gesundheitsamt in Berlin. German social reform, as reflected in French eyes, was thus synonymous with intervention by the national state. For this reason imperial Germany could be neatly located at an ideological pole opposite that of English liberalism. This juxtaposition generally suited French liberals, who could all the more easily accuse their political opponents of advocating the Germanization of the republic.[61]

3. *Successful.* All pioneers have their problems, and the Germans were correctly assumed by the French to be suffering from false starts and social conflicts. Yet the German statistics were striking. They seemed to substantiate a steady amelioration of public health that correlated with the extension of social insurance. That conclusion was repeated constantly in reports by French investigative missions sent to Germany and by delegations that attended dozens of international congresses gathered during the decades before 1914. All indications were that Germany had no peer among nations in the construction of new hospital facilities, university clinics, popular sanatoria, and specialized asylums for the insane, the chronically ill, and alcoholics. Whatever one might think of imperial Germany for other reasons, its medical and scientific accomplishments were impossible to deny.[62]

4. *Popular.* The German success was not only theoretical and institutional, it was also beginning to reach the mass of the population. As insurance coverage expanded and compensation was increased, the Bismarckian social legislation was gaining wider acceptance even among the potentially dissident working class. Granted, Bismarck's intentions may have been duplicitous; but the long-term results were undeniably salutary for the standard of living and sense of security among the laboring poor. The French observed, as a consequence, that public opposition to state interventionism in Germany was dwindling, not only among the liberals (who were supposed in any case to have been co-opted by Bismarck) but also in the rank and file of Social Democracy. The revisionist character of German socialism was accurately appraised by the French in terms of an increasing eagerness to demand social security benefits and thus to cooperate with the imperial regime. This phenomenon was not without direct impact in France, where like-minded popular leaders such as Jean Jaurès displayed a growing tendency to praise German social reforms and to advocate their adoption by the republic.[63]

5. *Appropriate*. The type of social reform inaugurated under Bismarck seemed particularly well suited to the disposition and temperament of the German people. Dealing as they often did in generalities, the French were inclined to see all Teutons as disciplined beyond anything conceivable in a Latin country. From the grain of truth in this assumption sprouted innumerable theories about the comparative national character of the French and German peoples. It was inevitably supposed that the latter were more readily militarized and that they tended to tolerate regimentation unacceptable in freedom-loving France. In caricature the German model could therefore evoke the nightmare of an imperial state unleashing squads of ruthless inspectors to pry into everyone's privacy—and of their being welcomed by an obedient populace![64]

Whatever the degree of distortion, Germany's example provoked a variety of responses in France. Some French were of course hostile to everything German. Many found the German system enviable but infeasible for France. Others became persuaded that a healthy dose of Germanic discipline was exactly what the French needed in order to cope with the social question. We should not imagine that the German model elicited solely a negative reaction in republican France, or that a pervasive atmosphere of revanchism existed throughout the half century after 1870. Just as they confronted the military or scientific prowess of their most formidable neighbor, the French responded to the precedent of German social reform with a mixture of apprehension and admiration. Opinions were openly and deeply divided. Precisely what influence the perceived model would have in France therefore remained uncertain.

Chapter 4

The Sources of Social Reform

The first centennial of the French Revolution was a splendid occasion for the entire nation and especially for Paris. As the danger and excitement of the Boulanger Affair receded, the populace could breath more easily and again exude the charm that has always captivated visitors to the capital. The great world's fair centered at the Trocadero represented, far more than its predecessor in 1878, a declaration of independence and a notification that the French had at last put military defeat behind them in order to reclaim their leading status among the powers of Europe. France stood on the threshold of the Belle Epoque, prepared to look forward once more and to savor the rewards of progress. Yet this celebratory mood was crossed, almost imperceptibly, by a dingy shadow. The social troubles of the time could be temporarily repressed but not altogether ignored. To be sure, the Parisian police were under orders to prevent begging on the exposition grounds and to sweep away vagrants from the city's center. But an inquisitive tourist might have taken a bus ride to its terminus in the Paris suburbs, visited the shabby streets of Belleville, or wandered aimlessly on the outer slopes of Montmartre. Poverty was there, even if it was not visible from the platforms of the Eiffel Tower.

Only three years earlier, in 1886, the government had consolidated a number of separate agencies into the Bureau of Public Health and Hygiene within the Ministry of the Interior. Appointed as the first chief of this new welfare administration—a crucial post that he would occupy for nearly two decades—was Henri Monod, who promptly set about to convene an international congress on public health in conjunction with the 1889 exposition. Although the proceedings of the congress could be characterized as only an exercise in verbosity, the very fact that delegates met in Paris to discuss their mutual social problems was symptomatic of a growing awareness that public health was everywhere becoming an irrepressible issue. Accordingly, the congress concluded with the unanimous adoption of a sonorous resolution favoring the introduction of a compulsory system of public welfare throughout "the civilized world." A curiosity was that Germany, the only nation already to have conceived the embryo of such a plan, was not represented at the sessions and consequently cast no vote. The conspicuous absence of a German delegation was overlooked by no one, of course, and was politely attributed to French national pride. After all, it would surely be unseemly for a foreigner to suggest that France was no longer in the vanguard of civilization.[1]

French reformers themselves were often less squeamish. For them, as we shall often record, the German example was undeniably relevant and insufferably goading. The new impetus to social reform in France doubtless had roots in a recognition that the national performance had been heretofore inadequate. But it was also in part a response to the international standard established by Germany in the early 1880s.[2] It is therefore fitting to locate the major forums of this initial French venture into state welfare and to inquire about the mixed motives of those who sought social reform.

State Administration

Although the formal beginning of France's welfare program may be dated from 4 November 1886, when a presidential decree created the Bureau of Public Health and Hygiene, several more years transpired before there was any tangible effect of this administrative innovation. Henri Monod, who had previously made a name for himself as a health official in Le Havre, accepted the directorship of the new central agency in early 1887 and began at once to assess France's organizational problems. The results of his survey were bleak. *Bureaux de bienfaisance* functioned in 15,250 of the nation's communes but were totally lacking in 19,111. Some form of free medical assistance was available in forty-four French departments but not in forty-two others. In sum, about half of metropolitan France had no public welfare whatever. Agencies were more or less well established in the larger cities, yet they were completely absent in many smaller towns and across broad stretches of the countryside. Because the French system was voluntary instead of compulsory, as Monod explained to Premier Charles Floquet, "everything depends on the goodwill of administrative committees." If financial help was not forthcoming from above through the prefectoral corps, the cost of hygienic measures fell directly on the communes. There the vote of a municipal council was decisive, Monod complained, and this local body "usually makes use of it to refuse welfare." Consequently, public health functioned irregularly in the cities and "it is virtually nil in the countryside."[3]

Largely at fault was the absence of state aid. Monod estimated the total welfare allocations for all of France in 1885 at 185 million francs. But of this amount only a pittance of 7.5 million was budgeted by the central government, most of it to support mental patients and foundling children.[4] Clearly the state's financial participation would need to be increased. Yet how should it be administered? The three obvious possibilities were either to leave the *bureaux de bienfaisance* under communal control, to place them under departmental prefects, or to create an entirely new bureaucratic structure of welfare agencies directly responsible to the Ministry of the Interior. Each of these proposals had its advocates, but there was no consensus as to the most viable solution.

Essential to the success of welfare reform, in Monod's view, was the creation at the national level of an executive body that would deliberate on social issues, draft appropriate legislative measures, and apply pressure on the parliament to pass them into law. At his urging such a directive agency was created by presidential decree on 14 April 1888: the Conseil Supérieur de l'Assistance Publique (CSAP). We may be certain that this title was not chosen at random, because analogous groups had already operated to good effect in the preparation of military and educational reforms: the Conseil Supérieur de la Guerre (CSG) and the Conseil Supérieur de l'Instruction Publique (CSIP).[5] Monod's intention was clearly to replicate these two bodies and thereby to found a kind of general staff for public welfare. The original CSAP consisted of sixty-seven members—of whom barely half regularly attended its meetings—divided almost equally in number between Paris and the provinces. Later reduced to the round figure of sixty, this collection of notables included eighteen parliamentarians (six senators and twelve deputies), twelve lawyers, and a remainder of persons with "special competence," which ordinarily meant mayors of larger cities, prominent physicians, or seasoned public health officials.[6] The membership was divided into four standing committees on children; indigents, including those who were ill and required hospital care; the aged and invalid poor, who might be lodged in hospices; and mental patients, beggars, and vagrants. Visible from this cursory listing was a de facto definition of what was generally understood by the concept of welfare as well as an implicit agenda of social legislation yet to be drafted.[7]

The principles by which the CSAP would be guided were disclosed during an inaugural ceremony in Paris, gathered appropriately in the conference room of an institute for the blind, on 13 June 1888. The CSAP was greeted by Prime Minister Charles Floquet, who recalled the primitive state of French public health and recited statistical evidence of the unequal distribution of existing welfare agencies. The featured speaker, however, was Henri Monod. He regretted that the practice of compulsory health care underwritten by the state had not yet penetrated into French legislation, thus leaving the nation "without order, without method." The French must first contemplate their own inadequacies, then learn from the example of others (notably England and Germany), and finally adopt reforms compatible with Gallic tradition and temperament. France had few laurels to rest upon. Monod recalled an earlier article in the *Revue des deux mondes* in which Jules Simon had aptly summarized the situation: "When one regards the totality of aid administered by the *bureaux de bienfaisance* throughout France, one is struck at the same time by the immensity of the effort and the nullity of the result." What the French lacked in comparison with their neighbors, Monod reiterated, was "organization, method." Only by an act of national solidarity, namely the approval of an obligatory welfare system, could the Third Republic close the gap.[8]

The course of the CSAP was thereby set. The key word in Monod's statement was "obligatory," by which he acknowledged the inadequacy of private charity and advocated adoption of a minimum of medical care for every needy French citizen. Behind these broad objectives, and motivating them, was a manifest assumption that the nation was falling behind its chief competitors. Left unstated were the precise implications for legislative action. But these were indicated in a report prepared for the CSAP by the chairman of one of its four sections, Dr. Lucien Dreyfus-Brisac. In the absence of a national health plan, he confirmed, medical care in the French provinces was poorly distributed and frequently unavailable. This fact was "particularly shocking in a democratic country." There was only one remedy: "We need public welfare methodically organized; and in order to reach this goal, the state must intervene." What form should such intervention take? Dreyfus-Brisac presented demographic data to demonstrate that the public health schemes of both England and Germany—contrary to fears that they would be flooded by demands from the poor—had actually reduced the number of welfare recipients. Moreover, also against all expectations, the participation of private charity had not declined. But Dreyfus-Brisac believed that the British example, with its sorry precedent of workhouses and poor laws, was problematical. "Infinitely more than the 'poor law,'" he concluded, "the present organization of public welfare in Germany may be compared with the system that we want to see adopted in France."[9]

We cannot infer that the CSAP was from its inception a united and enthusiastic proponent of the German model. Yet there was a recognition that a purely voluntary organization of public health could not function effectively. To some extent the state would need to draft mandatory regulations. Henceforth the question was not whether to adopt them but how. In general terms the example of Bismarckian social legislation was known to members of the CSAP, and the majority of them—an exact count is impossible—favored its basic principle of obligatory public assistance. A dual problem nonetheless remained: to define the concept of obligation within the French context and then to implement it. Agreement on the direction of reform was altogether desirable, as Charles Dupuy observed at an early session of the CSAP, but the real issue was to determine in what manner "this entirely new [mandatory] principle could pass from the realm of philosophy to the realm of reality."[10]

The initial efforts of the CSAP were ostensibly quite successful. Within a few months of its first regular session in January 1889 it could claim to have sponsored a parliamentary measure providing increased aid to abandoned children. Flushed with this quick victory and spurred by the concurrent public health conference at the Paris exposition, the CSAP decided to draft and demand passage of a law to guarantee free medical care for every needy French citizen. The opening words of this bill (*"Tout Français . . ."*) echoed those of earlier legislation that established universal military conscription and compulsory primary education. The objective was consciously identical: to spread the same rights and obligations of all French citizens uniformly across the land. In the domain of health and hygiene, practically speaking, this meant that the new law was intended to extend to rural France the minimally necessary medical aid already available to many urban dwellers. Every one of the French communes would thus be obliged, with the support of the departments in which they were located, to provide adequate facilities and financial support for its residents. With parliamentary approval of these provisions on 15 July 1893 France took, in theory at least, an initial step down the path toward a mandatory national program of public welfare.[11]

Whereas the CSAP remained primarily concerned with the formulation of policy, the more menial tasks of public health were left to another administrative body: the Comité Consultatif d'Hygiène Publique (CCHP). Like many other institutions concerned with welfare, this group could trace its lineage to the Second Republic. Initially attached as a thirteen-member advisory board to the Ministry of Agriculture and Commerce, the CCHP grew in size if not in influence under the regime of Napoleon III. Repeatedly reorganized before and after 1870, it did not begin to acquire real administrative clout until its presidency was assumed in June 1884 by Dr. Paul Brouardel, dean of the faculty of medicine at the Sorbonne and one of the most significant social reformers of the early Third Republic. An organic connection with the CSAP was cemented in 1889, when the CCHP was transferred to the Ministry of the Interior. The tandem of Brouardel and Henri Monod thereafter constituted the core of the reform movement within the French bureaucracy. This vital center remained intact until shortly after 1900, when Monod's resignation and Brouardel's declining health created a temporary hiatus and led to an eventual restructuring of administrative machinery.[12]

The CCHP's continuous expansion of membership was ratified by a statute in 1902 that fixed the number at forty-five. Of these, sixteen were named directly by the Minister of the Interior, six represented other related bodies (including the Academy of Science, the Academy of Medicine, and the CSAP), and twenty-three served ex officio because of various administrative duties. Especially numerous, as one would anticipate, were medical persons, public health inspectors, pharmacists, veterinarians, and architects—those charged with the more practical aspects of social hygiene. A list of topics regularly treated by this group reflects its pragmatic bent: vaccination procedures, inspection of mineral water, disinfection of lodgings and factories, control of pharmaceutics and drugs, and so on. The fact that its meetings were weekly (rather than a series of biannual sessions like the CSAP) also indicated the workaday routine of a bureaucratic corps, not the loftier preoccupations of a policy-making board.[13]

In assuming the presidency of the CCHP in 1884, Paul Brouardel was perfectly frank about the desultory performance of the committee in years past and, above all, about the need to revitalize France's entire system of public health. Local sanitation agencies (*conseils d'hygiène*) either did not exist in the communes or "their meetings are ill attended, their opinions seldom or not at all respected; they lack authority."[14] A subsequent survey confirmed this evaluation. Sanitation agencies were of some consequence only in northeastern France and in a few provincial capitals elsewhere. The difficulty was that neither moral encouragement nor financial incentive was provided by departmental authorities (*conseils généraux*), who too often failed to comprehend the ecological importance of clean air and water. Their inaction, in turn, was partially predetermined by the tepid attitude of the national government. Brouardel singled out the salutary role of the *Reichsgesundheitsamt* in Berlin, which was equipped with its own laboratories and was able to dispatch competent young physicians to the German provinces whenever an epidemic threatened. Unless similar steps were taken immediately, he argued, the French nation would find itself confronted by "rivals who would soon assume the front rank in a science of completely French origin."[15]

Under pressure from the CCHP a legislative bill was drafted and adopted in the mid-1880s that intended to multiply local health agencies as well as to provide regular state inspection of their sanitation efforts. By 1889 Brouardel also obtained his coveted laboratory in Paris, of which he was inordinately proud, as he boasted, because it "now permits us to suffer with dignity a comparison with analogous institutions that function abroad."[16] But local politics proved to be more intractable. Despite years of cajoling by the CCHP, many mayors and municipal councils remained indifferent to the fine art of bureaucratic reporting. Questionnaires were left unanswered, statistics incomplete, and regulations unheeded. Before the turn of the century, Brouardel wrote with some bitterness, the CCHP was "very often badly or insufficiently informed." As a consequence, he lamented, "the committee [was] unable to make a decision."[17] No doubt administrators at any time or in any country could only empathize with Brouardel's frustration. But for him the pain was rendered particularly acute by the worry, often repeated, that "all of the neighboring peoples have taken a lead over us."[18]

Such sweeping protestations of French inferiority must be received with caution. In regard to certain communicable diseases, notably smallpox and typhus, there is indeed statistical evidence of French retardation before 1900. But we have seen that the total mortality rate in France was gradually declining. Arguably, then, the battle for better water and air was slowly being won.[19] Nagging problems nonetheless remained, and the CCHP generally reinforced the CSAP in urging stricter sanitary legislation and mandatory implementation. A characteristic example was the question of disinfection. This procedure was thought at the time to be the surest method to check contagion. But it required proper fumigation equipment, which was not always available. A report by Henri Monod in 1892 counted twenty-two French departments with only a single disinfection unit, another thirty-three with none. Statistics, moreover, showed an ominous correlation: of those departments without any sanitary equipment whatever, three-quarters registered more deaths than births. Thus the demographic data again provided a grim prompter that France's public health was far from sound. They suggested to reformers that more vigorous state intervention would be required if the republic were to mount an adequate response.[20]

City Government

What was transpiring at the national level, in terms of an increasing awareness of public health, had a certain parallel among the large municipalities of France, especially in Paris. Also worthy of mention in this respect were Lyon, Marseille, Bordeaux, Lille, Montpellier, and Grenoble. Yet none of these was remotely so critical as the capital, which alone accounted for about half of the nation's total population growth in the period from 1870 to 1914. The social problems of Paris thus reflected the rest with an unmatched intensity, because the city's centrality and magnitude could not fail to have the maximum impact on broader policies of public welfare.[21]

During the first part of the nineteenth century public sanitation had been generally deplorable. Wracked by cholera epidemics and other infectious diseases, the municipality of Paris responded erratically with a series of improvised measures.[22] Some public assistance reached the ill and the indigent through the *bureaux de bienfaisance*. Such inadequate aid, however, went to assuage the immediate needs of the poor rather than to forestall the underlying causes of their plight. Leaders of the Second Republic recognized that a major effort would be required to renovate the capital's infrastructure, but precarious political circumstances did not allow for a sufficient investment of time or capital to achieve it. That task soon fell to Louis Bonaparte and Baron Haussmann. Within a fortnight after the coup d'état of 2 December 1851, a governmental decree created new sanitation committees (*commissions d'hygiène et salubrité*) administered under the Prefecture of Police. These agencies of public health were nominally separated from those of state welfare (*bureaux de bienfaisance*); but the boundary between their functions was never carefully drawn. They existed side by side in the various arrondissements of Paris, although both were overshadowed by Haussmann's heavily financed and far better publicized reconstruction of the city's sewers, aqueducts, and streets.[23]

This complex arrangement was suddenly placed into question by the collapse of the Second Empire and the eruption of the Paris Commune. A report in the spring of 1871 by Citizen Treillard, director general of the Commune's administration of public assistance, charged that the old *bureaux de bienfaisance* had been nothing but handmaidens of charity. They had failed to respond to "sentiments of civic solidarity" and had become "instruments in the struggle against social ideas." Worst of all, they had fallen under "clerical influences," openly favoring families within the Roman Catholic flock and thereby sowing hypocrisy and suspicion among the Parisian populace. Accordingly, Treillard proposed to abolish the existing agencies and to replace them with a set of new "welfare offices" (*bureaux d'assistance*) in each of the capital's twenty arrondissements. But the ephemeral character of the communard regime, like that of the Second Republic, left these ambitions unrealized.[24]

Paris was unique among French cities, besides the obvious reasons of size and national politics, because of the long disruption of its public services during the war, which accounted in part for a frightful smallpox epidemic in early 1871. The new republican cabinet under Adolphe Thiers needed quickly to restore bureaucratic as well as military order, and it consequently fell back on experienced functionaries who could manage France's most troublesome municipality. This retrenchment coincided with the emergence of the Municipal Council of Paris (CMP) as an autonomous and often truculent political factor. Thereby the terms were set for a recurrent conflict that was to endure throughout the Third Republic. Paris was allowed no mayor but was administered jointly by the prefect of the Seine and the CMP. The moderate leanings of the former were repeatedly challenged by the more radical demands of the latter, thus playing out a long aftermath of civil conflict between state and city that was a legacy of the Paris Commune. This clash was first announced in strident terms by Georges Clemenceau when assuming presidency of the CMP in 1875, and it persisted long after his passage into national politics a year later.[25]

The public health system of Paris meanwhile regrouped. Neighborhood sanitation committees resumed their functions and were placed under an executive council (Conseil de Surveillance), which oversaw the municipality's health efforts. That body, whose records are one of our best sources for the city's attempt to cope with disease and death, provided a meeting place for Parisian doctors, architects, and city councillors. In addition, it recruited wealthy businessmen and property owners to consult on questions of sanitation and construction. At the same time, the *bureaux de bienfaisance* resumed their role of dispensing state welfare benefits and supervising home care as a necessary supplement to the overcrowded hospitals and hospices of Paris. Despite doubts expressed in the CMP about the utility of administering welfare funds though these agencies, their range of services and hence their budgets continued to expand. In 1879 they introduced a food-stamp program; and in the early 1880s they were instrumental in extending vaccination procedures in the city.[26]

Not before the late 1880s did the demand for an overhaul of the French welfare structure begin to boil over in the CMP. Two reasons were prominent. The first was an increasing strain on the city's budget created by the growing needs of sanitation and social welfare.

Members of the CMP contended that the capital was being forced through immigration from the provinces to carry a disproportionate share of the national burden; a revision was therefore essential to channel more funds through the Paris municipal government, while for good measure granting it a greater freedom in their distribution. Implicit in this plea, we cannot avoid noticing, was the self-contradiction of simultaneously seeking more state aid and less state control.[27] A second theme was polemically if not practically as important: an insistence by the CMP that the city's hospitals and health services should be totally secularized. The militant anticlericalism that had flared during the Paris Commune was scarcely tempered in the years thereafter. Initially the CMP hectored the central government to "laicize" Parisian public schools. Once that objective was attained, and after Eugène-René Poubelle had become prefect of the Seine in 1884, the emphasis of the CMP's criticism shifted from primary education to public health. By a ballot of 65 to 7 in June 1887, the CMP ratified a motion for the "immediate [and] complete secularization" of all state-supported hospitals and welfare agencies. The majority favoring this resolution ascribed France's "shameful" record in public hygiene to the "pure anarchy" of the state administration. Prevented from being masters even in their own house, the citizens of Paris had to suffer inefficiency and incompetence that contrasted starkly with the well-conceived sanitation programs of such German municipalities as Munich and Berlin.[28] But for their part, opponents of the proposed anticlerical measures stressed the significant role of traditional charities in France, the long hours of dedicated service by religious personnel in the hospitals, and the inevitable rise in administrative costs that would follow their expulsion. This defense was eloquently stated by one Catholic city councillor, Georges Berry, who expressed to the CMP's majority his fear that "your hatred for everything that concerns God will bring the ruin of public welfare."[29]

Such acrimonious debate in the CMP thus provided a counterpoint to the harmonious but vapid resolutions meanwhile adopted in 1889 by the international welfare congress in Paris. Leading the charge was a Socialist councillor, Édouard Vaillant, whose name still recalled his youthful role in the Paris Commune. It was now Vaillant's contention that state intervention was essential to the solution of social problems. No one any longer contested the propriety of enforcing uniform regulations for schools and, he argued, "it is the same for public welfare." Paris needed to provide free medical dispensaries in every quarter of the city. Beyond such immediate practical measures, Vaillant exclaimed, "public welfare should be reorganized in its entirety."[30] This outburst had resonance especially on the CMP's standing committee for public welfare, which reported to a plenary session on 15 November 1889 that "the administration" (meaning that of the national government) had been guilty of "unjustifiable negligence." Particularly in regard to secularization, the demands of the CMP had been ignored, and hence many hospitals and health agencies were still "in the hands of nuns." Ever since Monsieur Poubelle's appearance as prefect of the Seine, the state bureaucracy had "cooperated with the opponents of secularization." The obvious polemical and personal edge on these accusations did not detract from the point that a large majority of the CMP wanted a major legislative reform. This wish was expressed in two motions adopted that same day: one in favor of free medical care for all ailing persons in need, and another to guarantee a monetary subsistence for the aged and infirm. In a primitive form these resolutions prefigured the essential principles of legislation later passed by the French parliament in 1893 and 1905.[31]

For the time being, however, the mandate of the CMP was necessarily more modest. Councillor Paul Strauss reminded his colleagues that it was not a legislative body and that the duty of drafting social measures was best left to the CSAP: "our hands are tied."[32] A more pertinent issue was the distribution of financial aid to the poor of Paris. The CMP hoped to fix a monthly minimum of ten francs for all residents enrolled on the administrative list of indigents, even though it was evident that this amount was inadequate. Such a dole, as one councillor remarked, could only condemn the needy to begging, which was "unworthy of a civilized society and especially of a democracy."[33] Yet it would certainly be better than nothing and a decided improvement over existing circumstances in which some of the city's desperately poor were allotted no more than three francs a month—just enough, Vaillant snarled, to assure a slow and painful death in the midst of winter. He added again that they were manifestly saddled with a welfare system that "functions badly" and that required a total revision.[34]

What practical form could a change take? The answer was twofold. First, it was crucial to compensate for the uneven distribution of funds and facilities among the city's twenty arrondissements. Areas around the Paris Opera and the Champs Élysées, for example, received not only a share of public welfare allocations but could also rely on generous private donations and legacies from their wealthy residents. Other sections, notably those on the city's northeastern perimeter, lodged a large population of paupers and poor workers but contained far fewer charitable institutions of any consequence. Sentiment ran strong in the CMP to redistribute public funding more fairly throughout the metropolis. Yet to reduce state aid, say, to the prosperous ninth and sixteenth arrondissements would only discourage philanthropic gifts there, because the indirect effect of reallocation would be to siphon away private money to other quarters. By the end of 1893 a formula was devised by which three-fifths of public funding through the *bureaux de bienfaisance* was equally dispersed among all of the arrondissements, while the remainder was designated solely for the disadvantaged districts of the capital. Yet this provision scarcely began to alter the existing imbalance, and the CMP was repeatedly confronted with requests for emergency appropriations. For Paul Strauss this inscrutable problem was further evidence of a need "to reform the entire organization of public health" in order to curb "crying abuses" and to end "this state of anarchy."[35]

The CMP's other puzzle, apart from the distribution of welfare funds, was finding a means to render public assistance more cost-effective. For this purpose the Elberfeld model seemed to some councillors to offer a feasible solution. This was one of the proposals submitted by Édouard Vaillant in June 1892 to counter the "manifestly deplorable lack of resources and organization."[36] The basic notion of the proposed plan was to harness volunteers who would, without remuneration, constitute a corps of social workers, regularly visiting the poor and catering to their individual needs, reporting to welfare and sanitation agencies, and thereby assuring efficient allocations without undue administrative overhead costs. This suggestion was discussed and endorsed by the CMP's welfare committee, whose reporter Raoul Bompard cited "the truly remarkable results obtained in certain foreign cities, notably in Germany, by the application of the so-called Elberfeld system." Especially encouraging were statistics indicating that the absolute number of welfare recipients under this scheme had actually been reduced by over half since its inception in the 1850s, enabling the city of Elberfeld to reduce the tax burden on its residents. The secret was simple: "to assist the poor properly, one must know them well." Bompard concluded his committee's recommendations by stressing that "there is in the structure of the so-called Elberfeld system no special feature that cannot be successfully imitated elsewhere."[37] Presumably this included Paris. But as desirable as the Elberfeld model may have appeared, it violated established bureaucratic procedures in Paris and required an optimal amount of neighborhood initiative that was altogether uncharacteristic of the city's administration. Only a single pilot project was launched in the third arrondissement, which functioned well enough for a time, but without ever setting a precedent for the entire municipality or for others.

In evaluating the beginnings of social welfare in France, it is well to guard a sense of proportion. True, if one measures in terms of the monthly allowance received in 1893 by an aging and unemployed widow in a working-class district of Paris, public welfare was still inadequate. Yet the aggregate expenditure projected for public assistance programs in the capital during the year 1894 was nearly 20 million francs—that is, almost three times the amount allocated in the national budget for all of France only a decade earlier.[38] If benefits were not yet sufficient for the needy individual, there was nevertheless a detectable movement by the collectivity to cope with the problems of urban crowding, communicable disease, and inveterate poverty. Political conflicts between city and state notwithstanding, the municipal government of Paris henceforth represented a potent ally of reformist elements within the national administration who were seeking to construct the foundations of a welfare system.

The Medical Community

In regard to the medical profession, as in so many other respects, Paris was preeminent. One must only review the recruitment and training of students to comprehend the reasons. With the loss of Strasbourg, only two regular medical faculties remained in 1871: Paris and Montpellier. Four others—Nancy, Lille, Lyon, and Bordeaux—were founded before the end of the decade; but they were slow to organize and to offer complete facilities for education. Thus in the years from 1875 to 1880 nearly 83 percent of all French medical graduates were trained in Paris. By the end of the 1880s the annual proportion had declined to about 60 percent, without greatly altering the extreme centralism of the system. This structure of medical schooling was likewise reflected in the geographic distribution of personnel: as late as 1890 over two-thirds of France's communes lacked a local physician. Rural medicine still was a rarity.[39]

Entrance to a medical career first required successful completion of the baccalaureate degree in a classical *lycée*. Thereafter, because the curriculum of these secondary institutions provided little preparation in the natural sciences, aspiring students needed to absorb a year of elementary tutoring at the university before gaining formal admission to the faculty of medicine. Finally, after a minimum of four years, they were prepared to seek state accreditation through a competitive test (*concours*) that led to a license to practice. Understandably, the rigors of this selective process left the typical French physician only faintly inclined, after nearly a decade of studies in the city, to accept the rude life of some rural outpost. An overwhelming majority of French physicians remained urban dwellers, and about one in five practiced in Paris. This situation had been somewhat mitigated in the early nineteenth century by the presence of less intensively trained health officials (*officiers de santé*), who served as medical surrogates. But this category was already diminishing by 1870 and would be abolished altogether in 1892. France thus approached the end of the century with a medical corps that was poorly distributed, socially elitist, and traditionally oriented in education and outlook.[40]

At the pinnacle of the medical hierarchy stood the Academy of Medicine. Founded by royal decree in 1820 as an advisory body to the Restoration monarchy, the Academy continued to perform that function for successive regimes thereafter. Allegedly a national institution, it presented in actuality a mirror image of the medical profession's centralization. The Academy's regular membership was virtually synonymous with a listing of clinic chiefs in the major hospitals of Paris. The number of resident members was fixed in 1835 at precisely one hundred, to which were added another hundred "associates" and "correspondents," both French and foreign. In 1856 the category of *correspondants nationaux* was vastly augmented in an ostensible attempt to deflect criticism of political domination by Paris, but such second-class status did little to alter the existing reality.[41]

A concern for questions of sanitation and welfare was already apparent before 1848 in the Academy's organization. At that time there were eleven standing committees, of which the eighth was specialized in matters of public health and hygiene. This body advanced a suggestion in 1881 that a separate and unified administrative bureau for public assistance be created, an initiative that resulted in Henri Monod's appointment as director of that office several years later. Meanwhile, as we have witnessed, the Academy gained considerable public attention through the depopulation debate, which brought France's most prestigious medical opinion to bear on important aspects of public policy. It became common practice in the 1880s for the republican government to request a professional opinion from the Academy on such matters as infectious disease, alcoholism, drugs and tobacco, or tuberculosis. On these issues the line between scientific opinion and social commentary was often imperceptible. Hence it was not altogether out of character for the Chamber of Deputies in April 1890 to solicit an appraisal from the Academy of Medicine about the effects of women's night work. The resulting report confirmed that the extreme fatigue of female laborers was a probable factor in France's insufficient birth rate. In addition, the deleterious impact on family life was worrisome to Academy members. Such moral concerns obviously transcended a strictly delineated realm of medicine. The Academy thereby began to assume a certain public role in promoting social reform, as in its unanimous resolution that the nocturnal labor of women might have, for their health, "the most disastrous consequences."[42] From this pronouncement to a legislative proposal was but one more stride.

A word must be added about the relationship between elitism and reformism, which was less simple than one might suppose. To put the matter rather uncharitably, members of the Academy had nothing to lose. They were all ensconced in comfortable senior professional posts. If not immortals, they were untouchables. Nothing is more conducive to ostensible impartiality than prosperity, and it is arguable that proceedings of the Academy were relatively free of special pleading for private interests. Thus it should not surprise that the medical elite was not totally hidebound about innovations in public health and welfare. Despite fierce internal dissension from time to time, the majority of the Academy adopted progressive stances on such crucial issues as mandatory smallpox vaccination and compulsory notification of tuberculosis, both of which we must later explore in detail.[43]

That granted, however, it is only fair to say that the Academy's first priority was nonetheless to protect or enhance the authority of the medical profession. Questions of status, medical fees, and executive prerogative were certainly not beneath the concern of leading physicians, who therefore found reason to worry about reforms that might radically alter the structure of private practice or the organization of their hospitals and clinics. In certain regards, consequently, social reform might appear to doctors as a threat. This negative tone became particularly evident once extensive measures of social insurance were contemplated or enacted. Conflicts arose between medical practitioners and mutual aid societies, as well as between both and the state. Before 1914 these disputes complicated the cause of social reform and tended to blunt its impetus.[44]

The role of the medical profession was to be further vexed by syndicalization, which was in one of its aspects an organized revolt of provincial physicians against the monopoly of Paris. Although the medical syndicates were decidedly antielitist, they were not consistently proreformist. Conservative in some regards, they favored more "democratic" procedures in others, especially in training and licensing of doctors. From the standpoint of social reform, therefore, their record was mixed and complex. Because French physicians did not speak with one voice, their reformist message was necessarily blurred.[45]

Legislative Committees

A peculiarity of the social history of the Third Republic was that most pieces of major welfare legislation were voted by the parliament with virtual unanimity, even though the basic principles of such laws were highly controversial. Therefore, as one commentator has observed, the parliamentary proceedings of the time must frequently be regarded as a deliberate "deception" (*trompe l'oeil*) of the electorate. In reality the facade of political harmony covered a profound conflict about the conception and implementation of social reform.[46]

From this fact a methodological implication inescapably follows: it is not primarily to published debates that one must turn to uncover the motives of political reformers and their opponents, but rather to the records of parliamentary committees that labored *in camera* to achieve a consensus before legislative proposals ever entered the public arena. Of particular significance in this regard were the proceedings of standing committees in the Chamber of Deputies, the minutes of which were inscribed by hand in small green-bound ledgers and later deposited in the Archives Nationales. The real story of social reform is to be found in these manuscripts. Here and not elsewhere we may discover which politicians actually favored what specific measures and why.[47]

One main difficulty of reform initiatives was institutional discontinuity. After the initial confusion of the early 1870s, the French parliament settled down to a regular rhythm of quadrennial sessions punctuated by legislative elections:

1871–76	National Assembly
1876–77	First legislative period
1877–81	Second legislative period
1881–85	Third legislative period
1885–89	Fourth legislative period
1889–93	Fifth legislative period
1893–98	Sixth legislative period
1898–1902	Seventh legislative period
1902–6	Eighth legislative period
1906–10	Ninth legislative period
1910–14	Tenth legislative period

Each time a new legislative period began, all parliamentary committees had to be reconstituted, sometimes but not always under the same chairmanship. Thus with every new cycle a certain period of adjustment was required before committee members were sufficiently initiated so that discussions could resume their course. Likewise, in the waning months of a term, it was common that uncertainty about the continuity of a committee might offer a plausible excuse for delay. Thus the only fertile period for enactment of reform bills was usually restricted to a few months midway through the ephemeral life-span of a given legislature.

This problem, common to most democratic assemblies, might not have been unduly debilitating had it not been for two others. One was the chronic instability of the republican cabinet system. The unrelieved political turmoil of the Third Republic was perpetually disruptive during regular parliamentary cycles, because it was precisely the more active committee chairmen in the Chamber of

Deputies who were most often called upon to serve as cabinet members or administrative officials. The normal legislative terms were consequently syncopated by crises that were in effect a structural disruption of the legislative process. A related problem was the bicameral framework of parliament. Legislative bills frequently shuttled between Chamber and Senate, each time incurring the risk of a prolonged interruption. As a rule, legislative initiatives for social reform originated in the lower house, whereas the Senate played exactly the moderating (not to say obstructionist) role foreseen by the drafters of the 1875 constitution. The usual pattern was for a committee of the Chamber to offer a bill to a plenary session for approval. Once adopted there by a majority of deputies, the legislative draft went forward to the Senate, where it was almost certain to be modified. Once a bill returned to the Chamber, the deputies then faced an agonizing dilemma: should the law be accepted in its altered form, or should it be sent back to the original committee for reconsideration? This classical pattern of bicameralism, with elaborations, was repeated many times over after 1876 and contributed importantly to the lags and frustrations known to every member of parliament, if not always to the public.[48]

As the personnel of parliamentary committees constantly shifted, so did their focus. One must not imagine a single and slowly evolving assembly of notables, such as the Conseil Supérieur de l'Assistance Publique or the Academy of Medicine, but a highly complex and never consolidated network of deliberative bodies, often overlapping and always political. Some of them were convened on special issues and were thus limited in their scope and sporadic in their importance: committees and subcommittees that met to discuss mental illness, foundling children, mendicity, prostitution, alcoholism, or tuberculosis. These had the fault of their virtue. They could treat specific problems, but they sometimes lacked a broad enough context to evaluate them or to conceive viable legislation. Their efforts were therefore liable to be checked by other pressures outside the purview of one small committee chamber. More crucial for our purposes, therefore, were the debates of four of the standing committees in the Chamber of Deputies. These, despite the disjunctures already suggested, managed to maintain some continuity throughout the early phases of the reform era.

FINANCE

The tax structure of the Third Republic rested on the base laid for it during the presidency of Adolphe Thiers. By no means a radical departure from the past, it depended largely on indirect taxes—for instance, on alcohol and tobacco—as well as a few forms of direct taxation, such as the infamous levy on doors and windows. These had in common that they permitted the state to collect revenues without entering private dwellings or businesses. France had a tax system, in other words, that took exclusively into account public transactions and visible signs of wealth. It did not permit inspectors of finance to delve into confidential ledgers. This sacred liberal principle remained unchallenged until 1887, when the then minister of finance Albert Dauphin presented a bill designed to separate personal and property taxation. Although the precise implications of this fiscal proposal were at first uncertain, it unquestionably hinted the ultimate intention to establish an income tax.[49] We shall later examine the problem of introducing a more progressive revenue plan, but here it is already noteworthy that such a measure had first to run the gauntlet of various parliamentary committees, where it quickly became entangled with other reform issues concerning savings banks, insurance companies, and retirement pensions. In 1891 one deputy, Pierre Papelier, commented that France's entire financial structure still depended on the notion of individual liberty, whereas the only obvious alternative was mandatory regulations "more or less similar to those adopted by neighboring nations and in particular by Germany." France needed tax reform, he believed, but it must be in accord with "the habits and needs of our race." To this familiar formulation Papelier added another: "In Germany obligation is imposed; here, to the contrary, under our structure of liberty, every citizen should have personal autonomy as his sole precept."[50] This glance into the opening arguments offered in a committee room of the Chamber before 1893 is sufficient to suggest that the spirit of orthodox liberalism was far from exhausted in France and that the entire agenda of fiscal reform was certain to face intransigeant opposition.

LABOR

The earliest investigation by the republican National Assembly into the conditions and practices of labor, conducted between 1871 and 1875, revealed that French workers were usually ill-housed, unduly alcoholic, and little inclined to participate in voluntary savings plans.[51] Later governmental studies, based on questionnaires returned by departmental officials, corroborated these conclusions and consequently emboldened those who favored increased state interventionism. In 1884 Richard Waddington presented a committee report supporting the enactment of a maximum ten-hour working day and the imposition of special restrictions on the labor of women and children.[52] These issues were intensively researched and debated during the years following by the Chamber's labor committee, whose records afford an incomparable prospect of daily life among the French working population. Above all, they disclose the total inadequacy of voluntary insurance and pension plans to meet the needs of a growing labor force. According to one well-versed committee member, Fernand de Ramel, the *caisses de vieillesse*, created in 1850, had a total enrollment after four decades of only 400,000 among France's 9.6 million workers, employees, and domestic servants. Ideally one might prefer a pension scheme independent of the state, Ramel allowed, but practical experience demonstrated the necessity of increased state participation.[53] The weight of this opinion was to be further enhanced after 1893, as we may already anticipate, when Alexandre Ribot and Jean Jaurès joined the labor committee and brought its deliberations more forcefully to bear within the Chamber of Deputies.

PUBLIC HEALTH

From a third key committee emerged in 1889 the first coherent legislative proposals to provide more state aid to alleviate the effects of sickness, accident, and old age. Although not adopted in the comprehensive form known in Germany, they did lead to passage of the 1893 omnibus law on free medical assistance. The prestige of this committee, and therefore the seriousness of its recommendations, was strengthened by the presence of nationally known politicians such as Jules Siegfried and Édouard Lockroy. Members were quite conscious that they were advocating "a new path" of welfare reform, but they were careful to define the concept of "obligation" in institutional rather than personal terms. That is, communes and departments should be required to offer medical care to their residents, but such compulsion "did not entail, as quid pro quo, the right to [public] assistance."[54] Whether this neat concept could be sustained, and just how much state subsidization would be necessary, no one could confidently predict. Yet one early consensus was clearly detectable among those deputies who wrestled with questions of public health: there was little hope that France could address welfare needs successfully so long as matters were left entirely to local officials and private initiatives.

SOCIAL INSURANCE

It is well to cite the full title of this committee, which was after 1893 to become by far the most central and influential parliamentary group dealing with welfare legislation. The Commission d'Assurance et Prévoyance Sociales (CAPS), as the designation indicates, was devoted to social insurance rather than public assistance as such. This distinction, always somewhat artificial, became necessary in legislative practice in order to secure passage of the 1893 law on free medical care. Problems of insurance and pensions had to be detached from a minimum guarantee of medical aid for the indigent in order to obtain a majority vote in the Chamber. Measures of curative medicine were thus to be distinguished from those of prophylactic health care. The broader and farther-reaching implications of the latter were thereafter left to CAPS, which struggled for years under the presidency of Léon Bourgeois to weld glaring ideological differences into some form of social legislation. The list of those who served at one time or another on this committee was virtually a roll call of France's most distinguished social reformers of the late nineteenth century. Besides Bourgeois, these included the names of Jules Siegfried, Léon Say, Jean-Honoré Audiffred, Louis Ricard, François Jourde, Paul Guieysse, Jean Jaurès (transferred from the labor committee), and Raymond Poincaré. Together they formed a wide and representative spectrum of political power under the republic. Accordingly, no documentation of this time yields more detailed and revealing information about the central motives of reform than the minutes of CAPS, which well illuminate the dialectical tension that existed between the principles of liberalism and the practical necessities of state interventionism. They also display the considerable extent to which that second pole was associated in the mind of reformers with a German model.[55]

The foregoing overview of the committee structure of the Chamber of Deputies, in reference to welfare, allows us to anchor the social question within the French political process. Perhaps there is some case to be made for a thesis that the evolution of society is an autonomous development upon which political considerations exercise at most a marginal influence. But the bulk of evidence gathered for this study suggests otherwise. The political structure of a nation, its regions, and its locales has a direct and often decisive bearing on the character of social change. The fine distinctions of pace, tone, timing, and quality cannot be appreciated apart from the political options that affect them. The course of welfare reform in the early Third Republic is therefore an exemplary case study in the relationship of politics and society, especially when placed into juxtaposition with that of France's most powerful and influential neighbor.

Pressure Groups

The notion of a pressure group may seem inappropriate to describe a large number of the congresses, committees, and public leagues that appeared in late nineteenth-century France. We ordinarily think of pressure groups as well-financed lobbies operating in a nation's capital, covertly though not always subtly seeking to obtain some advantageous legislative provision on behalf of specific economic interests or professional coalitions. True, this conventional definition does not quite fit the case, least of all in its sinister implications of easy money. Yet neither is it appropriate to speak of welfare groups in the Third Republic as if they were collections of individuals devoting their time solely to religious or philanthropic causes. The difference was that many of these new organizations aimed not only to assist the poor and the ill but also to modify the society that was neglecting them, and they sometimes intended to do so through the encouragement of state intervention.

A thorough history of French pressure groups has never been reconstructed and cannot be attempted here. But it is fair to observe, because such formations were born to agitate, that they tended to cluster around passionate and conflictual causes. Three of these were particularly conspicuous in the decades after 1870. Naturally one type was the nationalistic league embodying resentment over the treaty of Frankfurt and especially the annexation by Germany of Alsace and Lorraine. In its earliest incarnation, this revanchism was largely expended by the end of the 1870s, when the enrollment of irredentist groups began noticeably to dwindle.[56] Other chauvinistic movements later replaced them by concentrating on the more durable themes of colonialism, anti-Semitism, or just old-fashioned patriotism. Here the names of Georges Boulanger and Paul Déroulède come immediately to mind. Because such groups fed on the political scandals and public crises that abounded before 1914, their stories lie close to the surface and have been frequently told.[57] A second category of pressure group was concerned with the French Kulturkampf. The most obvious example was the Ligue de l'Enseignement that conspired with Léon Gambetta and Jules Ferry in the campaign to secularize French public education. This effort was countered in turn by several Catholic societies that worked to arouse resistance, circulate petitions, elect conservative deputies, and gather funds for parochial schools.[58] A third set of associations rallied about the banners of public health and, almost indistinguishably, public morality. Of these the temperance league was archtypical: local chapters banded into a national congress that tried to mobilize opinion against the evils of drink, to solicit parliamentary action in prohibiting certain "poisonous" beverages such as absinthe, and to urge control of the production or consumption of others. Not surprisingly, this agitation also provoked its contrary in the form of liquor lobbies supported by growers, distillers, and distributors.[59]

In imitation of the temperance movement, and closely affiliated with it, pressure groups were meanwhile founded to promote various other welfare causes. The generally assumed etiological link between alcoholism and tuberculosis encouraged a close relationship among reformers concerned with them. Similarly, antisyphilis leagues (which discreetly avoided that designation) arose to denounce the nefarious effects of bars and cabarets on public health and to demand stricter regulation of prostitution. A host of smaller societies joined the growing welfare crusade: associations to aid pregnant or abandoned women, orphans, the blind, deaf, and dumb, the mentally retarded, the crippled and incapacitated, the indigent, and the unemployed. Most of these nascent movements may perhaps be seen as secular counterparts to long-existing Catholic societies. As such, they represented a conscious recognition—or, better said, an accusation—that traditional modes of private or confessional charity were no longer adequate. To reiterate the essential point, they often proposed not only to aid the needy but to transform the entire conception of welfare. Hence they may be properly identified as pressure groups for social reform.[60]

Unfortunately, any attempt to derive a typology of philanthropic societies and to define their objectives may exaggerate the coherence of the phenomenon they represented. The character of these groups was variegated, their organization irregular, their funding limited, their influence dubious. They lacked above all a leadership that could focus and coordinate dispersed activities. In some instances it is arguable that the persistence of one pressure group tended to complicate or indeed cancel the campaign of another. If, for example, the "three great scourges" of tuberculosis, alcoholism, and syphilis were indeed inseparable, then restrictive laws and financial expenditures to deal with but one of them would not suffice; all would need to be treated together. Not until the 1890s did an unofficial executive board of reformers emerge as patrons of a new journal, the *Revue philanthropique*, created by Paul Strauss. Well connected within government and without, this list included such eminent names as Léon Bourgeois, Émile Cheysson, Ernest Lavisse, Henri Monod, Jules Siegfried, Théophile Roussel, and Féix Voisin. It was Strauss, however, who mainly supplied the missing mortar. A man of tireless energy and great tact, he was surely among the handful of most important social reformers of the early Third Republic. He seemed to be everywhere. He was for many years the chairman of the CSAP, longtime member of the CMP, later elected to the French Senate, honorary fellow of the Academy of Medicine, and sponsor of countless welfare leagues and committees. These attachments made his journal a clearinghouse of information about reform meetings and movements as well as welfare legislation (or lack of it) in France and abroad. Strauss's regular editorials, often cited by others, provided a running commentary on the many reform proposals advocated by various pressure groups. Withal, through its extensive coverage of extraparliamentary activities during the years before 1914, the *Revue philanthropique* ranks as a historical source of the first order.

In the inaugural issue of 1897 Strauss set forth the program he envisaged for the crusade by "the knights of welfare and solidarity." His editorial policy would be as impartial as possible, he claimed, but the journal's efforts on behalf of "this great and noble cause" would obviously side with "the good, the humane, the altruistic" against "the indifferent, the hardened, the egotistical." The common task of reform groups was to alleviate suffering, to battle pauperism, to combat illness and unemployment, and to overcome alcoholism, tuberculosis, venereal disease, and "psychological misery." These were the metaphors of a militant. They were also a frank admission that France had failed so far to cope with its social problems and should regroup "in light of the example of foreign countries." The French needed to study the accomplishments of others, Strauss advocated, for "no science is more international than that of welfare."[61]

By following the pages of the *Revue philanthropique* one discovers a broad panorama of social concerns and of the organizations that supported them. The depopulation debate was constantly under review. Strauss found that France's demographic stagnation justified "all the alarms" emanating from the Academy of Medicine; the theme of French "inferiority" to Germany was hence recurrent.[62] Another of the journal's major subjects, to which Strauss was personally dedicated, was care for working mothers and foundling children. The campaign against infectious diseases, particularly tuberculosis, was also featured. Nor were alcoholism and venereal disease neglected. Moreover, two problematical questions received extensive coverage: public versus private schemes of health insurance and the financing of cheaper public housing. On all of these issues Strauss remained a strong advocate of state interventionism, seeing no other means by which France could successfully meet the material needs of its population, regain moral and intellectual momentum, and match the sanitation and welfare advances of its main competitors. His journal was in all these ways illustrative of a time when the French nation was gradually drifting away from the pole of orthodox liberalism without possessing a clear sense of just where it was heading.

Part Two

The Intersections of Reform

Chapter 5

Men and Women

The Belle Epoque cannot be described as a great age of women's liberation. Male dominance of French society, securely framed by the Napoleonic Code at the beginning of the nineteenth century, remained virtually unshaken until the onset of the First World War and was relaxed but gradually thereafter. That French women did not gain the suffrage until 1944 was only the most egregious characteristic of a general circumstance that was largely taken for granted. It is remarkable, in fact, how little the inferior status of women in French society was challenged before 1914 by members of either sex. With few exceptions or qualifications, the natural order of things appeared to place men on top.[1]

Yet women were at the center of attention in the movement for welfare reform in France. Their role in society was incessantly a subject of discussion among those whose public task it was—as committeemen, city councillors, medical experts, or parliamentarians—to ameliorate the health and prosperity of the general population. This stated concern had little or nothing to do with feminism.[2] Nor should it be automatically ascribed to a growing sense of social injustice. The most fundamental motive for bettering the lot of women did not obviously emerge from the internal functioning of French democracy. Rather, it was a tangent of the late-century demographic crisis and of an urgently felt need to salvage whatever possible of France's power and prestige as a great nation. The emotions of patriotism, and specifically of a desire to compete with Germany, provided the primary motor force of reform pertaining to women. To put the matter somewhat bluntly—but no more so than the expression of many men engaged at some level of public affairs at the time—the essential consideration was that women performed the singular function of producing children, half of whom might later become soldiers.

Sexism and the Single Woman

All the framers of France's welfare institutions were men, whereas the great majority of persons receiving public assistance were women. Until adolescence male and female recipients of aid administered through the *bureaux de bienfaisance* were equal in number. But among adults, about the year 1900, women constituted roughly two-thirds of those drawing regular welfare payments. One major explanation of this imbalance presumably lay in the longer life expectancy of women, because nearly half of all beneficiaries were widowed. The other most conspicuous category was unwed mothers. Alone, destitute, and usually unemployed, a woman was far more often than not the subject of social welfare.[3]

At the time few persons found it a curiosity that exclusively men made the decisions and struck the bargains that determined the fate of thousands of helpless women. No woman, of course, sat in either house of parliament. Nor was there a female member of the Academy of Medicine, the Municipal Council of Paris, or the Ministry of the Interior. In short, one seeks in vain for any significant input from women within the government or its welfare administration before 1914. Rare exceptions tend only to corroborate this rule. A few women were called to comment before parliamentary committees on questions such as night labor or homes for foundling children; but the testimony of those invited (one must wonder how representative they were) had no demonstrable effect on the already-established drift of discussion. Two women did finally become members of the Conseil Supérieur de l'Assistance Publique in 1906—well after the CSAP had ceased to play a crucial role in the formulation of reform legislation.[4] Several female volunteers were also recruited in Paris to serve as *dames patronneuses* in an attempt to expedite the distribution of welfare funds. And a handful of women, for whom it was necessary to invent the neologism *administratrices*, were employed as staff members of welfare agencies. These were exotic creatures. The only positions customarily occupied by women within the welfare system were those of midwives and nurses. Otherwise it remained a male preserve.[5]

What, then, was the attitude of French reformers toward the distaff objects of their attention? The answer to that question, although necessarily impressionistic in its nature, falls into a fairly consistent pattern, which is best gathered not in theoretical tracts but from the transcripts of meetings where the substance of welfare measures was actually negotiated. However grotesque the scene may now appear to us, it was then common for a caucus of ten to fifty elderly gentlemen—without any women present—to discuss in detail such matters as breast-feeding, birth control, abortion, prostitution, and venereal disease. Invariably they shared the view that women were the weaker sex, unable to compete equally with men in the marketplace, and thus in need of protection and aid. Women were thought to be less durable, more subject to fatigue that adversely affected both their performance on the job and their aptitude for reproduction. Male reformers generally concurred in the proposition that a woman's place is in the home and that factory labor is somehow unnatural and degrading at the least, or an unfortunate necessity at best.[6]

A second cluster of typical male assumptions could be described as moralistic. During the extensive debates after 1870 over the care of unwed mothers and foundling children, it was frequent to hear references to the "fault" of a young woman who had become pregnant, fled her village, and sought refuge for herself and her illegitimate offspring in the city. This worn scenario was never free of the notion that a female's frailty was compounded by her special capacity for sin. Repeated countless times, such melodramatic episodes acquired the collective status of a social problem. To be sure, men were sometimes to blame—although one fellow of the Academy of Medicine maintained that they were "more often seduced than seducers."[7] But most reformers were troubled by the thought that state assistance might be exclusively channeled to help single female sinners, who surely deserved to suffer the consequences of their actions, whereas properly married and putatively virtuous mothers were left to manage without public aid. There should be, as a member of the CSAP observed, "no privilege for misconduct."[8]

Third, women were presumed to be congenitally sentimental. They were consequently unsuited for executive positions in the welfare administration, which required a keen sense of social justice unsullied by emotionality. Besides, women were less able to deal with hooligans and rowdy teenage boys. It might be useful to have female auxiliaries in the *bureaux de bienfaisance*, because some women welfare recipients felt more at ease with their own sex; but this arrangement could not be permitted to place an excessive burden on the budget. Hence it would usually be better to deploy women volunteers, both to save funds and to avoid "a certain humiliation" for men placed under female supervisors.[9]

Precisely how deep and wide such attitudes were rooted in the psyche of welfare reformers can never be established. We can only confirm that discussions of public health remained unmarked by demands for a basic restructuring of gender relationships. Social reform was conceived as a means to help women—and therewith ultimately the entire French nation—to survive under existing conditions. It was not intended as a vehicle to alter their social status. We should also recall that the same was essentially true of simultaneous educational reforms, which were designed to ratify, not to remove, male dominance.[10] In 1893, for example, a program of moral education for girls' primary schools was drafted by the steering committee of the Conseil Supérieur de l'Instruction Publique. It was to be similar to that for boys' schools, apart from the emphasis on "certain particular duties" of women: namely, the chores of homemaking. Instruction for young women would center not on the phrase *lutte pour la vie*, as for boys, but *concorde pour la vie*. More revealing still was a first draft considered by the CSIP, which contained a clause, for girls only, about "the eminent virtues of silence." This expression was later removed, but it was perhaps more objectionable in theory than in practice.[11]

Such general observations offer no more than an initial approach to the subject. To proceed we must investigate more closely some specific categories of women singled out for social welfare. Three of these were most prominent: mothers, workers, and prostitutes.

Mothers and Infants

Foundlings had long been a social problem in France. For some decades just before the end of the Old Regime, their annual number has been estimated at 40,000.[12] Meanwhile, the practice of wet-nursing was implemented on a large scale. By one reckoning as many as a third of Parisian newly borns were placed with *nourrices* in the late eighteenth century. Becoming a mother, to modify an old proverb, was manifestly less difficult than being one.[13]

To deal with these abandoned or relegated infants, two institutions were developed in the first half of the nineteenth century, both of which were visibly collapsing before 1870. The first was a makeshift system of *tours*. The appellation was literal: specially designated hostels were outfitted with revolving cylindrical boxes (much like the receptacles for packages in modern French post offices) into which an unwanted baby might be placed on the outside by a mother or her surrogate, who then rang a bell and disappeared anonymously before a nurse on the inside swiveled the crib and received the deposited swaddling. By avoiding the distress of having an illegitimate child for whom she could not provide an adequate home, the young mother was free to return unencumbered to her rural village or urban employment. Once the transaction was completed, however, the infant was left to the mercy of strangers whose good intentions could not always compensate for the absence of maternal attention. This entire arrangement raised moral and financial questions. Did not the *tours* represent an encouragement to profligacy? And who was to pay for the care and maintenance of hundreds of neglected waifs left to the charge of the community? Worst of all was the appallingly high mortality rate among abandoned children, probably twice that of infants raised in families. For these reasons the *tours* fell into disrepute and were legally abolished in 1860.[14]

The other institution that failed to endure was the *direction des nourrices*. Attached to the public welfare administration of Paris, this bureau fulfilled the task of locating wet nurses in the countryside and placing sucklings from the capital city with them. But the wealthy Parisian bourgeoisie increasingly preferred to employ wet nurses privately and, by paying them more generously than public agencies, to secure the best. The placement office consequently became in effect a temporary refuge for indigent mothers, and its quality declined correspondingly. As the Paris chief of public welfare complained, it was no longer possible to recruit *nourrices* except among those unable to find lucrative private employment; and they were "third-class," that is, often dry and capable only of giving a bot-

tle. The administration was left to run an expensive baby-sitting service for the poor. Unable to stem a rising mortality rate among its
infant clients, the office was finally disbanded in the 1870s.[15]

Such institutional atrophy, worsened by the dislocations of the
lost war, was apparent to everyone as the Third Republic began. It
was therefore appropriate that the first piece of postwar social legislation was the Loi Roussel, which regulated wet-nursing and urged
every French department to provide a minimum of public assistance
to mothers and infants.[16] Although the provisions to implement this
law remained rather vague, the principle that was supposed to guide
republican policy was thereby clarified: whatever their marital status,
young mothers were encouraged to bear, keep, and nurse their own
children. To this end a committee "for the protection of young children" was established in the Ministry of the Interior, which was later
merged into the national health administration. As Dr. Gustave
Drouineau described it, the committee's purpose was to regain a grip
on the social problem of illegitimacy by steering a course between the
"severe and humiliating" alms of private charity and the "blind aid"
of an impersonal state bureaucracy.[17]

The initial postwar decade, then, was a time for regrouping and
reformulating general objectives. But by 1885 it had become abun-
dantly clear that amelioristic policy statements and official blan-
dishments would not suffice. During a debate at the Academy of
Medicine, Dr. Joseph Lunier reviewed the latest statistics on France's
demographic decline since the beginning of the century. In 1801, he
reported, the average French family had produced 4.24 children, in
1850 it was 3.45, and the figure recently stood at 3.10. The most
plausible explanation of this decline was that the majority of the
population had progressively adopted voluntary birth control, which
Lunier chose to call "preventive abortion." In addition to traditional
prophylactic methods, above all coitus interruptus, now condoms
and the recent invention of the diaphragm (*pessaire de fond*) were
also available. "Women seek to avoid pregnancy without forgoing
sexual relations," Lunier lamented, "and they succeed." The suppression of the *tours* had unquestionably increased France's deficit, he
believed, because the number of alleged stillbirths had risen from
31.57 per 1,000 in 1840 to 44.70 in 1881. In reality, Lunier declared,
many of these cases were "disguised infanticides." To combat this tendency, France should take vigorous action by "vibrating the chord of

patriotism," demonstrating that "Malthusian practices" of birth control were harmful to health, and strictly enforcing the Loi Roussel throughout the land—measures that might save the lives of 80,000 infants annually. In the implementation of public health laws, Lunier believed, decentralization could be dangerous: "When it is a matter of general interest, the state alone has the capacity to command and to act. In this regard, for very good reason, it should be armed with absolute power when addressing a question that touches the very existence of the country [and] the national security."[18]

In this discourse we overhear only one man's opinion; and certain aspects of it, insofar as they could be construed as interference in the privacy of the family, did not go unchallenged by some of Lunier's medical colleagues. Yet the thrust of his remarks—that France was a nation in crisis and that demographic stagnation was a clear and present danger—was irrefutable. That same conclusion underlay repeated efforts in the parliament during the early 1880s to obtain a bill that would extend and strengthen the original Loi Roussel, especially by creating a category of "morally abandoned" children who, though not technically orphaned, had been neglected or mistreated. As one reporter in the Chamber of Deputies noted, a similar enactment by Prussia in 1878 had brought "excellent results almost immediately." He also repeated the findings of a parliamentary inquiry that the French nation, formerly a pioneer in public welfare for children, had lately been outdistanced by others.[19]

Rather than pursue in narrative detail the wending course of reform, we may concentrate here on three controversies that emerged from it. First, there was the proposal of a return to the *tours*. Their disappearance, as we saw, had coincided with an apparent rise in the rate of infant mortality and was assumed to be a principal cause of it. Because nearly half of French departments operated no welfare service whatever, many pregnant girls and unwed mothers literally had nowhere to turn. The result, in the words of Dr. Henri Thulié, a member of the CSAP and former president of the Municipal Council of Paris, was "a crying social injustice."[20] Some favored reestablishment of the *tours*, arguing that they would be better than nothing. But others proposed a bolder alternative: to require every department to provide a bureau for single mothers and their infants, thereby founding an entirely new welfare structure that would stress the virtues of maternity rather than promote sexual promiscuity and moral irresponsibility (as, they claimed, did the *tours*). Social reform, argued Lucien Dreyfus-Brisac before the CSAP, must be "as profound [and] as radical as possible." The French should not hesitate to make public assistance available "for everyone and everywhere."[21] This sweeping contention, it should be recalled, came from a man well known as an outspoken advocate of the German model. At least insofar as child support was concerned, he now gained the backing of the national director of welfare, Henri Monod, as well as other active proponents of social legislation such as Paul Strauss. They were forced, however, to endure a barrage of harsh criticisms: that a compulsory plan would be a coercive departure from the liberal precepts of laissez faire; that the cost of its implementation would be prohibitive; and that it would be neutralized in practice by the "habits and customs" of the French people.[22] On all sides it was agreed that no solution was feasible that did not allow fugitive mothers to retain their anonymity. Monod and other reformers therefore urged an "open door" (*bureau ouvert*) policy that would offer asylum to any woman who applied, no questions asked. Naturally it was to be feared that lifting all restrictions for admission would considerably inflate welfare costs. Monod waved this objection aside by grandly observing that "human capital is more precious than financial capital." Yet potentially hard budgetary choices nonetheless remained.[23]

A second unresolved issue concerned the paramedical care of pregnant women and abandoned children. Cynically known as "angel makers" (*faiseuses des anges*), the midwives of France were much maligned. Among the men who debated reform, it was thought that midwives routinely collaborated in abortions or infanticides. The statistician Jacques Bertillon estimated that France registered relatively three times as many stillbirths each year as elsewhere in Europe, and a large number of them were presumably deliberate.[24] Wet nurses were in no better repute. Those *nourrices* who served with welfare agencies were ordinarily awarded a small bonus for each infant in their care (thirty-five francs in the Department of the Seine). To survive, they were forced to accept more sucklings than they could nurse. Many babies were therefore bottle-fed with cow's milk, and a high proportion of them suffered death through gastrointestinal complications. The innuendo was that the *nourrices* were often guilty of neglecting sickly infants, after collecting a subsidy for them, in order to make room for more. One French deputy claimed that such infant mortality was "a hundred times more frequent" among the poor than the rich.[25] In truth, these rumors lacked any statistical base whatever. But they were nonetheless sufficient to strengthen the government's resolve to include more stringent regulations as an integral part of reform. To protect the innocent against abuse was both "just and necessary," Henri Monod wrote; "here the intervention of the state is legitimate." Opening a national welfare congress at Lyon in 1894, Henri Thulié amplified the point. France's demographic slide was not simply a result of "maternal negligence," he said, but stemmed from problems of administrative personnel and organization. Tighter regulation was essential to set the nation back on a path of population growth. The lesson of the lost war was that the French must multiply to survive: "*L'année terrible* gave us cruel proof that the number of men constitutes not only the wealth of a country but also its safety, and that lacking an adequate quantity of soldiers, a valiant, intelligent, and wealthy people is destined to perish." Again, one must comment, as did Thulié himself, that speeches and congresses alone were of little avail without the application of well-crafted social legislation.[26]

A third question was emblematic of the rest. What of fathers? Often welfare agencies were actually dealing with abandoned women as well as abandoned children. Having sired an offspring, a man might with impunity disappear and leave his unmarried sexual partner on her own to cope with the consequences. Other nations had long taken legal measures to hold males accountable, but the Civil Code of 1804 prohibited the police from tracing truant fathers (*recherche de la paternité*). Women had no right to sue for child support. Thus an unwed mother, if indigent, had only the recourse of charity or public welfare—unless she chose some more drastic means to escape her plight. While reviewing these all too familiar circumstances before his colleagues at the Academy of Medicine, Léon Lefort cited a shocking statistic: the illegitimacy rate in the Department of the Seine stood in the 1880s at 235 per 1,000 births, whereas in London it was only 5 per 1,000. He ascribed this remarkable discrepancy to two factors: the much tougher paternity laws in (supposedly liberal) England; and the English social morality, which allowed greater freedom before marriage, whereas in France "liberty for women begins with the day of marriage."[27] The rebuttal to this argument was predictable and categorical: that it would be unworthy of the republic to open a witch-hunt for errant fathers, and that French sexual mores were in any event immutable.[28] Without attempting to arbitrate this recurrent dispute, we can easily perceive how it implicated both the basis of a male-dominated society and, specifically, that of a totally masculine medical profession. By much later standards the paternity question was clearly an issue of women's rights. Yet its emotional tenor at the time derived from a different source, namely, the approach of a demographic disaster. As Gustave Drouineau pointed out to the CSAP, during the decade of the 1880s France would have recorded an absolute population deficit had it not been for the steady accumulation of illegitimate births. He reiterated the lugubrious theme commonly heard in reformist gatherings: "A nation that ceases to grow is wounded; it is doomed before long to perish."[29]

This pessimistic message was also at the core of a long report submitted in 1898 to the Conseil Supérieur de l'Assistance Publique by Émile Rey. In this document, which would serve as a reference point for future legislation, Rey reviewed France's entire welfare effort during the past three decades, particularly in regard to assistance for poor mothers and their infants. Until the first welfare congress in 1889, he recalled, "the state displayed virtually no interest in this imperative duty" and had provided only minimal care for orphans. Not only was that earlier lack of solidarity unworthy of a democracy, it also represented a danger for the "national defense." The French could not continue to accept a decline of their population, confronted as they were with "the terrifying spectacle of all the nations of Europe growing and multiplying with rapidity, whereas we remain inert." Apart from the enormous demographic growth of Russia, since 1870 Germany had increased by 12.5 million inhabitants, England by 10 million, Austria by 6 million, Italy by 5 million, and France "painfully" by but 2 million. In these numbers, Rey continued, "there is an immense danger for the future, indeed for the existence of France." Ever since the Franco-Prussian war, "the miseries of 1870 and the menacing development of our neighbors" had hovered over the nation's destiny. A downward spiral was not yet arrested. The time had therefore arrived to adopt broader measures of social welfare reform in order to encourage larger families, to provide better health care, and to lower the rate of infant mortality.[30]

The Rey report represented an epitome of reformist thinking in

France about the turn of the century. It offered an unabashed advertisement for motherhood and provided a rationale for national solidarism. The urgency of Rey's proposal for legislative action, approved by the CSAP in 1900 and forwarded to parliament, derived not from a demand for women's rights or for the realization of republican democracy. It arose, rather, from the necessity of national survival on a crowded continent where the French population was falling alarmingly behind the rest of Europe. Some day men might be called to fight for France. But first they needed to be born and raised.

Women in the Work Force

Let it be said at once that French social reformers showed little interest in peasant women, except as they entered the urban market. Quiet desperation in the countryside was only of marginal concern. Thus the majority of working women, whose employment was still in agriculture, were scarcely affected by measures that came under consideration to improve the conditions of labor.[31]

The first serious effort to introduce stricter regulations into the workplace can be dated from 1885 when Martin Nadaud introduced a bill to the Chamber advocating a ten-hour working day. That factory hours for children should be limited was a foregone conclusion. The real issue was whether a distinction should be made between men and women. Should they both be regarded as adult laborers and treated alike? Or should women be protected by special provisions, unlike male workers who were obliged to bargain with their employers through trade unions? In a sense, the difference was between a viewpoint that stressed class and one that emphasized gender.[32]

The labor relations committee of the Chamber began deliberations on this matter in March 1887. The principal proponent of "total regulation"—meaning that legislation should apply to the sexes equally—was a Catholic notable, Albert de Mun, who contended that all workers were virtually defenseless against their *patrons*. The only weapon available to the trade unions was a strike, a means of agitation still disapproved by society. Hence de Mun believed that the state should intervene with laws "to protect the weak against the abuses of exploitation of which they may be victims." Such help to the working class should be extended, he was careful to specify, without lapsing into state socialism. Philosophically de Mun thereby rested his case on what he termed "legitimate liberty," which existed somewhere between the "absolute liberty" of a pure laissez-faire economy and the opposite extreme of excessive state interventionism.[33]

The strongest objection to this argument was stated by a deputy, Fernand Faure, who supplied the committee with a straight dose of liberal orthodoxy. He, too, favored a legal reduction of working hours from the twelve-hour day set in 1848, but this change should not be achieved through governmental intrusion. The state's only legitimate function was to defend the feeble. But since permission had been granted to organize trade syndicates in 1884, adult male workers no longer required such protection. The value of an individual in the marketplace always depends on personal initiative, the mark of a mature sense of responsibility. As an example of the self-regulating function of a free-market economy, Faure cited, in authentic liberal style, the British experience: "They counted on the initiative of individuals and arrived at a better result than that demanded by the Comte de Mun."[34]

So much for principles. As always, the devil resided in details. Such was the reminder of Richard Waddington, who had recently directed a parliamentary inquiry into French labor practices. Waddington favored an eleven-hour day for all workers on the grounds that a ten-hour day was currently unenforceable. His study showed, contrary to a widespread contention, that most French workers did not already have a de facto ten-hour day. That was often the case in metallurgy but not so, for instance, in the textile industry. Literally a moderate in this regard—midway between the existing statute of twelve hours and the proposed reduction to ten—Waddington nevertheless advocated the state's intercession into labor relations. It was simply unrealistic, in his view, to count on emotional appeals to the humanity of employers: "The *patrons* will never voluntarily accept and will never themselves adopt a measure that causes them certain losses and runs contrary to their interests." Against their recalcitrance, especially outside a few big cities and industrial centers, the labor unions remained powerless. The state must therefore draft a national reform and enforce it.[35] Waddington's reasoning coincided with that of Martin Nadaud, except that the latter continued to plead for a ten-hour day. He had only contempt for the liberal view that the entire matter should be left to the automatic mechanism of the market: "French society always seems to be uninterested, or nearly so, in the welfare of the workers. At least the bourgeoisie has never done anything." He therefore joined de Mun and Waddington in support of "total regulation."[36] The labor committee, however, remained unconvinced; and in May 1887 it decided by a narrow vote to exclude adult male workers from any limitations on hours of employment that would be applicable for women and children. One deputy, Charles Achard, a strong advocate of state intervention, attempted to summarize the central theme that had emerged: whether "the principle of liberty itself should be regulated and limited by the superior principle of social justice." It was precisely here that the committee hesitated. Its close ballot therefore suggested a need for the further search of a suitable compromise.[37]

Accordingly, a series of investigative committee hearings was conducted in the next year. These sessions were strictly among men, both deputies and witnesses, until late November 1888, when a group of female textile workers from the Department of the Vosges offered to testify. This proposal touched off a symptomatic procedural debate. "We have never heard a delegation of women workers," commented one committeeman in support, adding that it would be "impolitic" to respond negatively "in this day and age." But, not coincidentally, three members opposed this view: Waddington, Nadaud, and Achard. Relatively speaking, this trio represented the most leftist element present, and one might have expected them to welcome the direct testimony of women. However, precisely because they supported limitations on labor for all workers, male and female, they were disinclined to single out one sex for special consideration. We are left to speculate about another possible motive for their dissent. Very likely, the three may have suspected that the women's testimony would prove unfavorable for reform altogether. In any event, their objection was overruled and for the first time since the founding of the Third Republic a female voice was heard within the walls of the French parliament.[38]

The Vosgesian women provided a detailed account of their daily lives as textile workers in eastern France, where an important part of the industry had relocated after the loss of Alsace and Lorraine. They were earning about half the wages of men. A female tending spools (*bobineuse*) was usually paid fortnightly at a rate of thirty to thirty-five francs, whereas her male counterpart received about four francs per laboring day. Women were frequently consigned to the night shift, especially if married, enabling them to alternate with their husbands at work and meanwhile keep the family intact at home. A mother of seven testified that she was generally on the job six nights a week from 5:00 P.M. to 7:00 A.M., including two hours of rest. She had maintained that pace for six years, she said, and was feeling fit. She expressed gratitude to her employer for the "excellent" bouillon provided during her breaks. She and her fellow females actually preferred night work, although (other than occasionally passing him at the factory gate as the shifts changed) she saw her husband only for eighteen hours on the weekend. Another woman corroborated this account and went on to describe her daily routine after leaving the factory at 5:00 A.M. She did household chores for two hours, slept three and a half, devoted herself to the children between 10:30 A.M. and 2:00 P.M., slept for another two and a half hours, then arose to prepare herself for the next shift commencing at 5:00 P.M. When women laborers became pregnant, the committee learned, they usually worked through the eighth month. Because they returned to work within two months after birth, they were able to nurse their infants at most for a few weeks. As a rule, no *crèches* or other child-care facilities were available.[39]

This glimpse into an existence scarcely imaginable to Europeans a century later was not without its ambiguities. If one might well conclude that social reform was indispensable, of what sort should it be? Far from condemning night work for women, those testifying pleaded that it be continued. Otherwise many women would lose their jobs and, with only the husband's wages remaining, they would be unable to maintain their families. The productivity of French industry was also bound to suffer from the suppression of night work and the curtailment of hours. By adopting severe restrictions, the parliament might therefore succeed merely in harming the national economy and forcing thousands of women into dependence on welfare relief. As for the demographic crisis, never absent from such considerations, French deputies had to weigh these factors against opinion emanating from the Academy of Medicine, which favored the abolition of women's night work and the reduction of their hours on grounds that the fecundity of females was significantly reduced by the fatigue of prolonged factory labor. In addition, as Dr. Rochard stressed, the moral consequences of women's night work were clear to see: "The child in the street, the father in the cabaret, and the daughter who knows where."[40]

Reform proposals soon became stalled in the parliamentary process. A measure passed by the Chamber of Deputies in 1890 foresaw a maximum working day of ten hours for all laborers; but this provision was stricken by the Senate. When the bill returned to the Chamber's labor relations committee for reconsideration, its members voted overwhelmingly (15 to 1) not to accept the Senate version. A deadlock thereupon ensued for the next several years. In an effort to break the impasse in 1894, the committee, under its new chairman Alexandre Ribot, devised a compromise formula of twelve hours per working day for men, eleven for women, and ten for children. Also, Ribot's committee recommended that a maximum of ten hours for women be phased in by 1897.[41]

It is noteworthy that for the first time French Socialists gained prominence in these deliberations. They were usually consistent both in supporting greater state intervention to regulate labor practices and in urging that limitations of the laboring day be established uniformly for men and women. Thus Jean Jaurès, as an active member of the labor committee in the mid-1890s, was willing to accept a temporary bargain, but his clearly stated objective was to gain a ten-hour day for all.[42] Jules Guesde, although not a member of the committee, appeared before it to present his more radical motion for an eight-hour day. Needless to elaborate, Guesde's plan encountered disbelief and skepticism among most of the assembled deputies. At least it had the utility of making Jaurès appear moderate by comparison.[43]

The Socialist politician who unquestionably exercised the most determinant influence on the outcome, however, was Alexandre Millerand. After Jaurès's transfer from the labor committee in 1898, it was Millerand who steered his colleagues toward a solution. Polished and pragmatic, he possessed a realistic sense that legislation must above all be practicable. Further investigations by the labor committee into the textile industry revealed that production could not be effectively organized if workers were not on identical schedules. The 12-11-10 formula was frequently inapplicable, it became evident, because some skilled labor (especially by men) could not be accomplished without assistants (often women and children). If the length of the working day were to be unified, in that case, how soon and at what level? Millerand was able to obtain a resolution to enforce a maximum eleven-hour working day by January 1900, which would be reduced to ten hours within three years.[44]

The meandering pace and complexity of this story should not obfuscate its moral: the fates of men and women in the labor force were inseparable. Ultimately it was neither sexism nor socialist theory that prevailed, but the nature of the marketplace.[45]

Prostitution and Exploitation

In the nineteenth century prostitution became primarily an urban phenomenon of industrial nations. Hence it could not fail to gain in importance. The statutes regulating prostitution in France had been drafted in the early days of the Napoleonic empire. They required a regular examination for venereal disease and therefore made registration with the police mandatory. As in many a growth industry, however, the rules were seldom strictly observed. By the 1890s the prefect of police in Paris estimated that women "submitted" to administrative control (*filles soumises*) were outnumbered by freelance prostitutes (*insoumises*) at a rate of three to one.[46]

The reasons for this lively trade were not mysterious. They were well explained by Jules Simon in a book on female workers that had become something of a best seller by 1871, when it was published in its seventh edition. The expansion of urban markets, especially in Paris and the larger port cities, had attracted thousands of young women as laborers, salesclerks, office personnel, and domestic servants. Invariably they were ill-housed and poorly paid. Whenever rents and living costs rose, many of these females were forced to the margin of society, where they were left with but one means of financial survival. Usually, of course, this meant a loss of independence, an increased exposure to communicable disease, and a moral stigma that came with the calling of a prostitute.[47]

Soon after its founding, the Third Republic adopted a stance of deregulation. The disgrace of the preceding imperial regime bolstered the belief that France had been subjected before 1870 to an excess of administrative meddling. Once the initial trauma of the Paris Commune and its public repression had faded away, the national government consciously began to relinquish its grip: witness a law in 1880 that relaxed the licensing of bars and cabarets dispensing alcoholic beverages. Consumption climbed accordingly, and so too did the prostitution with which carousing was always associated. Not that prostitution was perceived as unproblematical. To the contrary, young women displaying their wares in windows of the rue François Miron, right behind the Paris city hall, represented a "permanent scandal" for municipal officials. Still more disturbing, a parliamentary inquiry into working conditions concluded that most male laborers showed little inclination to save money through voluntary retirement programs and preferred to spend their wages on more enticing and alcoholic pleasures.[48]

The movement toward deregulation was thus no sooner confirmed than it came under challenge. In 1881 Théophile Roussel, Jules Simon, and others submitted a bill to the Senate in favor of legal protection for abandoned and mistreated children. Among the social concerns expressed in justification of such a law was the widespread, albeit unquantified, prostitution of minors. To gain a more precise picture of this practice, a special committee of the Academy of Medicine undertook an investigation for which the principal source was an administrative study of prostitution and syphilis during the decade from 1878 to 1887. This analysis, based on police reports, admitted that there was no possibility of establishing the real extent of clandestine prostitution. But of the unregistered women taken into custody and medically examined, it was determined that more than a third carried venereal disease; and these constituted about half of all syphilitic prostitutes. The committee therefore concluded that the introduction of more rigorous surveillance was imperative and that the national state would need to intervene. A resolution to that effect was thereupon adopted by the Academy of Medicine. A sort of neoregulationism thus made an appearance in the early 1890s, just as other welfare reforms were being considered to meet France's demographic crisis.[49]

On the last day of October 1891 the new minister of justice, Armand Fallières, proposed a bill in the name of "public morality and social defense" to tighten controls on drinking establishments that facilitated prostitution. This draft soon entered the parliamentary arena and was thoroughly aired in an ad hoc committee created by the Chamber of Deputies. Records of the confidential deliberations of this body reveal that the members' primary objective, as a committeeman said, was the "energetic repression of pimps." The common goal of combating the scourge of syphilis was of course evident, but the intention to protect rather than to punish prostitutes was surprisingly enlightened, whereas, as another deputy commented, pimps "merit no consideration."[50] These laudable motives did not alter the fact that prostitution was uncontrollable without stringently enforced state regulations. Within the city limits of Paris alone, according to the prefect of police, there were in 1892 nearly 5,000 officially registered prostitutes and probably another 15,000 freelancers. The city had 60 public houses of prostitution and 654 bordellos. Moreover, these establishments were doubtless outnumbered by small hotels and bars that also catered to such commerce. Little wonder, then, that no one could devise a feasible solution to recommend to the Chamber. Further study was required.[51]

It may seem odd to mention brothels and nurseries in the same breath, yet they both prompted political questions about state regulation. They were also implicated in complaints against the exploitation of women and minors. And both became connected with the depopulation crisis, which increased fears that creeping moral degeneracy and inadequate public hygiene were crippling the healthy family life essential for sustained demographic growth.[52]

Private and especially church-sponsored organizations became targets of those who believed that the absence of any state control inevitably led to abuses. On a scale of villainy, independent childbirth clinics (*maisons d'accouchement*) were thought to be the most sinister because, as Dr. Gustave Drouineau charged before the Conseil Supérieur de l'Assistance Publique, they "often encourage abortion and infanticide." A motion that the clinics should become "the object of special regulations" was duly adopted by the CSAP in 1892.[53] Hardly less dubious than maternal clinics were orphanages where, it was alleged, children were forced to earn their keep by excessive hours of labor in what were in effect cottage industries. Not only did the youngsters sometimes suffer from exhaustion, they were too often indoctrinated rather than properly instructed—an accusation brought with increasing frequency against Catholic institutions during the anticlerical campaign for the separation of church and state.[54] Least troubling but nonetheless problematical were the *crèches*, which we shall examine more carefully in another context. Essentially daytime centers for preschool infants of working women, they boasted an honorable history of private enterprise since 1844, but they could not escape the scrutiny of reformers who criticized their uneven quality of medical care and irregular hygienic standards. No one denied that the *crèches* met a social need. But exactly for that reason many reformers thought it essential for the state both to subsidize and to regulate their operation.[55]

The decade bisected by the year 1900 may be described as a time of public leagues, national committees, international conferences, and parliamentary maneuvers. Throughout, the woman question remained prominent, especially in regard to prostitution, and it was concisely enunciated from the beginning by Léon Bourgeois: what was to be the nature and extent of state intervention?[56] Emerging as it did in bits and drabs, the answer never achieved clarity. Perhaps the simple truth was, as one historian has concluded, that prostitution remained "virtually impervious to reform attempts" and that legislative proposals therefore had "not the slightest chance of passage—at least not directly."[57] Yet that judgment begs the issue: why not? Ultimately the explanation lay deeply implanted in the ambiguous character of the republic, which was forever wavering between liberal precepts and future prospects for a much more highly regimented society. French reformers had an excruciating choice between the unbearable consequences of laissez faire and the seemingly unacceptable implications of authoritarian control. A pair of legislative bills to regulate prostitution—an antipimping code and a general statute for the protection of minors—fell squarely between these two stools. We cannot be surprised by a report, distributed in 1912 by the Ministry of Labor to the prefects of France, that analyzed the ill effects of a mass exodus by young women from countryside to city. After all that had been said and done, the report stated, prostitution remained unchecked and had reached the proportions of "a disastrous social phenomenon." For French reformers before 1914, these were obvious grounds for discouragement.[58]

Maternal Care and Family Assistance

The agitation for reforms that aimed to reverse France's alarming pattern of demographic decline achieved a legislative victory in 1904. Two laws were passed in that year to provide state aid for maternity cases. One bill required every department in France to create for needy mothers a special hostel (*maison maternelle*) that would offer free facilities for prenatal care and delivery. At public expense the hostel was to be staffed by a physician, a small group of social workers, and a female officer of admissions. This legislative act was supplemented by a second bill, which afforded a modest subsidy for women who breast-fed their own babies. The objectives of these measures were forthright: to fill the lacuna left by abolition of the *tours*, to offer a readily available alternative to abortion or infanticide, and to undercut the high infant mortality associated with abandonment of illegitimate children. More significant than the specific provisions of this legislation was the obligatory principle they embodied. The French state thereby committed itself to a welfare program that was mandatory throughout the land. Implementation, as we have so often seen, was another matter. But at least the legislature no longer balked at the very notion of imposing uniform regulations in the name of national solidarity.[59]

The actual impact of these reforms was nonetheless limited. They made it possible for a few women, especially in rural areas, to receive encouragement and temporary assistance heretofore unavailable. But the 1904 laws did not address the needs of the growing female labor force in the cities. Nor did they help parents struggling to support their families on a meager income. Reformers therefore set their sights on two additional measures of social welfare for women, both finally adopted in 1913, that were also designed to halt France's demographic recession. One granted financial aid for pregnancy leave to working women; and the other established a monetary subvention for married couples producing more than three children.

To appreciate this culminating burst, later to be treated in detail, we need to step back and view it in the total perspective of the final quarter of a century before 1914. The origin of the proposal for direct state assistance to expectant mothers may be chronologically situated with precision in the year 1890, when Jules Simon attended an early welfare congress in Berlin. This event, reverentially mentioned in later years, proved to be of practical importance when Simon returned to Paris and began to lobby for the organization of maternity assistance. He urged that the republic respond to the unanimous resolution of the Berlin congress (at which the French delegation alone had abstained) in favor of a minimum of four weeks of state-sponsored postnatal sabbatical for mothers. Imperial Germany was already implementing such a plan, soon to be followed by Austria-Hungary and later by other west European nations.[60]

In the summer of 1892 a legislative proposal was forwarded to the Conseil Supérieur de l'Assistance Publique, of which Jules Simon—his health now failing—had long been a leading member. Here a debate developed that at first revolved on the nature of liberal principles. The bill represented a "colossal danger," one opponent said, because it would offer state aid even to unwed women, thereby weakening public morality and the family. The state should intervene to assist a person in difficulty only when it was "not his fault," continued Loys Brueyre, and should not tamper with an individual's private destiny: "I absolutely reject collectivism however it appears, whether it is in the form of state socialism or in the form claimed by the Catholics." This assertion was countered by two CSAP delegates who were also members of the Academy of Medicine. For one, Jules Rochard likewise professed to be a defender of liberalism, but he disputed Brueyre's rigid definition of it. There were humanitarian reasons to protect helpless mothers and to save their infants. It was also a patriotic duty, because the French could thereby add 28,000 conscripts annually to their army. Léon Lefort concurred. Given the obvious insufficiency of private charity, he argued, the state should reimburse its debt to the poor, who were helping to produce the national wealth and to defend the national territory. Lefort remarked that liberals made no objection when the state interceded to protect private property or to prevent crime. Why boggle at maternity assistance? If this constituted state socialism, Lefort added caustically, "then we have a duty to create state socialism."[61]

It is unnecessary to unravel any further these familiar recitations. They are enough to confirm that the motivation and conception of this particular reform proposal was identical with the others we have examined. It was above all a means to offset France's demographic deficit and to render the republic capable of competing as a major European power. In the already cited report of Émile Rey in 1898, the twin objectives of lowering infant mortality and raising larger families were firmly anchored in this context. While explaining his report to the CSAP in 1900, Rey was even more optimistic than his medical colleagues Rochard and Lefort. He believed that the implementation of far-reaching social reforms could ensure the survival of an additional 100,000 children each year and therewith greatly enhance the "security and grandeur" of the nation.[62] When motions to protect pregnant mothers and newborns were introduced to parliamentary committees, the same rationale obtained. To surmount "decadence" and return to the first rank of European states, French deputies were told in the bill's preamble, it was necessary to establish "a strong and powerful nation."[63] These repeated emotional appeals to French pride at every stage of the legislative process cannot be dismissed as chauvinistic drivel or as merely a packet of convenient debating points meant to override the objections of reluctant liberals. Rather, they expressed one of the deepest motives of those reform advocates who were nudging France toward an ethic of public welfare.

Chapter 6

Physicians and Patients

The profession of medicine was crucial for any effort to raise the standards of public health. If new hygienic measures were to be effectively implemented, it would be necessary to have a sufficient corps of well-trained medical personnel. According to some accounts, this was scarcely a problem throughout much of the nineteenth century. If anything, it has been suggested, France suffered from a glut of doctors who emerged from the best system of medical education in Europe.[1] The reality was otherwise. The French nation never had remotely enough qualified physicians to meet the medical needs of its entire population. Perhaps the rich were properly treated in Paris. But indigents in the city and rural folk across the countryside were always neglected. What perpetually characterized the French medical profession was maldistribution of doctors, inadequacy of facilities, and lack of funds for expansion.[2]

These conditions were fully exposed by the war of 1870. From that time on, the realization that France was facing a medical crisis began to spread. This new awareness focused at first on the fact that the country lacked enough medical schools. With Strasbourg detached, only the faculties of Paris and Montpellier remained. Hence a program was launched in the 1870s to create additional centers of medical instruction in Nancy, Lille, Lyon, and Bordeaux.[3] Yet this effort, important as it surely was, begged a number of ulterior questions. What kind of training should medical students receive? How should they be deployed? What institutional innovations would be required to support an expanded scheme of public health? These were just a few of the issues that came under consideration in the early decades of the Third Republic, to which we may append another: how was France to sustain medical leadership in competition with the flourishing scientific enterprises of imperial Germany?

A complex story of challenge and response emerges from a study of these problems. Medicine, then as now, represented a host of established procedures and vested interests. Controversies were consequently sharp, often bitter. Reputations rose or fell like shares on some volatile stock exchange. There were conflicts among physicians; between them and their patients; among politicians, health officials, and insurance funds; and invariably between bureaucratic regulations and popular resistance to intrusions on privacy. The course of reform was therefore erratic as the republican leadership felt its way uncertainly toward a coherent scheme of social welfare.

A Need for Change

Signs of malaise in public medicine were manifest by 1880. One had only to visit a Paris hospital to perceive them. Chronic overcrowding was evident from the number of stretcher patients (*brancards*) who clogged the aisles or lay squeezed between the beds. There were not nearly enough wards to meet the demand, and in those that existed the ill were parked indiscriminately, regardless of the type of their malady. From a statistical standpoint this chaos was readily explicable: in the two decades since 1859 the population of Paris had increased 69 percent, whereas the number of beds in the city's hospitals and hospices had multiplied on an average of less than 20 percent. Thus in 1859 Paris had provided one bed for every 164 residents, but by 1879 that ratio had declined to one per 231.[4]

Outside the capital the situation was different but no less disturbing. In the first postwar decade the number of licensed physicians was apparently declining. They were, moreover, mostly concentrated in urban areas where medical practice was adequately remunerated and reasonably comfortable. The life of a country doctor was considerably more strenuous and sometimes impoverished. To some extent the slack of rural medicine was taken up by "health officials" (*officiers de santé*), who compensated for their lack of formal training by tireless service to the needy. Yet a felt need within the profession to upgrade medical standards, while buttressing the prerogatives of physicians, brought pressure to abolish this ancillary personnel, even though a large majority of France's nearly 36,000 communes still had no resident medical authority whatever.[5]

A searching discussion followed. Several of the leading medical personalities of the time, including Dean Paul Brouardel of the Sorbonne, initially opposed a motion to suppress the *officiers de santé* on grounds that their place in the countryside would only be taken by charlatans, who already abounded in areas without qualified medical personnel. To eliminate semiskilled health officials, Brouardel argued, would be to reduce the medical corps by a quarter, and that "at a moment when this number is already insufficient"[6] (see Table 4).

Two other developments in the 1880s were symptomatic of growing discomfort. One was a strident demand by the Municipal Council of Paris that all of the capital's medical establishments be secularized. This tendency, although resisted sporadically by various national governments over the years, nevertheless evolved and later culminated in the campaign to separate church from state. Such rancor tended to cloud reform questions with large infusions of ideology.[7] Another controversy surrounded the inception of medical "syndicates," of which we must take further note. Here we may simply register that the medical profession was agitated by internal dissensions as well as external pressures, both of which eventually complicated efforts to achieve social reform.[8]

These stirrings of the medical community were directly related to the organization of a central Bureau of Public Health and Hygiene in the Ministry of the Interior. This agency, we have observed, was conceived by its director Henri Monod as the hub of a campaign to revitalize France's entire sanitation and welfare system. But several divisive policy issues immediately arose, over which the new health administration hesitated. Their common source was confusion as to whether France should consolidate an entirely new branch of welfare bureaucracy throughout the country, with its own staff of inspectors who would report directly to Monod's headquarters; or whether the additional services would be attached to existing departmental offices and supervised by the prefectoral corps. Illustrative of this unresolved dilemma was a quarrel over the relative merits of home care (administered by the *bureaux de bienfaisance*) and of hospital treatment. Ultimately at stake, of course, was the degree of permissible administrative centralization and state interventionism, matters on which a consensus was still lacking.[9]

Table 4 / *Number of French Medical Personnel,*
1847–1881

Year	Physicians	Officiers de santé	Total
1847	10,643	7,456	18,099
1853	11,172	6,859	18,031
1857	11,065	6,392	17,457
1866	10,254	5,568	15,822
1876	10,743	3,633	14,376
1881	11,643	3,203	14,846

Source: Paul Brouardel and A.-J. Martin, "Exercice de la médecine," CCHP,
Recueil 16 (1886): 86–137.

Behind these principles lurked the practical problem of assuaging the effects of population growth in Paris. Basically the options were three: to move medical patients out to the suburbs or provinces; to construct spacious new facilities in Paris; or to inaugurate a vastly improved system of home care, thereby relieving congestion in the capital's hospitals and hospices. For related reasons, the first of these proved to be infeasible: most of the ill and aged did not want to be moved from the city, and residents of outlying districts did not want to receive them. Private persuasion and public oratory were usually to no avail in gaining the cooperation of patients who preferred to remain in the city. Besides, what community in the Parisian *banlieues* would cheerfully accept a recuperation center for persons with contagious diseases in its midst? Alarmed protests rebounded from Bobigny against the proposal to locate a smallpox clinic there. Another effort to create a ward for scurvy patients in Créteil aroused "the emotion of the population." The Paris director of public health therefore concluded that any attempt to populate suburban hospitals with "contagious Parisians" was certain to be resisted "in the most energetic fashion."[10]

As for the second possibility, of course, the real sticking point was expense. Rural and suburban patients entered Paris for treatment but brought no supporting funds with them. The capital had the power neither to oblige other communes to pay for their ailing emigrants nor to build their own medical facilities to keep them. Meanwhile, the municipal budget of Paris was climbing precipitously, at an average annual increment of a million francs in the decade after 1880. In the 1870s two large hospitals (Laennec and Tenon) had been opened, but in the 1880s only two small ones (Bichat and Broussais) were founded. The city's finances were stretched merely to maintain existing facilities. The national government, in charge of pari-mutuel funds and other major sources of revenue, was reluctant to increase subsidies for a municipal administration with which it was often in conflict. And so it went, with needs forever outstripping resources.[11]

A third option remained, and there was much talk of it: a complete revision of France's health system to render home care more effective and thereby to relieve pressure on the crowded medical facilities. Every year about 3,000 requests were received—mostly from the aged—for admission to Parisian hospices, but barely a third of these could be placed. Also, although supposedly intended for short-term treatment, hospitals were overflowing with the chronically ill, whose extended care kept out new patients. And the stretcher cases continued to encumber the rest.[12] These difficulties were compounded by the tendency of many physicians to send clients, especially those on welfare relief, to the hospitals rather than to care for them at domicile. The underfunded *bureaux de bienfaisance* were apparently helpless to offset this imbalance, because doctors commanded only minuscule fees for home visitations and patients usually received no more than five francs monthly in sickness compensation, a sum inadequate for survival. Clearly changes were necessary, but of what sort? In November 1889 the welfare committee of the Municipal Council of Paris presented a plan. Its spokesman explained: "What we propose already exists—do not forget, gentlemen—in several German cities. At Elberfeld quite generous assistance is provided to disabled workers as well as to their widows and to each child. In a city as rich as this one, it should be fairly easy to do what has been accomplished in Elberfeld."[13] In fact it was not. Although a pilot project based on the Elberfeld model was started in the third arrondissement of Paris, a totally revamped welfare procedure remained a mirage.

In the early 1890s the winds of reform nonetheless began to gust. This was the period, we recall, when the republic was moving toward the adoption of legislation to guarantee free medical assistance for every needy French citizen. Such a measure was necessary, Paul Brouardel contended before the Academy of Medicine, both on behalf of the "general interest" and for "national defense."[14] Some specific facets of the political process that led to the law in 1893 should not escape our attention here. There is abundant evidence, first of all, that competition with Germany remained firmly fixed among the motives of French reformers. Brouardel's allusion to the needs of national defense was not exceptional. Reporting for the welfare committee of the Municipal Council of Paris in the summer of 1892, Raoul Bompard discoursed on the success of Germany's welfare agencies in reducing overhead costs while yet increasing individual subsidies for medical patients. "The Council knows," Bompard said, "what truly remarkable results have been attained by certain foreign cities, notably in Germany, by the application of the Elberfeld system."[15] Likewise, in the final months before passage of the law, Émile Cheysson urged members of the Conseil Supérieur de l'Assistance Publique to throw their influence behind the reform. It was not adequate, he stated, to administer welfare benefits solely on the basis of "statistical generalities." One needed to establish close contact with indigents and to examine "how they live, how they eat, how they are housed, how they are dressed, and that in every district. That is what is done at Elberfeld. . . . I think that what is good for Elberfeld would also be good for us [*ce qui est bon à Elberfeld le serait aussi chez nous*]."[16]

Yet the French conception remained fundamentally different from the German, of course, because it did not mandate group insurance for every worker. "Obligation" in French terminology was a bureaucratic notion that applied only to the communes and departments, which were required after 1893 to provide a minimum of gratis medical aid to indigent patients. Beyond such public welfare payments, however, health insurance in France remained optional. Thus the 1893 law did not depart far from the liberal precept of self-help. Still, it is permissible to evaluate the new legislation as a telling wrinkle of erosion on the liberal surface. It opened a crack for legitimate state intervention and thereby provided a possibility of further governmental intrusion. Just as Germany had adopted national welfare measures immediately after a shift to economic protectionism about 1880, now a decade later the French reform followed acceptance of the Méline tariff in 1892. The common denominator of these enactments was a slippage of laissez-faire orthodoxy. It was essentially to this fact that the French premier Charles Dupuy referred with some hyperbole when he announced: "We are in a sense making the first step into a new world."[17]

Doctors and Reformers

The onset of social reform was bound to pose a threat to traditional medical practice. As a rule the French doctor was self-employed, working alone or with a helper in his small office, much like an artisan in his atelier. But now the specter of socialized medicine suddenly loomed at his door in the guise of governmental regulations, state inspectors, welfare agencies, and insurance companies. Most physicians understandably responded with a certain consternation. One proposal, for instance, was to divide Paris into medical districts, assign practitioners to them, and oblige welfare recipients to seek consultation with the doctor nearest their residence. This reorganization would rationalize administration of the 1893 law, but it was also likely to curtail the venerable principle of free choice. Would it go so far that patients could no longer select their family doctor, or that physicians would be prohibited from retaining the fees of their long established clients? If so, the confidence of their relationship was certain to suffer.

Here honest opinions sharply diverged, as the debate over wet-nursing well illustrated. Some argued that the only way to control *nourrices* and to end malpractices that held down the French birth rate—meaning abortions and infanticides—was to implement an extensive program of state inspection. But others rejected such bureaucratic interference and maintained that greater power should be vested in local physicians to punish and correct abuses. To offer French babies "the breast and nothing but the breast," as a member of the Academy of Medicine exclaimed in a spurt of sloganeering, the undiminished authority of the doctor must be safeguarded.[18] Because these differences were deep and persistent, it is dubious that the Parisian municipal councillor Dr. Auguste-Louis Navarre was justified in claiming at the end of 1895 that "a sort of revolution in the organization of public welfare" was in progress.[19] Most of the evidence speaks to the contrary. Rather, one must be struck by the longevity of medical attitudes and habits, by the unrelieved crowding of hospital wards, by the slowness of institutional reform to penetrate the provinces, and by the continuing clashes over policy questions.

As for Paris, as late as 1905 the secretary-general of the CSAP, André Mesureur, openly conceded the "lamentable condition" of the city's physical plant. Old buildings were not suited for innovative procedures. Nor was it usually possible to upgrade the quality of hospital personnel, for whom "nothing, or almost nothing, has been done."[20] The need for a "complete reorganization" was also admitted by Poubelle's replacement as prefect of the Seine, Justin de Selves.[21] Yet the cost appeared prohibitive, and old practices died hard. The custom of tipping personnel in the hospitals, though officially discouraged, was zealously guarded by nurses and orderlies; thus patients who refused often found no response from the staff to their pathetic calls for a bedpan in the night.[22] The needy who failed to gain admittance to a medical facility were likely to suffer still more serious discomfort. A report to the Municipal Council in 1900 estimated that 36,000 Parisians, dependent on welfare, were receiving aid for home care at a monthly rate of three francs in the summer, five in the winter. One councillor qualified this dole as "a disgrace and a scandal." Another, André Lefèvre, blamed such penury on the *bureaux de bienfaisance*. He noted that only in the capital's third arrondissement, where the Elberfeld plan was being tried, were unsalaried welfare workers effective in reaching the indigent population. The entire system needed recasting, he argued, because as things stood "public welfare, gentlemen, cannot resolve the social question." Called upon to defend the administration's record against these mounting criticisms, Henri Napias could only place the onus on "insufficient resources" that left Paris in "an extremely painful situation."[23]

Circumstances elsewhere in France were naturally more disparate and could be disaggregated only by intensive local studies. A revealing source, however, is provided by the minutes of the Academy of Medicine, which tracked responses to social legislation across the nation. The Academy's acknowledged expert on such matters was Dr. Charles Porak, who reported extensively to his colleagues late in the year 1900. His tone was pessimistic. Problems in rural France began with the lack of reliable statistics because of negligence by local mayors. The same was often true of physicians, who were expected to work long hours, travel immense distances on primitive roads, and then return at nightfall to complete bureaucratic forms.

"Statistics," observed Porak about the country doctor, "are odious to him." Because the great majority of communes had no trained medical personnel, physicians were generally assigned to cover broad districts. But the boundaries were often ill-defined and the burden unevenly distributed. The supervision of wet nurses by doctors consequently tended to be irregular and incapable of preventing fraud. The maldistribution of resources and responsibilities led to altercations between doctors and communes; and the mode of welfare payment—whether according to the patient's department of origin or department of residence—likewise produced conflicts among the communes. Moreover, there was a question of how conscientiously a physician should probe alleged malpractices and enforce the law of the land. This was, Porak admonished, "a serious issue that might impinge on the liberty of everyone and the inviolability of private domicile."[24]

In the details of Porak's account we catch glimpses of the rigor of rural life, and we sense the difficulties encountered by any social legislation in sinking roots beyond the city limits of Paris. Above all, we see that social welfare and private medicine did not always mix. Passage of reform measures was a sine qua non of meaningful change, but it did not assure that daily medical practice would soon be transformed.

Public Health and the Smallpox Scare

The greatest ally of welfare reform was contagious disease. So long as debate could be delimited to a narrow range of abstract principles, the liberal philosophy of rugged individualism maintained a certain plausibility. But when faced with a raging epidemic, fastidious insistence on self-help verged on absurdity. Lone persons, families, or communes were helpless to contain infections, which by their nature respected no local or regional borders. The obvious recourse— and, given the political configuration of late nineteenth-century Europe, possibly the only feasible recourse—was for each national government to adopt measures of public sanitation and hygiene that had some chance of protecting its population. The solution, in short, was state intervention. No special aspect of the social question more clearly illustrated such apparently inescapable logic, or better revealed the differences between France and Germany, than the eruption of a severe epidemic of smallpox (*variole*) during and after the war of 1870. The previous history of the disease has already been capably chronicled.[25] Here we need to examine at closer hand the postwar decades and to relate this medical episode to the rest.

In the late summer of 1870 Prussia entered the war against France with an inoculated army, even though the Prussian civil population was not yet under a mandatory program of vaccination. On the other side, neither the French army nor the citizenry had been systematically protected against smallpox. The result was, during the siege of Paris late that autumn, that the Prussian forces lost fewer than 500 men; whereas the defending garrison suffered more than 23,000 smallpox casualties within the city walls.[26] After concluding an armistice in the winter, however, Prussian troops began returning to Germany, taking with them hundreds of French prisoners of war. Thereupon a frightful smallpox epidemic occurred in Prussia and adjacent areas that claimed thousands of lives in the two years following. From this experience the new national state drew an appropriate conclusion. In 1874 the Reichstag accepted the government's legislative proposal to require of every German citizen an inoculation against smallpox. Before the end of that decade the disease had virtually disappeared east of the Vosges.[27]

In the Third Republic circumstances were otherwise. During the 1870s and well into the 1880s public health was still considered a matter primarily under local aegis. We have seen how the state maintained its liberal orientation. No less significantly, it lacked a dynamic administration for public health and hygiene: there was no real French equivalent of the *Reichsgesundheitsamt*. Although the lesson of the siege of Paris was patent to the French, of course, they were thus ideologically and institutionally unprepared to adopt mandatory procedures on a national scale. In certain French cities efforts were mounted to enforce vaccination of children and revaccination of adults, despite some resistance among the "unenlightened classes," according to police reports. By 1882 Paris had opened inoculation centers in all of its twenty arrondissements.[28] But the picture outside of the capital, as always, was kaleidoscopic; and it was precisely this absence of national coordination that was so keenly deplored by reformers. Such regret was evident in 1887 when Minister of the Interior René Goblet finally proposed to create the national Bureau of Public Health and Hygiene. He stressed the importance of requiring all French physicians to report incidents of infectious disease to the state's sanitation authorities. "This obligation exists in several countries," he noted: "This is the point of departure for any hygienic reform."[29]

Strong support for this initiative came from two quarters. The first was the Municipal Council of Paris, where a report on contagion in the capital showed a persistently high rate of mortality there and blamed it on the "pure anarchy" of the nation's health and welfare administration. In Munich, the report added, annual deaths from typhoid fever had fallen to 12 per 100,000, whereas in Paris the comparable number ranged between 70 and 90. It was not smallpox alone but health care in general that needed improvement. The government must take action: "Results attained abroad confirm this assertion." The report continued: in Paris hospitals infectious patients were still placed in public wards with others, "an example of the most culpable negligence," which could only induce "a feeling of shame" among the French. Stricter measures of public sanitation should be implemented, the report stated with special reference to smallpox. For this effort an example was provided by "the irreproachable manner" in which certain German cities had acted, especially Berlin, where there already existed a central office of sanitation "by which we have been inspired."[30]

The second impetus emerged from within the state bureaucracy, notably in the persons of Paul Brouardel and Henri Monod. The French nation was, according to Brouardel, continuing to lose many thousands of its citizens every year to smallpox. These losses were "compromising the national defense." During the war of 1870 the army had lost the equivalent of a division to the disease, and perhaps five times that many had fallen ill. German statistics proved beyond any doubt that the entire population, civilian as well as military, must be vaccinated and revaccinated to make a significant dent in the death rate. "It is up to the government to insist on it," Brouardel admonished: "It is the duty of the state."[31] Monod expressed his support in almost identical terms. He contended that smallpox was the easiest of all communicable diseases to control because of available vaccines. Yet France refused to make inoculation procedures mandatory, thereby leaving "a deficit in our legislation." He could cite some startling figures: the German army had not lost a single man to smallpox since 1874, and the mortality rate among civilians in

Berlin in 1884 was an incredibly minimal 0.33 per 100,000. Brouardel underscored this point with a disarming comparison: in 1886 France incurred 15,000 deaths through smallpox; all of Germany, but 225. His colleague at the Academy of Medicine, Dr. Adrien Proust, promptly corroborated these findings and added a seemingly irrefutable commentary: the experience of nearly two decades had demonstrated the "incontestable superiority" of German legislation.[32]

Yet if this conclusion was all that obvious, we are left to wonder again why the French did not at once follow the German lead? To gain a precise impression of the ideas, pro and con, that were then circulating in press and parliament, it is well to trace them to their source: the Academy of Medicine. There it was once more the unrelenting Paul Brouardel who began in 1890 a debate that would preoccupy French medical opinion for over a decade. Somewhat scaling down his earlier estimates, Brouardel claimed that infectious diseases —particularly smallpox and typhoid fever—were causing 30,000 unnecessary deaths each year. This attrition could only be halted by an obligatory program of vaccination and revaccination, he believed. Already under such a plan, most of the major German cities had suffered no smallpox mortalities whatever in 1888. The English option of leaving the problem to local sanitation officials, Brouardel demonstrated, was globally less successful: London had only 8 smallpox fatalities in 1888 but Sheffield lost 408. Meanwhile in France, although complete statistics were unavailable, the annual casualties of such contagion were still to be counted by the thousands.[33]

Rising to oppose Brouardel was a renowned Parisian physician, Dr. Léon Lefort, who delivered an impassioned rebuttal that required thirty-seven printed pages of the Academy's minutes. Lefort's essential message was a defense of individual liberty. To make vaccination mandatory, he said, would be "a severe blow against personal freedom." The state should not assume the right to force inoculation on an unwilling patient, nor should it require a reluctant doctor to wield a needle. Beyond the question of volition, there were many practical problems to countenance. Although vaccination centers were now installed in the capital city, "outside of Paris there exists nothing, absolutely nothing." Lefort presented a depressing picture of conditions in the countryside, where peasants might travel seventy or eighty kilometers with their infants to find the nearest medical station; or doctors would be pressed into making long journeys over rough terrain to reach them. "Until the [French] peasant finds, as does the German peasant, once a year on a day announced in advance and at a distance not exceeding five kilometers, a doctor who will vaccinate free of charge anyone who appears . . . , we will not have the right to demand a law of obligatory inoculation." It would be, Lefort argued, a "flagrant injustice" to require conformity with such regulations without first providing the facilities to implement them.[34]

But these practical objections were not the heart of Lefort's message. He praised the English example of refusal to impose a national vaccination scheme, because its people resisted the intrusion of the state. On the other hand, "Prussia is always being cited, and because mandatory vaccination has been accepted in Prussia, one imagines that it would be the same in France. That is a gross error. The law would be no more accepted in France than it has been in England." Lefort thereby came to the crux of his refutation by charging Brouardel with a "vaccinal fanaticism," which he compared to religious zealotry: "You no more have the right, over my objection, to baptize my child with the intention of saving his soul than you have the right, over my objection, to vaccinate him for the purpose of protecting his body." Lefort correctly predicted that, whatever the Academy of Medicine might decide, the French parliament would long hesitate to adopt such controversial legislation that would be certain to provoke public indignation. What was possible in Germany had been rejected in England because it was "contrary to the liberal genius of the nation." As for France, Lefort left his auditors with a rhetorical question to which, for him, the answer could not be in doubt: "Is our national character more similar to Prussian discipline or English liberalism?"[35]

It is unnecessary to recapitulate here another lengthy altercation in the spring of 1891. Within the Academy of Medicine Léon Lefort's contentions failed to find broad support, despite his not unfounded charge that Paul Brouardel and others were shifting away from purely scientific grounds to the realm of politics. He, of course, was doing the same when he exclaimed: "Here we are no longer confronted with a simple question of medicine; it is a matter of the rights of a citizen." But he erred with a concluding prediction: "You will never obtain this law."[36] In fact, most Academy members were persuaded that adoption of procedures like those in Germany was unavoidable, and in May 1891 a resolution to that effect was endorsed. Parliamentary approval was another and more protracted matter. Not until 1902 did a national program of vaccination become obligatory. In the meanwhile an estimated annual average of 10,000 French men and women continued to die of smallpox, a mortality rate that began to decline almost at once after the passage of legislation.[37]

In a variety of ways the smallpox issue was superbly illustrative of the time and place. Public emotion, which had been largely spent on cholera epidemics earlier in the century, was briefly focused on *variole* in the wake of war in 1870, to be displaced in turn by tuberculosis around 1900. The French reaction was thoroughly predictable, insofar as it proceeded from a liberal premise that individual rights must be protected at all costs. But the increasing clout of a new social reform movement became evident as the nineteenth century moved to its close. Perhaps most striking in this dialectical clash of medical opinions was the international shorthand in which it was expressed: to reject national health measures was to hark back to the British example, whereas to advocate them implied acceptance of German interventionism. The lesson of the smallpox episode was that the question of a choice between "English liberalism" and "Prussian discipline" could not remain forever rhetorical.

The Specialization of Medicine

Given its antiquated hospital facilities and outdated health regulations, the Third Republic inherited more medical problems than it could manage. In addition to smallpox, other contagious diseases periodically ravaged the country. Perennial killers such as tuberculosis and syphilis were rampant. Cases both of ancient disease (leprosy) and of new malady (polio) were sporadically reported. Even cholera did not disappear: one severe epidemic erupted at Le Havre in 1873 and another in Marseille two decades later. If a case of measles was often less than lethal, the incidence of that infection was extraordinarily high—it was estimated at eight times that of smallpox in Paris during 1889—and it contributed steadily to infant mortality.[38] Typhoid fever likewise recurred with alarming frequency, particularly in the mid-1880s and again after 1900. These outbreaks suggested to reformers the relatively unevolved status of scientific medicine in

France and thereby threw the French into an unflattering light by comparison with Germany. Official statistics were incomplete but indicative. In the decade after 1897, for example, the city of Paris alone had about 25,000 reported cases of typhoid fever causing nearly 4,000 deaths, whereas in the same period Berlin recorded barely 4,300 cases with 664 deaths.[39] There were two manifest explanations for this unfavorable contrast. One was that the Germans had generally adopted stronger sanitation codes for water and sewage disposal. "With a vigor that we lack in France," Dr. Louis Vaillard admitted to the Academy of Medicine, they had enforced hygienic measures "better and more ardently than we." The other reason was no less troubling. An investigation showed that three-quarters of French typhoid victims were left in common hospital wards, where they remained a mortal danger to their fellow patients. It was above all this latter failing—the lack of special facilities for various infectious ailments—that soon became the principal focus of medical reform.[40]

Until 1893 little had been accomplished to create isolation wards, suburban hospices, retirement homes, asylums, inebriation centers, or sanatoria. All would cost enormous sums of money. Moreover, once completed, they would force a reorganization of France's entire hospital system and therewith alter the structure of public medicine. Such financial and professional issues now formed the nexus of reform controversy. Ideally each infectious disease should have its own quarters for quarantine and cure. But as everyone knew, that goal was not to be achieved overnight.

We may attribute three basic attitudes to French reformers: they recognized the difficulties of expanding and modifying medical services; they were nonetheless determined to do so; and they acknowledged that in many respects Germany was already setting precedents for what they hoped to achieve. If one were to make an elaborate collage of the statements and writings of Henri Monod during his two decades as the chief administrator of French public health, these interlocking notions could be amply documented. And many others in the various forums of social reform shared his wish to revise the still-operative regulations of 1840 governing hospitals and hospices. Until that was accomplished, as an official report in 1901 concluded, existing medical conditions would remain "unworthy of Paris, unworthy of France."[41]

Everything depended ultimately on doctors. Without their cooperation no meaningful change was possible, whatever legislators
might decide. Specifically, the issue was posed as to what extent the
state should intervene into the confidential relationship between
physician and patient. The conservative elite of the profession, men
such as Germain Sée, considered the absolute discretion of medical
personnel to be inviolate; but, as a colleague in the Academy of
Medicine reminded him, that principle needed to be tempered by a
respect for "scientific truth."[42] These abstractions were brought to a
test in 1893, following passage of the bill guaranteeing free medical
assistance to the needy, by a request from the government that the
Academy of Medicine draft an official list of infectious maladies.
Such an enumeration had been informally compiled before, but now
the impact would be more serious, because doctors would be legally
required to notify public health officials at once of any occurrence of
a disease on the list.

That issue was but the beginning. A spate of old and new questions begged for response. Should the cities be divided into medical
districts with a stipulation that patients be obliged to consult with
the physician nearest their place of residence? What, then, of free
choice? Should consultation be strictly separated from treatment,
thereby avoiding the potentially corrupt practice of having a doctor
assign wealthy patients to himself and slough others off to the hospitals? And should the state's welfare agencies be reorganized and
rebaptized as *bureaux d'assistance* in an attempt to coordinate hospital
service more effectively with home care? Advocates of the latter reform, incidentally, were able to point out that the less densely settled
city of Berlin had over 2,000 welfare administrators, whereas Paris in
the early 1890s had only 253 to deal with more than 120,000 indigents on the official relief rolls.[43]

Yet how much surveillance and coercion was permissible? Opponents of strict regulation conjured ludicrous scenes of bureaucrats
and sanitation police hounding the ailing to their hovels at night.
Some rejected as unenforceable a compulsory declaration by doctors,
while others agreed that such measures were likely to founder on
"the categorical opposition of the family and of the patient." Collusion between physician and patient made the law easy to circumvent,
as in the frequent cases of tuberculosis victims who, fearing social
ostracism, were obligingly reported by their doctors to be suffering

from chronic bronchitis. Nevertheless, a list of twenty-two infectious diseases was compiled in February 1902. Of this number, the first thirteen were subject to mandatory declaration and the others were optional. Fourteenth on the list was tuberculosis.[44]

Then the problem was to obtain compliance. Comments from those closely involved with enforcement did not inspire great confidence in the efficacy of legislation or of statistics derived from it. The most obvious difficulty was that none of "the three great scourges"—tuberculosis, alcoholism, and syphilis—was carefully reported. Even more than consumption, of course, venereal disease carried a moral stigma that many families chose to suppress. And alcohol-related death was commonly ascribed to kidney or liver ailments. Only 149 mortalities from drink were counted in all of Paris for 1904, although, as one physician remarked, he had observed at least that many in his own hospital alone.[45] Paul Brouardel, albeit an advocate of regulation, sympathized with the delicate personal situation of the physician who risked dismissal by a family whose sordid medical history he dared to reveal. While serving as coroner at the Paris morgue, he had frequently been implored by families to remove any mention of venereal infection or of alcoholism as a cause of death; and he recalled a doctor in Melun who registered a male corpse as the victim of excessive drink, only to be sued for 10,000 francs by his family.[46] Henri Monod's Bureau of Public Health and Hygiene thus found itself in a permanent bind. Without compulsory declaration of communicable diseases, it was impossible to demand mandatory disinfection. But because reporting was irregular, enforcement even of the existing code, as Monod admitted, was "very insufficient."[47] Documentation from the period confirms these difficulties again and again. The 1902 regulations on infectious disease were, as a member of the Academy of Medicine put it, "the capstone of our sanitary edifice," yet declaration of diseases on the official list was "not made at all or made badly." Whether from a sense of confidentiality or of futility, French doctors could simply not be relied upon to disclose the full truth.[48]

Dissatisfaction with "this comedy" (in the expression of a French deputy) eventually provoked a controversy not over the principle of obligatory declaration but the question of who should be required to make such a declaration. One legislative proposal was to place that obligation on the head of the family, rather than on the doctor. "Physicians are not functionaries," intoned the bill's sponsor.[49] Skepticism about that solution, which was more likely to confirm noncompliance than to alleviate it, led Joseph Grancher to offer another suggestion: it should be the property owner's responsibility to notify public authorities of the presence of any infectious malady on his premises. This idea, too, failed to stir much support. By 1913 the issue was as yet unresolved, the medical profession remained divided, and the parliament still lacked a formula to break the impasse.[50]

The medical problem of mental illness was both exceptional and symptomatic. A special status had long been accorded to *aliénés* in France, and already under the Old Regime the state had assumed some responsibility for their care. Yet at the end of the eighteenth century the only asylum exclusively for the mentally impaired was the one at Charenton made famous by the internment there of the Marquis de Sade. In addition, there were two small wards at the Hôtel Dieu. Special facilities for the insane were also created in the early nineteenth century at Sainte-Anne, Ville-Evraud, and Vaucluse, plus some designated sections in the large hospitals of Bicêtre and Salpêtrière. Yet all of this allocation was not nearly enough; and, as in other regards, the Third Republic began in arrears. In Paris space was available for scarcely a third of registered mental patients, which left the remainder unattended. Elsewhere in the nation, as ever, the confusion was literally incalculable. The indefatigable sleuth Maxime Du Camp estimated that France contained 50,000 demented individuals. He saw the problem, whatever the actual numbers, to be that French methods of treatment of the insane had for a long time remained "stationary," and mental patients were consequently "neglected almost everywhere." Du Camp's conclusion therefore anticipated that of republican reformers who came to address the issue: "Here the state can and should intervene."[51]

The first comprehensive legislative project to extend state-sponsored care to the mentally ill was submitted in 1881. It was based on the assumption, inherent in the simultaneous campaign for the Ferry educational reforms, that private (primarily religious) care was inadequate. Hence the bill stipulated that every department in France should within ten years construct a mental asylum or else contract with another department for care of patients declared insane. Despite a recognition that the need was urgent and that more specialized facilities were imperative, the measure languished in parliament for the balance of the decade.[52] As he reviewed this record of inaction in 1890, the deputy Joseph Reinach pleaded that the moment had finally arrived for the French to advance. Unless they did so, he said, they would "resign themselves to conserving the law of 1838, to lagging behind other peoples, [and] to ignoring the very science that was born in France." Reinach thereby sounded a recurrent theme of reformers that the French nation, formerly in the vanguard of Europe, had now dropped to the rear.[53]

We begin to touch here on what was typical in the problem of mental health. In the first place, like the statute for mandatory declaration of infectious diseases, it raised the fundamental issue of individual freedom versus state intervention. How, for instance, would it be decided to commit a mental patient to an asylum? In the past this decision was left to a consultation between family and physician. But there were repeated stories about malpractice and mistaken admissions—such as the husband who took this convenient means to rid himself of a troublesome wife—and therefore the sentiment grew that a court judgment should first be necessary before committal was approved. This legal requirement was favored by Reinach and his committee in the Chamber of Deputies, and it was supported by Monod in the Ministry of the Interior. A disturbing drawback, however, was stressed by Paul Brouardel: as a rule, French judges and justices of the peace were totally unqualified to render a decision on insanity. All that would be accomplished by the proposal was to displace the potentiality for error from one dubious venue to another.[54]

Second, and closely related, the traditional role of the doctor was placed into doubt. Rather than an exclusive confidant of the patient's family, he would henceforth become part of a social welfare system and thus subject to its regulations and restrictions. Worse, his omniscience came under challenge. Not his word alone but that of judges and bureaucrats would weigh on treatment of *aliénés*. Some distinctions needed to be made among types of insanity, with separate facilities constructed to accord with them. The curable should not be left indiscriminately with the incurable; and the criminally insane must be isolated from the others. These matters of public and private concern required professional competence, for which most French physicians were now declared unfit.[55]

Third, the consideration of mental health care again raised the embarrassing reality of France's retardation compared with the progress of Germany. This theme was forcefully presented, during a public welfare conference in the summer of 1894, by a group of French physicians who reported on the far higher degree of specialization among German psychiatrists. Not only had the Germans developed new methods of treatment, but the imperial state was also providing sufficient funding to implement them. Singled out was the new facility at Friedrichshain in Berlin, which one French doctor unhesitatingly called "the current model" of psychiatric treatment.[56] That opinion was corroborated in the first important survey of mental disease in France by Dr. Paul Sérieux, published in 1903 after several years of investigation. Unlike France, said Sérieux, Germany required of all medical students an internship of six months in a psychiatric clinic, of which there were then twenty-six at the German universities. France had no such clinics, possessed only four chairs of psychiatric medicine, and required no internship as a regular part of medical training. Could France hope, under these conditions, to keep up the scientific pace in mental health? Sérieux did not shrink from the obvious answer: "It is painful to admit that this is far from being the case." He went on to diagnose the reasons for France's "state of inferiority" that could only appear "somewhat humiliating." French medical practice was overcentralized, mired in tradition, and stalled by prejudice—all compounded by ignorance of foreign languages and an unwillingness to travel or study abroad. Thus, Sérieux charged, the French "ignore or disdain foreign innovations, [whereas] the Germanic spirit, to the contrary, is thoroughly organizing and assimilating." In the end, his indictment ran, the relative deficiency of French medicine could therefore be traced to "the different geniuses of the two races."[57]

In reading Sérieux's abrasive prose, which was bound to irritate many French physicians, one must of course bear in mind that such was precisely his purpose. Reality and rhetorical excess were artfully mixed to achieve the effect of shock that might dislodge the recalcitrance of antireformists. Facts and statistics were deployed selectively. One illustration was a report to the Conseil Supérieur de l'Assistance Publique by Dr. Paul-Maurice Legrain, director of the asylum of Ville-Evrard, who related that the cure rate for mental patients was significantly higher in Germany than in France. Further inquiry by the CSAP confirmed these findings but also exposed the flaw of such a general comparison. If the alleged rate of successful treatment of mental patients in Germany was an astounding 63 percent against only 19 percent in France, that tabulation was falsified by differences in the organization of psychiatric medicine. Given the higher degree of specialization in Germany, it was normal procedure there for potentially curable patients to be preselected, whereas the hopelessly insane were separated for perpetual detention. In France all were incarcerated alike, and few were ever freed to return to normal life.[58]

The implications were not hard to summarize. France needed to revise medical education, to require psychiatric training, to promote more specialized methods of treatment, to provide financial assistance for cases of mental illness, and to look abroad—that is, to Germany—for a model of such reforms. All of these assumptions rose to the surface before 1914 in discussions about revising the 1893 law on medical assistance by extending coverage to the mentally ill. As it happened, this proposal remained one more item on France's long prewar agenda of unfinished business. Yet at least the direction, the objective, and the rationale of medical reform were being set.[59]

Medical Syndicates and Mutual Societies

A movement to organize French physicians into medical syndicates began in 1879. Despite some explicit references to the model of industrial trade unions, the term *syndicat* was somewhat misleading. In actuality, the notion of a guild seems more appropriate, for the first concern of these new formations was to protect the privileged status of the profession. Beyond that, the syndicates were a form of protest against elitism within the profession. Some doctors, it seems, were more equal than others.

The syndicalization of physicians caught on quickly, good evidence that the concerns it represented were widespread. By the early 1890s syndicates had enrolled over 10,000 members, about 70 percent of the nation's entire medical corps. It is noteworthy, however, that less than 20 percent belonged at that time to groups that were affiliated with the French Union of Medical Syndicates, the seat of which was of course in the capital. Two decades later, by 1909, the percentage of such affiliations was much higher, about half, but we can conclude that the origins of the movement were mostly local. Only gradually did it become a national organization. To speak of a revolt of rural doctors may be overwrought, yet the syndicates gained their impetus precisely from those physicians who regarded themselves as relatively underprivileged, overworked, and sorely tried by encroachments from Paris on their independence.[60]

These concerns, as earlier suggested, had a dual aspect. One was a desire to secure the authority and prerogatives of the profession as a whole. The most obvious manifestation of that effort was a campaign to abolish the paramedical category of the *officiers de santé*, thereby establishing a monopoly of doctors who had been fully trained and licensed through university medical faculties. The second facet of early syndicalist activity was an attack on the privileged few in certain sectors of the profession. This thrust was directed in part against the Academy of Medicine and the overbearing elitism of Parisian physicians. But it also sought to challenge local elites, such as clinic chiefs in provincial hospitals who supplemented their private practice with salary and prestige gained from positions financed through *bureaux de bienfaisance* or cantonal medical programs. Many doctors believed that the medical field was becoming overcrowded, despite statistics to the contrary, and worried that their existence was threatened by increasingly severe competition for clients. They therefore feared that further intervention by the state in the form of social medicine would only make matters worse. These concerns created the curious paradox that medical syndicates professed to favor reform and yet generally opposed the expansion of welfare.[61]

All of these currents came to a confluence in the Medical Practice Act (*Loi Chevandier*) of 1892. This legislation ratified three goals of the syndicates: formal abolition of the *officiers de santé*, legal sanctions against medical charlatans, and official recognition of physicians' right to unionize. What the law did not specify was no less significant. It left open issues about the nature and extent of state-sponsored medical care. When, in the following year, a bill was passed guaranteeing free medical assistance to every French indigent, this problem became unavoidable and acute.

Two intersecting issues formed the center of controversy: medical fees and free choice. The first was bound to bring most country doctors into conflict with welfare officials. Whereas the former wanted to be paid as handsomely as possible for each consultation with individual clients, the latter hoped to hold down costs and to do so whenever feasible through a prepaid cooperative medical plan. The most fundamental interests of private practice and social welfare were thus at odds. This dichotomy was likewise evident in differences over the organization and distribution of medical practitioners. Should they be entirely free, literally as members of a liberal profession, to reside anywhere they wished and to treat only clients whom they chose? Or should they be constrained to accept an assignment in a certain district and obliged to receive patients who were expected to seek treatment from the physician nearest their place of residence? These alternatives may sound abstract and extreme when summarily stated. Yet they defined the two ideals between which French medicine sought a niche.[62]

This clash of principles was enormously complicated by the simultaneous growth of mutual aid societies. With their basic premise of voluntarism, these health insurance groups were thoroughly liberal in principle. But their welfare function and implicit sponsorship by the state often placed them at odds with the syndicates. Conflict started with cost. Insurance agencies invariably sought to limit expenses and often employed their own company doctors who were under instructions to keep this consideration in view. The ordinary practitioner, examining a few clients daily in his tiny *cabinet*, had reason to expect a suitable reward for private services, but he now faced an unfavorable comparison in cost-effectiveness. Understandably, prepayment programs (*abonnements*) joined by a large number of patients proved to be more economical than individual care, thereby producing a deflationary pressure on fees and depriving the personal physician of clients. The very purpose of the mutual societies was thus inimical to that of the syndicates.[63] The traditional precept of free choice was also threatened. When mutual societies were small and isolated, they usually employed a single doctor, and a client's decision to join a particular insurance group was tantamount to selection of a certain physician. But larger societies located in more densely populated areas often boasted a staff of several doctors, among whom the patient might no longer be free to choose. Just as in state welfare agencies, it was frequently an administrator upon whom the decision about a doctor-client relationship would depend. Hence, as one syndicate spokesman complained, the situation had been made "more difficult and more painful."[64]

Another complication was pointed out by Jean Jaurès. Speaking to a parliamentary committee that was investigating current medical practice, Jaurès suggested that a second-class citizenship was being created among the ill. If a doctor working for a mutual society were called at the same time to treat one patient on insurance and another on welfare, he would invariably favor the former.[65] For reasons that we must later analyze in detail, this objection cut close to the core of French health procedures. Because there was neither totally unregulated medical practice nor a highly developed system of public health, inequities of status among patients were unavoidable. Preferential treatment was inherent in the entire structure of mutual societies but invariably deplored by medical syndicates.

A favorite target of the syndicates was medical education. Foremost among the critics was Dr. Henri Huchard, who—although he gained a hospital post in Paris and became a member of the Academy of Medicine—was editor of the *Journal des praticiens*, the Union of Medical Syndicates's most influential organ of information and propaganda throughout the nation. Addressing an annual congress of syndicate doctors in 1907, Huchard excoriated France's "lamentable system of medical instruction" and advocated a "revolution" in both curriculum and certification. Reform should begin in the secondary schools, where science still trailed classical studies. A change there would permit abolition of the introductory year in basic physics, chemistry, and biology. A poll conducted by his journal indicated that nearly two-thirds of French physicians supported these alterations. The fundamental difficulty remained, however, in medical training itself. Huchard scorned the medical caste system perpetuated by the French institution of *concours d'agrégation*, a state-controlled competition for certification. Not only did this procedure of examination produce "abuses and scandals," he charged, it resulted in a stifling elitism. Far better, in Huchard's view, was the German system in which the importance of medical research was emphasized. German medical education was "more rational and more democratic." France would do well to imitate this model, Huchard believed, and to adopt what he called, in a neologistic burst, "*le privat-docentisme*."[66]

If the exact meaning of this alien term was far from certain, the assembly of syndicalists was nevertheless swept with enthusiasm for it. Huchard's remarks were seconded by the secretary-general of the national union, Dr. Émile Leredde, who complained that the position of elite physicians too often depended "not on real merit, on service rendered, on scientific research, but strictly on state examinations."

The declining international prestige of French science, he added, could be directly traced to "the crisis of medical training." Another delegate doubtless expressed the opinion of many present when he also supported Huchard but admitted some confusion about his inventive terminology: "I don't know whether *privat-docentisme* is German [or] whether *agrégation* is French. In any event, I know that the *agrégation* has run its course."[67] Without reiterating the entire transcript of the 1907 medical congress, we may record an apparently paradoxical consensus that the structure of medical practice in imperial Germany was more progressive and less elitist than that of republican France. "If the German organization is not yet perfect," Dr. Étienne Bazot summed up, "it is at least many times superior to our own." Then he concluded: in Germany physicians were finding a hearing for reforms beneficial to the profession, "whereas here nothing of the sort exists [and] nothing is accomplished."[68]

At least three caveats must be entered against these expressions of discontent. First, the pretension of the medical syndicates to champion the cause of democratic progress was undercut to some extent by their barely disguised interest in securing wealth and privilege for the profession. It was the function of the union to lobby for a monopoly, no less, and to prevent measures that might hinder the doctor's access to his affluent clients. Second, it must be said that the syndicates were not nearly so thwarted in this effort as some of their spokesmen protested. Elimination of the *officiers de santé* was only the beginning of a largely successful campaign to anchor private medical practice in France and to check the drift toward what was castigated as "bureaucratic medicine."[69] Finally, the much acclaimed Teutonic example was, to say the least, ambiguous. The international prestige of Germany's research-oriented science was undeniable; and the demonstrably higher degree of specialization in German medicine justified its claim to greater modernity. But these developments were surely not attributable to a democratic surge within the Kaiserreich. Rather, as we have so often witnessed, the active patronage of an imperial state and the financial impetus provided by a national welfare scheme fueled the German advance. And precisely these were, at bottom, the mortal enemies of the French medical syndicates, whose aim was to hinder public agencies from interfering with the sacrosanct relationship between physicians and patients.

Chapter 7

Parisians and Provincials

Tocqueville once remarked: "It is no exaggeration to say that Paris *was* France."[1] While this obiter dictum was shrewd as a political assessment, it did not well epitomize the nation's social development. In fact, the contrary was true. The more that Paris concentrated the power and prestige of France, the less it resembled the provinces in social structure and daily existence. In these respects, at least, France was not Paris. Since Tocqueville's time this theme has attracted a very substantial bibliography; and it remains a topic with which no serious history of France can entirely dispense.[2]

In general one may assume that the French countryside suffered a decline in prosperity during the 1870s. A change for the worse about that time was not solely attributable to military defeat, indemnities paid to Germany, or the amputation of Alsace and Lorraine—although those losses were not negligible. Another stunning blow in that decade was the devastation of a phylloxera epidemic, which crippled the entire economy of southern France for several years. Less significant perhaps, but symptomatic of French vulnerability, was the simultaneous influx of cheap grain, mostly American wheat, which tended to depress farm prices and revenues. All of this must be viewed in the political context of the early Third Republic, which experienced a diminution of the vitality it had inherited from the Second Empire. As the economic and demographic growth rate slackened, an internal migration from hills to valleys and from rural areas to cities became intensified.[3] Of course it was Paris—only to a lesser extent Lyon and other provincial capitals—that felt the major effects of these developments. Because France's first city had both incomparably more wealth and obviously more poverty than else-where, circumstances there were both far better and much worse than the French average; and in any event the rhythm of life of Parisians was altogether different from that of rural folk.

For social reformers these manifest discrepancies, which were magnified after 1870, created any number of perplexities. Health and sanitation regulations designed for the capital city did not apply equally well to the countryside, and vice versa. What could be con-ceived, financed, administered, and enforced in Paris could not al-ways be implemented in Toulouse, Amiens, or an isolated village in the Alps. Hence, with very rare exceptions, the impetus for reform came from the center, but the inertia of rural France constantly threatened to choke it. In theory, improvement of public welfare depended on the cooperation of communes, departments, and the state. In practice, however, efforts of social amelioration often bogged down in confusion or conflict between Parisians and provincials.

The Principle of Obligation

The sacred cow of public health was the commune. We tend to forget how much of the French countryside was sparsely settled, as it still is. The first major administrative reform of 1789 envisaged a vast network of some 35,000 urban and rural communes throughout France. A century later about 17,000 of them still had fewer than 500 inhabitants, of which many were far removed from main roads and railways. This fact, as much as the democratic tradition of the Great Revolution, bolstered the view that sanitation measures were best trusted to municipal authorities—a notion, as we have seen, often raised to the level of ideological dogma in the prevailing ethos of liberalism. Consequently, insofar as anything worthy of the name ex-isted before 1870, health care was usually left to local or clerical hands. That was the French way.[4]

The crisis of charitable institutions inherited from the final years of the Old Regime was never surmounted. Even where they func-tioned, such institutions basically treated the effects of poverty; they did not address the causes of mass indigence, deficient infrastruc-ture, poor hygiene, and insalubrious dwellings. In the opening de-cade of the Third Republic, as we witnessed, it was the housing ques-tion that drew the special attention of legislators. With his pleas for reform in the early 1880s, Martin Nadaud gave a cheerless rendition of rural France. In English he offered his fellow deputies a maxim (of dubious authenticity): "As the homes, so the people." Held to this standard, he stated, most provincials were surely in miserable straits. Nadaud and his supporters spared no details of daily life in the French countryside: lack of light and ventilation, absence of adequate heating, leaking roofs and mud floors, primitive outdoor toilets, impure water, and more.[5]

This *cahier de doléances* immediately preceded the creation of the Conseil Supérieur de l'Assistance Publique. Initial statistics compiled by the CSAP placed the rural population of France at 27.5 million. So paltry was public assistance to them that the monthly average per capita allocation for health care was all of thirty-eight centimes. In reality, state aid meant that a few special cases were awarded some help, as Henri Monod noted with transparent disgust, while the others were "left to the whims of charity."[6]

Without attempting to reconstitute in detail the series of long debates that ensued, we can easily sketch a few of the main arguments that emerged from them. Monod and his reformist allies deplored that departmental assistance to the communes was poorly organized and inadequate. From all that was known, there were "enormous lacunae" both in provincial towns and their environs.[7] Monod himself stressed the necessity of national legislation that would extend social welfare and public hygiene beyond urban areas, because meaningful aid was "virtually nil in the countryside." Out there the representative bureaucratic institution was still the *dépôt de mendicité*, where the ill and the indigent were randomly quartered with criminals, vagabonds, and beggars.[8] Premier Charles Dupuy raised with the CSAP the possibility of closing the *dépôts* and relying on the penal system. He related that a recent police razzia on mendicants had produced more than 14,000 arrests. Yet Dupuy recognized that repression alone was not the answer. The problem would find no solution, he said, until "the day when public welfare is completely organized." Such sentiments could only lead to one conclusion: the state would need to intervene and to impose an obligatory system of health care throughout France. A resolution to that effect, exempting Paris and Lyon because of their already existing municipal welfare organizations, was adopted by the CSAP in February 1889, thereby solidifying what was clearly the majority opinion of reformers.[9]

An intermediate and less categorical position was associated with the name of Jules Simon. It was he who had formulated the frequently cited axiom that state intervention was legitimate "everywhere it is necessary and only where it is necessary."[10] But the problem, of course, was to define necessity. The two most fundamental reforms of the early years of the republic, universal military conscription and compulsory primary education, had been accepted on all sides because they were thought essential to the survival of the nation. Both rested on the principle of obligation. Now Simon in effect favored elevating the welfare question gradually to a similar status by implying, but not pushing, the thesis that increased state intervention would ultimately be required. He reminded the CSAP that he was a Breton by birth and proud of his provincial heritage. Yet he was unwilling to leave certain matters, such as the inspection of public schools, in local hands. The suggestion was clear, despite Simon's caution, that other social issues would eventually need to be regarded in the same light.[11]

A third standpoint, most conspicuously represented by Jules Crisenoy, underscored the practical difficulties of imposing any national scheme of public health. There was, to begin, the question of cost: who was to pay the still-uncounted sums that proponents of a mandatory system would squander? If the simple reply was the state, then the next issue was to ascertain by what means it would raise the new revenue required. Second, the fragile relationship of public institutions to private charity would be placed into doubt. Seldom spoken in polite company was the subliminal issue of church and state. But this friction was certain to be exacerbated if compulsory procedures were forced on provincial authorities by a secular state. Finally, a multitude of administrative difficulties might impede the implementation of stringent measures. Crisenoy claimed to have evidence, for example, that a fusion of hospitals and *bureaux de bienfaisance* was infeasible, and moreover that it was opposed by a majority of medical personnel. Therefore, he concluded, "it cannot be a question of creating for all of France a uniform organization."[12] This last reservation was by far the most widely shared among members of the CSAP. One of them, a physician, sustained Crisenoy's objections by challenging the majority on pragmatic grounds: "You are certainly going to encounter insurmountable difficulties."[13]

In the minds of Henri Monod and the majority of reformers,

the decisive point was to establish the principle of obligation. It would be up to the parliament to devise means of financing public health provisions and up to the bureaucracy to implement them. What counted for the CSAP was the resolve to change France's welfare policy and to set the machinery of the state in motion. The rest would follow. By 1890, despite all, Monod had reason to believe that he had attained this primary objective and that a new phase of reform was about to begin.

The First Gap: From Conception to Legislation

Expressed in grandiose terms, the vision of French reformers was to restore their nation to the foremost rank among European states. Ideally, they wanted nothing less than a compulsory system of health, sanitation, and welfare for every French citizen. Thus, with one legislative package, France would outdistance the Bismarckian reforms of the 1880s and regain a preeminent international status worthy of the world's greatest democracy. Such a program would rescue the struggling urban masses, extend help to the most remote corner of the countryside, and provide temporary assistance to the ill and injured as well as permanent care for the invalid and the aged. Avid reformers not only hoped to realize this grand conception, they wanted to do so soon. "It would be deplorable," as the chairman of a parliamentary committee said, "if we in France were the last to apply the principles of public welfare."[14]

We know that the reform bill of 1893, important as it was in some regards, did not nearly approach this encompassing design. The obvious incongruity between optimal intentions and legal enactments requires our careful attention. Perhaps the first explanation of that gap was already implicit in the statement just quoted: a mistaken assumption that "the principles of public welfare" were already fixed and that all one needed to do was work out the details. Such optimism was especially prevalent among members of the Conseil Supérieur de l'Assistance Publique, of whom a majority had swung by 1890 to Henri Monod's notion of reform. True, as he conceded, there remained a number of nagging questions, but he and his close associates remained confident that the answers to them would soon be devised.[15]

The total picture was in actuality more clouded than Monod admitted. Practical difficulties began with a shortage of personnel. We have already examined two instances: the paucity of physicians in rural France and the complete absence of any welfare offices in nearly half of French departments. The CSAP was eager to remedy these deficiencies instantly by creating dispensaries in neglected areas that would provide prescriptions and medical advice to those in need. Yet Paul Brouardel pointed out the sobering fact that France lacked enough registered pharmacists to staff the project. One-quarter of the cantons (groupings of communes) had no druggist whatever, and another quarter had but one. Brouardel estimated that it would be impossible to enforce the envisaged program, even if adopted, in three-quarters of French territory.[16]

So far as sanitation was concerned, a lack of equipment posed similar problems. The shocking reports of insalubrious housing had touched off a fumigation craze in the late 1880s. If slums could not be cleared, at least they could be cleaned. Some cities had acquired the requisite equipment (*étuves*) for such a systematic undertaking. Yet these scattered attempts again revealed the unequal distribution of urban and rural hygiene. An investigation by Henri Monod in 1892 disclosed that thirty-three departments had no fumigation apparatus at all; and twenty-five of them annually recorded more deaths than births. The need was clear, but the solution would be neither simple nor rapid.[17]

Concerns about how far health care could be extended were nothing new. The familiar objective of founding a *bureau de bienfaisance* in every commune was reconsidered by an ad hoc committee in the Chamber of Deputies and duly approved. Likewise, the proposal that within a decade each department should accept the responsibility to create some specialized facilities for the treatment of mental patients was endorsed by the CSAP. Thus, even before the political slogan of national solidarity gained currency, it was beginning to acquire shape in the legislative process.[18] Were reformist ambitions to be fully realized, welfare institutions would be spread throughout the countryside. But did this mean that compulsory accident insurance might be provided for French peasants or, as some advocated, should it be restricted solely to certain "dangerous industries"? When that issue came before the labor committee of the Chamber of Deputies, the German precedent soon became the center of controversy. The earliest national legislation in Germany had excluded the peasantry. Gradually the view prevailed there, however, that all types of work were potentially dangerous, including agriculture, and the Reichstag moved accordingly to expand coverage to farm workers. From this scenario French deputies drew divergent conclusions. One faction claimed that the German example implied the importance of first gaining the principle of an obligatory law and only later extending it to the peasantry. Another group contended to the contrary that the German experience showed the folly of restricted coverage at the initial stage of implementation. As one deputy put the latter view: "The progress realized by foreign legislation is an argument in favor of one proposal forming a totality." Although a majority of the Chamber's labor committee gravitated to this opinion, they had to take strong opposition in the Senate into account. For the moment, as a consequence, neither side gained a decisive edge.[19]

In the end, all of this debate about administrative changes was related to their cost. If the CSAP could feign insouciance about finances, parliamentary committees and bureaucratic agencies could not. For them budgetary limitations were all too finite. Speculation abounded. Would the measures currently envisaged treble or quadruple the state's outlays for welfare assistance? And then? The truth was that nothing was certain and that one hunch was nearly as plausible as another. A pungent odor of irrationality wafted over the entire proceedings. The safest wager was that, if reforms were pushed anywhere near their maximum potential, the financial capacity of communes and departments would be quickly exhausted. For some this implied the perfectly acceptable result of state intervention; for others, it conjured the appalling monstrosity of state socialism. This testy ambience helps to explain the frequency of references to the German precedent. When it came to the hard questions of francs and centimes, the French had no experience and consequently no reliable statistics on which to base their projections. The Germans had both. And meanwhile, deep in the bowels of the French bureaucracy, "difficulties" were already being reported because of a shortage of welfare funds. Even without more costly reforms, it seemed, discomfort caused by the social question was bound to grow.[20]

Apart from these general considerations, the legislative process leading to the reform bill of 1893 forced the French to focus on three specific issues that would determine the course of social welfare. The first, implicit throughout, was to decide whether a single set of mandatory regulations should apply everywhere in the nation, or whether the law might allow for local and regional differences. The ideological bent of most reformers, beginning with Henri Monod, was to insist on unity—that is, as it came to be codified, "solidarity"—and to stress the necessity of obligation for all. But neither before nor after 1893 was that outcome self-evident. The records of parliamentary committees reflected continuing objections to standardization on a national basis. In the labor committee of the Chamber, for instance, vigorous opposition was expressed against uniform regulation of working conditions without regard to the size, location, or nature of enterprise. Unlike the factory, labor in agriculture was ordinarily seasonal, more intense at some times, more lax at others.[21] In the social insurance committee (CAPS) criticism was much the same: rules that were applicable to large industrial firms were often unsuitable for small businesses and for agriculture.[22] By means of the 1893 law France nonetheless opted for a unitary precept of free medical care for all needy French citizens. Anxieties about the impracticability of this omnibus measure were eased by a conspicuous and possibly cavernous loophole. Article 36 of the bill's final version allowed exemption from national regulations for communes able to demonstrate that they were providing sufficient hospital and health care under existing local arrangements. We shall shortly examine the consequences of this provision, which, it may be said in advance, diluted but did not nullify the notion of general medical assistance.

If one may see in this qualified victory for reform a step away from liberalism and toward state intervention, the same was not true of the decision concerning a second principle. Even before the idea of obligatory medical aid was passed into law, it came under challenge. An 1891 report to the CSAP by Hermann Sabran gave an exceedingly unfavorable evaluation of France's hospital and home care system, which was still plagued by maldistribution of physical facilities, inequities in the treatment of patients, and "numerous difficulties" in the allocation of financial resources. The resulting muddle of existing legislation, which left much discretionary power to the communes, was "a painful spectacle." Even when they could afford better health services, many provincial towns did nothing. And the government's efforts to persuade the departments to apply more pressure were often ignored. Sabran and the subcommittee for which he reported therefore favored the principle of obligatory assistance. But they called attention to a further dimension already embodied in the German legislation of the 1880s. If possible, Sabran wrote, the French should espouse not only a national program of medical assistance but they should, like the Germans, also advance to "prudential" insurance (*prévoyance*). In other words, the ultimate objective should not merely be to treat illness, accident, and infirmity but to prevent them. Indeed, the report argued, the more completely preventive medicine was implemented through compulsory insurance, the less significant would be the expense of administering public assistance. Sabran did not believe that the French nation was as yet prepared to imitate the German model, and he explicitly refrained from advocating the immediate adoption of a mandatory system. His concluding remarks, however, expressed a hope that the concept of *prévoyance* would ultimately gain acceptance and thereby displace *assistance* altogether.[23] Without following the discussion beyond this point, we can observe that the 1893 law avoided any mention of a state insurance plan. Coverage beyond the minimum provided by welfare agencies remained a private matter for the mutual aid societies. Thus a fundamental cleavage remained between the German and French conceptions of social reform.

A third issue was linked to the second. It also separated France from Germany. The German social legislation had appeared in three separate but complementary packets on illness (1883), accident (1884), and then permanent disability and old age (1889). It escaped no one that the first two, which offered coverage for temporary incapacitation, were detachable from the third, which was in essence a pension plan for invalids. In France, a land without mandatory insurance, it was uncertain how a long-term commitment to thousands of infirm and aged welfare recipients was to be managed. Resistance in the parliament to such a provision was unyielding, and reformers were finally persuaded to separate it from the proposal lest the entire law be thrown into jeopardy. One need not speak of a retreat. Rather, this outcome represented a sensible consolidation of what was actually attainable at the moment. But an altercation was thereby stirred in 1893 on the question of pensions, and a resolution of it stretched off into the unforeseeable future.[24]

The Capital and the Communes

Before surveying the effects of the 1893 reform as it was implemented, we need to examine the special status of Paris in public hygiene. At the outset three background factors may be taken for granted: the existence since the early nineteenth century of an autonomous municipal health administration in the capital; the tragic conflict in 1871 between the Paris Commune and the fledgling government of the French republic; and thereafter a long antagonism of city and state over the secularization of public education. With the adoption and implementation of the Ferry reforms in the early 1880s, the school issue subsided. But it was soon replaced by another: the secularization of hospitals. Beginning about 1885, that is, the political focus in Paris became public health. As this latter phase began, the national government was represented by a new tough-minded prefect of the Seine, Eugène-René Poubelle, whose unsought fame as king of the French trash can made him a conspicuous target for the Municipal Council. Rancorous and bitter at times, this turbulent confrontation is a tale already told elsewhere.[25]

Here our concern is centered on the implications for further welfare reform. In this respect, too, the CMP was thoroughly hostile to Poubelle and accused him of worsening the capital's social problems by protecting the conservative interests of the wealthy. In his inaugural address as president of the CMP in June 1887, Alexandre Hovelacque expressed disdain for "counterrevolutionary, antirepublican institutions" headed by "functionaries of the state." Formed in "a Bonapartist mold," he charged, an administrative autocracy had been imposed on Paris that could not fail to produce "a permanent conflict." Hovelacque singled out the prefect of the Seine and the prefect of police as obstructionists, and to the applause of his fellow councillors, he offered them a challenge: "If the state is unable to realize these republican and social reforms, then it should allow the communes to act!"[26] If one may admire the pluck of this outburst, it is necessary to recall that the military verdict of May 1871 remained unchanged. The pretension of the CMP that the city of Paris should somehow bypass the national government and directly inspire the rest of France to democratic reforms was a delusion. Political myths are sometimes useful, but they seldom endure without an adequate budget.

There was a still more serious difficulty: the communes of rural France remained singularly unreceptive. Trouble began in the Paris suburbs. A petition signed by 773 residents of the commune of Créteil in 1887 vigorously protested a proposal to locate there a clinic for the treatment of smallpox and scurvy, the purpose of which was to alleviate crowding and prevent spread of contagion in city hospitals.[27] Such opposition, echoed many times from neighboring departments in the years following, repeatedly stalled efforts to relieve demographic pressure in the capital. Yet suburban communities staunchly insisted on the right to send patients into Paris for medical treatment. In the summer of 1889 Poubelle attempted to force the mayor of Neuilly to increase his commune's annual contribution to the Paris welfare administration from 2,700 to 16,550 francs in order to offset the increasing cost of hospital care. This demand drew a flat refusal from the incensed Neuilly Municipal Council.[28] An alternative was for Paris to contract with provincial hospitals to accept a certain number of patients who would agree to be transferred there. That suggestion, however, had two complications. One was a dubious and paradoxical financial policy whereby the city was flooded with rural immigrants seeking free medical care at the same time that it was required to subsidize hospitalization of Parisians in the countryside.[29] Another problem was the recalcitrance of urbanites to accept reclusion in a distant exile. The CMP considered a program to expel elderly and chronically ill persons who were without family support and therefore dependent on welfare assistance. This measure was debated for years without a resolution because municipal councillors shrank from unacceptable consequences of a mass deportation from Paris.[30]

Only one course remained. The city had to raise more revenue, and the readiest manner to do so was to obtain increased subventions from the state. This effort became a long and sad tale of conflict between the CMP and the Conseil de Surveillance, which was charged with overseeing communal welfare in Paris. The municipal government had modest success in attracting special subsidies through the Ministry of the Interior: 900,000 francs in early 1890, for example, and another 253,000 in 1891.[31] But such allocations did nothing to alter the structural problem that the national state jealously protected its purse strings. The CMP's attempts to seek a larger regular share of pari-mutuel proceeds from the Paris racetracks failed, despite the plausible contention that the bulk of that money was skimmed from wealthier residents of the capital. Consequently, through the legislative process, the national regime could increase the municipality's financial obligations for public welfare without automatically providing adequate means to meet them. A perfect illustration was the impact of the 1893 reform of medical care for the destitute, a measure that was bound to affect Paris in particular. It did so at a remarkable rate. In the succeeding decade the municipal welfare budget rose from about 30 million francs to 57.5 million by 1903.[32]

In view of this imbroglio, the CSAP was called upon to evaluate the situation. A report presented to that body in late 1892 by Henry Fleury-Ravarin described Paris as a city inundated by "a veritable army of professional beggars." The archaic municipal welfare system was unable to cope with more newcomers, and it manifestly required "prompt and urgent reform." The report stressed that the city's public health agencies were still functioning under the regulations of an 1849 national law that was no longer appropriate to their needs, especially given the "enormous discrepancy" of resources available to the various arrondissements. Fleury-Ravarin therefore favored a special statute for Paris that would allow greater flexibility in managing its own financial affairs.[33] Yet the CMP found itself caught in two contradictions, one old and one new: the capital was simultaneously demanding greater state subsidies but fewer state controls; and it was seeking a separate status at a time when the French republic was moving toward more uniform welfare legislation in the name of national solidarity.

Meanwhile, constant bickering between city and state officials continued. Paul Strauss spoke dejectedly of a "veritable antagonism" that did nothing to correct "crying abuses."[34] But such complaints from reformers constituted only half of the story. No doubt the Paris public health administration stood in need of reorganization and required better financing. The capital was nonetheless far in advance of other French cities (with the possible exception of Lyon), and it still offered an example to the provinces. A detailed report by Dr. Gustave Drouineau to the CSAP in 1897 described Paris as "the avant-garde of our progress in welfare." He added that "the same preoccupations have appeared abroad, where science has likewise finally prevailed." Drouineau singled out as examples the German cities of Berlin, Munich, Leipzig, Breslau, and Erlangen. Even by the standards of this elite company, he implied, Paris did not cut too bad a figure. Yet he left unstated a disconcerting corollary: within the French nation Paris was inevitably unique; and, insofar as health care and sanitation were concerned, the countryside represented a drag.[35]

In 1898 Dr. Henri Napias became the new director of public welfare in Paris. He immediately set about to define the city's problem and to solve it. His definition was simply that the capital's hospitals and health facilities had not kept pace with its demographic growth. The solution was less obvious. Napias was not notably more successful than his predecessors in obtaining an increment in state subsidies. Yet the number of Parisian indigents continued to grow. The welfare committee of the CMP estimated in 1898 that 32,000 destitute residents were currently receiving an average of but four francs a month in direct public assistance. By 1900 the number of Parisian paupers was placed at 36,000, which a reporter for the CMP frankly called "a disgrace and a scandal."[36] The committee's urgent recommendation that a monthly individual subsistence level be set at a twenty-franc minimum seemed almost utopian by comparison. The more the CMP addressed the real needs of the aged and infirm, however, the greater their financial plight appeared. After long debate the rate was finally fixed at thirty francs. A motion that the distribution of this aid be contingent on an increase of state subsidies to the city was rejected on the humanitarian grounds that the needy should have a right to existence, no matter what the resulting fiscal discomfort for the municipal administration. But a recognition that high-minded principles do not defray expenses was wryly expressed in a comment, variously attributed, that circulated like some Chinese proverb: "He who seeks reform should be prepared to pay for it."[37]

After 1900, to bring this aspect of the story to a close, the CMP adopted a more conservative tone. Yet the financial strain only worsened, and the influx of provincials in search of medical care did not abate. The national government made an effort, through its prefects, to enforce 1893 regulations that required the rural population to apply for admittance to hospitals nearest their place of residence. Orders to that effect were then issued directly from the prefects of each department to mayors in the communes.[38] The intention of activating this bureaucratic chain of command was clear but the effect was slight. An accurate tabulation of those arriving in Paris primarily for medical reasons is impossible, but the telltale symptoms of overcrowding and underfinancing remained evident. Thus one of the elemental realities of nineteenth-century France went essentially unchanged. It was most cogently articulated by Ambroise Rendu, chairman of the CMP's standing committee on public health: "The departments . . . are invading the capital."[39]

The Second Gap: From Legislation to Action

The imperfections of the 1893 law on free medical aid for the poor were apparent to everyone. Among its severest critics, in fact, were those reformers who had worked hardest to obtain the bill, because they regarded it as only a first step toward a more comprehensive and compulsory plan of public health. No sooner was the legislation adopted, therefore, than agitation began to augment it with another measure (not passed until 1910) to extend coverage to the aged and permanently disabled. It was this conception of a retirement pension that had been detached from the 1893 law in order to hasten parliamentary action. The next major objective of social reform was thus assistance for long-term invalidity, because existing French legislation applied only to temporary unemployment through accident or illness.

First among the major obstacles to that end, in the phrase of reformer Émile Rey, was the "crying disproportion" between city and countryside. "Hence," he wrote, "in a nation such as ours that claims to be democratic, where the principles of equality and fraternity are so frequently and loudly proclaimed, there still exists this shocking inequity." Rey saw only one solution: "The state must intervene to restore equilibrium in the name of national solidarity."[40]

A more immediate concern was to implement the 1893 bill. The progress of this effort was of course closely watched by the Academy of Medicine, to which Dr. Théophile Roussel reported in March 1895. He noted that the law had been drafted specifically to provide "medical aid in the countryside." But unfortunately, Roussel observed, "practical difficulties have already been encountered in its application."[41] Two provisions were causing particular trouble. One was a stipulation that communes must draft a list of destitute residents so that health administrators could determine the amount and distribution of necessary financial allocations. This procedure created no undue confusion for small communes with a relatively stable population. But in areas of urban density and greater mobility, the lists were invariably incomplete or out of date. In this respect, at least, the law suited the countryside but not the cities. The mayor of Reims, Henri-Alfred Henrot, testified before the CSAP to this effect, urging that "great latitude" be accorded to municipal officials.[42] Others observed the same phenomenon yet drew an opposite conclusion. As the deputy Jean-Baptiste Bienvenu-Martin said, many communes seemed to be inspired by "narrow considerations" that led them to be either too parsimonious or too generous with public funds.[43] In practice the dilemma appeared insoluble. If the national regime attempted to enforce a system of lists with strict controls on payments to the poor, it was sure to be met with resistance and damned as autocratic; but if it allowed complete discretion to municipal councils and mayors, the result was certain to be chaotic. Not until after 1900 did the Waldeck-Rousseau cabinet develop a proposal to set a floor and ceiling for local welfare appropriations with the explanation that provincial communes should not be permitted, in effect, to dictate the amount of state subsidies.[44]

Another paragraph of the 1893 law also created much consternation. Article 35, as noted, permitted communes to apply for exemptions from state regulations if they could demonstrate that they were already providing sufficient health services under local aegis. The original intent of this provision was to allow some leeway for urban arrondissements, especially in Paris and Lyon, that already had their own system of municipal welfare agencies. Instead, it proved to be the rural communes that sought release from state control—thereby forgoing state subsidies, as a member of the CSAP complained, although "they have great need." By the beginning of 1896, 454 communes located in 43 different departments had already invoked Article 35, enough to arouse fears that the intention of the law to create a safety net for all the poor of France was being thwarted. Those communes, said another CSAP member in responding to the statistics of exemption, were placing themselves "in defiance of a compulsory system." Such apprehensions grew as the numbers rose. This "bad tendency" represented a "real abuse" in the eyes of a third CSAP member, who detected "a spirit of resistance" in the provinces. And a fourth concluded gloomily: "Solidarity no longer exists."[45] By 1901 over 1,000 requests for exemption under Article 35 had been received by the Ministry of the Interior, and there was reason to worry that the law would be battered into oblivion. Yet we know in retrospect that the tide was cresting and would thereafter recede. The reasons are uncertain, but presumably most communes eventually found it convenient to accept state subsidization in return for what proved to be only a token of state intervention.[46]

These difficulties of implementation had important policy implications. At stake was the entire concept of obligation. As one specific issue after another came before the CSAP, opinion increasingly polarized on that primary issue. Naturally it was Henri Monod who led the chant for thoroughgoing reform. He remained convinced of "the insufficiency of private charity" and the necessity of a "comprehensive plan" that embodied a "spirit of method."[47] His colleague Loys Brueyre also stated the need for a national solution to the social question and deplored that the state had too long "remained inactive."[48]

The reiteration of these customary themes was countered by those who contended that strict state regulation was wrong in principle, inapplicable in practice, or both. Among numerous examples two should suffice. In 1898 the CSAP was the scene of a sharp exchange between reformer Paul Strauss and some of his more conservative colleagues. Strauss was critical of the perfunctory manner in which physicians often visited *crèches*. It would be far better, he contended, to require that nurseries have resident doctors and to remind them that a *crèche* is "not a cloakroom." This sarcasm drew a retort that such regulation might make sense for Paris, with which Strauss was familiar, but it was completely unrealistic for provincial France. The retired mayor of Rouen, Maurice Lebon, concurred with this rebuttal: "In such delicate matters," he said, "the best method is to leave a lot of liberty."[49] Meanwhile, in the Chamber of Deputies, committee hearings were beginning on the vexed question of extending mandatory health care to the aged and infirm. Jean Jaurès was a strong advocate of a compulsory scheme, but he faced repeated contradiction even from deputies who generally favored social reform. Jean-Honoré Audiffred estimated that nine-tenths of the communes would be incapable of financing such a plan. And Paul Guieysse pointed out the complexity of the French labor force, which made it difficult to determine eligibility: "The problem seems to me to be too complicated to be resolved in a general manner."[50] These objections, and many like them, indicated that passage of the 1893 law had been less than an unmitigated triumph for the forces of reform and that the principle of obligation was far from secure.

One of the chief motivations for pursuing a national health care plan had nothing to do with soaring principles and eloquent parliamentary debates. From all accounts, the rural byways, town squares, and city streets of France were increasingly populated by vagabonds and mendicants. A study of this conspicuous social issue, which was presented to both the CSAP and the Chamber of Deputies in 1899 by Jean Cruppi, suggested that the republic had actually retrogressed in this regard. The number of beggars—"this army of 30,000 men"—had quadrupled in the second half of the nineteenth century, according to Cruppi, who added a deliberately jolting comment: "In this matter, as in many others, we have allowed ourselves to be outdistanced by neighboring countries." Ideally, the proper response should be to provide specialized facilities to meet the individual causes of mendicity: more hospices for invalids, *maisons de travail* for the temporarily indisposed, and new prisons ("they are terrified of the cell") for criminals. Yet, as always, the irrefutable objection was that provincial communes could not possibly support such a program, since they were already "overloaded with taxes." Nor was it feasible, while begging was increasing "in disquieting proportions," to lock up every undesirable presently at large. The cost would be prohibitive, Cruppi told the CSAP, and thus "parliament would not listen to us." Although he expressed support for compulsory welfare legislation to mitigate poverty throughout the land, Cruppi was brimming with encouragement rather than with optimism: "My heart is with you as you attempt to place France on a par with other countries, for we are behind from this viewpoint."[51] A commentary on vagabondage in the *Revue philanthropique* more precisely remarked that it was above all Germany that preceded France on "the path of social progress."[52]

Despite all the extravagant public celebrations, then, the twentieth century began on a note of deep dissatisfaction among French reformers. With its administrative loopholes, unenforceable regulations, and tepid inspection procedures, the 1893 law was failing to consolidate more uniform health care. Furthermore, its central principle of obligation was in question. Paris was still plagued by inadequate funding, which exacerbated "the miserable condition of public welfare," in the words of the mayor of the city's seventh arrondissement, Charles Risler.[53] Arguably, public hygiene in the French countryside was even worse, added Paul Brouardel, who mocked hackneyed notions about the fresh air and healthy conviviality of rural life.[54] In a memorandum to the Waldeck-Rousseau cabinet in March 1900, Henri Monod attempted to lend some statistical substance to these generalizations. Since 1885, he specified, the state budget for welfare expenditures had risen over 30 percent. Yet the annual average allocation per resident in Paris was 11.11 francs; for other cities over 100,000 in population it was 4.52 francs; and for 397 towns under 100,000 it was 2.12 francs. No accurate data existed for the remainder of rural communes, but it was known that about 20,000 of them still had no welfare agency whatever.[55]

These numbers suggested neither adequacy nor uniformity. As for the government's social policy, Monod confided to the CSAP, it was "not without a certain emotion" that he detected growing opposition to the principle of obligation. He understood that term to mean the self-imposed duty of the state, the departments, and the communes to provide sanitation and health services for every French citizen—without, however, admitting the individual right of each person to demand medical care and a minimum subsistence. Yet this fine distinction was difficult to maintain. As a colleague reminded Monod, "this word [obligation] does not have the same meaning in every mouth and in every meeting."[56] Monod was nonetheless determined to press on with social reform, and on 15 February 1902 he was able to register another parliamentary victory with the passage of a law on public sanitation. Previous legislation had been optional in principle, leaving it to provincial officials to decide whether instances of infectious disease should be reported to Paris. This procedure had proved ineffectual, as Monod bluntly said, because "the mayor did not do it." Now the new bill made such declaration mandatory for all towns with a population over 20,000. Each would be required to have a committee of sanitation and to report any outbreak of contagion as defined by an official list issued from the Ministry of the Interior on the advice of the Academy of Medicine. These stipulations were not without their own problems, as later events would show, but at least they represented a reaffirmation of a compulsory principle in public health. Monod had renewed reason to hope that these regulations would afford "more solid bases" for welfare efforts.[57]

Looking back across the decade since the enactment of the 1893 law on free medical aid, we must acknowledge that this note of optimism was only marginally justified. Monod's Bureau of Public Health and Hygiene was undoubtedly making headway. Yet the record left no question that a chasm separated the letter and the reality of social legislation. As ever, the principles of the French Revolution commanded less than unanimous consent.

An Uneven Balance

In the years before 1905, the various republican governments of France succeeded in passing into law three social reforms of overriding importance. They were the Loi Roussel of 1874, basically a bill to regulate wet-nursing and the care of foundling children; the law on free medical assistance of 1893, which guaranteed aid by physicians and pharmacists to the needy who were temporarily disabled by illness or accident; and the sanitation reform act of 1902 that mandated the creation of committees on public hygiene in all communities over 20,000 (and spas over 2,000) and required them to report any instance of infectious diseases specified on a list prepared in Paris. All of these legislative enactments had the common purpose of extending health care to the French countryside. Each had only moderate success in doing so.

In a sense, the apparent decline of wet-nursing during this period may perhaps be taken as testimony that stricter regulation did have a salutary impact. Yet, for one simple reason, we cannot be certain: the available statistics are fragmentary. The closer one looks, the less dependable the data appear. As late as 1908 a report to the Academy of Medicine conceded that fifty-eight of France's eighty-six departments were derelict in providing useful tabulations concerning application of the Loi Roussel. "Is that not deplorable?" asked the reporter, Dr. Armand Gautier, without bothering to pause for a reply.[58] No doubt it was deplorable, and it remains so for the historian. Any account that claims statistical exactitude in this matter must therefore be suspect. We can read only the bottom line of the balance sheet: that the French birth rate continued to fall. Meanwhile the mortality rate barely improved, and the nation reached its demographic nadir just as the new century began. How the population trend might have progressed had the war of 1914 not intruded, we cannot of course know. But there is no reliable evidence that the Loi Roussel significantly altered the total pattern for the better.

As for the 1893 law, we are likewise left to draw inferences from incomplete returns. Bureaucratic reports do give us assurance that this measure gained increasing acceptance after 1900 and that the number of new exemptions sought by communes under Article 35 dropped to a negligible quantity. Thus earlier fears that the entire conception would crumble were unjustified. One looks nonetheless in vain for any statistical proof that might gauge the program's effectiveness in rural areas. All we have is hearsay, much of which is ambiguous. In 1912 Léon Mirman, then the national director of public health, reported to the CSAP that, although the legislation had made little difference in the cities, it had presumably been of importance elsewhere; after all, it was "a law made for the countryside." Unfortunately, Mirman presented no serial numbers to support this assumption, because, one suspects, none existed. Even if we take at face value his evaluation of health and hygiene in the capital city, which he knew well, no special credence need be accorded his surmise about the rest, for which he had little proof.[59] The recorded impressions of Henri Monod, probably the person most qualified to judge, did not reflect such optimism. Monod continued to view with skepticism the monetary capacity and ethical standards of most provincial communes, where personal rivalries and special interests always complicated or indeed negated application of the law. Particularly troublesome, he thought, was the perennial feud between private charity and public assistance. He was disturbed by reports that some medical patients were slyly accumulating financial aid from both, thereby curtailing the help available to others. By its nature, such a consideration is unquantifiable in its consequences, and we can therefore not hope to arrive at an unassailable measurement of the truth.[60]

For the third of the major reform bills in question we have testimony frequent and variegated enough to establish that it had scant impact in the countryside before 1914. Because this legal measure was mandatory only for larger population centers, that conclusion should not be surprising. But health officials had openly expressed hope that the entire nation would be swept by a new impetus for public hygiene. That did not happen. In his final report as president of the Comité Consultatif d'Hygiène Publique in 1903, Paul Brouardel regretted that sanitation services outside the cities still suffered from "too frequent negligence" and that they were often organized "scarcely or not at all."[61] A.-J. Martin, a member of the CSAP and of a special task force to fight tuberculosis, agreed with Brouardel that administrative machinery was generally lacking to implement the law and that its enforcement would take a long time.[62] In 1905, shortly after Brouardel's retirement from the CCHP, his former colleagues received an extensive memorandum on the condition of hygienic services in the Midi, roughly between Grenoble and Montpellier, which concluded that three years under the new sanitation law had produced "not the slightest progress."[63] A similar report from the Massif Central found sanitation there "absolutely deplorable" and blamed inertia on the indifference of prefects and subprefects: "Those who work [on problems of public hygiene] are the exception, and those who send us informative documentation . . . are even more rare."[64] Such depressing news led to an administrative shakeup, with Brouardel's former committee assuming in 1906 the more august title of Conseil Supérieur de l'Hygiène Publique (CSHP). But a statistical profile of improvement was lacking in the next decade, while qualitative reports continued to weigh notably in the negative.

Maybe all that France needed was a firm hand. That, in any event, was the opinion of Georges Clemenceau, who became minister of the interior in 1906 and immediately requested his prefects to demand stricter enforcement of the 1902 law, reminding them of its "obligatory character."[65] With the kind of mordant humor that was his trademark, Clemenceau observed the irony that everyone now seemed to want application of provisions for public assistance (so as to receive payments), but no one cared much about regulations on public hygiene. Such lack of compliance, he fumed, was apparent not only in the countryside but in some of the larger cities, and he intended to end it.[66] The reasons for frustrating lags in application of the 1902 reform were ticked off in a report to the CSHP by Albert Bluzet, who, as an inspector general, was closely acquainted with actual conditions in the countryside. He listed six: the lassitude of the local population, a spirit of routine among provincial officials, the insouciance of communal administrators, a reluctance of medical personnel, the undue complexity of bureaucratic regulations, and a lack of adequate funding and equipment.[67] One could hardly expect to improve on this summary, especially as it was reconfirmed by other officials in the Ministry of the Interior whose task it was to sift through information reaching Paris from the provinces. If anything, further evidence gathered by the CSHP suggested that the unchecked spread of certain communicable diseases, particularly tuberculosis, was resulting from the "greatest inertia" of rural communes and that France was reaching a "critical situation."[68]

Admittedly, though it was indicative of serious difficulty, such alarmism remained inconclusive. The minutes and supporting documents of the CSHP constitute an extensive body of evidence. Yet the difficulty of evaluating the data was always the same: "the absence or inexactitude of these statistics."[69] Still, the cumulative weight of reports, memos, public statements, and unguarded exclamations cannot be discounted. We are therefore able to speculate with some certainty about the total impact of reform legislation on the relationship between city and countryside. It seems safe enough to conclude that the urban population, despite the unsolved problems of crowding, benefited more immediately and directly from new welfare measures than the rest of France. This phenomenon was partly a matter of tradition (the fact that Paris and a few other urban centers already had an infrastructure in place), partly the inherent nature of a centralized bureaucracy, and partly a result of the cumbersome legislative process. But mostly it was the product of the local intransigeance or physical inaccessibility of many rural areas. After all, the main culprit was the commune. There is a paradox in this conclusion, to which so much documentation attests. The Third Republic's legislative program, conceived primarily in the hope of expanding the direct benefits of improved public hygiene and health care, and intended thereby to reach the more remote areas of the land, in reality touched mainly the cities, and above all the capital. Hence, in the time between the wars of 1870 and 1914, the distance between Paris and the provinces actually widened.

Chapter 8

Managers and Workers

The story of the slow emergence of an organized labor force after the Paris Commune has often been narrated. Too seldom, however, has it been related to the simultaneous development of public welfare. Just as in Germany, where proscription of socialism throughout the 1880s was accompanied by legislative measures to ameliorate the lot of workers, a combination of repression and reform was also manifest in France.

In a number of identifiable ways, of course, the context of French labor was markedly different from the German situation. France's republican form of government left a wider berth for the eventual integration of a socialist movement into the ruling consensus. A greater latitude for labor was likewise afforded by the ethos of liberalism in France, which contrasted with the ubiquity of an imperial state in Germany. The mandatory character of Germany's social insurance programs created a circumstance there unknown in France, where voluntarism remained the rule. The German system rested on a far broader base of heavy industry, whereas the French work force was less numerous, less concentrated, and generally less susceptible to politicization.

Yet many issues in the two nations were similar. On a political level there was the always-problematic question of reconciliation between radical elements and a regime that had deliberately persecuted them. The status of trade unions and the nature of socialist political representation therefore had to be elaborately negotiated in both countries. Of obvious mutual concern, too, were labor's demands to augment wages and reduce working hours, inescapably implying some kind of regulatory function for the state. Entwined with the rest, finally, was the daily experience of most workers everywhere in Europe: poor sanitation, wretched housing, industrial accidents, poverty, and disease.

This potpourri of social problems contained one basic ingredient: every potential solution was complicated by an inherent clash between employers and employees. We need fall neither into quibbles about nomenclature nor into debate about Marxist theory to recognize that a conflict of interests frequently marked relations between management and labor. But it is also wise to avoid a mindless reductionism that distills every labor dispute into the same essence of class struggle. Above all, the ambiguous performance of the French republican state should be observed without preconception. One must not assume from the outset that it was solely dedicated to serving the captains of industry. What existed instead was an intricate triangular configuration of uneasy compromise.

Confusion and Repression

The insurrectionary outbursts in the spring of 1871 did not come unannounced. The immediate provocation for the Paris Commune and other provincial uprisings was clearly a popular sense of betrayal by the Napoleonic leadership—coupled of course with a fear of the foreign conqueror—but this phenomenon also had its antecedents in a wave of industrial strikes that had occurred in the final years of the Second Empire.[1] At that time one writer in the *Revue des deux mondes* already referred to the situation in France as "pregnant with peril," by which he meant labor unrest rather than the menace of war with Germany.[2] When a major strike was declared at Le Creusot in early 1870, Charles de Mazade characterized it as "only the manifest expression of a more general movement," adding that indiscipline among French workers was apparently "becoming a habit."[3] Another commentator, Paul Leroy-Beaulieu, concluded that "these subversive ideas and these frequent material disorders" were attributable to a "spirit of radical hostility against the existing order."[4] There was, in short, ample indication that the Paris Commune was not simply an anomaly of wartime and that deeper structural problems lay embedded at its base.

After the Commune, however, the French population was forced to live under martial law. Police records leave no uncertainty about the repressive intentions of the Thierist regime or the ruthlessness with which it carried them out. Scarcely a day passed during the first three years of the republic without news of arrests, expulsions, or occasional executions. By the summer of 1872 more than 33,000 citizens had been arraigned because of their alleged participation in insurrection, and the number continued to rise.[5] In a few instances public emotion erupted in the working-class districts of Paris. But the most notable fact was that the laboring populace as a whole remained docile and dispirited. Antagonism toward Adolphe Thiers was prevalent but muted. And there was little sign of a radical fringe after most of its adherents had been eliminated or exiled. The prevailing spirit of the early 1870s was thus one of distress and disorganization. According to police reports, French artisans and laborers were generally cowed, even when, "following the example of German workers, they demand an augmentation of their wages." If there were any serious political fissures in the social structure, they were provisionally plastered over. As another police memorandum put it: "The bourgeoisie thinks only of business; the workers, only of wages."[6]

It should be recalled that the first formal antisocialist legislation of postwar Europe was enacted in France in 1872. This law came into being after abortive efforts by the Quai d'Orsay to arrange an international summit meeting to draft a united program of repression against the First International. When Bismarck refused to cooperate in this project—presumably on the grounds that he needed no help from the French and preferred to isolate them—Foreign Minister Charles de Rémusat still hoped that each nation would contribute to an "ensemble of measures" to contain radicalism. He had heard that the Germans were already contemplating such unilateral action. "We should precede them on this path," he asserted, and thereby "give to other peoples an example of reform that . . . has become necessary in face of the great social peril to which all nations are exposed at this time."[7] Besides, France badly needed to save face by reassuring everyone, at home and abroad, that another Commune was out of the question. "To refuse," wrote the Marquis de Gabriac from his diplomatic post in Berlin, "is perhaps to revive against us the reproach of lacking energy vis-à-vis the threat of revolution and to justify to some extent the misgivings of Europe."[8] Thus a bill was adopted by the French Assembly in Versailles on 14 March 1872 that made membership of a French citizen in the International punishable by imprisonment for two to five years.[9]

Repression reached flood tide by the summer of 1873. By then more than 45,000 criminal dossiers from the Commune had been considered in the courts. A new category was created that swelled the statistics: "refusal to inform." Nearly 9,000 persons were booked for failure to offer testimony, a rate of more than one hundred indictments a day during two years. Such numbers may be shocking. But the truth was that the Thierist government had erected an elaborate machine of repression. Measured by the more brutal standards of the twentieth century, let it be said, this regime fell far short of a police state. There were no allegations or evidence of torture. Yet one must observe that the early acquiescence of the French working class after the Commune was reinforced by the gavel, the guard, and the guillotine.[10]

A parliamentary investigation of French working conditions in the early 1870s revealed the depth of disarray among the laboring population. The composite portrait that emerged was hardly flattering. Workers were described as laconic and conservative, concerned only with their most immediate needs, shiftless, suffering from chaotic family circumstances. They were mostly illiterate, often alcoholic, and above all vulnerable to the slightest personal misfortune. Their plight was compounded, reports said, by the "distressing condition" of the economy, which increased unemployment, mendicity, and prostitution. If this collage of impressions nearly approached the social reality, as surely it did, the conclusion could not be surprising that the workers were in no posture to help themselves out of misery: "This goal must be achieved by other means."[11]

Welfare, in other words, would need to originate elsewhere. Perhaps one should look to employers? But there were several difficulties with such an expectation. Despite organization through chambers of commerce and professional associations, industrial managers (*patrons*) were far from forming a united front. Differences between bosses of large and small firms ran deep, with the former willing to tolerate some social welfare efforts and the latter usually resisting them.[12] In the absence of any collective recourse, wealthy entrepreneurs sometimes mounted individual efforts to improve housing and sanitation for their employees. Yet the findings of parliamentary inquiries acknowledged that even the best-intentioned attempts of industrialists could not provide an adequate solution. Still operative, furthermore, were the liberal principles and practices of the era, according to which the state could legitimately quell public disturbances harmful to commerce and industry but not infringe on the right of a private business to determine its own labor policy. This dictum was well illustrated by a correspondence in the autumn of 1872 between Adolphe Thiers and Eugène Schneider, the almighty steel magnate of Le Creusot. Without bothering to request governmental approval or to gauge the national implications of his decision, Schneider merely informed the French president in a personal letter that he was exercising "a certain influence on the question of wages," hoping thereby to avoid any recurrence of the labor trouble in his region: "I have been able here [Le Creusot] to produce a great appeasement." Rather than to question, still less to challenge, Schneider's independent initiative, Thiers expressed his approval of "vigorous discipline" to "contain" the workers. "Force and justice," he wrote, "are the only resort of society against disorderly passions."[13]

This exchange typified the earliest phase of the republic and its anxious conflation of laissez faire with law and order. Organized labor meanwhile seemed nowhere in sight until mid-decade, when some changes became visible. Labor strikes now reappeared and at the same time discussion of what was already called "the social question" began. In the foreground were demands for higher daily wages and for the workers' right to take collective action to obtain them. "This terrible question," as the police well recognized, was not strictly a French problem; it was "the single point toward which all nations are tending."[14] Actually there were still broader implications: not just wages but working and living conditions, and not only male workers but women and children. In addition, a growing awareness was evident that the state could not avoid being drawn into disputes between management and labor. Both sides sought out government officials to settle unresolved conflicts. Because a regular procedure did not exist, these first awkward exercises in labor arbitration were extemporaneous happenings. In March 1876 a group of angry carpenters argued for hours with their employers in the office of the prefect of police in Paris. Clashes also occurred among laborers when those on strike tried to prevent others from attempting to continue work, causing the latter to request police protection.[15] Similar incidents were reported from the provinces. For instance, the prefect of the

Nièvre, southeast of Paris, described his effort to arbitrate for stone-masons who "requested my intervention in fixing their wages." When their bosses failed to cooperate, negotiations collapsed and the workers went out on strike.[16] These scattered episodes soon became too frequent to be ignored, and they suggested that the republic would not long avoid some degree of enforced regulation. Nor would French labor fail to seek a more appropriate forum to express its collective grievances.

The First Stirrings of Socialism

Rehabilitation of the Socialist movement began with the convocation of a workers' congress in Paris in 1876. This gathering was the brainchild of a Parisian activist, Charles Chabert, who was well known to police agents as an audacious orator and an advocate of political amnesty for the exiled communards of 1871. The launching of Chabert's project was simultaneous with his founding a new popular journal, *La Tribune*, which promptly made preparations for the congress into headline news. The leftist response was by no means unanimously enthusiastic. An established rival daily, *Droits de l'homme*, contested the utility of such a large meeting, especially in view of the tight security restrictions that were sure to be imposed on it, and suggested that Chabert's scheme was primarily a publicity stunt to boost sales of his newspaper. Likewise, in *Le Rappel*, Léon Gambetta's crony Édouard Lockroy criticized the project as ill-timed. As it turned out, this internecine wrangling delayed but did not deter the momentum for a meeting.[17]

Naturally police agents were on the *qui vive* and set about to assess the motives of Chabert and his colleagues. The finding of their investigation was that the congress represented an effort to resuscitate a labor movement that was nearly comatose. Workers had already begun to tire of strike agitation that so frequently proved to be ineffectual. A symptom of this "lassitude" was the low attendance at protest rallies, which were routinely monitored by detectives. Although Chabert had promised to exclude controversial political demands from the agenda of his planned assembly, the police correctly surmised that he intended to encourage clandestine caucuses "to create the bases of an electoral organization." Hence the Paris congress in itself was bound to become a political event that would revive working-class spirits and raise expectations of reestablishing a rapport with international socialism.[18]

Curiously contributing to this malaise were stories, often related in unintentionally comic detail, about recent contacts between French and German workers at the centennial celebration of the American Revolution in Philadelphia. Visiting French delegates had the unnerving experience of being greeted there by German-American marching bands playing the *Marseillaise*; and German Socialists in attendance took the occasion to pin red cockades on the lapels of their French comrades. Thus it was on the soil of Philadelphia beer gardens where the first postwar fraternization occurred between workers from opposite sides of the Rhine. Much of the revelry was meaningless, and some of it ended with hard feelings and fisticuffs. But in Paris French police officials were not amused by what they perceived as a dangerous precedent for renewal of socialist internationalism. Their worry was deepened by rumors that certain sections of the International, especially in Geneva, were meanwhile increasing efforts to establish contacts with labor leaders in Paris.[19]

Yet the Paris assembly was inauspicious. Chabert's *Tribune* printed long excerpts from its proceedings, although one must wonder to what effect, since they were hard to match for sheer boredom. Perhaps with a smattering of sour grapes, *Droits de l'homme* offered only a summary of the opening session on its second page. Some interest was aroused by a discussion of women's rights, but most delegates soon had a surfeit of speeches and spent more time in cafés and restaurants. These activities were exhaustively covered by the police, who found little cause for alarm and no reason to intervene. The only disturbing note was the announcement of a second congress, scheduled for the following year in Lyon, and of plans to convene an international conference of workers in conjunction with the projected Paris Exposition of 1878.[20]

By November 1876 the Prefecture of Police had gathered a compendium of information concerning the first congress and its impact. It had been attended by 332 delegates, of whom 237 were Parisians. The official minutes confirmed that the meeting, as advertised, had avoided inflammatory declarations about political issues. Few real workers and no peasants were involved in the proceedings, which had been dominated by newspaper editors and other intellectuals. But on the fringes of the gathering there had met discrete groups that possessed the potential to spur Socialist activity "to a very high degree." The International had left no visible trace, but it was implicitly present. Police agents noticed that many personal addresses were exchanged. The Paris congress was therefore not as harmless as it may have appeared, they concluded; indeed, it represented the opening of "a war on religion and capital."[21]

To test this hypothesis, the Prefecture of Police ordered in late 1876 a survey of labor organizations in the major industrial centers of France. It is instructive to register a sample of reports in the same chronological order that they arrived in the capital and were transmitted to the French cabinet.

7 November: In Limoges the Paris meeting had created "a considerable impression on the working population," and the labor movement there was beginning to assume "a real importance."

13 November: In Grenoble and the Department of the Isère workers were displaying "radical tendencies that become more pronounced each day."

18 November: Because of the moderate opinions and sober habits of the working population in Lille, the influence of Socialist agitators in that city remained "mediocre."

20 November: Lyon, by contrast, was the scene of numerous labor groups and "dangerous tendencies," to which the government must pay close attention.

22 November: Although the majority of workers in Saint-Étienne held "radical opinions," they were generally nonbelligerent except under the influence of drink, which sometimes led to "deplorable excess."

In sum, Socialist leaders were making clear progress, and workers' candidates would have "serious chances" in the next general elections.[22]

These returns spoke of a labor movement still in its adolescence. But when multiplied several times, they could give no comfort to a government drifting inexorably into an internal crisis and feeling constant pressure from a formidable neighbor. We may leave aside here a narration of the *seize mai* episode in 1877 and the republican electoral victory that ensued from it. What is particularly relevant is that these developments transpired in France on the eve of a dramatic shift of political fronts in Germany, right after two attempts on Kaiser William's life in the spring of 1878. By obtaining anti-Socialist legislation at that time, and thereby escalating the precedent set by the 1872 law of the Thierist regime in France, Bismarck assumed the distinction of taking the lead in persecuting labor. Repeating an old cliché, one French agent reported to Paris that the German chancellor "had his hands everywhere." Another claimed to know that Bismarck was urging European governments "to decide on the Socialist question and to accept or refuse a united league against social revolution."[23] For such a grand diplomatic design there was and is no proof. Yet circumstantial evidence gave it some credibility when a German diplomat, the Count von Wesdehlen, directly confronted French premier Jules Dufaure with an incident that had allegedly transpired in 1877 during the workingmen's congress in Lyon. According to German sources, a coffeehouse plot was conceived there "to eradicate the sovereign houses of Europe," beginning with Germany. If given a literal interpretation, this rumor might mean that French radicals were actually implicated in the attempted assassination of the Kaiser. Wesdehlen demanded that the French open an investigation.[24]

However farfetched such imputations may have seemed, they could not be ignored by the government at a time when the Paris Exposition of 1878 was in progress and when another gathering of workers' delegates was scheduled to assemble in the capital. The Prefecture of Police observed that this meeting, unlike the first two labor congresses in Paris and Lyon, was frankly identified as an "international" event. Surely, "above all after the attacks in Berlin," the cabinet should not tolerate "a veritable implantation of the Socialist International on French territory." The police therefore recommended that the convocation be cancelled. Following a fortnight of further consideration, the Ministry of the Interior concurred that "the government finds itself confronted by an illicit association" that was explicitly forbidden by the law of 14 May 1872. Orders were correspondingly issued to prevent the gathering; and they were strictly enforced in September 1878 by the arrest of Jules Guesde and thirty-eight other Socialist sympathizers who attempted to defy the ban by meeting in rump session.[25]

There was something anomalous about the fact that, under German prodding, the republican government invoked its own restrictive legislation at precisely the moment when the French press was deploring with virtual unanimity the passage of anti-Socialist measures in Berlin. German ambassador Chlodwig zu Hohenlohe made specific complaint of this inconsistency, pointing out that the German action was being criticized in France even by politicians and editorialists who had approved the execution or deportation of communards only a few years before. He also reported that the Bonapartists were taking advantage of the turmoil to divert popular agitation to their own ends. "With the naive, easily excited, and frivolous French nation," Hohenlohe commented with some condescension, "such intrigues find a fertile soil."[26]

We may draw other conclusions. It is evident, first of all, that the political origins of modern French Socialism may be traced to that postwar decade in which Germany still dominated France. Thus the entire ambience of the earliest attempts at labor organization was permeated by the hopes or fears—depending on one's perspective—of a reinvigorated Socialist internationalism. For French Socialists this largely meant the possibility of establishing attachments to German Social Democracy, which was widely admired for its strength and organization as well as, after 1878, for its heroic resistance to persecution. In the *mentalité* of French leftists there was, of course, much ambiguity about Germany. Admiration for the SPD was always mixed with generous doses of Germanophobia, and in that respect French Socialists were little different from their compatriots. Clearly, Karl Marx to the contrary notwithstanding, the workers did have a homeland. Yet the international constellation of the 1880s—specifically including the anti-Socialist campaign in Germany—removed much of the psychological conflict for the French. To espouse an internationalist outlook in France before 1878 seemed both dangerous and disloyal. Thereafter, once Bismarck had outlawed Social Democracy, it could appear merely as the sensible support of a fellow underdog against the overwhelming power of the German Kaiserreich. French Socialism was thereby freed of any antinationalistic onus, a circumstance that facilitated a full amnesty of the communards in 1880 and expedited, as part of a general wave of deregulation, the legalization of syndicalism in 1884. At the very time that the labor movement was suffering through its worst period of repression in imperial Germany, therefore, French workers were able to assume a place within the broad political spectrum of the Third Republic.

Very Delicate Questions

The fortunes of organized labor in France were profoundly affected by three intimately related changes that occurred about 1880: the end of the government of moral order after the conservative electoral defeat of 1877 and the resignation of Marshal MacMahon from the French presidency at the outset of 1879; the relaxation of overt oppression, announced by the extension of a blanket amnesty to convicted communards in 1880 and followed by the legalization of labor syndicates in 1884; and the beginning of serious consideration by the French parliament of social welfare measures for workers. The third of these is difficult to date, because it was characterized in the 1880s by protracted deliberations rather than bold enactments. By the middle of that decade, in any event, the government's good intentions were firmly stamped on the record. The primary objective, stated by Minister of Commerce and Industry Maurice Rouvier in February 1885, was to obtain "the betterment of the material condition of the laboring classes."[27]

It remained to do so. The succeeding years were a time of intense discussion, most of it out of public view in legislative committees where the principles and details of reform were thrashed out without resolution. Reformers began with the same issues that were deemed most urgent by the workers themselves: hours and wages. Closely attached to these, as we have already documented, were the questions of child and female labor. A motion to establish a maximum ten-hour day for all was brought to the Chamber of Deputies on 10 March 1884 by Richard Waddington.[28] Although the initial airing of this measure was inconclusive, it ignited an intermittent debate over "total regulation" (whether adult male workers should be subject to the same restrictions as women and children) that preoccupied the labor committee of the Chamber of Deputies in the following five years. At least this altercation served to clarify opposing positions and to polarize French deputies into recognizable factions that reflected the ideological dichotomy of the day. The two sides, as Charles Ferry put it in 1889, comprised those who favored "the liberal solution" and proponents of "the authoritarian solution."[29] In this respect, labor reform was not far different from other social issues on the republic's agenda as the Belle Epoque began.

It may appear almost too convenient to speak of a new reform impetus in the early 1890s, but this fitted a familiar pattern. Completion of the vaunted German social legislation, convocation of an international welfare conference during the Paris Exposition of 1889, and consolidation of Henri Monod's Bureau of Public Health and Hygiene had all directly preceded this moment, and political leaders were conscious of passing over a threshold. French premier Charles de Freycinet expressed the prevailing mood in a message to the Chamber: "Gentlemen, we are in an era of social transformation when the condition of the workers is justifiably the object of our preoccupations."[30]

The government's determination was soon to be tested over the question of accident compensation. Previously we saw how existing regulations held owners of industrial enterprises liable for accidents only when they were shown to be at "serious fault." Workers were required, in effect, to sue their superiors, with the burden of proof resting on the prosecution. This conception was now sustained in the Senate but challenged in the Chamber's committee on labor. Reformist deputies basically wanted a no-fault system that would eliminate long and costly judicial proceedings. Otherwise, as committeeman Louis Ricard said, "the manager and the worker will be constantly at odds." The labor committee concurred, and by an 11 to 2 margin it was decided to reject the Senate version in favor of a plan that would "profit equally the manager and the worker."[31]

One question, however, led to the next. The no-fault bill presented by the cabinet and supported by the labor committee was, as the Socialist deputy Émile Jamais noted, "inspired by provisions of the German law on accidents." But a crucial difference was that in Germany all industrial workers were under an umbrella of mandatory insurance, whereas their French counterparts were not—"a lacuna of French legislation," Jamais commented.[32] Should France nonetheless guarantee workers a fixed indemnity, as in Germany? The government advocated such a proposal, and the labor committee was prepared to recommend it. Yet, if so, at what rate? The government asked that anyone disabled through industrial accident be awarded only 50 percent of salary during convalescence. But the committee, observing that the level was 60 percent in Austria and 66 percent in Germany, decided instead to set the subsidy at two-thirds of a worker's regular wages.[33] Through such details we are able to decipher at close hand the nascent character of French welfare for workers, with its distinctive admixture of voluntarism and compulsion, and to define more precisely the attempted compromise between a "liberal" and an "authoritarian" solution. We can also confirm yet again that the latter was associated in the minds of most reformers with the German model.

The same may be said for early discussions of a pension plan, which began in the 1890s, although they did not culminate in legislative action until two decades later. Several different proposals came under scrutiny at the same time. As one author of a pension bill, the deputy Pierre Paplier, explained: "All of these systems are more or less similar to those adopted by neighboring nations and in particular by Germany." Paplier went on, however, to specify how his own scheme would differ: "In Germany obligation is imposed; here, to the contrary . . . , individual liberty must be respected."[34] Just how, without compulsory membership, a comprehensive pension plan could be conceived and financed was still uncertain. Nor did it as yet have sufficient political backing to pass through parliament. We may therefore defer unwrapping the legislative package finally adopted in 1910. Let it nevertheless be noted here that the eventual success of any pension program was sure to require the mutual cooperation of labor and management as well as some measure of subsidization by the state. The young Raymond Poincaré summed up: "There are still very delicate questions to be resolved."[35]

Three issues remained especially vexing in the late 1890s: hours, wages, and the right to strike. Most French legislators agreed on the necessity of adopting a uniform workday, but they disagreed on its optimal length. Conservatives argued for twelve hours or, preferably, for no regulation at all.[36] The Senate favored eleven hours; the majority of the Chamber, ten. Moderate Socialists such as Jean Jaurès would settle for nine, but more radical leftists like Jules Guesde and Édouard Vaillant urged that the maximum be lowered to eight. If matters were left on a local or voluntary basis, Guesde contended with an unsubtle twist of irony, the workers would remain subject to the "goodwill or gentle whim of their managers."[37] This broad range of parliamentary opinion provided a useful instrument for measuring the relative ideological position of French politicians. But, given the diversity of views and the laxity of enforcement, it betrayed little about actual working conditions, which forever lagged behind hypothetical discussions of them. A representative of the Federation of

Parisian Workers testified before the labor committee, for instance, that legal restrictions for women were not being enforced in the case of typesetters and newspaper folders, who would otherwise be driven into unemployment. For them, among others, night labor and long hours were still the norm.[38] As this example suggested, hours and wages were inextricable. Women typesetters received 30 percent less than men. Their employers wanted to keep that arrangement rather than raise the price of their journals and risk losing circulation; and many women employees, spurred by the threat of dismissal, agreed.[39] Male workers at the bottom of the pay scale, including foreigners, faced the same dilemma. When a daily minimum wage of five francs was established in Paris for street sweepers, half of them were let go for lack of an adequate budget.[40] Objections to a minimum wage were cogently stated by the prefect of the Seine during a rhetorical duel with Jean Jaurès in the labor committee. Managers had an obvious interest in engaging the cheapest labor possible, Monsieur Poubelle remarked, and they were therefore reluctant to accept any legislation that would limit free competition for jobs. Likewise, although restrictions on the workday might be suitable for factories with a large labor force (and thus, presumably, with the capacity to organize shifts), they were infeasible for small enterprises and for outdoor seasonal employment. This last point was conceded by many deputies outside the Socialist camp, such as Jules Siegfried and Léon Bourgeois, who otherwise supported labor reforms. As a consequence of these complications and divisions, proposals for a standard of shorter hours and higher wages tended to bog down.[41]

The strike issue was no less complex, and it provoked similar disagreements between Socialist and non-Socialist reformers. In 1896 Gustave Mesureur, then the minister of commerce and industry, brought a bill to the Chamber's labor committee that would require arbitration proceedings before a strike could be declared. Against this proposal formed an opposition, led by Jean Jaurès, which raised two pertinent objections. First, it was a matter of timing: the success of a labor strike often depended on its spontaneity and swiftness. Mesureur's plan would delay any direct action by workers and allow their bosses to prepare countermeasures. Second, there was ambiguity about whether arbitration would be binding: if so, it would be coercive; if not, it would be ineffectual. Mesureur responded that he did not wish to cripple the syndicates but solely to prevent wildcat strikes. He hoped only to require that the parties attempt arbitration before stopping work. Jaurès countered once more: "I am struck by the discrepancy between the subtlety of your hypotheses and the simplicity of reality." In fact, he argued, organized labor had no interest in wildcat strikes started by a few excitable individuals. Collective bargaining predicated on the right to strike, not on prior binding arbitration, was therefore the answer.[42] Further discussion failed to produce agreement about implementation of the Mesureur plan. The labor committee finally "declared itself in favor of the principle of obligation," yet it declined to specify how the workers should be represented or who should be chosen to constitute a board of arbitration. Adoption of a motion for "a compulsory attempt at conciliation"—over the protest of Jean Jaurès and one other member of the committee—did not clarify these intractable questions.[43]

The State as Arbiter

The weakness of existing welfare institutions persuaded nearly everyone by 1900 that some government assistance was indispensable in solving the social question. Yet to what extent was state intervention permissible into spheres that had traditionally been private? That classic question, little closer to a solution than thirty years before, was of course not unique to France. It had been directly addressed in Pope Leo XIII's remarkable encyclical *Rerum novarum* of 1891, which encouraged all political regimes to offer special aid to the poor. And it was debated in the forum of the Second International with reference to ministerialism, specifically meaning the participation of the French Socialist Alexandre Millerand in a liberal bourgeois cabinet. The problem was also intrinsic to a third current international perspective: the wide attraction of the German welfare model, which seemed to offer important benefits to the working population of Europe through a deliberate strengthening of state prerogatives.

Each of these aspects was controversial during the opening decade of the twentieth century. But most lives are led in less abstract terms, and it is well to broach the subject with more mundane matters such as the minimum wage. This controversy continued to absorb the Chamber's labor committee, which approved the proposition that French communes and departments had the right to fix the salaries of their own employees. But if municipalities could establish a scale of wages for *directly* contracted labor, should they not do so for *indirectly* employed workers as well? Apart from the convoluted problem of classifying laborers into such nebulous categories, objections were raised against this suggestion even by those who favored an active role by the state in regulating the marketplace. Albert de Mun thought it best to leave minimum wages entirely to negotiations between entrepreneurs and syndicates. His colleague Pierre Baudin agreed, stating that creating an obligation for communes and departments to intercede in settling salary disputes would be "an antiliberal measure."[44] The sensitivity of the cabinet to these criticisms was apparent in testimony by Premier Charles Dupuy, who conceded that uniform regulations on a national basis were infeasible. He offered a list of desiderata: minimum wages and maximum hours should be adjusted to the "normal" standard of separate regions; they should be applied only in public enterprises, not in the private sector; and communes should retain an option to require that certain industrial managers pay their workers in accordance with the established wage scale of a given region. Minister of Commerce and Industry Paul Delombre amplified Dupuy's remarks by explaining that the government was seeking a way between the extremes: "It is not an absolute theory of doing nothing, nor is it the contrary theory that the state should do everything; it is the idea that there exists an evolution and that the state should encourage it."[45] These words conveyed a conception of the state as an agent of solidarism. The republican government would act as an honest broker between management and labor, taking the side of neither, serving the interests of both. Such a stance of impartiality was appropriate enough, it seemed, but could it be maintained through sharp theoretical contradictions, bitter labor disputes, and crippling strikes?

A test case was presented by a statute passed into law on 30 March 1900 that set the standard of a ten-hour working day for women and children, with adult male workers to be adjusted at that level within four years. The regulatory intention of legislators was patent, but subsequent reports from state inspectors showed the variability of actual practice and the difficulty of securing a grip on the problem. A survey of nearly 40,000 factories visited by inspectors in the Paris region in 1899 indicated that workers in more than half of them were still on the job for at least eleven hours a day. In Marseille the percentage was slightly lower, and many urban workers had already become accustomed to a ten-hour day; the Marseille inspector therefore cautioned against any authorization of twelve-hour shifts, lest it touch off strikes in the port. But another inspection report from the Limoges area stressed the seasonal character of labor there and pleaded for greater "tolerance" in the enforcement of restrictions.[46]

In truth, the government had little choice. Attempts to crack down on employers provoked their hostility or outright resistance. In 1903 Albert Congy submitted a motion to abrogate regulatory provisions of the 1900 law on grounds that it should be brought into conformity with the "reality" of the French labor market.[47] That reality also had an international context, which was forcefully expressed by a spokesman for the owners of metal and mining industries. If shorter working hours were imposed in France, including an already-proposed eight-hour day in the mines, he said, the nation would become industrially less competitive in Europe, the price of French finished goods would rise, imports would increase, and higher taxes would surely ensue—all of that merely "to give to certain persons [that is, syndicalists] a satisfaction that has been accorded them in no other country in the world."[48] These worries were especially relevant to Germany. Throughout most of the 1870s France had maintained a positive balance of trade with its eastern neighbor. But this favorable position changed abruptly in the 1880s after Bismarck's switch to a high-tariff policy, which sharply reduced the flow of imports from France without slowing the movement of German industrial products westward into the relatively unprotected French market. Application of the Méline tariff after 1893 was in part intended to correct this imbalance. But by then the bulging strength of Germany's industrial sector had far surpassed that of France, which could ill afford any self-imposed disadvantage in production and trade. Such alarmism was perhaps unjustified. True, the French economy sputtered for several decades and was statistically overmatched by the German surge. Yet France's own economic upswing after 1893 was not negligible, and it is not demonstrable that the limitation of working hours was a handicap, particularly as that trend was everywhere evident in western Europe and the United States. We may nonetheless observe that, among French industrialists, German competition created anxieties with which reformers had to reckon.[49]

That Germany was admired as well as feared meanwhile became apparent in discussions of accident insurance. A bill holding employers liable to pay a modest indemnity to injured workers was, as we earlier saw, enacted by the French parliament in 1898. But this measure pleased almost no one. After "seventeen years of sterile debates," contended the deputy Georges Graux, the French had succeeded only in assembling bits and pieces of a coherent welfare program. "We have unsystematically borrowed from Germany some fragments of legislative texts, neglecting those institutions that assure on the other side of the Rhine the regular operation of a well-coordinated law." Graux added that, despite the "incontestable merit" of German legislation, its enforcement had nevertheless created "frequent difficulties and numerous protests," even in a country "where the spirit of discipline reigns." Still, the basic difference was that Germany provided for its citizens broad state-sponsored provisions of social security that France lacked; hence the French arrangement failed "to give the same guarantees to industrialists" against abuses by workers who were careless, who falsely claimed to be incapacitated, or who unduly prolonged their convalescence. Graux urged that the 1898 regulations be amended so as to prevent such "demoralizing and ruinous frauds," pointing out that the French parliament had blindly adopted German accident insurance rates without considering the long-standing national differences in salary scales and in the structure of enterprise.[50]

Thereafter the debate proceeded on two levels. One involved the principle of allowing the state to function in effect as a huge insurance agency, with all the attendant technical questions about the relationship between public and private financing. This issue we may properly leave for a later analysis of the French system of mutual aid societies. The second facet, more directly germane here, concerned the confrontation of management and labor in the courts. Ambiguity still existed about exactly which workers were eligible for indemnification in case of an industrial accident, what amount of assistance they could expect, and whether they could obtain it without presenting legal proof of incapacity. The result was the continuation of courtroom scenes in which managers and their clever lawyers faced barely literate workers who found themselves, in the words of a Socialist deputy, "disarmed, badly defended, often deceived, and in the end doubly victimized."[51] Whatever their scruples in matters of principle, many French politicians were moved by the undeniable veracity of this rendition. In presenting a revised accident compensation bill in February 1901, Léon Mirman cited the case of some workers injured and unemployed since June of the previous year while their claims were still under litigation. For them the 1898 code was already a "dead letter," because they were "incontestably deprived of any means of defense." Hence, charged Mirman, they would be forced to jeopardize their future just in order to survive by accepting a meager out-of-court settlement from the employer.[52]

In June 1901 the Chamber of Deputies approved a revised law and sent it on to the Senate. After the usual disputation between the two houses, a final version was enacted on 10 June 1902. Its purpose was to extend the coverage of the 1898 code to broader categories of workers and to clarify their claim to indemnities. For his part, Mirman left no doubt about the model that French reformers had in mind: "That is what happens in countries—Germany, Austria— where obligatory insurance has been instituted; that is what would happen in France if the aim forthrightly affirmed by the Chamber were to prevail."[53]

The Millerand Era

During the initial decade of the twentieth century, the pivotal figure of French socialism was Alexandre Millerand. Granted, Jean Jaurès doubtless enjoyed greater popularity among French workers and appropriately emerged as the acknowledged leader of a united Socialist political party, the SFIO. But in parliamentary circles Millerand's presence was more central and also more controversial. If a less illustrious figure than Jaurès, whose oratorical skills he could not match, Millerand provided a more sensitive barometer of Socialist progress.[54]

We are not primarily concerned here with the well-chronicled debate over ministerialism, which culminated in 1904 when the Amsterdam congress of the Second International censured Millerand's previous participation in the Waldeck-Rousseau cabinet, thereby placating his critics in the German Social Democratic party, like Karl Kautsky, who invoked the supranational fraternity of the labor movement. Rather, our attention is turned to those perennial questions that had long preoccupied social reformers bent on reconciling the competing claims of management and labor.

Hours and wages remained most prominent among them. On such issues Millerand revealed himself as one of those revisionist Marxists who regarded politics as the art of the possible. Accordingly, his influence was consistently exercised to obtain a standard ten-hour day without a reduction in wages. In these efforts, as usual, Millerand risked being outflanked by more vociferous Socialists such as Jules Guesde and Édouard Vaillant, who continued to ply both labor syndicates and parliamentary committees with arguments for an eight-hour day and the establishment of a minimum wage.[55] Seen strictly through a Socialist prism, of course, Millerand could appear fainthearted. But it is necessary to read the entire record and to take full account of the continuing pressure from well-financed groups of employers. The Paris Chamber of Commerce, for instance, was emphatic that entrepreneurs in the capital were unreconciled to state interference into business. As late as 1907 its *Bulletin* still advocated the maintenance of a twelve-hour workday and insisted that private commercial establishments should remain totally free from further government regulation of hours and wages.[56] This resistance among French *patrons*, if anything, became all the more extensive and explicit as the government attempted to require compliance with restrictions. A gathering of presidents from ninety chambers of commerce listened to their chairman explain his "intimate conviction" that the French worker was less assiduous and more easily distracted than German or English laborers: "You will recognize with me that he is not a great producer." It followed that France would be more seriously disadvantaged than competitor nations by a limitation of working hours. After discussing a proposal to endorse a maximum of twelve hours a day and 3,000 hours a year, the assembly adopted instead a lapidary resolution that rejected all state regulation of adult male labor.[57]

Just as managers used the argument of international competition to oppose the ten-hour day, so did some reformers employ it to resist proposals for an eight-hour day. Léon Bourgeois, while minister of labor, appeared at the Palais Bourbon to plead for an exemption of certain metal industries that needed fires to be tended around the clock. Vigorously attacked for sacrificing the interest of manual laborers engaged in "painful" tasks, he was prodded by Albert de Mun about advancing to an eight-hour workday (thereby permitting three daily shifts instead of two). Bourgeois demurred: "We cannot hope for an eight-hour day without international agreement."[58]

A discernible pattern might be suggested by these details: management was hostile to state regulation, militant Socialists supported it, and moderate parliamentarians like Millerand and Bourgeois shifted uneasily between them. But political motives were in fact mixed; and from the standpoint of social reform, one should be wary of awarding facile approbation to those who appeared progressive. Particularly dubious was the Socialist stance toward foreign laborers in France. Bills were introduced in 1898, 1906, and again in 1910 to establish state regulation of wages for immigrant workers at the same level as for the French, with an explanation that employers would then "have no interest in preferring the foreign element."[59] Although statistics continued to show that by far the most numerous contingents of aliens were Belgian and Italian, supporters of this measure were not beyond stirring xenophobic aversions against an easier target: the "veritable invasion" of German workers.[60]

There were also objective reasons for the apparent increase of labor strife around 1900. Despite signs that the French economy might be recovering momentum, the rate of unemployment was higher than ever. In the thirteen years from 1890 through 1902, over 25 million days of labor were lost by layoffs and lockouts; and more than half of that total occurred in the final four years (see Table 5). Strike activity was likewise accelerating rapidly if erratically. The number of recorded strikes stood at 313 in 1890. By 1900 this figure had nearly trebled, and in 1904 for the first time it exceeded 1,000. The number of enterprises involved and the total of laborers who protested in this manner thus grew accordingly (see Table 6).[61] The growth of syndicalism provided a third measurement. After reappearing in scattered fashion in the 1870s, as we have noted, trade unions were granted legal status in April 1884. Local and regional syndicates gradually emerged thereafter until the formation of the Confédération Générale du Travail (CGT) in 1902. By the end of that year over 9,000 syndicates had enrolled nearly 1.5 million members. It should be added, however, that only half of these were industrial workers, properly speaking; approximately one-quarter of the

Table 5 / Days of Unemployment among French Workers, 1890–1902

1890	1,340,000
1891	1,717,200
1892	917,680
1893	3,174,850
1894	1,062,480
1895	617,469
1896	644,168
1897	780,944
1898	1,216,306
1899	3,550,734
1900	3,760,577
1901	1,862,050
1902	4,675,081

Source: Édmond Michel, Les habitants *(Paris, 1910), p. 155.*

Table 6 / Labor Strikes in France, 1893–1906

Year	Number of Strikes	Number of Firms	Number of Strikers
1893	634	4,286	170,123
1894	391	1,731	54,576
1895	405	1,298	45,801
1896	476	2,178	49,851
1897	356	2,568	68,875
1898	368	1,967	82,065
1899	739	4,290	176,772
1900	902	10,253	222,714
1901	523	6,970	111,414
1902	512	1,820	212,704
1903	567	3,246	123,151
1904	1,026	17,250	171,097
1905	830	5,302	77,666
1906	1,309	19,637	438,466

Source: Pierre Colliard, "Rapport fait . . . au nom de la Commission du Travail,"
16 June 1910, AN Paris, C 7486.

Table 7 / Membership in French Trade Syndicates, 1903

	Number of Syndicates	Number of Members
Management	2,767	205,463
Labor	3,934	645,426
Mixed	146	33,431
Agriculture	2,433	598,834
Total	9,280	1,483,154

Source: Édmond Michel, Les habitants (Paris, 1910), p. 148.

organizations were managerial and another quarter were designated as agricultural groups (see Table 7).[62]

The cumulative effect produced by these increases of unemployment, labor strikes, and syndicalization generated a new round of reformist debate after 1900. This time it was Millerand himself who helped draft and defend a bill to make arbitration mandatory before a strike could be called, an arrangement castigated only a few years before by Jean Jaurès. Receiving mixed signals from its leadership, the rank and file of labor syndicalists remained divided on the issue. Many of them, according to Millerand's cosponsor Pierre Colliard, were opposed to the bill. But they had also previously balked both at trade union regulations and at rules for accident compensation. Thus Colliard was confident: "The workers will accept [arbitration] once they understand it." In 1904 the Chamber's labor committee went on record in favor of the new plan, although the parliament was still not persuaded to enact it into law.[63]

Before the end of the decade four other legislative proposals to regulate labor strikes had joined the Millerand–Colliard bill on the Chamber's docket. On behalf of the labor committee, Colliard was appointed to offer an analysis of these five conceptions of the problem. His report, henceforth central to the committee's deliberations, compared the strike statistics of the previous fifteen years in Germany (see Table 8) with those in France.[64] Colliard contended that strikes were not caused by syndicates; rather, both were by-products of "the struggle between employers and their employees." He also rejected the charge that the recent militancy of French syndicates had resulted from an infiltration of anarchists, noting that anarchism

Table 8 / *Labor Strikes in Germany, 1893–1906*

Year	Number of Strikes	Number of Firms	Number of Strikers
1893	116	—	9,356
1894	130	—	7,318
1895	204	—	14,032
1896	483	—	128,808
1897	578	—	63,119
1898	985	—	60,190
1899	1,288	7,121	99,333
1900	1,433	7,440	122,803
1901	1,056	4,561	55,262
1902	1,060	8,437	53,912
1903	1,374	7,000	85,603
1904	1,870	10,321	113,480
1905	2,403	14,481	408,145
1906	3,328	16,246	272,218

Source: Pierre Colliard, "Rapport fait . . . au nom de la Commission du Travail,"
16 June 1910, AN Paris, C 7486.

played no role in the trade unions of Germany even though the number of strikes there had also increased in the early 1890s. Colliard cited with evident approval an alternative theory advanced by Charles Rist, professor of law at Montpellier, who saw exports as a crucial economic indicator for France and "especially for Germany." Whenever exports rose in the two countries, unemployment would sink and strike activity would increase; whenever they fell, the inverse was true. This simple paradigm did not apply well to England, Rist believed, because the British Isles were not sharing equally in the gathering prosperity enjoyed by France and Germany. But on the Continent, Colliard concurred, workers were inclined to press for higher wages when managers had need of them and to desist from agitation when the labor market was stagnant: "This explains the recurrence of strikes in Germany and France in periods of prosperity and their decrease in periods of crisis."[65]

Colliard then turned to an evaluation of the role of the state in strike settlements. In the distant past, he wrote, "the state in effect intervened in strikes for the benefit of the owners [and] against the workers." Ostensibly that spirit had changed. The liberal state was now supposed to allow labor disputes to run their course and to intercede only to maintain order. Colliard observed, however, that it was always the workers who took to the streets and who blocked traffic, not their managers. Hence, he concluded, all the legislative proposals before the Chamber of Deputies shared a common hypocrisy: "this pretended neutrality of the state." Despite recognizing the manifest ineffectuality of existing regulations to prevent strikes, Colliard recommended that France reject mandatory arbitration, except perhaps in the case of workers directly employed by the state, the departments, or the communes. Otherwise arbitration should remain optional.[66]

It is unnecessary to elaborate on the timidity of Colliard's conclusion, which only reaffirmed the status quo. We may also omit any commentary on the strained plausibility, not to say banality, of his rendition of Rist. The point to retain here is the framework of the analysis itself, for which the comparability of France and Germany was basic. Such thinking, reflected in documents central to the deliberations of the Chamber's foremost committee on labor relations, was thus placed squarely in the mainstream of French parliamentary debate, not left on the periphery. This observation should have nothing surprising about it, given the paramount role of German Social Democracy in the political movement of the Second International as well as the simultaneous precedent of the German social welfare system. Before 1914, in other words, Germany was both a natural comparison and a defining element in the progress of organized labor in France.

Part Three

National Crisis and

Social Security

Chapter 9

The Funding of Reform

The connection between public welfare and public wealth is self-evident. If the French state were to assume prodigious new responsibilities in providing financial aid to the needy, some additional means of funding would have to be found. Free medical care for the poor, subsidies to unwed pregnant women, workers' compensation for industrial accidents, assistance to invalids and the aged—such measures, among many others, were ardently desired by social reformers. But each was to be obtained only at a price that was certain to rise with every passing year. To advocate reform was implicitly to sanction increased budgets and hence to raise a question about the sources of state revenue.

Although these elemental truths were apparent when the Third Republic began, and even before, they did not become acutely uncomfortable until the late 1880s. It was no coincidence that serious parliamentary discussion about an income tax started at the same time as the inauguration of a central Bureau of Public Health and Hygiene and the formation of a Conseil Supérieur de l'Assistance Publique. Virtually simultaneous, moreover, was the start of deliberations about state regulation of alcoholic beverages, in which the symbiosis of health and finance was equally striking. We shall see how the income tax issue played off against the alcohol question, without either reaching a firm conclusion. Moreover, in the absence of major new tax increments, a third source of additional income (and curtailment of expenditures) became enticing: the confiscation of church property. To reduce the religious controversy solely to its financial aspect would, of course, be a terrible simplification. Yet this facet of French anticlericalism should not be sundered from the rest.

In the midst of these fiscal considerations it may be well to reflect on the problem of public "mores" (*moeurs*). This characteristic French term can be variously understood as manners, morals, customs, or conventions. It indicated a sense of how things were actually conceived or accomplished in daily life—as opposed to what was alleged to be ethical and valid "in principle" (*en principe*). Such commonplace notions lead us close to admitting that national character does have some explicative value, not because it may be substituted for an analysis of structural factors but because contemporary historical personages so often resorted to it either to justify or to challenge the status quo. If republican politicians were agonizingly slow to adopt the solution of an income tax before 1914, it is relevant (albeit insufficient) to note one of the reasons why: they were French.

The Income Tax Issue

Traditionally the fiscal system of France rested on an idiosyncratic mixture of direct and indirect taxation. Consolidated during the period 1791–1816, the former were referred to as "the four old maids" (*les quatre vieilles*), the senior and most formidable of which was a land tax (*impôt foncier*) that accounted for nearly half of direct state revenues as late as 1914.[1] Indirect levies fell on raw materials and consumer goods, including alcohol and tobacco, thus serving as a kind of national sales tax that produced increasing income for the state through the economy's slow expansion. At the local level these two financial categories were reflected respectively by the so-called *centimes* (calculated like the *quatre vieilles*) and by the *octrois urbains* (municipal surcharges on consumer items), which were still collected in about 1,500 French towns and cities on the eve of the First World War.[2] If these various modes of taxation were overlapping and confusing, not least for those obliged to contribute to them, they shared one common feature: all were approximations based on public transactions or external signs of wealth. That is, French law condoned no rigorous state inspection of personal fortunes and private finances. Precisely this proved to be the central issue raised by the proposal of an income tax.

In matters financial, Adolphe Thiers was thoroughly conservative. Although he tended, if anything, to favor protectionist tariffs, Thiers had little success in budging the general orientation of free trade inherited from the Second Empire, both because of liberal leanings in the Assembly at Versailles and because of constraints imposed by the most-favored-nation clause of the Frankfurt treaty concluded with Bismarck in May 1871. The only noteworthy fiscal innovation of the Thierist regime was therefore a 3 percent tax on personal property (*valeurs mobilières*) adopted in June 1872. But as the German ambassador Harry von Arnim remarked at the time, that legislation was actually a "weak surrogate" for an income tax to which Thiers remained adamantly opposed.[3] Early proponents of an income tax, such as Henri Germain and Léonce de Lavergne, were consequently thwarted by the first president. Nor, later in the decade, did Léon Gambetta's advocacy of a proportional tax on personal revenue find much resonance. During the 1870s, then, the nation's finances remained focused on modest tariffs, limited taxation, and a balanced budget.[4]

A reconsideration was required in 1879 when imperial Germany completed a decisive shift to protectionism. The details of the French reaction are superfluous here, except to note that an income tax was again excluded. Instead, Gambetta and Léon Say reached a compromise with the new man of the hour, Charles de Freycinet, who thereupon launched his famous program of railway construction and public works. When, after great expense and investment, this massive project suddenly collapsed at the Paris Bourse in 1882, France entered a phase of economic lethargy that lasted until the turn of the century.[5]

Throughout this time the issue of an income tax remained under consideration. One of the first probing summaries of it appeared in the *Revue des deux mondes* in 1880, written by a former minister of finance, Pierre Mathieu-Bodet, who argued that "the necessity of increasing revenues" was placing an intolerable strain on French tax procedures. He reviewed the existing forms of direct taxation, especially criticizing the practice of calculating the value of housing by counting the number of doors and windows, because the poor were thereby constrained to live in hovels without light or fresh air. Mathieu-Bodet advocated separating property from personal revenue for purposes of taxation, but he stopped short of endorsing what was called in atrocious franglais "l'income tax." That term was unjustly scorned in France, he felt, pointing out that versions of it had already been introduced in England, Prussia and other German states, Austria, and Italy. Such a system had "incontestable advantages," but it must not be simply superimposed on the current battery of indirect and direct levies. A major overhaul of the entire fiscal structure would be necessary if an income tax were to succeed.[6]

The case for such an enactment was also pleaded by Charles de Mazade, publisher of the *Revue des deux mondes*, in his regular fortnightly editorials. By 1880 French recovery from the war had noticeably slowed, he wrote, and a decline in exports betrayed signs of economic fatigue. Meanwhile, expenses for public works and schools were annually increasing the national budget by at least 50 million francs: "At every turn we are verging on excess." This deteriorating financial condition was further worsened by the "colossal sums" extracted to finance the Freycinet plan, which Mazade estimated at 4 billion francs, and by outlays necessary to implement the Ferry laws on compulsory primary education. Legitimate as they might be, all of these allocations were becoming "exorbitant," well beyond the available means of the state and the communes. The clear implication was that France would need to adopt a far more stringent fiscal policy, to find significant new sources of revenue, or both.[7]

Such elevated discussion among intellectuals probably counted for little in parliamentary circles, but it both reflected and better defined the dilemma created by the rising cost of government. After Léon Gambetta's political debacle and premature death in 1882, the legislature seemed almost paralyzed, clinging to liberal principles and fiscal austerity. There the matter stood—exception made for a short-lived tax proposal submitted by Paul Bert in 1885—until the movement for social welfare began to gather momentum.

An initial skirmish occurred when Albert Dauphin, minister of finance in the cabinet of René Goblet, submitted a new tax bill in February 1887. Dauphin's wording was so vague, not to say evasive, that his ulterior intentions were called into question. But Goblet frankly dispelled any existing doubts about his colleague's motive: "it is an attempt [to establish] an income tax."[8] After that confession, in the absence of any compelling argument for the necessity of such radical change, Dauphin's motion was allowed to die in the Chamber's committee on finance. By early summer, without ever coming to the floor, it was formally withdrawn by President Jules Grévy.

The following year seemed to augur a different story, and that difference—even though the outcome proved to be identical—was instructive. By October 1888 Goblet had been replaced as premier by Charles Floquet and Dauphin in the Ministry of Finance by Paul Peytral. The new team was determined to press for an income tax, especially after consolidation of Henri Monod's social welfare admin- istration in the Ministry of the Interior. Such taxation, Peytral claimed, was "urgently demanded" by public opinion. He hoped to allay fears that collection procedures would create a serious breach of privacy. The French citizen, he underscored, should be taxed *"without obliging him to make a total declaration of his fortune."* Peytral offered assurances that his ministry would reject such a measure, "even though it is applied in various nations, notably in Germany."9 In De- cember a new finance committee was formed in the Chamber of Deputies. Ominously, its chairman was Jules Roche, who had been an acerbic critic of the Dauphin bill. By Roche's own count, all but two members of the committee opposed Peytral's proposal, and he ex- plained why: "One must recognize that all peoples do not have the same character. In Hamburg, for instance, an income tax exists." But a law that might be acceptable to German burghers would prove unsuitable for the French if it were "inimical to the character of our race." Roche therefore spoke for the majority in rejecting the "in- quisitorial spirit" of the legislative project, which he thought "abso- lutely inapplicable" in France.10 Peytral's disclaimers were to no avail. His denial of any draconian intent was sharply contested by the dep- uties: "Whatever one may say," cried one committeeman, "it is an inquisitorial tax." And when Peytral characterized his bill as only a modest experiment, he was charged with deception because the ini- tial rates of taxation were certain to be raised whenever the govern- ment needed to meet higher expenses for welfare. In reply, he con- ceded that the proposed law should render the republic capable of "responding to any necessity." In the end, however, Peytral was left with the lonesome argument that an income tax was functioning in neighboring countries and was therefore feasible for France. For rea- sons that Roche had already made plain, that point was insufficient to shake the committee from its negative stance.11

At this juncture national politics confirmed what had as yet only been writ small in a single committee room of the Chamber of Depu- ties. A new round of parliamentary elections in 1889 dealt a setback to the Radical party and effectively created a four-year hiatus in its efforts to obtain tax reform. We may therefore take leave for that interim, except to note the continued references in various reform bodies to the international context. France was not a fiscal island, least of all in treating social problems for which the solution was bound to be expensive. This basic proposition and its rebuttal remained the same. When, for example, Paul Guieysse pointed out in the Chamber's social insurance committee (CAPS) that Germany was dealing with the welfare question on a much broader scale than France, Louis Ricard retorted that the "French temperament" was repelled by "domestic inquisitions" and that all attempts to pass an income tax were doomed for that reason.[12] Multiplication of such instances here would be possible but supererogatory.

Another continuity of the period before 1893 was equally evident and closely related. Because of social welfare measures incorporated in the law on free medical care, pressure to increase public revenues was intensified. This phenomenon was particularly discernible in discussions of the reformist Conseil Supérieur de l'Assistance Publique, where discomfort became more pronounced with the facile assumption that the CSAP should draft legislative provisions regardless of their potential cost. The difficulty of that approach was its flagrantly apolitical character. What was decided in Paris would never play in Perpignan unless it could be financed. Because it would be folly to depend on the communes to raise local *centimes* to pay for additional costs, the obvious solution seemed to most CSAP members to be some revenue scheme like those abroad. As the former mayor of Reims, Henri-Alfred Henrot, said, "I do not see why an income tax does not exist in France, whereas it has been established in England and Germany." After all, he added, the expenses of social reform would somehow have to be met, even if "it would change our habits."[13] This consequence was exactly what French legislators were still reluctant to advocate. They were gradually coming to concede that the state must intervene to aid the needy, but they were as yet unwilling to alter the tax structure fundamentally in order to do so. Accordingly, the medical assistance bill of 1893 was passed into law without adequate provisions to pay for its potential cost.

The Alcohol Question

Deregulation of the sale of alcoholic beverages was widely hailed in 1880 as a liberal triumph. Restrictions on the licensing of *débits de boissons*—bars, bistrots, and cafés—had been inherited from the Second Empire and maintained by republican regimes under conservative presidents Thiers and MacMahon. The new law could therefore be viewed as an emphatic rejection of state interference with the French right to unrestrained conviviality. Hence alcohol now became big business. In the next quarter of a century the number of legal drinking establishments rose from 354,000 to nearly 470,000; and these, by official count in 1904, were supplied by 8,894 distilleries, 3,382 breweries, and over 30,000 wholesale distributors. France thereby provided a bar for every eight-five inhabitants or, more meaningfully, one drinking locale per thirty adult males. Consumption climbed apace. Statistics varied, but we may fairly estimate that the French wine market doubled from 1850 to 1900 and that the sale of hard liquors quadrupled.[14]

For more than a decade after 1880 alcohol was not a major public issue. Records of the Academy of Medicine showed only a flickering interest among physicians about the deleterious effects of drink on personal and public health. One member, Dr. Étienne Lancereaux, several times rose to challenge the popular notion that drinking, especially of wine, was actually nutritious and fortifying. He warned that alcoholic excess would only produce the premature senility of individuals and the debility of nations, "for their decline is assured." But such caveats had little visible effect on public comportment or conventional wisdom.[15]

At the same time there was frank recognition that excise on alcoholic beverages was a staple and indeed indispensable source of public revenue. In the Academy, Théophile Roussel calculated the annual income from this form of indirect taxation at 400 million francs. He recognized that it was the Academy's assignment to weigh medical questions and to leave the national budget to the cabinet and parliament. Still, if increasing consumption of alcohol was good for finances, it was ultimately bad for health. This fact, Roussel admitted, was "a great and deplorable contradiction."[16] It was nonetheless impossible to detect any early movement, within the Academy of Medicine or without, to curtail the production and distribution of alcoholic beverages. Rather, the opinion developed that the state should only take steps to encourage the consumption of wine at the expense of *eaux-de-vie* and other noxious drinks. This principle was built into the taxation proposals submitted in 1888 by Minister of Finance Peytral, who urged lowering some levies on so-called hygienic beverages and raising them on the rest. We saw, however, that this bill bogged down in the parliamentary process and had to be withdrawn.[17]

Following passage of the 1893 law on free medical aid for the poor, the need for an increase of tax revenues became imperative. There were three ostensible ways to obtain them: by raising the excise on alcohol, through introducing an income tax, or with some mixture of both. In February 1894 an omnibus tax reform bill, drafted by Gaston Guillemet and cosponsored by more than one hundred French deputies, was presented to the Chamber. The self-avowed principle of the measure was "if not to suppress alcoholism, at least considerably to attenuate its dangers." Although financial income was allegedly secondary to this concern, Guillemet estimated that annual revenues through augmented taxation of alcoholic beverages could be raised to 900 million francs, thereby more than doubling their current level, through the establishment of a state monopoly on distillation and distribution.[18] When this far-reaching proposal encountered fierce opposition, it was eclipsed by an alternative bill from the deputy Henry Fleury-Ravarin, who dismissed any thought of a state monopoly and advocated a milder policy of "hygienic control" on alcohol. He compared this scheme to regulations adopted recently by the German Reichstag (after a similar failure by Bismarck to secure a state monopoly in 1887). "This seems to us extremely interesting," Fleury-Ravarin noted, "because Germany is to our knowledge the only country that has attempted to establish legislation analogous to that which we propose." Its implementation in Germany was still defective, but "we persist in believing the principle to be excellent." Thus, he concluded, "in borrowing their idea, we may prevent ourselves from falling into the errors committed by our neighbors."[19]

Parallel to these complex deliberations, the finance committee of the Chamber was also considering a separate bill on tax reform prepared by Godefroy Cavaignac. Most of the other states of Europe, Cavaignac argued, were moving to a progressive system of taxation.

Paramount among them was Prussia, which in 1891 had realized "a quite remarkable effort of internal reorganization that should inspire the most serious reflection." The key to the Prussian example was a proportional tax based on obligatory declaration of income. Although Cavaignac mentioned several other variations on this theme —England, Austria, the Netherlands, Italy, and certain cantons in Switzerland—his attention remained fixed on the Prussian analogy.[20] In early November 1894 Cavaignac was elected chairman of the Chamber's finance committee, where he continued to call for "the very prudent experiment" of a Prussian-style income tax. The extensive minutes of his group and its subcommittees constitute a record of protracted dispute resulting in split votes on a variety of specific issues: 11 to 10, 13 to 7, 7 to 6, 8 to 6, 12 to 11, and so on.[21] When on 28 November a plenary session of the finance committee, by a margin of one ballot, rejected a motion to adopt Cavaignac's conception, he abruptly resigned. Then a week later, reassured that the committee's decision was only provisional, he resumed his chairmanship. Yet the truth was that his initiative was blocked and his ephemeral prominence was ended.[22] The obituary of the Cavaignac bill was pronounced in October 1895 by the new minister of finance, Alexandre Ribot, who deemed it to be too radical in its requirement of an obligatory declaration of personal revenue. Ribot admitted that "such is the procedure in Prussia, where one encounters the classical type of a global income tax." But as for France, he said, the state's "inquisitorial investigations" of private fortune would surely be "intolerable for our national character."[23]

These tergiversations set a political precedent for the unstable years following and, in fact, for the entire period until 1914. Much like the question about compulsory declaration of communicable diseases to public health officials, the major problem with tax reform was the mandatory reporting of private income to state inspectors, which would be necessary to assure its feasibility and fairness. Those who favored such a measure habitually cited foreign models, above all that of Prussia, while those who opposed it invariably insisted on the inviolability of French liberties and customs. For example, after the initial confrontation between Cavaignac and Ribot, a second major fiscal reform initiative was launched in February 1896 by the succeeding minister of finance, Paul Doumer. He supported "a profound reform of our financial system" following "the formula adopted by the majority of our neighboring countries." Doumer's tenure in the cabinet proved to be brief, however, and by that summer his tax bill was denounced by yet another minister of finance, Georges Cochery, as "a means incompatible with our national character and the condition of our mores." Echoing Ribot's earlier rejection of Cavaignac, Cochery dismissed Doumer's bill by maintaining that France needed "an *evolution* and not a *revolution*."[24]

Similarly, on the eve of the new century, a third round of altercation developed between the deputy (and later minister of commerce) L.-L. Klotz and Paul Peytral (who had accepted the portfolio of finance in 1898). Klotz, a disciple of Léon Gambetta, openly identified his own income tax bill with those of Cavaignac and Doumer before him. But Peytral refused to support administrative appraisals of personal wealth except on the basis of "external signs" such as rental values or the retention of servants, horses, and carriages. He consequently favored direct taxation "without vexation or inquisition of any sort."[25]

These repeated cycles of conflict about the nature of reform brought the republic little closer to a solution, even while the cost of welfare continued to mount. All the more, therefore, was the importance of revenues from alcohol consumption magnified. The connection between these two factors and the dilemma they represented—that "great and deplorable contradiction," as Théophile Roussel had once remarked—were perfectly apparent. A conspicuous but by no means unique example was Georges Cochery, whose opposition in 1896 to a Prussian type of income tax has been recorded. At that time, while still minister of finance, he introduced a bill to control distillation of alcoholic beverages and alcohol-based industrial products. He stressed the necessity of strengthening the state's grip on one of France's foremost health hazards, "which threatens to compromise the very future of the race." But he also acknowledged that the government could not countenance legislation that would limit the substantial revenues gathered through the taxation of liquor sales. Above all, the alcohol industry represented an integral element of the French economy. The livelihood of millions, as well as their pleasure, depended on it. Cochery thus ended on an equivocal note: "it is an extremely complex question impinging on very large interests."[26]

An intervention by the Paris Chamber of Commerce illustrated Cochery's point and exposed the difficulties of obtaining a state monopoly. In a report submitted to parliament, the Chamber of Commerce argued that in France, "a country of vines and fruits," no one phase of alcohol consumption could be controlled without adopting a totally repressive system of regulation. Some reformers wished merely to limit distribution, whereas others advocated restrictions solely on distillation. But distribution of alcohol could not be effectively separated from production, the report contended. To curtail the sale of alcoholic beverages without simultaneously cutting back on production would be to create a huge surplus that was sure to provoke more fraud and illicit traffic. Yet to restrain production in certain regions or by specific growers and distillers would require tyrannical enforcement of rules that would infringe on individual liberties. Thus it would be far better to respect "the natural laws of commerce," in other words, to sanction the supply and demand of a free-market economy. Because effective alcohol regulation must be total, there was cause to reject any state intervention. Besides, the report concluded on a peremptory note, "it is impossible."[27]

The sequel after 1900 was deadlock and confusion. In part, these paltry results were the work of lobbying by such groups as the National Federation of Beverage Retailers and the Union of French Brewers, whose representatives appeared at parliamentary committee hearings to sketch a lurid picture of the devastating effects to be expected of excessive state regulation. But the basic problem remained a lack of legislative consensus. The implicit contradiction between the needs of health and of finance—in the absence of a breakthrough on the income tax issue—was compounded by more technical disputes about the relative merits of regulating the production and distribution of alcoholic beverages. In addition, there were confounding legal problems. If, for instance, certain bars or bistrots were to be closed, how would they be selected and expropriated? Alas, the complications seemed endless.[28]

On a single regulatory matter French politicians and physicians could reach virtual unanimity before the First World War: an absolute ban on absinthe. The medical profession was categorical about the damaging effects of this concentrated green drink; and both the Chamber of Deputies and the Senate were inclined to forbid its sale.

Yet this beverage, too, had its lobby of growers and retailers, who argued their case with persistence and were able to delay legislative action until 1915. Even if we were to regard this enactment as a belated concession to the campaign for state regulation, rather than as an extraordinary wartime measure, it represented an interdiction of only one very small sector of the nation's global alcohol production. Moreover, it culminated less obviously in the context of alcohol regulation than as part of a movement to prohibit open purchases of certain addictive drugs. Thus many antiregulationists could be persuaded to make an exception for absinthe by classifying it along with opium, morphine, and cocaine.[29]

The same rigorous standard was not extended to the rest of France's alcohol industry. The influential wine and liquor lobbies were undaunted and continued with success to oppose reform. When Jules Siegfried attempted to rally support for new regulations on liquor licensing in 1913, he was met by protests from an organization elaborately entitled the Congress of the National Federation of Beverage Retailers, Restaurateurs, and Hotel Proprietors. Appearing before a legislative committee of the Chamber of Deputies assembled to consider the Siegfried proposal, one lobbyist claimed to represent more than 200 affiliates of the congress engaged in the distribution of alcoholic beverages. "Our federation cannot accept your project, which is imperfect," he told the committee bluntly; and he added a plea: "We ask you not to legislate hastily." With that, truly, the Third Republic could not be charged.[30]

The Conundrum of National Character

Speculations about national character are old and plentiful. This is not the place to fabricate a general theory, nor to flay one. But as we have already taken frequent note of references to French *moeurs*, either by the French themselves or by those who observed their behavior at close range, it is perhaps useful to address directly the elusive problem of public morality. Although any historian must hesitate to generalize about the attitude of an entire people, it may be legitimate to gather from available sources some scattered allusions to the character of the French nation and to ask what bearing they had on the development of public welfare before the First World War.[31]

First let it be noted that the self-evaluation of the French bore close resemblance to the image formed of them by foreigners. This fact was particularly striking in the case of German representatives who dealt with the republican leadership, beginning with Bismarck's disparaging reaction to the rhetorical style of Adolphe Thiers: it was, the chancellor once wrote, like the thick layer of foam on a glass of beer that one had to swallow before reaching the liquid.[32] Other German observers were given to uttering similar asides about the French people in general. Thus the picture emanating from across the Rhine was much as we might expect: the Germans were direct and disciplined, the French were not. Probably most other Europeans thought (and continue to think) of the two peoples in similar terms. This cliché, after all, provided the simplest explanation of German triumph and French defeat in the war of 1870. It conveniently separated victors from vanquished.

The French themselves tended to believe firmly in theories of national character, if we judge by the many public statements already cited. They, too, were inclined to draw a sharp contrast between themselves and the German people, which was naturally the most pertinent of comparisons after 1870. But the self-depiction of the French was more nuanced. Granted, the Germans were better disciplined. The manner in which the French differed from them, however, could be judged in a more or a less flattering light, depending on the predisposition of the observer. At their worst the French were egoistic, unruly, vacillating, and disorganized. But at their best they were individualistic, original, nonconformist, and stout defenders of personal liberty. Such conflicting self-conceptions did not always follow ideological lines. Besides, it was altogether possible to combine them into what might be called a patriotic despair, as if the French were somehow being punished for their virtues.[33]

Tidy configurations were therefore precluded. Yet at least four attitudinal clusters may be identified that suggested the inherent suppositions brought by the French to the issues of welfare and taxation. None of these factors was uniquely French. Yet their peculiar combination was characteristic of the now prevailing climate in which republican social reform was nascent.

A PRONOUNCED SENSE OF SOCIAL HIERARCHY

To begin with the most obvious fact of public life, French society was highly structured. That this reality was so rarely made explicit by reformers or their opponents probably indicated a tacit understanding among them that required no mention. With few exceptions, after all, French politicians were middle-aged, middle-class men with a classical education and a host of common assumptions. As if by an act of nature, they constituted an elite. Gender and class distinctions were therefore pervasive in the public sphere even when unspoken.

Women, as we earlier saw, were usually regarded as objects of various welfare measures intended to raise France's sagging demographic profile. Suffrage for females—still less their full participation in legislative reforms that so directly affected them—was literally inconceivable to most of the men involved. Moralistic attitudes about the "fault" of unwed mothers were often expressed, seldom challenged. It was taken for granted that most women should be paid less than men and that they should generally be assigned to menial labor without any prospect of advancement. Women were thought to be flighty by nature and lacking in independence of character. They were physically, intellectually, sexually, and morally weak—and hence they were often victims of their own frailty. The fuss about wet-nursing, the controversy over foundlings (whether to abolish the *tours*), and the ugly rumors of abortion and infanticide were all related to these male perceptions. So was prostitution, associated with venereal disease in a manner suggesting that syphilis originated with women rather than men.[34] In France there appeared to be, as a member of the Academy of Medicine put it, too much "liberty of seduction," to which French women easily fell prey—whence the uncommonly high rate of illegitimacy. And illegitimacy, in turn, meant an elevated toll of infant mortality. Other nations had comparable problems, to be sure, but none of them displayed the same demographic incapacity as the French people, whose lasting infecundity seemed to be a special national trait.[35]

Workers fared no better. Like the poor in general, they were thought by bourgeois reformers to be "difficult, unstable, and given to constant complaining."[36] Some presumptuously demanded the *right* to public assistance, rather than accepting it meekly as a latter-day form of alms. The congenital rowdiness of the French lower orders, so it was said, impeded a solution to the shortage of working-class housing, because publicly funded dwellings were likely to be trashed by their proletarian residents. The disorderly and destructive behavior of French workers in this regard was sometimes contrasted with the respect for property evinced by their German counterparts. The laboring class also had a manifest weakness for drink. Alcoholism had long been widespread in the laboring population and was alleged to have been responsible for all manner of excess during the Paris Commune. Since then, the proclivity for heavy drinking had only worsened in France, more than elsewhere, with the predictable ruination of the nation's health. There was a popular saying that "lung disease is caught at the bar" (*la phtisie se prend sur le zinc*); and estimates were that at least 70 percent of tuberculous patients were alcoholics. The impression deepened that workers were basically infantile and incapable of "prudence" (*prévoyance*). Thus they were wanting in precisely that concern for their future so essential to welfare through self-help.[37]

If those who debated reform usually held these views, consciously or unconsciously, they could still disagree about the correct inferences to be drawn from them. Committed reformers looked upon the inferior estates of French society with benevolent paternalism. What the poor, the weak, and the afflicted could not do for themselves should be done for them; the state therefore had a clear moral duty to intervene on their behalf. Opponents of extensive reforms were no less ready to raise questions of morality, but with contrary conclusions. Why should huge sums of public wealth be expended on derelicts and drunkards who had willfully precipitated their own degeneration? And why must upstanding citizens, who had worked steadfastly to secure a personal fortune, be forced to share it with fallen women and whores, especially when virtuous mothers were neglected by welfare agencies interested solely in cases of illegitimacy?[38]

Such opposing contentions and objections, to repeat, were not exclusively French. But they had particular urgency in a nation that was arguably the most sexist and alcoholic in western Europe, and where, for reasons that defied totally rational explanation, the birth rate was by far the lowest. It took but a small step to posit that French national character was somehow a contributing factor.

A SUSPICION OF INSTITUTIONS

While France has been among the most centralized of modern states, observers have often remarked on a penchant of the French people to mistrust government officials and to worry about what "they" might perpetrate in the name of a national administration.[39] We have seen how an inveterate hostility toward public affairs could be extended, especially among the rural population, to hospital care and to medical practice. Although not without a rational kernel, the French aversion to institutionalization was perceived by reformers as a paranoia with which they had to reckon. From the standpoint of welfare, a major part of the problem was the extreme importance attached to the confidentiality between physicians and patients, analogous to that between priests and parishioners. The doctor's office was a kind of confessional, to which state health officials should have no access. Therefore attempts to implement compulsory declaration of certain diseases were frequently met with a stolid resistance that caused reformers to back off.

This attitude affected government policy toward the construction of popular sanatoria. The rapid expansion of the sanatorium movement in Germany around 1900 had no parallel in France, partly for political reasons that we shall explore, but also because many French vehemently objected to institutional regulations that required an individual to be separated from family and friends. To a lesser extent, this may also have inhibited the establishment of inebriation centers for the treatment of chronic alcoholics.[40] In both instances moralism played a part. To be committed to an institution was to accept a social stigma and the risk that one's family would be humiliated or ostracized. The same, of course, applied to workhouses and prisons. The theory that beggars or vagabonds could be rehabilitated through forced labor was not implausible, but workhouses—despite several attempts at pilot projects after 1870—never caught on in France. They were commonly dismissed as a fiasco of English welfare unsuitable for the French. Prisons were not usually considered as welfare institutions, although they did permit the separation of criminal types from others. One curious twist, however, was created by incidents of the poor attempting to gain admission to warm prisons in the winter months, even if it meant deliberately smashing windows with rocks in order to provoke their own arrest.[41]

Whatever the public institution, there was an intimate connection between morals and money. They were inseparable at the time and they cannot be neatly disaggregated in retrospect. Most French people (not alone) had no desire to pay higher taxes in order to employ more government inspectors to meddle in their private affairs. Such objections were registered whenever a government official complained about unsanitary food served in a Catholic *crèche* or the lack of safety measures in an artisan's workshop. To many, inevitably, the public sphere seemed in such instances to be impinging unduly on the private. On a grander scale, too, this defensive attitude bore on questions about the bureaucratic structure of welfare: whether new administrative offices should be founded in every French department or whether public health and hygiene should just be left to the prefects. In late nineteenth-century France, less often seemed better.

A TENDENCY TO EXCLUSIVITY

Liberalism had tenacious roots in the ordinary French family. A guarded stance against external interference applied not only to institutions but to outsiders in general. In their self-perception the French were exceedingly generous with their own but penurious toward others. The family—or, by extension, the local community—was a discrete clan with its own special rituals, hidden complicities, and unwritten code of ethics. To these a stranger was denied any direct access.

Such a generalized portrait might, of course, suit any number of social units. We can only record that the French family was among them and that a sort of tribal mentality was common. This trait was a repeated source of frustration for Henri Monod's Bureau of Public Health and Hygiene because of the reluctance of local communes to comply with national regulations. If peasants were becoming Frenchmen after 1870, they seemed to be doing so at an infuriatingly slow pace. It was an old story: if public assistance was left to the communes, they would refuse to take action; but if attempts were made to enforce uniform measures, local officials would complain and balk. Thus optional programs were usually ineffectual and compulsory programs often proved unenforceable. Monod constantly despaired about the lack of cooperation from mayors and municipal councils, who appeared more concerned to maintain local prerogatives than to improve sanitation and health care.[42]

Likewise, the most adamant objection to the introduction of an income tax was its "inquisitorial" nature. The thought was horrifying that state inspectors should physically enter private lodgings or businesses to check the veracity of fiscal records. This defensiveness was probably typical above all of the wealthy bourgeoisie, who had most to fear and most to lose from strict controls on the accumulation of personal wealth. Yet it would be a mistake to ascribe this attitude to a single class. Prejudice against tax collection was (and remains) a popular phenomenon transcending social status. Dr. Henri-Alfred Henrot put it best: the underlying problem was that "the communal electors refuse to support councillors who threaten them with new taxes."[43] This bedrock political reality restrained efforts to innovate public health reforms, which were constantly forced to swim upstream, as Charles Dupuy said, "against habits and against customs."[44]

In this connection it is proper to add a word about racism. The tendency to exclude "strangers" undoubtedly existed in France, but one should guard against the overinterpretation of random statements. On numerous occasions, of which several have been cited, speakers arose in political meetings to reject compulsory measures of social welfare in France on the grounds that they were incompatible with "the habits and needs of our race."[45] Such remarks were ordinarily intended to establish that the French were different from the Germans (or, far less frequently, the English), not racially superior to them. In saying so, those who opposed reform were attempting to meet the argument that progressive taxation and mandatory welfare were feasible because they functioned successfully abroad. Their most disarming and rhetorically unassailable rebuttal was to insist that the French were not Germans. Repeated many times over, this contextual usage of the term "race" was simply a coded reference to familiar distinctions of ethnic diversity, whereby the Gallic and Germanic peoples were assumed to have separate identities and thus to require different modes of governance. There was in these traditional notions much of Tacitus and little of the viciousness of twentieth-century racism.

That said, one cannot pass in complete silence over a visible smudge of xenophobia that rose to the surface of the Belle Epoque. Agitation against foreign workers was not uncommon in the industrial cities, and overt discrimination often touched Italians, Spaniards, and Belgians as well as Germans. Thus such prejudice did not derive solely from resentment about the lost war of 1870 or from fears of overbearing German military and economic might. It was xenophobic. We need not belabor the implications of the Dreyfus

Affair in order to add that anti-Semitism also contributed a racist component to the rest. For the time being, with the future hidden, it was still possible to regard France as the European nation most allergic to strangers, foreigners, and Jews.[46]

AN ASSERTION OF INDIVIDUALITY

Everything added up. For better and worse, the French considered themselves a people lacking in collective discipline, loving privacy, honoring confidentiality, maintaining integrity of the community and the family. In sum, France was a nation of individualists. No generalization about the French people has been more durable or better earned. It might almost appear, after all the tumult of the early nineteenth century, that in the chaotic parliamentary regime of the Third Republic the French had finally found the government they deserved. At last, one could plausibly conclude, the national character and the nation-state had been properly fused.

All conjectures about the collective identity of nearly 40 million diverse people are necessarily tenuous. But they do not seem altogether fanciful when examining the record of welfare reform in France. Just as art may simultaneously reflect and distort nature, political myth bears a refracted similarity to historical reality, and the two are often difficult to distinguish. The incessant complaints of reformers about the intractability of French public opinion cannot be dismissed as pure invention. Otherwise we should have to suppose that French individualism was nothing more than a convenient fiction to excuse repeated legislative failures. The contention that the republican political structure itself was defective and partly to blame is undoubtedly correct. But the lament of reformers was directed less against the edifice of government itself than at the public morality forming its foundation. Why was there for so long in France no mandatory smallpox vaccination, no effective clearance of slums, no movement for popular sanatoria, no income tax? The ultimate answer lay in the convictions and conventions of an entire people.[47]

Fiscal Reform and Religious Strife

Church leaders regarded the establishment of the Third Republic with apprehension, and for good reason. Stories about pillaging, personal attacks, and the confiscation of church property during the

Great Revolution were of course known to everyone. When that spectacle was revived by the Paris Commune, along with frank demands for the separation of church and state, the Roman Catholic hierarchy recoiled into a defensive posture and quickly made its peace with the regime of Adolphe Thiers. The first president's enforced resignation in May 1873 was not a threat to the Vatican, because the succeeding government under Marshal MacMahon was, as advertised, equally dedicated to the maintenance of moral order. But radicalization of the Municipal Council of Paris soon renewed fears of secular aggression, especially when Georges Clemenceau assumed presidency of the CMP in 1875. At his inauguration Clemenceau unfurled the banner of anticlericalism.[48] The earliest stage of that struggle does not directly concern us here. Let only two of its salient features be noted. First, it occurred at a time when the Vatican was preoccupied by the German Kulturkampf. France was thus temporarily insulated from the most strident arena of religious conflict during most of the 1870s, because French anticlericals could not risk a charge of playing the dupe for Bismarck. Second, the school issue, around which the initial debate in France centered, nonetheless proved to be an irrepressible source of contention. With passage of the Ferry educational reforms after 1879, the French Kulturkampf therefore erupted and began to displace the German controversy as the focus of religious dispute in Europe.[49]

A second phase of altercation can be dated from 1883 with the appointment of Eugène-René Poubelle as the new prefect of the Seine. Poubelle was brought to that post by the government with malice aforethought to throttle the pretensions of the CMP to dictate the pace of secularization. Attention meanwhile shifted from schools to hospitals—that is, from public education to public health. A resolution adopted by the CMP to dismiss all religious personnel from the staff of Paris hospices and hospitals was annulled by Poubelle in 1885, along with several other municipal enactments, on grounds that the Council had thereby "exceeded the limits of its competence."[50] The prefect's stance was strengthened by a petition, signed by 1,157 patients at the suburban hospital of Ivry, requesting that Catholic nuns be retained there as nurses. This incident touched off an acrimonious discussion in the CMP that ended with a motion, adopted by 75 to 11, that condemned the national regime for "not taking greater account of the wishes of the Parisian populace and of the Council in the question of secularization."[51] The result was to return the issue of separation of church and state to the political agenda, where it remained for the next twenty years. "It is certain," one municipal councillor warned, "that the battle between the clericals and us is no longer a latent struggle. It is a war."[52]

Wars are expensive. Frank recognition of that fact was one explanation for the government's restraint. The Conseil de Surveillance, charged with administrative control of the capital's public health system, took due note of the rising costs of replacing religious with lay personnel, an estimated 250,000 francs in the three years from 1885 to 1887. Yet this body was willing to approve of the CMP's policy providing the city would pay its own bills. There were also legal complications, however, as in the case of the Hôtel-Dieu and the hospital of Saint Louis in Paris, both of which enjoyed a special legal status dating back to the Old Regime. Repeated motions by the majority of the CMP to move ahead were therefore stalled for years while litigation was left dangling in the Conseil d'État.[53] Polemics meanwhile continued. Poubelle was castigated as a "defender of nuns" by some members of the CMP, whose spokesman Henri Rousselle urged "immediate [and] complete secularization" of hospitals.[54] The conservative minority of the CMP countered not only with the customary legal and financial objections but with a moral caveat as well: leftist ideological cant was taking precedence over health care of the population. Municipal councillor Georges Berry, a staunch Catholic, confronted the majority with his worries that their "hatred for everything that concerns God [may] bring the ruin of public welfare." By 1890, it is accurate to say, the two sides had been staked out.[55]

Yet much of the following decade was spent marking time. Heretofore confined mostly to Paris, the secularization controversy became national in scope as its epicenter wandered from the CMP to the Conseil Supérieur de l'Assistance Publique. In the process, questions that began as models of simplicity—how soon can nursing nuns be shown to the door of the Hôtel-Dieu?—assumed a more complex form. Above all, the enormous fiscal implications of anticlericalism became clearer. Rhetorical denials of added cost were often repeated by reformers, but they acquired a hollow ring as the facts became known. A good example was the clinic at Berck-sur-Mer, maintained on the Atlantic coast by the Paris municipal government to treat urban children suffering from consumption and other respiratory ailments. In real terms, the policy of secularization meant recruiting, training, moving, and housing a staff of nurses and orderlies brought in to replace religious personnel. During the summer of 1892 the Conseil de Surveillance reviewed this project and approved a special subsidy of 18,000 francs to fund it.[56] As a consequence, the last nun left Berck-sur-Mer that November. In the following spring, however, Poubelle presented the CMP with a bill for precisely 55,922 francs to meet the initial conversion costs, more than three times the original allocation.[57] Added maintenance expenses were more difficult to gauge within the total welfare budget. A municipal finance expert stated that the annual increment (mostly in salaries) because of secularization in the city of Paris had reached nearly 200,000 francs by 1892, although he admitted that other estimates placed the figure as high as 800,000 francs. Such numbers were still round and rather abstract, but it was already evident that the precedent of Paris, if extended to the entire nation, would create a major new strain on the finances of the republic.[58]

The future of charity was concomitantly thrust into doubt. How far could an anticlerical campaign go without disrupting the flow of funds through private donations and legacies? A complete census of charitable institutions had never been conducted, but France was known to possess a vast network of them supported by philanthropic contributions. In its debates the CSAP remained well aware of the significance of private charity and the delicate nature of its relationship to public assistance. The problem was, as one member obliquely said, that charitable enterprises often tended to be "jealous" and "narrow."[59] Translated into political terms, this meant that most of them were controlled by the Catholic church. Thus the effort to promote cooperation between private and public welfare was undercut by threats of a separation between church and state. This stark contradiction was the central theme of dozens of meetings, inside of government and out, where reform was debated.

Before 1900 the official policy of successive republican cabinets was to pacify church-state relations and to sponsor only "concordi-tary legislation."[60] But Henri Monod's Bureau of Public Health and Hygiene was far less fastidious and urged increased state intervention to monitor private institutions such as orphanages that were suspected of abusing or exploiting children in their care.[61] There were rumors that private donors would retaliate by closing their purse. As Henri-Alfred Henrot remarked, "an excessive number of rich people do not like the republican government."[62] The Baron d'Haussonville spoke for them, arguing that public assistance should be operative only in instances when private charity was demonstrably insufficient.[63] Reformers naturally took the contrary position that religious alms were a relic of times past and that Catholic institutions were both self-seeking and untrustworthy; hence they must be carefully watched. So while one side denounced the "tyrannical demands" of the state, the other charged that "incalculable miseries" were being created by the church. These exchanges became so heated in the CSAP that Monod found it necessary to issue explicit denials that there existed any "plot against private charity" or that stricter measures of surveillance by state inspectors might be only a prelude to the "confiscation of charitable institutions." Yet these disclaimers could not fail to stimulate the anxieties they were intended to allay. At the least they showed that the ultimate consequences of the French Kulturkampf were increasingly easy to articulate.[64]

The impact of the Dreyfus Affair is difficult to assess with exactitude. For a time after the arrest of Alfred Dreyfus in October 1894 that episode distracted public attention away from the religious question and permitted the church to participate in a brief conservative resurgence. But once the case began to break and events were set into motion that led to the pardon of Dreyfus in 1899, anticlericalism regained its thrust. A contemporaneous incident, apparently unrelated, accentuated this pattern. At Nancy a news story appeared on the exploited labor of children boarded in the orphanage of Bon Pasteur. Reformers promptly seized on this "scandal" as confirmation of their suspicions about the unaccountability of Catholic charities. The CSAP convened to draft tighter restrictions on the state's licensing of private institutions and to urge increased latitude for state inspectors investigating them. The same chords were vibrated in the press, notably by Paul Strauss, who editorialized that "the necessity of a regular [and] permanent inspection is indisputable."[65]

After 1900 the active campaign to separate church and state resumed. Visitors to an international welfare conference in Paris were taken aback by the vehemence displayed between the respective proponents of private charity and public welfare in France. The famous German philanthropist, Dr. Emil Münsterberg, later recalled "the most ardent and passionate polemics" within the French delegation, which contrasted so conspicuously with the harmonious climate of the Kaiserreich.[66] Münsterberg's lengthy study of the German welfare system, translated into French in 1902 under the spare title of *L'assistance*, was meanwhile reviewed by a frequent contributor to the *Revue philanthropique*, Louis Rivière. While the French tried to cover their internal discord with "platonic resolutions," Rivière wrote, "Münsterberg shows us how it functions in Germany" and how factions there had succeeded in "substituting for passions stirred by the Kulturkampf an atmosphere of peace, tolerance, and public tranquility." Rivière hoped France would profit from "the example of Germany" to restore religious harmony.[67]

But there was little chance of that once the cabinets of René Waldeck-Rousseau and Émile Combes began to transform anticlerical agitation into government policy. Legislation of stricter state controls over church establishments, following recommendations of the CSAP, was forthcoming despite protests from Catholic deputies that it constituted "a veritable seizure by the state of private charity."[68] The author of this bill, Jean-Baptiste Bienvenu-Martin, brushed aside such objections by citing the precedent of the Prussian law of 1879 on regulation of philanthropic enterprises. Demonstrably, he contended, a lack of controls allowed exploitation of child labor and thereby created competition for certain industries. "Based on that factor, and by the argument drawn from foreign legislation, we may discount criticism about aggressive innovation and abusive state intervention." As he threw his government's support to Bienvenu-Martin's bill in October 1902, Prime Minister Combes followed the same line of reasoning in advocating "permanent inspection" and "serious protection" for all those under the care of religious charities.[69]

We need not recapitulate the ensuing conflicts that led to the final act of separation in 1905. It is worthwhile, however, to confirm that financial considerations were never far removed from them. Rabid advocates of secularization wanted to eliminate religious institutions entirely from municipal and state budgets, but they had to worry about Catholic sensibilities and the real danger that private charities might withhold funding and thereby compound the burden of public assistance. Not for the first time, disputes also raged about the overlapping spheres of public and private welfare benefits: if Catholic citizens were recipients of financial aid from church sources, should they simultaneously draw the same state subsidy as the needy who were accorded no religious charity?[70] Without a doubt the most disputatious proposal of this sort was to convert Catholic monasteries and convents into tuberculosis sanatoria. That measure, its author argued, would provide "an immediate remedy" for an obvious lacuna in French health care.[71]

From a fiscal standpoint such legislative squabbles were clear evidence of one of France's most basic political problems: the parliament's refusal to modify the nation's tax structure in order to generate revenues sufficient to underwrite welfare reform. When discussion in the Chamber's finance committee returned to the urgency of an income tax, the concurrent religious controversy left no room for the compromises necessary to enact it. Joseph Caillaux, temporizing as ever, therefore suggested that the taxation question be deferred until the separation of church and state was accomplished. Although the deputies present could not gainsay the advisability of further delay, they were openly dismayed about the repeated frustration of fiscal reform. One of them questioned whether the committee's efforts were not being entirely wasted in charades: "We are the laughing stock of the country."[72]

The ultimate act of separation in 1905 neither diminished the republic's financial deficit nor ended its ideological discordance. The fate of private charity remained moot, and the daily reality often went unchanged. A discussion in the CSAP of problems in the staffing of mental asylums was illustrative. Complaints were registered that too many physicians remained beholden to the church and refused cooperation with state inspectors. One member caustically described the scene: "When you ask them, they reply: 'The Mother-Superior will give you complete information.' But she never does." Reformers thus found plenty of reason to grumble about religious obstructionism, to which they ascribed blame for statistics alleging that the German recovery rate for mental patients was two or three times higher than that of the French.[73]

An appropriate summation for this history was formulated by Henri Monod shortly before his retirement in 1906: "The pressure toward secularization could not fail to invade the domain of charity."[74] If that development was indeed inevitable, its effects were mixed. They were perhaps salutary for public welfare insofar as the confiscation of some church property may have abetted an increase in the number of *bureaux de bienfaisance*. But there were losses as well as gains, especially for patients whose nursing nuns were unceremoniously expelled from hospitals throughout France. The cooperation of private charity and public assistance thus remained tenuous, while the cost of health care continued to climb.

A Matter of Money

Only after 1900 did a clear distinction begin to emerge between state aid for the poor (*assistance publique*) and social insurance (*assurance sociale*). The latter notion, imported from Germany, remained ambiguous but was increasingly centered on the question of pensions for the aged. Even though reformist orators and their opponents often confused the terms, it is crucial to note the differences in principle and to distinguish carefully between the laws of 1905 and 1910.

In essence the 1905 reform bill was designed to extend existing measures of free medical assistance to the poor, which had been on the books since 1893. Henri Monod first announced that intention in his speech to an international welfare congress gathered at the Sorbonne in 1900. This initiative was supported in the year following by the CSAP on grounds that current funding from the communes was inadequate to care for many convalescents who were aged, infirm, or incurable; the state would need to assume a larger role. The principal objection to such supplementary legislation was its cost. "Everything," said one member of the CSAP, "comes down to a matter of money."[75] But the prevailing view was that it was the CSAP's primary task to define France's social needs, whereas finance was a function of the parliament. The majority was strengthened in this convenient sentiment by an endorsement for its efforts from Émile Cheysson, who remarked that the Germans had resolved the matter in a "magnificent fashion." He added hopefully if somewhat stiffly: "It is not too much to presume of our nation's generosity to believe it capable of the effort made by Germany."[76] But how generous must it be? Monod estimated the additional annual cost to the state, departments, and communes at about 16 million francs. Adopted on 14 July 1905 with this assumption in view, the new law granted subsidies to all needy invalids over seventy years of age, either in the form of hospitalization or home assistance to be fixed by the appropriate municipal council at a rate between five and twenty francs per month.

Similar benefits would be available for all those under seventy who were totally incapacitated by accident or illness.[77]

One need not belittle this enactment to observe that it confirmed rather than altered the French conception of public welfare as an augmented and secularized form of charity. The motion for a national pension plan was otherwise, because it did not propose merely to funnel more funds through government agencies into poor relief. Rather, in the name of "prudence" (*prévoyance*), both workers and employers would be required to contribute to a common account, which was then with state subsidization to be deployed as a national retirement pool available to every French citizen reaching a specified age. Directly inspired by the German social legislation of 1889, this new departure had been temporarily derailed in 1893 to clear passage for the much less controversial law on free medical aid. But it was resubmitted to the Chamber of Deputies in 1897 by Jean Jaurès, who recommended that all retired workers over sixty years old should be awarded an annual minimum pension of 500 francs. To defray the enormous expense of this project, Jaurès was frank to say, France would doubtless need to adopt a progressive income tax.[78]

The policy of the Radical party, and of the successive cabinets dominated by it after the turn of the century, now became of critical importance. The key figure was Joseph Caillaux, who as minister of finance in the Waldeck-Rousseau government in 1900 submitted a legislative bill circumspectly labeled as a "reform of direct contributions." In recent years, the preamble read, other nations of "the civilized world" had completely transformed their tax structure "in accordance with the temperament [and] the genius of each race." Germany, England, Scandinavia, Switzerland, and Holland had all done so, whereas France "remained outside this movement of reforms that has agitated Europe." The reason for French recalcitrance was easy to identify: "To a system of obligatory declaration, which is enforced in a great number of foreign countries and notably in those of the Germanic race, it has been objected that this is incompatible with the customs and genius of our race." The French people might be willing to accept an increase of taxation, but they would not submit to state intervention into their personal affairs. "We are persuaded," Caillaux concluded, "that they would rebel against the interference of fiscal authorities, to which they are unaccustomed."[79] Therewith Caillaux secured his place in a long line of politicians who favored the principle of an income tax but not the practical measures necessary to implement it. If Jaurès was correct that the introduction of an income tax was prerequisite for another major step in social welfare, his reform proposal had something less than Caillaux's full concurrence.

At this juncture attention turned once more to the Chamber's Commission d'Assurance et Prévoyance Sociales. While reporting for that committee in January 1902, Paul Guieysse succinctly outlined the "two general conceptions" that had so far emerged: either an obligatory pension system supported by increased direct taxation; or, "absolutely to the contrary," an optional retirement plan financed by mixed taxes and mainly administered through voluntary mutual societies. Despite strong opposition within the parliament, the majority of CAPS remained favorable to a mandatory pension arrangement that would require matching contributions from workers and their managers. Guieysse indicated his preference for a guaranteed annual pension of 360 francs for those retired after the age of sixty-five.[80] If these terms fell short of the more lavish proposal by Jean Jaurès, they went nonetheless well beyond the boundaries set by Joseph Caillaux. Once more, however, as in 1893, the pension debate was suspended by common consent so that the less ambitious extension of public assistance could be passed into law in 1905.

The retirement of Henri Monod as director of the national Bureau of Public Health and Hygiene marked a brief pause but not a change of direction in the course of reform. His successor, Léon Mirman, was an independent socialist who was skeptical about extracting prepayments from the salary of workers and who therefore emphasized the necessity of raising additional revenues through the introduction of an income tax. Accordingly, a new spate of taxation bills was submitted in 1906 to the Chamber of Deputies, where they were channeled to a special committee formed to consider them. Its chairman, Camille Pelletan, inaugurated the proceedings by expressing his astonishment that France had still not adopted a progressive tax structure, "whereas it exists in so many neighboring monarchies." Passage of an income tax, Pelletan said, had become essential for the realization of a workers' pension plan. Good intentions would no longer suffice. Now parliament must find the practical means to implement them. This statement was seconded by Jean Jaurès, who demanded immediate and vigorous action.[81]

By 1907 a pattern became established. A leftist faction around Jaurès and Pelletan was pushing for a maximalist package of taxes and pensions. Meanwhile the more moderate government, represented by Caillaux, continued to preach caution. Although widely suspected and often accused of dilatory tactics, Caillaux presented an income tax bill in February. But he was promptly criticized by Pelletan for hawking the "rather false idea" that it would be possible to avoid a mandatory declaration of wealth. Jaurès attempted to moderate between the two by praising the outline of Caillaux's proposal as "excellent" while expressing reservations about certain "rather weak" details. These, as it turned out, included the question of obligatory declaration, still regarded by most Socialists as indispensable. In closed committee hearings Jaurès made note that in Germany such a measure was required for all those earning more than 3,000 marks a year. Then the transcript dryly recorded his unambiguous comment: "M. Jaurès declares that he would be partisan to an analogous system."[82]

For his part, Caillaux, though invited, initially refused to appear before the committee or to engage Jaurès directly in debate. Functionaries from his ministry performed in his stead. One of them explained that Caillaux opposed erecting a barrier of 5,000 francs (slightly more than 3,000 marks) because it would only encourage a division into social classes. Besides, he rejected the principle of an obligatory declaration because most French businessmen "do not like to say clearly what they do," and they would therefore "prefer another taxation even [if it were] a bit excessive." Caillaux supported a fixed scheme of tax assessment on commerce (called *patentes*) based solely on external signs of wealth. Jaurès, in turn, was willing to concede that there was popular resistance to governmental intrusions into private affairs. But, he countered, "we should be preoccupied less by the feelings of those concerned than with their real interests." In any event, he added, it would be deplorable to perpetuate "the unjust and inequitable system of *patentes*."[83]

To narrate the foregoing scene and to capture its exact language is to approach as closely as archival records permit to the core of the social question after 1905. The traditional liberal inhibitions against virtually any form of state intervention into public welfare were no longer the primary issue. Rather, the problem was to determine just how much farther government regulations should be extended.

Above all, and finally, it was a conflict over finances. To pass from a modicum of public assistance to a mature system of social security was sure to be horrendously expensive. Beyond that, it would involve a very different set of assumptions about the prerogatives of the state and the predilections of the French people. The evidence is prima facie that politicians like Jean Jaurès, Camille Pelletan, and Léon Mirman—a second generation of leftist reformers now advancing to the forefront—regarded the German model as their ultimate goal. They did not imagine that France would adopt a program of workers' pensions identical to that of imperial Germany, but it would ideally be, just as Jaurès said, "analogous." Joseph Caillaux and others in the cabinet adopted a more defensive posture, which rested less on the tired maxims of liberalism than on appeals to national unity. Here we can grasp the real meaning of the vaunted slogan of solidarism: the French would be French (and not Germans); the conflict of classes would be avoided (or simply denied); the rights of individuals would be balanced against the imperative needs of society; and the price of welfare reform would be strictly limited. This was the path that now stretched toward the future of France.

Chapter 10

The Dilemma of Mutual Societies

Among the many unresolved problems of public health in late nineteenth-century France, none was more crucial than the fate of mutual aid societies (*sociétés de secours mutuels*). Indeed, it is surely correct to say that mutualism represented the most reliable bellwether of the social question. Its evolution would indicate the outcome of reformist efforts in France after 1870 to construct a national health system worthy of the name.

Curiously, this subject has heretofore received scant attention from historians. No comprehensive study of mutual societies exists, despite the conspicuous fact that they became a quintessential French institution well before 1914 and remained so throughout half of the twentieth century.[1] Although it is beyond the scope of this work to recount that long and complex story, there is reason to sketch its main outlines and to delve into some of its details. Specifically, we need to determine how the development of the French mutual society differed from that of the German *Krankenkasse*, to which it posed a characteristic Gallic counterpart.

One of the clues to this analysis, already suggested by the discussion of matters financial, was an increasingly manifest polarization of the political spectrum toward right and left. The former espoused doctrinaire liberalism, opposed the income tax, and supported the mutual societies. With equal consistency, the latter professed socialist principles, favored a progressive reform of the tax structure, and regarded the mutual societies at best as an interim solution pending adoption of social security. Between these opposite poles the transient political regimes of the early Third Republic shifted in search of a middle ground on which to rest a viable government. One cannot fail to remark in retrospect how little this broad configuration of French politics has changed ever since.

A Clash of Principles

The origins of mutualism may be traced back to the religious confraternities and artisanal *compagnonnages* of the Old Regime.[2] But the scattered appearance of mutual societies after 1800 must be understood primarily as a response to protoindustrial conditions during the Restoration and July monarchies. Following the tumult of the Great Revolution, the pace of manufacturing began to accelerate, resulting in confusion and anxiety within the ranks of labor. Such is the impression one gains from reading the statutes of the societies formed before 1848. Few of them had an avowed political purpose. They were, rather, small groups of relatively prosperous breadwinners—the membership was overwhelmingly male—who joined together to protect themselves against the menace of illness or accident. In return for a modest initiation fee and the defrayment of a monthly premium, they were guaranteed compensation in case of temporary incapacitation. The mutualist gospel of self-help appealed mostly to a stratum of urban artisanal workers at a time when they could look neither to private charity nor to state welfare. As a group of mutualist advocates expressed it in 1846: "Only the *mutualité* can assure the future of the worker and inspire in him the habits of order and temperance." Thereby was born a primitive system of independent insurance companies that enrolled about 100,000 members by the mid-nineteenth century.[3]

The sobering experience of 1848 strengthened the opinion that workers should earn their stake in society through "labor and savings." This was the slogan of Jean-Baptiste Dumas, minister of agriculture and commerce under the republican president Louis Bonaparte in 1849, who condemned the "dangerous illusions" of the recent past, meaning the seductive doctrine of a guaranteed right to work. Instead, the laborer should be encouraged to set aside a few centimes each day to assure a future for himself and his family. Dumas conceded that such a program could not be totally autonomous, because it would no doubt require a modicum of state regulation, but he expressly rejected the principle of obligation. It was, rather, the willing cooperation of labor and management that would promote among workers a sense "of order, of economy, and of regularity in the conduct of their life."[4] In these elegant homilies we of course hear the unmistakable reverberations of classical midcentury liberalism. But Louis Bonaparte himself had somewhat different ideas, and he moved quickly to implement them after his seizure of power in December 1851. On the following 26 March a decree from the "prince-president" stipulated that mutual societies should henceforth be considered public instruments of social betterment. If his intentions were firm, the implications were unclear. Minister of the Interior Fialin de Persigny attempted to explain. Until the present, the state had maintained a benevolent neutrality toward mutual societies: "its intervention has been only unofficial." But the new dispensation had now changed "the nature and character of this institution." The chief executive wished to expand mutual societies across the nation, to mobilize local mayors and *curés* in their support, and to engender a public ethic of "prudence" among the working class, as was evident in England. This last reference suggested that Napoleon III had a model of British friendly societies in mind, but documents of his reign continued to refer vaguely to the "new character of these institutions" and to praise him effusively as "the founder of mutual societies."[5]

An official census of mutualism, sent to the emperor in 1853, afforded a notion of its growing national importance. By then nearly 2,500 separate voluntary societies existed in seventy-seven departments of France. Their ranks usually remained small: only 16 of them had more than a thousand members, and most were closer to a hundred, often less. Before 1870 the total membership barely exceeded three-quarters of a million. If that figure appeared mediocre for a national population of over 35 million, it did not prevent the boast (printed on posters displayed by Paris kiosks to announce a mutualist gathering at the Sorbonne in 1861) that the societies represented "one of the great benefits from the liberal and intelligent initiative of the emperor's government."[6]

Although the intelligence of Napoleon III's regime may be a subject of some dispute, an increasing political pressure of liberalism in the 1860s was certainly evident. For the balance of the Second Empire, therefore, the voluntarist character of the mutual societies remained intact despite the state's active patronage of them. The rationale of mutualism was forcefully adumbrated by the Vicomte de la Guéronnière in a speech to a mutual society, La vraie humanité, of which he was appointed president by Bonaparte in 1859. His was an inspiring message of self-help and the salutary value of labor. "To work," said the Vicomte grandly, "is to ennoble oneself." It was also a law of God. But individual labor is enhanced through association. By freely joining in a common effort, workers could secure their own well-being amid the vicissitudes of life: "Assistance is thus substituted for alms." Ideally, the mutual society "belongs to everyone, profits everyone." This vision, to be sure, had not yet been fully realized, and further efforts were still needed to spread the gospel of mutualism, especially among the young.[7]

The final relevant innovation of Napoleonic administration was the creation in 1868 of state insurance funds (*caisses d'assurance*) that would offer indemnities against accidents and death. Accident coverage, with its implicitly contentious question of fault, had always been problematical for the mutual societies. Life insurance was likewise rare and, when available, remained generally confined to those wealthy enough to afford expensive premiums. Now these measures, as the current minister of agriculture and commerce Adolphe Forcade said, were to be instituted "under the guarantee of the state."[8] For two reasons, however, this formulation was never clarified. One was that a definition was lacking of the relationship between the old mutual societies and the new *caisses*. And the other was that application of the law became moot once France plunged headlong into war with Germany.

In several regards the decade of the 1870s constituted a hiatus. Many records of the *mutualité* disappeared in the flames of the Paris Commune. Besides, the financing and functioning of individual societies were disrupted for months or sometimes years after the conflict. Statistics were fragmentary during that time, but there is evidence that membership temporarily declined below pre-1870 levels.[9] Reports indicated that administrative efforts to establish a program of accident and life insurance were resumed. Yet that attempt, as one official memo admitted, "does not rest on a sufficiently solid basis." This faint reference was not solely to funding but also to fears that a mandatory plan of state insurance for workers would only encourage "utopian" ideas that were "still too widespread."[10] It is certainly no strain on the evidence to extrapolate from such statements a conclusion that the Commune had briefly unleashed the specter of state socialism and that the first cautious governments of the Third Republic wanted nothing of the sort.

The 1880s thereupon provided a respite for regrouping and growth. During that decade two extensive surveys of the mutualist movement were conducted by the Ministry of the Interior, which offered an evaluation of its recovery. The first, gathered by René Waldeck-Rousseau in 1882, tabulated exactly 7,279 mutual societies in France, of which 5,188 were "authorized" by the government. This number was growing at an annual rate of nearly 300. Of the total, 71.4 percent were for men only, 2.84 percent for women only, and 25.92 percent were mixed. The survey also showed that the *mutualité* was largely an urban phenomenon, with the largest concentrations in Paris, Marseille, Lyon, Bordeaux, and Lille. The departments surrounding those five cities accounted for somewhat more than a quarter of all mutual societies. Twelve departments had none. One other statistical result is noteworthy: the societies provided very few pensions. The figure for all of France still fell short of 15,000 in 1882. Thus the essential character of mutualism was reconfirmed as a voluntary form of sickness insurance, since many mutual societies did not cover accidents and few of them allowed pensions.[11] A second survey under Armand Fallières in 1887 corroborated these tabulations and documented a continued expansion. By 1890, we can presume, the mutual societies had attracted well over a million members (see Table 9).[12]

Before proceeding it is important to mention briefly the parallel development of savings banks (*caisses d'épargne*) in France and to distinguish these from the mutual societies. The two institutions were often in competition, actually, because few workers could possibly afford both. The mutualist principle dictated that workers must risk some of their wages in what was essentially a gamble: if they fell ill, a substantial subsidy would be theirs; if not, a portion of their hard-earned income was gone. But at a savings bank they could safely deposit all of their surplus capital, earn a small dividend, and perhaps obtain a modest loan. For many in the labor force or in small private business firms, the *caisses d'épargne* therefore presented an attractive alternative. Originated in Paris in 1818, they had grown into a network of nearly 1,700 affiliate branches by the late 1880s. Even so, as Édouard Lockroy informed the Chamber of Deputies, it

Table 9 / Growth of Mutual Societies, 1852–1902

Year	Number of Societies	Number of Adult Members
1852	2,488	239,501
1857	3,609	416,881
1862	4,386	565,163
1867	5,829	750,590
1872	5,793	691,241
1877	6,078	814,393
1882	7,279	1,017,225
1887	8,427	1,130,463
1892	9,662	1,288,021
1897	11,335	1,539,104
1902	13,673	2,073,569

Source: *Anatole Weber*, À travers la mutualité. Étude critique sur les sociétés de secours mutuels *(Paris, 1908), p. 29.*

was elsewhere, particularly in Prussia, that the savings bank (*Sparkasse*) had come into its own. Through astute investment of funds and generous extension of credits, it had become a conduit for the recent surge of German agriculture and industry. "We believe that the moment has come," Lockroy commented, "to endow our country with a system that has succeeded so well among our neighbors." As it proved, the growth of the *caisses d'épargne* in France was considerable. Before the turn of the century they were to enroll nearly a quarter of the French population.[13]

By 1890 these affairs had entered the tortuous parliamentary process. A series of preliminary debates in the labor committee of the Chamber revealed a familiar dichotomy among deputies. An avowedly liberal faction declared its antipathy to "dangerous" proposals that industrial firms be obligated by law to insure the labor force against illness and accident. "It is an inadmissible objective," said one of them. "We are slipping into state socialism," charged a second deputy, who added: "It's all terrible." But it was Gustave Dron who most succinctly stated the case against tighter state regulation of private enterprise with the lapidary phrase: "I am a partisan of liberty."[14]

The other side was equally adamant, arguing that protective

measures for labor would be ineffectual unless available for all. Without such a comprehensive insurance plan, contended Louis Ricard for the reformers, "the owner and the worker will be constantly at odds." Another deputy, Émile Jamais, cited the example of Germany and observed that the current reform initiative in France was "inspired by provisions of the German law on accidents." As he recognized, however, the guiding precept of German social insurance legislation was its mandatory character, which ill accorded with the voluntary structure of French mutualism. Yet Jamais was among those prepared to adopt an entirely new obligatory system "just as it is in Germany and Austria." In principle, at least, the ultimate implications of doing so did not go unstated: "There is," Jules Mercier insisted, "no other solution to the problem except insurance by the state."[15]

We need to allow for the full complexity of all this disputation. Also evident were the hesitations of those deputies whose views did not correspond precisely with either of the opposing camps. Conspicuous among these was the Comte Albert de Mun, who considered a highly centralized scheme of obligatory insurance to be a "detestable [and] dangerous path." He preferred some sort of regional system that would provide a compromise between the extremes, as he saw them, of absolute liberty and state socialism.[16] Yet the committee needed to bring the question to a closure, and it did so by adopting Louis Ricard's general motion in favor of obligation. The wide margin of victory, 13 to 2, was deceptive insofar as it failed to allow for a centrist position. It should be added, moreover, that this skirmish had avoided any discussion of the practical effects that adoption of a German-style system of insurance would have on the French *mutualité*, whose representatives hurried to the Chamber to make known their dissatisfaction with the labor committee's initial decision. More acrimony ensued. Once again, although details of the debate were elaborate, the pattern was identical. Those who supported a major reform insisted that a compromise was illusory and that an effective insurance plan, whether central or regional in its administration, would need to be mandatory. Their opponents charged that this outcome would mean abandonment of the mutual societies, which was unacceptable. For those who hesitated Paul Guieysse spoke with more hope than confidence: "All these modes of insurance are not incompatible."[17]

By February 1891 four different parliamentary bills were pending that collectively defined the range of options. The first, authored by the liberal Gustave Dron, presented a mandate for mutualism and dismissed the principle of obligation. This draft was the only one to advocate a stand on the unmitigated voluntarism of the mutual societies. Diametrically opposed was a second proposal from Pierre Richard, which foresaw the "obligatory solidarity" of management and labor under state regulation. Richard spared no sarcasm about "the sad example [of] nonmandatory insurance," and he suggested that those who defended mutualism should "cast a rapid glance at the colossal monument so recently and so rapidly constructed by our neighbors." The models of Germany and Austria, he contended, were proof that "the difficulties provided by the creation of compulsory insurance in a large country are not as insurmountable as apparently believed in France."[18]

The controversy was thereby stretched between these two antagonistic positions. In comparison, the other pair of bills seemed almost moderate, although both of them favored adoption of an obligatory arrangement in the sense that employers would be required to provide coverage for their employees. A difference was in the proposed degree of administrative centralization. One version, offered by the Ministry of Agriculture and Commerce, wanted to coordinate the plan through bureaucratic offices in Paris; the other, jointly sponsored by Paul Guieysse and Louis Ricard, preferred more dispersed control by regions. Each of these two conceptions would have incorporated the mutual societies in effect as branches of a national welfare network. Exactly what impact this assimilation would have on the actual practice or philosophy of mutualism, though, was not explicit.[19]

In May 1891 all four bills were finally brought to a ballot. While reviewing the available choices, Louis Ricard argued that only two alternatives—the government's and his own—had any chance of passage through parliament. After some perfunctory discussion, a vote was recorded in the labor committee's minutes as though it were a conclusion foregone: "The system proposed by messieurs Guieysse and Ricard is unanimously adopted."[20]

There is a striking consistency in this sketch of mutualism. Attention to its pattern and its rhetoric enables us to trace a clear trajectory from a voluntarist doctrine, which remained the theoretical core of liberalism and mutualism, to a public ethic of social obligation, which was common to solidarism and socialism. But such an analysis necessarily suffers from three closely related deficiencies. So far, first, this story existed solely in the realm of ideology. What was being debated and decided before 1893 was a matter of principle, without much attention to the crucial details of implementation. Second, an important ambiguity remained about the concept of "obligation." Did it literally mean that every French worker and every employee in whatever enterprise would automatically receive adequate compensation in all cases of illness or accident? What of small artisanal shops? What of the self-employed, or domestic servants, or agricultural labor? These were a few of the precise questions that still awaited answers. Third, the issues raised before the Belle Epoque had not yet been exposed to pressures of the political process. The truth was that the labor committee of the Chamber of Deputies did not provide an accurate microcosm of the French nation or even of the French parliament. The status of the mutual societies was still far from settled.

Mutualism and Solidarism

Simultaneously with the passage of the 1893 law on free medical assistance to the needy, discussions began about a new statute for the mutual societies. Technically still operating under the Bonapartist decree of 1852, they were slated for a deregulation that would, as it turned out, enable the *mutualité* to thrive as never before. But of more proximate interest to most legislators was the problem of defining a role for the societies that was consistent with the emerging parameters of a national welfare system. In particular, the main issue was to decide whether the societies should be entrusted with expanded responsibilities for accident insurance and retirement pensions. As these questions grew in complexity, mutualism moved to the center of the political arena. If the labor committee of the Chamber could be thought eccentric, the Commission d'Assurance et Prévoyance Sociales was more broadly representative of French deputies. As CAPS went, ordinarily, so went the Chamber. However, once a bill affecting the mutual societies had cleared the lower house, it was sure to be subjected to critical scrutiny by the Senate, where the sentiment for reform was notably less cordial. The serious bargaining could now begin.

For different reasons, each of the three fundamental ideological positions was strengthened as this process moved forward. The Chamber had long ceased to be a citadel of liberalism, but the minority of deputies who might be labeled as liberals could always count on strong backing in the Senate. Thus their argument was stiffened that radical provisions in a legislative proposal were certain to doom it to interminable delay or to extinction; and a flawed bill, they insinuated, was better than none at all. The Socialist cause was meanwhile being buttressed by electoral returns, industrial strikes, and the organization of syndicalism. The French labor force was not nearly so united or massive as the German. But in Germany, because insurance regulations were mandatory for all, their implementation depended less on public approval. It was in a voluntarist ethos like the French that the cooperation of the workers was crucial. This fact explains the prestige and parliamentary clout of Socialist leaders such as Jean Jaurès, Alexandre Millerand, and Jules Guesde, who could claim access to vast reservoirs of labor support. Situated somewhere between liberalism and socialism were the still-incohesive adherents of solidarism. They benefited, as all centrists do, from the perceived excesses of their rivals on either flank, and also from an evident but vague feeling that some reform was desirable to deal with the social question as long as it did not upset existing institutions. The mutual aid societies were of course among these. Moreover, the solidarists now found in Léon Bourgeois the indispensable element of political leadership that they had heretofore lacked. Henri Monod was an effective advocate of reform within the bureaucracy, and Paul Brouardel exerted a measure of influence through the medical community. But neither possessed the national standing and oratorical skills that Bourgeois brought in the 1890s to the construction of a solidarist platform.[21]

On 19 January 1894 Léon Bourgeois became chairman of the Commission d'Assurance et Prévoyance Sociales in the Chamber of Deputies. During his inaugural statement he declared that the major challenge for his committee would be to determine "what the nature of state intervention should be and to what degree such intervention should be exercised."[22] Less than a week later the first test came. A proposal by Jean-Honoré Audiffred sought to recast the mutual societies by abrogating the 1852 guidelines: "In place of this oppressive regime, the legislative draft would substitute a liberal organization."

He proposed that the societies be unfettered to issue personal insurance policies against illness, invalidity, accident, and death. Their efforts would be coordinated by a new advisory board called the Conseil Supérieur de la Mutualité.²³ The objective of the Audiffred bill, in short, was to reaffirm the principle of voluntarism. But it was questionable to some deputies whether this aim was altogether compatible with the extension of a retirement program through the Caisse Nationale de Retraites, which was meanwhile under consideration. Some, such as Jules Siegfried and Léon Say, thought that pensions for the aged could best be administered by the mutual societies; but others, like Audiffred himself, considered that this combination would be "impracticable" and a "great imprudence." Bourgeois hesitated. First he divided CAPS into two subcommittees: one to draft a law on accident insurance and the other to deal with a pension plan. But as debate in plenary sessions grew more vehement, he finally admitted that "the two questions are connected and the solution of the one depends on the solution of the other."²⁴

Despite the intricacy of these discussions, it is not difficult to identify the central issue or to define the basic quandary of the solidarists. As ever, their essential plight was to integrate liberty with obligation. If insurance coverage and pensions were purely voluntary, they would reach only a limited portion of the population and would thus fail to protect many of those who needed help the most. Thus left to their own devices, mutual societies were likely to remain scattered and financially unsturdy, serving mainly the urban bourgeoisie and a laboring elite that could afford to meet regular premiums. Yet if a mandatory system were introduced, the mutual societies might soon become superfluous. Were all workers to be enrolled in a national health service, fully covered during their career and retirement, there would be little incentive for them to join a privately financed society and hence no rationale for the *mutualité*. The most cogent statement of this dilemma came from Louis Ricard: "The great question that divides opinion is that of obligatory insurance. . . . It is a singular pretension to create mandatory insurance through independent companies."²⁵ When Bourgeois put this issue directly to CAPS, the results were disconcerting. The committee voted unanimously to favor the principle of obligation, but it divided sharply about the mode of application through—or despite—the mutual societies. These perplexities were exacerbated by the bill on accident insurance. The Chamber's version favored full obligatory coverage under state regulation, whereas the Senate's draft espoused voluntary insurance that would leave the state to assume responsibility only for workers at high risk who were refused protection by private companies. Bourgeois made no attempt to minimize the contradiction. Undeniably, he said, the two plans were "separated by an abyss. They are deduced, the one and the other, from opposite principles."[26]

To study the solution of a specific problem may afford us a better perspective on solidarism than can be gathered solely from the epigrammatic self-definition of politicians. The ambiguity of the solidarist predicament was evident, for example, in the following two quotations. Audiffred: "We must accustom men to count somewhat more on their personal effort and somewhat less on the intervention of the state." Bourgeois: "The intervention of the state corresponds to a duty of social solidarity."[27] What such statements might actually mean in practice became clearer in 1894 when the government allocated a subsidy of 1.5 million francs for additional benefits to the elderly. The question immediately came under debate in CAPS whether these funds should be made available to all workers through the state's Caisse Nationale de Retraites or only to mutualists through the voluntary societies. Without following the twisting bypaths of this argument, which continued for a full year, we can see that its outcome was to fortify the notion of "prudence" (*prévoyance*) as the epitome of solidarism. True, it was shocking to refuse aid to suffering invalids. But for them, Léon Bourgeois stated, a separate welfare program was needed, as in Germany: "a service we hope to create in France." The immediate priority, however, must be "to save the principle of *prévoyance*." In this stance Bourgeois was strongly supported by Paul Guieysse and Louis Ricard. An amendment favoring a minimum subsistence for everyone without reference to membership in mutual societies was therefore rejected, as Ricard put it, because that would "deal a mortal blow to the spirit of prudence."[28] Theoretical confusion was not thereby ended, but this response to a hard question of policy at least placed the solidarists on record and helped them to establish an identity separate from liberalism and socialism. The state should by all means intervene to aid needy persons, but it might do so only to promote their individual initiative. In twenty-five words or less, such was solidarism.

In November 1895 Léon Bourgeois resigned as chairman of CAPS to become prime minister. Given the ephemeral career of most republican cabinets, his accession raised only feeble hopes that solidarist reformism had thereby gained supremacy. Still, it was an event not to be ignored, and opponents on both political extremes did not hesitate to make their differences with the government known. Five right-wing delegates from the national congress of mutual societies, convened that December in Saint-Étienne, arrived in Paris to present their case. They requested increased state subsidies to the *mutualité* in order to build a base of investment capital, and they urged a greater role for the societies in distributing retirement benefits. Thus the regime should collaborate with the mutualist movement without curbing its autonomy. This strategy was considered crucial by spokesmen for the societies, who feared that any strings attached to such official support might strangle them. Such apprehensions were well articulated by the arch-liberal Paul Leroy-Beaulieu, who praised the mutual societies as "a great progress" but who warned that state regulation of them was "useless, even dangerous."[29]

By contrast, the leftist politician Jacques Escuyer proposed a state pension plan that was, as he noted, based on calculations derived from the already-extant German system: "One finds in that operation exact numbers, 'experienced' numbers, so to speak." The putative cost would admittedly be enormous, eventually requiring as much as one-fifth of the French national budget. Yet the need for reform, Escuyer contended, was "great and urgent."[30] Minister of the Interior Louis Barthou inadvertently corroborated this opinion while reporting on a new census of the mutual societies in 1896. Although it had grown beyond a million members, the entire *mutualité* (as of the last day of 1894) was awarding pensions to only 35,415 persons, whose annual compensation averaged but 67.57 francs. That indemnity, moreover, had actually been declining somewhat as the number of beneficiaries slowly grew. Socialists were consequently loath to leave matters to the mutual societies. The Escuyer bill foresaw a fixed monthly contribution by employees, to be matched by their employers and subsidized by the state. All persons over sixty, whether mutualists or not, would be entitled to an annual minimum subsistence of 500 francs. It was on the basis of this plan that Jean Jaurès entered the parliamentary fray in 1897.[31]

By the late autumn of that year Léon Bourgeois was once more out of the cabinet and back as chairman of the Chamber's Commission d'Assurance et Prévoyance Sociales. As ever, the quarrelsome troika of liberalism, solidarism, and socialism was unsettled, and Bourgeois was given the unenviable task of driving them to legislative action on the question of mutualism. Whatever his reservations about the societies and their possible role in administering retirement pensions, Bourgeois could not contemplate their disbandment. In part, his attitude was determined by the incontrovertible fact that the *mutualité* had more than doubled in size since 1870. By the mid-1890s there were over 10,000 societies with more than 1.5 million members. But above all, Bourgeois and the solidarists were firmly attached to an ethic of *prévoyance* for which the mutualist movement had become a fitting symbol. This commitment was not shared by the Socialists. Indeed, Audiffred could plausibly contend that Jean Jaurès was "in absolute opposition to the system adopted by the committee." No matter how moderate or conciliatory on matters of policy, the Socialist leadership was perceived by solidarists as leaning too far in the direction of state intervention at the expense of personal initiative.[32]

For his part, during his personal encounters with Audiffred and Bourgeois, Jaurès did not depreciate the differences. "We set out from opposing points of view," he told Bourgeois, because "we [Socialists] do not believe it possible to establish a serious pension system without obligation." And he conjured a phrase that Bourgeois could not condone: "a pension for all."[33] Jaurès thereby exposed the basic ambivalence of solidarism and questioned the determination of Léon Bourgeois to establish a compulsory insurance system. In reality, perhaps, there were not three alternatives but only two. After all the dithering of the past decade, it was still to be demonstrated that the principles of voluntarism and obligation could be meaningfully combined in practice.

The Socialist Challenge

The 1898 accident insurance act created an official niche for the mutual societies. All industrial enterprises were henceforth obliged to carry insurance against mishaps on the job. They might do so by any one of three means: through a central state agency; by forming a private insurance company of their own, possibly in collaboration with other firms; or as part of the *mutualité*. In allowing that third option, French legislators consciously mandated the existence of mutual societies. This solution, in a smooth formula attributed to Prime Minister Waldeck-Rousseau, established "liberty within obligation."[34]

At least as far as the Socialists were concerned, Waldeck-Rousseau's slogan was more felicitous than convincing. No sooner was the accident bill passed than it was attacked as deficient by Léon Mirman and other leftists, who considered it unduly narrow in coverage. A series of motions for its modification therefore appeared before 1900.[35] The Socialists also wasted no time in renewing the campaign to obtain a compulsory pension plan. Already in June 1898 Alexandre Zévaès resubmitted the Escuyer–Jaurès proposal for a guaranteed minimum annual subsistence of 500 francs for every citizen over sixty years of age. As the new legislative period opened in July, this effort was endorsed at the first session of CAPS by the Socialist deputy Louis Puech, whose statement was blandly recorded in the committee's minutes: "He cites the example of Germany, which has preceded us. He approves a vast intervention by the state with the principle of obligatory insurance."[36] On the other hand, Auguste Gervais felt constrained to deny charges that he and like-minded leftists wanted to impose a German style of "state socialism." Rather, they saw it simply as "a superior morality." The time had come, Gervais urged, to move beyond the limited public assistance heretofore practiced in France and to embrace an obligatory program that would be "unambiguous, clear, and precise."[37] Finally, in that vein, Édouard Vaillant offered another compulsory pension scheme in March 1899, contending that "modern peoples"—of which he singled out the Germans—had long ago anticipated the French in assuring an honorable retirement for their elderly workers. Recent cabinets that presided over the destiny of France had created "a semblance of progress," but they seemed "in no haste to achieve this solution."[38] Thus, as the nineteenth century concluded, French Socialists were increasingly prone to challenge the current regime and to champion a German model of welfare reform.

The effect of this ideological barrage was to hasten the polarization of opinion about the mutual societies. Either they would have to be greatly expanded and sufficiently enriched to underwrite a national pension plan, or they would have to be restricted to a relatively minor function of handling short-term insurance claims for illness and accident, leaving retirement pensions to some other agency. Predictably, supporters of the *mutualité* urged the former course.[39] Most other deputies meanwhile cast about for some variant of the latter. Of these, the most arresting suggestion—which presaged the pension law finally to be adopted a decade later—was that of Louis Ricard. Like the Socialists, Ricard chose to cite Germany as the first foreign precedent, because there the problem had been solved "in a radical fashion" by social legislation that had culminated in 1889 with a broad state-sponsored pension program. Although France was not prepared to go to those lengths, Ricard assumed, neither was the nation willing to leave workers on their own: "The intervention of the state in such matters is almost universally admitted." Yet the government must make sure to encourage personal initiative, Ricard added, for "the individual [is] the artisan of his own destiny." If his prose thereby expressed the habitual self-contradictions of solidarism, Ricard's statistics confirmed the need for reform. He showed that less than 1 percent of commercial and industrial firms in France provided retirement pensions for their labor force, with fewer than 116,000 participants in all. That number represented only 4.35 percent of French laborers. By including miners and railway workers, who separately enjoyed automatic state pension benefits, one might reach a grand total of 660,000 pensioners—that is, barely 17 percent of France's nearly 4 million workers. Even granted this quite narrow definition of labor (agricultural workers, domestic servants, and white-collar employees were still omitted), it was patent that mutualism was failing to provide an adequate solution to the problem. What should be done? In answer, Ricard repeated an earlier tripartite proposal he had submitted with Paul Guieysse: that workers be given an option to contribute part of their wages regularly to a pension fund; that employers be required to match that amount; and that the state be expected to subsidize the fund, whenever necessary, to assure an annual minimum subsistence of 360 francs for all retirees over sixty-five and of 200 francs for invalids below that age.[40]

The Ricard bill, which gained government approval, was an excellent example of mainstream solidarism that sought to adopt a centrist posture between liberalism and socialism. As usual, it satisfied neither. Mutualists continued their attacks on what they regarded as excessive regulation that hindered their efforts to expand. And Socialists argued as before that fainthearted compromises would fail to assuage the plight of indigents or to gain wide support among workers. For our purposes it is particularly noteworthy that this leftist pole of reform so frankly associated itself with the model of imperial Germany. What was necessary in France, said Édouard Vaillant, was not merely an extension of public assistance but the adoption of "social insurance" as it was known abroad. "It is to the honor of the German nation to have been the first . . . to apply the principle of mandatory social insurance." He went on: "It is the unity of insurance that we must create, profiting from the experience of Germany and of other Germanic nations that have followed its example."[41] Numerous quotations of this sort could be cited, but one other source may suffice because of its subsequent importance. The author was Léon Mirman in the year 1900, not long before he succeeded Henri Monod as the director of the Bureau of Public Health and Hygiene. In the preambles of two bills that he had drafted to extend accident benefits, Mirman wrote of his regret about the "painful humiliation" of seeing Germany displace France in the vanguard of European nations. "May the French parliament compare [the situation] with the admirable effort accomplished by the German empire," which had so obviously surpassed all others "in this glorious path of social reform."[42] One may of course choose to interpret such passages as shameless hyperbole intended to squeeze out votes through appeals to national pride. But there was a genuine sorrow and a distinct touch of humility in Mirman's candid admissions, which kept the reformist movement from inertia or acquiescence.

The first few years of the new century were critical for the mutual societies, because their existence was threatened by mounting pressure for a mandatory insurance program. Sensitive to the political din among Socialists, the Radical cabinets of Waldeck-Rousseau and Émile Combes began to lean perceptibly in the direction of obligation. Yet they remained reluctant to cripple the *mutualité*. A possible way out was provided by the Bienvenu-Martin bill, discussed previously, whereby the existing benefits of public assistance would be extended to invalids and the aged. When Waldeck-Rousseau announced his support for this reform in 1900, he drew diverse responses that precisely followed the pattern already traced. To the left Édouard Vaillant and other self-avowed "revolutionary socialists" castigated the government's timidity. Rather than add another measure of social aid, he said, France should adopt a system of social security by "profiting from the experience of Germany."[43] To the right, meanwhile, mutualist leaders communicated to the cabinet their anxiety about the "dangers" of drafting more compulsory laws, and they admonished that "liberty is preferable to obligation."[44]

To obtain a quick reading of centrist politicians is less easy. But we may check the temperature of solidarism by plotting the pertinent editorials written in the *Revue philanthropique* by the veteran reformer Paul Strauss. Always well placed and connected, Strauss was closely acquainted with the mutualist movement and recognized it as a welfare factor to be reckoned with. Yet he also favored a compulsory program of increased public assistance for retired and incapacitated citizens, even though that might be at variance with the strict voluntarism of mutual societies.[45] The rub came for Strauss in regard to the long-term treatment of ailments like tuberculosis, as well as in the creation of a universal pension scheme that would adequately sustain the elderly for years after their retirement. For these problems, he believed, the mutual societies were insufficient, whereas "the German example is decisive."[46] Eventually France would need to adopt an obligatory welfare program on a national scale. If so, although the mutual societies were of considerable importance for the time being, they should be permitted neither to undercut public assistance organizations now nor to hinder the implementation of social security later. Strauss therefore looked forward to the adoption of what he termed "*prévoyance scientifique*," for which the mutual societies represented only an intermediate phase.[47] When the law of 1905 was at last adopted, Strauss hailed it as a "great event." But the total context of his writings makes it plain that for Strauss and other solidarists this praise was mitigated by a recognition that the social question was still in flux. In reality, the pension issue had only been deferred again, and the mutual societies were granted another reprieve.[48]

Toward a Pension Plan

By taking a comparative inventory of European social legislation in the year 1905, we might conclude that the Third Republic had moved relatively far to match the pioneering initiatives of the German Reich. What the Germans accomplished with their welfare laws of 1883, 1884, and 1889, the French had in their fashion replicated by the parliamentary enactments of 1893, 1898, and 1905. For the first time in French history significant financial compensation from the state was now available for the needy to defray medical expenses arising from illness, accident, invalidity, and old age.

With regard to welfare matters, however, there remained two basic differences between France and Germany. In the midst of so many fine details, programmatic statements, ringing orations, and complex proposals, it is well to keep both distinctions clearly in focus. First, whereas in Germany the principle of obligation clearly prevailed after 1870, in France it did not. The voluntarist *Hilfskasse* had steadily lost ground in the Kaiserreich to the compulsory *Zwangskasse*. Thus the German insurance funds were in effect parts of a vast state enterprise that guaranteed benefits to all workers and other needy citizens. Despite some admitted lacunae and the undeniable fact that reality never fully attained the promise of theory, it is nonetheless plausible to conclude that Germany had achieved a genuine system of social security by the outset of the twentieth century. The same could not be said of France. There the theory of obligatory universal coverage received strong support *en principe*, especially among assorted solidarists and socialists in the Chamber of Deputies. But the path to its implementation was obstructed. Part of the trouble was produced by the heated struggle between private charity and public assistance, which reached its boiling point with the separation of church and state in 1905. But equally difficult, and increasingly conflictual, was the relationship between the voluntarism of the mutualist movement and the mandatory structure of state aid. The growing numerical strength of the mutual societies and the unwillingness of most solidarist reformers to suppress them meant that obligation was still inoperative in practice. In France, to put the contrast with Germany as starkly as possible, it was therefore the *Hilfskasse* rather than the *Zwangskasse* that emerged victorious before 1914.[49]

The second difference was no less fundamental: France had not yet crossed the great divide to a national pension plan. As we saw, the 1905 law was essentially an extension of existing public assistance programs for the incapacitated and the aged, augmenting the previous legislation of 1893 and 1898. The issue of an automatic pension, in the sense of a minimum subsistence for all citizens beyond their date of retirement, had been repeatedly avoided. Apart from its unspecified but apparently enormous cost, the main reason for delaying such a project was uncertainty about its impact on the *mutualité*. Left as autonomous insurance agencies, dependent solely on the regular voluntary contribution of their members, most mutual societies were not financially capable of sustaining sufficiently generous pensions over a period of many years. If dependent on state subsidies, however, they would inevitably become subject to regulation. And they were sure to be objects of discord should their membership acquire extra benefits and privileges denied to impoverished nonmutualists who were wards of the state. Thus the flagrant contradiction in France between voluntarism and obligation remained irresoluble.[50]

This rapid summary is sufficient to establish that the development of the French mutual societies after 1900 constituted the central issue on which the social question turned. Were they compatible with the current welfare structure? Would they mesh with the eventual adoption of a pension system? These questions now required a response.

The connection between mutualism and welfare programs already in place was directly addressed by a motion from Jean-Honoré Audiffred to empower the mutual societies to administer free medical assistance under provisions of the 1893 law. Testifying before CAPS, Henri Monod explained the unwillingness of the Ministry of the Interior to accept this proposal. Audiffred was correct, he said, to assume that *prévoyance* was superior to *assistance* and should therefore be augmented. But the law stipulated that medical aid be available to everyone in need, and not solely to those who had chosen to meet monthly installments to a mutual society. Audiffred hoped that contact with the *mutualité* would encourage such foresight among workers. But one could just as well imagine the opposite effect: if any patient could obtain compensation through a mutual society without having paid regularly into it, members might well decide that their individual sacrifice was unnecessary, and they would resign. Monod's Bureau of Public Health and Hygiene therefore harbored two reservations: in principle a public service could not be administered by private agencies, and in practice the envisaged method of indemnification would be incompatible with existing welfare organizations, namely the *bureaux de bienfaisance*. Hence Audiffred's motion was infeasible.[51]

Further discussion only deepened these misgivings. Although he had been an early proponent of the Audiffred plan, reformist Émile Rey agreed with Monod's strictures, emphasizing the conflict of principles: "It appears difficult to confide a public service to a private organization." Alexandre Millerand raised a more pragmatic objection. The mutual societies might have become suitable if they had been deployed as welfare funds soon after passage of the 1893 legislation. But the *bureaux de bienfaisance* continued to exercise that function, Millerand said, and in the meantime France was moving on toward "obligatory assistance." It was too late. Reliance on mutualism would be retrogressive.[52]

Another incongruity between mutual societies and present modes of public health was described by Paul Brouardel. His objection, often restated in medical gatherings, was that the societies, by employing their own staff of doctors and binding members to a prepayment plan, were encroaching on the right of patients to choose their personal physician. As we earlier witnessed, this conflict of interests aroused many French doctors to oppose the extension of mutualism and to join in a movement for medical syndicalization. It was "humiliating" for the profession, said one speaker at a congress of practitioners in 1907, to allow the *mutualité* to fix a scale for fees, as had already occurred in Lyon. The congress thereupon adopted a resolution declaring it contrary to "human dignity" for any collectivity—obviously indicting the mutual societies—to impose the choice of a doctor on patients.[53]

Yet such static about the daily functioning of mutualism within the existing framework of private and public health institutions in France remained secondary to the debate over a national pension plan. Although the intensity of this altercation notably increased after 1905, the divisions remained much as before. Léon Bourgeois, with CAPS and the cabinet behind him, resumed his effort to erect a centralized system that would eventually supersede the voluntarist principle of mutual societies and thereby obviate their full participation. The societies should of course continue to exist, in his view, but only as adjuncts whose specific assignment was limited to private illness and accident insurance.[54] Socialist deputies generally applauded this stance, but the more radical among them charged that the government was failing to draw the proper conclusions from it. A truly adequate pension scheme, they contended, was certain to compound France's welfare budget considerably, which could then be met only by creating a state insurance monopoly. If so, the implication was plain that the mutual societies would eventually become obsolete once the total enforcement of obligation came into effect.[55] Defenders of the *mutualité* could agree with the Socialists that substantial cost increases were inevitable, but they viewed that likelihood as a reason to delimit and delay reform, or altogether to reject it. At lengthy meetings of the Conseil Supérieur de la Mutualité in April 1907, these alternatives were aired in an atmosphere of crisis. There was consensus among mutualist leaders that the government's pension proposal constituted both a "painful disappointment" and a "great danger." Yet the sentiment finally prevailed that the proponents of mutualism should avoid any obstructionist tactics and seek a practical compromise of liberty and obligation.[56]

Documentation thus confirms that a recurrent political pattern was deeply etched on the republic after 1900 and that the mutual societies remained objects of rabid partisan conflict. Yet remarkably little of that underlying controversy was evident in the public record. When the government-sponsored pension bill came to the floor of the Chamber of Deputies, debate was desultory and a ballot on 23 February 1906 produced the totally misleading margin of 501 to 5. Public controversy was further stifled when a special Senate committee under Paul Cuvinot succeeded in delaying action for another three years by raising two elementary objections. One was that the obligatory plan envisaged in the Chamber's version lacked popular support. To mark this point, Cuvinot sent out 30,000 questionnaires to various groups representing management, labor, agriculture, and the mutualist movement. Among approximately 10,000 respondents, a voluntary scheme of pensions was preferred over an obligatory plan by a substantial majority of nearly two to one. It should be noted, however, that more than half of the responses were from mutual societies, which were predisposed to favor voluntarism.[57]

The second reservation of Cuvinot's committee was fiscal. The Chamber's bill was inapplicable, Cuvinot contended, because "the expense would greatly exceed our financial capabilities." He estimated that the initial annual cost of the proposed legislation would reach an astronomical 282 million francs, that this figure would then rise to 545 million by the thirty-fifth year of implementation, and that it would finally level off to 425 million by the eightieth year. The government, for its part, was on record as favoring a ceiling of 100 million francs. This contradiction appeared intractable, and Cuvinot balked.[58] At last overcome with impatience, Minister of Labor René Viviani dared to attack Cuvinot in an open letter, blaming "defective methods" of the Senate committee for the intolerable delay. After raising the age of eligibility for a pensioner from sixty to sixty-five and lowering the direct contribution (*cotisation*) required of workers and their employers, the Senate at last approved the law. Rather than enter into another round of frustrating negotiations, the Chamber concurred and the pension bill was enacted on 5 April 1910. Hailed as a splendid victory for social reform, it was in fact an unstable compound that covered a lacework of jagged fissures just beneath its surface.[59]

An Uncertain Aftermath

The persisting contradiction between the principles of liberty and obligation was never more evident than in the months following passage of the 1910 pension law. While the government attempted in vain to enforce the new legislation, nearly everyone else sought to modify it. More than a dozen separate bills were submitted to the Chamber, each of which proposed to revise the law in some way, usually on grounds that the deputies had been unduly pressured into accepting the Senate version lest the entire measure again be delayed. Meanwhile, vigorous complaints came from various quarters, along with reports of noncompliance by both managers and workers.

If the 1910 enactment was indeed unenforceable, what direction should France take? Within the parliament there was sharp division, which was lucidly reflected by the Chamber's Commission d'Assurance et Prévoyance Sociales. One faction, led by the leftist deputy Jules-Louis Breton, favored the creation of a state insurance monopoly; another, behind Ernest Lairolle (who was also a member of the Conseil Supérieur de la Mutualité), rejected such political control as excessive, maintained that the existing law needed only some "touching up," and advocated an expanded participation of the mutual societies. When in November 1910 Louis Puech left the chairmanship of CAPS to become minister of public works, a ballot was necessary to name his successor. It was indicative of the legislative muddle that Breton defeated Lairolle for the post by the narrow margin of 16 to 14.[60] In the meantime the mutual societies continued to multiply. By 1911 they numbered about 20,000 with a total of nearly 5 million members who contributed some 65 million francs annually. Yet in the eyes of reformers, the congenital flaws of mutualism remained. As the definition of "worker" was greatly expanded by the 1910 act to include many office clerks, domestic servants, and agricultural laborers, voluntary coverage became hypothetically available to 17 million persons, of whom less than 35 percent were actually enrolled. And the average monthly compensation, at a rate of twelve francs per member, was insufficient to assure a minimum subsistence. Thus the perennial division recurred between representatives of the *mutualité*, who insisted that the societies could not meet the nation's needs unless completely freed to do so, and the critics of voluntarism, for whom nothing less than a compulsory state-operated insurance system could provide sufficient coverage.[61]

Criticism of the 1910 pension act came from several sources. Perhaps a single negative thrust could have been parried. But we can identify at least four simultaneous attacks that cumulatively undermined the measure from the moment of its inception and made its revision inevitable.

THE MEDICAL PROFESSION

Obviously it lay in the interest of the *mutualité* not to leave the level of medical fees to physicians and their patients, who might then be able to set exorbitant rates and present them to an independent insurance agency. As a rule mutual societies therefore required their members to consult with designated "controlling doctors," who determined whether it was permissible to seek special care from private "treating doctors."[62] Conflicts resulting from these attempts to restrict consultations and fees continued to sour relations between mutualists and the medical syndicates. Remarkably little protest emanated from members of the Academy of Medicine, whose brilliant careers in the clinics of Paris were scarcely affected by such financial squabbles. But those lower in the ranks or scattered across the countryside found themselves tightly squeezed between the expansion of state welfare and the growth of mutualism. A syndicate of French oculists, for instance, formally presented its grievances to the Chamber of Deputies. Members were being cheated out of their proper fees, so they claimed. The oculists were willing to aid the poor but not to tolerate restrictions imposed from without. They therefore protested "with all [their] might" against the "flagrant injustice" of the existing law.[63]

Records of parliamentary committees reveal many other such examples. Testifying before CAPS, an officer of the Union of Medical Syndicates of France summarized his profession's reservations: it was inadmissible that insurance companies should be allowed to operate "on the backs of physicians." Surgery fees were being held so low in hospitals that mutual societies found it convenient to dump victims of industrial accidents there. Among the resulting problems, this practice often led to overcrowding and a lack of facilities for indigents who were ostensibly guaranteed gratis treatment under the law of 1893. This "abusive situation," another syndicate doctor confirmed, was widespread in the provinces. Representatives from the Syndicate of Social Medicine in the Department of the Seine testified in detail about efforts by mutual societies to dissuade patients from exercising free choice of physicians, frequently forcing them to consult personnel assigned by their insurance agent. Such "maneuvers" included scheduling medical appointments so that only the "controlling doctor" could be present, thus putting the patient at his mercy.[64]

Whereas the negative character of such caveats became clear, it was less obvious exactly what scheme of social medicine the syndicates wanted instead. Presumably fairness for all could only be assured by an impartial medical jury—but by whom would it be nominated: the syndicates, the mutual societies, or the state? On that decisive question there was no agreement.

THE SOCIALIST FACTIONS

French leftists likewise failed to speak in unison. But they did share a common desire to see the republic continue with social reforms that would benefit broader segments of the population. The difficulty was that the 1910 pension plan required that workers first pay into the program for many years before they could finally become eligible at age sixty-five for compensation. Most would never live to see that day, and yet until their death they would nonetheless have a portion of their wages withheld. One bill cosigned by seventy leftist deputies therefore demanded the exoneration of all laborers earning less than 1.5 francs per day. This proposal was based on estimates by René Viviani that fully four-fifths of agricultural workers had an annual income of less than 300 francs. Some Socialist deputies joined with Jules Guesde in moving that the government, as "an act of social peace," find an additional source of revenue to relieve the poor by imposing a stiff new inheritance tax on the wealthy. This step, Guesde explained, would end the "nightmare" of workers in both industry and agriculture who justifiably feared that the 1910 law, however well intentioned, would only result in lowering their wages with little realistic hope of an eventual reward.[65]

These were but a few of the suggestions originating on the political left. A more complex proposal by André Honnorat attempted to establish a scale of payments whereby workers would be compensated for having a larger family through an increased subsidy for each child beyond the second. It was self-evident, Honnorat noted, that few laborers with families of four or five infants could possibly afford the withholdings necessary both for a state pension and for participation in a mutual society. Given the demographic crisis in France, it would therefore be an act of "patriotic foresight" to make allowances for fecundity. But even relatively moderate reformers like Viviani, Millerand, and Jaurès were not persuaded by Honnorat's amendment. While it might be excellent in principle, said Viviani, the result would be to change the conception of the law from *prévoyance* back to a type of public assistance, which might produce confusion and "flagrant injustices." Jaurès also deplored the "extreme complexity" of Honnorat's scheme and urged the simpler solution of reducing the age of eligibility from sixty-five to sixty, as the Chamber had originally intended. Otherwise, he said, workers were sure to be subjected to "new formalities" by the bureaucracy. Like Viviani, Jaurès wished to preserve the universal principle of a law based on labor, and not to allow it to depend on variables such as the size of families.[66]

These contentions displayed not only the disunity of the political left but also the deep apprehensions aroused by the uneasy combination of mutualism and mandatory pensions. Few workers and peasants could be certain where they stood in a public welfare system that seemed at odds with itself. They saw that all would give but that few would receive; and some, it appeared, might benefit substantially more than others.

The mutualist movement was not incompatible with solidarism. Both stood for the principles of self-help and social foresight inherited from liberalism. But the structure of mutualism had an inherent and irremediable deficiency: it lacked universality. Hence, as Édmond Michel expressed it so trenchantly, the mutual societies alone could not possibly resolve the social question, because they were "addressed to an elite of the workers behind whom are massed numerous groups of the increasingly miserable."[67]

To discover an example of reformist doubts, we may again follow the long paper trail left by Paul Strauss in his *Revue philanthropique*. Strauss recognized as well as anyone that the 1910 pension act did nothing to mitigate the clash of principles: "Some abhor obligation, others accept it as a necessity." More important, the entire welfare legislation to date had visibly failed to brake France's demographic decline. As a consequence, Strauss wrote in 1912, the republic was "gradually losing its numerical strength [and] allowing itself to be increasingly surpassed by younger and more prolific nations."[68] The very familiarity of these phrases, repeatedly heard in public forums since 1870, tended to exacerbate a sense of disappointment and futility. The mutual societies were seen by Strauss as imperfect and transient institutions, pending adoption of broader social legislation. Yet the longer they functioned and the more public acceptance they gained, the less likely conversion to a national system of compulsory insurance became.

It was thus *faute de mieux* that the mutual societies gained a place in the solidarist canon. In 1914, when summarizing the discussions of a welfare congress held that spring in Lyon, Léon Bourgeois referred to "social security, that is, under the current form of French health insurance, the *mutualité*."[69] In prewar France these terms, various though they were, had become virtually synonymous.

Administration of the 1910 law was largely unsuccessful. Workers were expected to purchase a stamp with each installment on their pension account and then to affix it on a card kept by their manager. Yet this procedure, copied from Germany, was sure to create friction whenever the two parties did not willingly cooperate or if either was reluctant to abide by regulations. To gain compliance, the government undertook to assign a new squad of state inspectors, but this project was initially underfunded and had to be scaled down from 764 to 376 and finally to only 59 additional functionaries for the entire nation. Thus, as Senator Armand Gauthier remarked, the traditional prefectoral system again became "the essential pivot" for enforcing welfare legislation. Prefects therefore received orders to prod workers about securing stamps and to prohibit managers from sabotaging implementation of the law.[70]

Apart from such procedural matters, the pension act had at times a deleterious effect on labor conditions, as we can gather from a cluster of reports from inspectors assigned to control the glove industry. Four of these located in major manufacturing centers—Limoges, Grenoble, Toulouse, and Dijon—gave a composite picture of increasing hardship. In order to escape the obligation for pensions, many managers were reducing factory labor by requiring workers to do their cutting or sewing at home and to deliver their production by the piece. The owner thereby incurred less overhead and little responsibility. Some laborers actually preferred this arrangement, because they could work for more than one company at a time and, by clandestinely increasing their hours beyond the legal limit, they might raise their wages. But many workers complained that they missed the warmth, light, and comradeship of their factory or atelier. Besides, under the circumstances, fewer apprentices were hired and unemployment rose, because laborers often had to maintain their own tools and hire their own helpers. Labor syndicates opposed these changes but could not prevent them. The result was, willy-nilly, that a retrogressive system was emerging in which there was less administrative regulation of laboring conditions and no recourse for many workers in case of accidents. Worse, given the lack of effective inspection by the bureaucracy, there was hardly a chance for enforcement of a pension plan.[71]

It is naturally impossible to measure the relative weight of these disparate critiques of the 1910 law, but their aggregate impact was enough to persuade all but the most intransigeant liberals that a strengthening of the pension act was imperative. On 7 November

1911 the government therefore submitted a bill to lower the age of eligibility from sixty-five to sixty and to raise the minimum annual allocation for retired persons from sixty to one hundred francs. The Ministry of Labor meanwhile instructed state inspectors to proceed more cautiously with enforcement of the existing legislation, awaiting its alteration, in an attempt "to dissipate misunderstandings and to end indecisions."[72] Even the imposing chairman of the Senate finance committee, Paul Cuvinot, was prepared to concede that difficulties of application had rendered the 1910 legislation inoperable and now required its revision.[73]

An amended version of the pension act was passed into law on 27 February 1912. Besides its lowered age requirement and increased benefits, the 1912 bill afforded greater flexibility in the amount of the regular installments to be paid by workers, matched by employers, and ultimately subsidized by the state.[74] At last, it seemed, France was taking a timorous step on the path to social security.

Chapter 11

The Parable of Tuberculosis

The greatest single threat to life in late nineteenth-century France was tuberculosis. This one disease killed more persons than all other infectious maladies combined. Precise statistics are lacking, but at its height in the Belle Epoque tuberculosis probably caused over 100,000 French mortalities annually, of which perhaps as many as 15,000 occurred solely in the city of Paris. If so, one must imagine that thirty to fifty Parisian families every day faced the tragedy of a consumptive death in their midst. Meanwhile, all across the land, the Big Killer had its way.[1]

Tuberculosis epitomized the French response to questions of public health and welfare. The magnitude of its impact after 1870 threatened to burst the rigid carapace of liberalism. Many traditional assumptions were unavoidably thrown into doubt: among them, that the state should desist from all manner of coercion in the private sphere, that the individual's personal life and health are strictly sacrosanct, that physicians must exercise total discretion concerning the condition of a patient, that social insurance ought to be a purely voluntary matter, and that direct taxation of family income in order to finance public hygiene should by all means be avoided. The tuberculosis crisis could not fail to test these limits of liberal ideology at a time when *laissez faire* was likely to mean *laissez mourir*.

Here it is pertinent to stress another aspect of the tuberculosis challenge: it brought the contrast between the German Reich and the early Third Republic clearly into focus. The relatively sluggish character of the French state was revealed by comparison with the strenuous efforts of the German empire to treat tubercular disease and to lower mortality through public agency. The hypothesis that somehow an "invisible hand" was moving across western Europe, automatically reducing the rate of tuberculosis fatalities through a general rise in living standards, was belied by the incapacity of France to protect its populace against the greatest scourge of the age.[2]

The Birth of an Epidemic

Public awareness of tuberculosis was minimal before 1870. Cholera seemed a far more terrifying contagion, striking swiftly as it did throughout the nineteenth century with immediate and violent symptoms that repeatedly frightened an entire nation.[3] By comparison, although it unquestionably claimed many more victims, tuberculosis appeared as a less dramatic, unobtrusive, and (in some literary fashion) almost elegant way of death. During the war of 1870 cholera was briefly replaced in the popular imagination by smallpox. Meanwhile, reporting of pulmonary tuberculosis was irregular, and public concern about it remained faint. There was confusion of terminology, and an inability or unwillingness to disaggregate tuberculosis from pneumonia, chronic bronchitis, or other respiratory ailments. Because families feared social ostracism, moreover, they demanded that doctors hide the truth of an unfavorable diagnosis from state health officials. Disorganization was thereby compounded by a conspiracy of medical silence.

For these reasons, origins of the postwar campaign for public health and welfare lay in a general concern about France's demographic crisis; they were not tuberculosis-specific. Only gradually did the realization emerge that the republic was suffering not only from a disastrously low birth rate, compared with that of other European states, but that it was also lagging in the reduction of tubercular mortality. Just how serious was the French retardation? An early indication was provided by a survey of sanitation in 1879. In an attempt to determine to what degree provisions of an 1850 law on the inspection of insalubrious housing had been enforced, the government requested reports from each of the nation's eighty-seven departments. Only fifty-nine of them complied, and of these but six claimed that conditions were "satisfactory." That is, fewer than one French prefect in ten could claim that sanitation commissions were functioning regularly in the major urban centers of his jurisdiction.[4]

Soon thereafter, the leftist deputy Martin Nadaud introduced a parliamentary bill to revise the 1850 legislation, calling it a "dead letter" and saying of state sanitation agencies: "In effect, they no longer exist."[5]

Because of this administrative disorder, it was impossible to measure precisely the status of public health or the part of tuberculosis in it. The statistician Jacques Bertillon wrote caustically in 1880 about the "defective method" of French data-gathering and the "imbecilities" that were frequently published in the guise of demographic analysis.[6] Little improvement occurred during the following decade. Reporting in 1883 to the Chamber of Deputies on the Nadaud proposal, Hippolyte Maze stated the conclusion of his investigatory committee that the nation's sanitary provisions were "absolutely insufficient." The committee therefore recommended that every commune in the country be required to create a commission to inspect housing and to enforce hygienic regulations. But legislation continued to lag.[7] Although the cabinet did urge French prefects to apply such a policy, rapid implementation was far from assured. When updating the Maze motion with a new public sanitation bill in 1887, Édouard Lockroy noted that results had so far been "virtually illusory." The basic problem, he recalled, was that most communities had no one competent to judge insalubrity, because 29,000 of France's 36,000 communes contained no medical personnel whatever. Even if mandated, therefore, local sanitation commissions would be ineffective. The only feasible solution would be a system of visiting state housing inspectors.[8]

These confusions and patent inadequacies prefigured the creation in 1886 of a central Bureau of Public Health and Hygiene under the direction of Henri Monod. It is germane to add that this important administrative innovation was consciously realized in direct imitation of a German model, the *Reichsgesundheitsamt*, which had been organized a decade before and which had already gained international prestige through Robert Koch's discovery of the tubercle bacillus. While discussing the German organization and its advantages—including a generous state subsidy for research, the systematic collection of statistical data for the entire nation, and a centralized laboratory for testing and experimentation—the deputy Pierre Richard made explicit reference to the potential value of such an office in combatting tuberculosis in France.[9] Thus, in regard to the tuberculosis question, the German precedent came to symbolize the pole of French opinion that favored increased state intervention. This perception stretched from a still-unformed general view about German social insurance laws of the 1880s to specific proposals for practical reform, such as Monod's new administrative bureau.

Another contemporaneous example was a suggestion in the Municipal Council of Paris by Édouard Vaillant, who had earlier been a student at Tübingen. He urged that the French capital inaugurate a program of polyclinics on the German plan, thereby making the benefits of university research more readily available to the public. Although this measure, too, was slow to be implemented, it indicated again that the eminence of German science was already concretely established in the French consciousness.[10]

Records of the Academy of Medicine before 1890 confirm these three impressions: that interest in reforms of public health was increasingly vocal; that concern about the imminent danger of a tuberculosis epidemic was emerging within the context of France's demographic crisis; and that the German example of scientific research and its application to medical practice was impinging on the French reaction. In the Academy a permanent committee was established to study tuberculosis and to draft a set of "instructions" about measures to halt propagation of the disease. A doyen of the medical profession, J. A. Villemin, reported for the committee. Whereas he continued to assume that the tuberculosis "microbe" might be transmitted by "direct heredity," Villemin emphasized that Koch's research placed the communicability of consumption beyond doubt. He estimated that one Parisian in four was infected with tuberculosis, and he outlined steps that should be taken to provide the citizenry with better sanitation, ventilation, and nutrition.[11] A full-scale debate followed the Villemin report in early 1890. There was general agreement that French alcoholism was a major villain. The pervasive danger of uninhibited spitting in public was also stressed by speakers. As for the recurrent dispute between the respective advocates of heredity and contagion, they appeared content to reach a vague compromise on the proposition that some persons displayed a greater "predisposition" to tubercular infection than others. Statistics showed that mortality rates varied among the quarters of Paris in accordance with the density of their population, and many members of the Academy urged that the government move more vigorously to improve drinking habits, working conditions, and housing construction.[12] All of this talk and good intention, however, committed the Third Republic to nothing. It was as yet unclear how France might proceed or whether the medical community should declare a national emergency in hope of stimulating further action. Despite growing worry among physicians, the Academy considered that its conclusions were, in Villemin's words, "still too alarming for the masses." More drastic measures of public surveillance, such as the mandatory inspection of schools, barracks, bureaucratic offices, and workshops, were rejected. The Academy's "instructions" were thus printed in its weekly *Bulletin* but not officially released for wider distribution to the public. If such restraint was reasonable in some respects, it would not long repress the badly kept secret that France was experiencing an epidemic.[13]

The Sanatorium Controversy

Just as the French demographic crisis drew attention to tuberculosis, so tuberculosis in turn inevitably emphasized Germany's example. In particular, it was now the sanatorium that took a place among such other objects of French admiration as the German university, the Prussian general staff, and the Wagnerian opera. Apart from that of Robert Koch, the fabled names of Hermann Brehmer and Peter Dettweiler also became widely known among European physicians during the 1880s, and the latter's sanatorium at Falkenstein near Frankfurt am Main was regarded in France as exemplary. The rates of tuberculosis cure obtained there, as Dr. Georges Dujardin-Beaumetz told the Academy of Medicine in 1890, were "truly remarkable."[14] At that time it was everywhere assumed that the only known treatment of the disease was fresh air, whether of the mountains or the sea, and that home care in crowded cities was usually ineffectual. Above all, patients with infectious diseases like tuberculosis needed to be isolated so that, healing or not, they would pose no immediate threat to society. For purposes both curative and prophylactic, therefore, placement in a sanatorium seemed to be the appropriate therapy.[15]

If anything might have undercut the sanatorium movement at an early stage, it was the discovery of a vaccine or a wonder drug that would eradicate tuberculosis altogether. For a brief moment in 1890 this possibility surfaced in the sensational form of a tuberculin serum developed by Robert Koch that was procured forthwith by the French for testing. One excited municipal councillor in Paris wanted it promptly dispensed to the city's populace, certain as he was that it promised "a veritable revolution in medicine."[16] But that bubble quickly burst when laboratory results proved to be dubious, and enthusiasm in the Academy of Medicine soon subsided.[17] The French were thus forced to enter the 1890s in the face of two disquieting facts. One was that available statistics showed tuberculosis mortality rates to be rising and reaching epidemic proportions. A report from the central Paris district of les Halles suggested that tuberculosis accounted for one death in every five and that one-third of Parisian hospital fatalities were consumptive. These numbers were "frighteningly eloquent," the report commented: "It is high time to react and to raise a cry of alarm."[18] The second hard reality was that physicians lacked either a vaccine to prevent or an antidote to cure tuberculosis. The sanatorium offered the only available therapeutic technique, for which Germany had set an international standard.

These circumstances explain the decision taken by the Municipal Council of Paris in March 1893 to construct the first major French sanatorium at Angicourt in the nearby Department of the Oise. Original plans called for the erection of two large hundred-bed wings in hopes of relieving crowding in Paris hospitals and matching the success at Falkenstein. But cost overruns soon became prohibitive, and the project was scaled back to one smaller fifty-bed unit. Even this facility proved difficult to complete. Its inauguration did not occur until 1900. Meanwhile, the municipality of Lyon also opened a sanatorium at Hauteville, and a few locations such as Berck-sur-Mer were designated to receive children suffering from pulmonary ailments. These beginnings were duly hailed by reformers as evidence that France was finally taking steps to close the therapeutic gap with Germany. Popular sanatoria "had demonstrated their merit abroad," said Paul Strauss, "and their utility is contested by no one."[19]

But medical opinion was in fact far from unanimous. The Academy of Medicine still hesitated to enter tuberculosis on the official list of contagious diseases for which notification to public health authorities was mandatory. A strenuous plea from the sanitation officers of four major cities—Le Havre, Lyon, Grenoble, and Saint-Étienne—failed to move the Academy to act.[20] Besides, doubts persisted about the infectious nature of tuberculosis and therefore about the efficacy of isolation. In 1896, two years before his election to the presidency of the Academy, Professor Sigismond Jaccoud characterized the contagion theory as "a mere possibility," because "the provenance of the bacillus remains in doubt." He contended that "absolute" methods of treatment were unjustified in view of the "ambiguity of the facts." For a government struggling to maintain a balanced budget, these remarks were not unwelcome. Even Léon Bourgeois issued orders that the creation of new medical facilities should not exceed approved fiscal allocations lest the state be saddled with a permanent deficit: "the government could not sanction such a procedure."[21]

Hopes and hesitations were carefully balanced in a report compiled in 1896 by Drs. Joseph Grancher and Léon-Henri Thoinot. This document, drafted at the request of the Municipal Council of Paris, specifically addressed the immediate measures that might be adopted by the capital city to combat tuberculosis. Some basic assumptions and broader implications were also evident. The Grancher–Thoinot report stressed that the disease was preventable and curable. Efforts of isolation, disinfection, and general sanitation were therefore desirable to prevent tubercular infections. Nonetheless, a proposal that private physicians must report any incidence of tuberculosis—let alone that victims should actually be required to enter a sanatorium if so ordered—was conspicuously absent.[22] All of which became the object of open debate during the waning years of the old century. In the Municipal Council there was a consensus, as councillor Raoul Bompard said, that sanitary conditions in several sections of Paris were "absolutely shameful." Yet politicians were reluctant to support drastic reforms because of rising costs, medical uncertainties, and fear of provoking a public reaction that would brand tuberculous persons as latter-day lepers. Hence it was premature to claim, as did Paul Strauss, that France was at last "following the example of foreign countries" by joining a "grand and noble cause" in the fight against tuberculosis.[23]

On 3 May 1898, two years after his initial report, Joseph Grancher submitted a sixty-page document to the Academy of Medicine on the "scourge" of tuberculosis, which he estimated was likely to contaminate one-quarter and to kill at least one-sixth of the French population. This statement, drafted after long deliberations by a panel of leading physicians and public health officials, represented a summary of responsible medical opinion on tuberculosis in the Belle Epoque. It passed rapidly over earlier conjectures about heredity and praised the remarkable bacteriological advances of J. A. Villemin, Louis Pasteur, and Robert Koch. Yet this second report again declined to recommend passage of a compulsory program for the identification and isolation of tuberculous patients. The committee, Grancher wrote, "very rapidly recognized that this new law, if it could be obtained, would encounter such difficulties—indeed such impossibilities—that it would be far better not to have the legislature intervene." Grancher therewith conceded that the ultimate problem was French *moeurs*, which he defined in this context as the "latent or explicit opposition of families who dread nothing so much as an intrusion into their affairs by public officials." Such recalcitrance was increased by the refusal of many physicians to comply with the state's health regulations. These obstacles, Grancher acknowledged, derived from persisting ambiguity in the medical community and the public about the etiology of tuberculosis: "The notion, relatively recent, of the contagiousness of this disease has not penetrated profoundly enough into all social strata to legitimate the draconian measures envisaged."[24]

A major boost for the sanatorium movement was provided in May 1899 by an international congress of physicians in Berlin. At this meeting, convened in the Reichstag building, the German medical profession displayed its antitubercular wares. The audience was impressed. The French delegation of Paul Brouardel, Louis Landouzy, and Joseph Grancher returned to Paris to praise the vast sanatorium facilities, the imperial patronage (including a dazzling reception at Potsdam by Kaiser William II), and above all the extraordinary results in Germany. According to the noted director of the pioneering sanatorium at Falkenstein, Dr. Peter Dettweiler, fully 20 percent of his patients were completely cured by rest and open-air treatment, and another 60 percent could be rehabilitated. Whether the French chose to replicate precisely the German procedures, Brouardel and Landouzy advised the Academy of Medicine after their return to Paris, surely they would need to open "numerous, very numerous popular sanatoria."[25] For his part, Grancher was moved to reappear before the Academy in March 1900 to announce a mea culpa. He had erred, he admitted, in refusing to support the inclusion of tuberculosis on a list of infectious diseases. Proper hygiene and fumigation procedures would only be possible if there were compulsory notification. Previously he had hesitated out of deference to public opinion. But now the alarm had sounded, and the Berlin congress, as he expressed it with a confused metaphor, had "aroused all those slumbering reverberations." The time had come for action.[26]

Political pressure also mounted. Most notably, Raoul Bompard, currently chair of the welfare committee in the Municipal Council of Paris, released an open letter to the French premier, René Waldeck-Rousseau, in which he urged that a coordinated antituberculosis campaign be started nationwide. In Berlin, Bompard commented, the Germans had offered an example of what was possible by "displaying with pride the immense effort of their private works and their public institutions." Waldeck-Rousseau responded by forming an extraparliamentary committee on tuberculosis control, led by Jules Siegfried and Paul Brouardel, that included nine senators, seven deputies, fifteen doctors, four municipal councillors, and a number of public health officers. Henceforth, at least, publicity would not be lacking.[27]

But in a series of articles in the *Revue philanthropique*, Paul Strauss pointed out the obvious: France required not more talk but increased allocations for sanatoria. The facility at Angicourt, finally opened, was admirable but insufficient. "The situation remains virtually as lamentable as before." If France could not copy the Germans, Strauss wrote, their example might nonetheless "excite our emulation." It was now up to the government to "give the signal for a crusade. . . . The hour has come to pass from words to deeds." Tuberculosis had become an "obsessive question" in France because of the "imperious necessity" for better health care and social insurance.[28]

Doubts and Initiatives

In retrospect it is clear that French enthusiasm for the sanatorium movement began to recede soon after the turn of the century. Despite all the public meetings, antituberculosis organizations, inspiring orations, and rhetorical outbursts in the press, swift progress was not detectable. Part of the trouble was the government's failure to make a forceful case for change. Even Henri Monod, a convinced reformer, was helpless to supply precise statistics on the alleged tuberculosis epidemic. In a summary of French mortality during the final two decades of the nineteenth century, he was able to show that the absolute levels of births and deaths in France were virtually on a par, and that the nation's population growth was therefore "vastly inferior" to that of neighboring countries. But the exact proportion of tuberculosis fatalities in that total was unknown. Monod offered detailed figures on other communicable diseases—typhoid fever, diphtheria, smallpox, whooping cough, and scarlet fever—but the reporting of tuberculosis, he admitted, was too approximate to justify firm conclusions. The mortality data attributed to consumption were actually exceeded by those listed as "causes unknown," and Monod could only add: "It is probable that a great number of these deaths are due to tuberculosis."[29]

Such ignorance aside, there were at least three other identifiable reasons why the impetus began to wane after 1900. First, the French treatment facilities remained inadequate, a condition that could not be quickly corrected without massive state funding. Serious limitations of the Angicourt sanatorium became apparent. It accepted only those Parisians designated as curable by doctors at the Laennec hospital, where a special tuberculosis dispensary was installed. Consumptives in other sections of the city and in the suburbs obtained no access. Another structure was opened at Brévannes, but it was designated for terminal patients and thus served only to remove some acute cases from regular hospital beds. Repeated attempts were made to arrange isolation wards for tuberculous persons, but this measure often met with opposition from chief hospital physicians who resisted any reorganization that might diminish their own administrative role. Assuming his duties as the new director of the Paris public health services in 1901, Charles Mourier described existing hospital facilities as "dilapidated, dirty, and repulsive, . . . unworthy of Paris, unworthy of France."[30] Naturally one must allow here for the self-interest of an administrator seeking funds for his particular bureau. Yet this statement did express a widely felt reformist need that was left largely unrequited.

Second, the sanatorium movement suffered from a lack of clear priorities. It was frequent in the Belle Epoque for orators to associate "the three great scourges" of tuberculosis, syphilis, and alcoholism. All were thought to have a common venue, the cabaret or bistrot, and each spawned a host of reformist leagues bent on eradicating a specific evil. Theoretically in collaboration, these groups tended in reality to compete for private donations and government subsidies. A good example was the activity of Émile Cheysson. As a leader of the French temperance movement, Cheysson made the conventional assumption that alcoholic excess and tubercular infection were causally linked. Accordingly, France should first make every effort to reduce the production and distribution (and therefore the tax revenues) of alcoholic beverages, rather than to invest heavily in the construction of sanatoria. Prevention, in short, should take precedence over cure. Cheysson lauded the "admirable institutions" of imperial Germany, "which merit our maximum attention." But the French, he said, should not adopt "a servile imitation." They should borrow procedures from abroad much as they had transplanted American grape stalks after the phylloxera outbreak of the 1870s. True, in Germany the popular sanatoria were flourishing under a national program of obligatory social insurance. But France had its own organization and its own principles. Hence, Cheysson maintained, "if the goal is identical, the method of attaining it must be in conformity with the genius of each nation."[31] These common notions, it must be added, did not go unchallenged. Sooner or later, retorted Édouard Vaillant, "we will be obliged to arrive at the German system of workers' insurance."[32] That day, however, had not yet arrived. Until it did, the proponents of popular sanatoria could not hope to realize their intentions.

Third, the medical picture became more blurred than ever. After the chimera of his tuberculosis vaccine had vanished, the reputation of Robert Koch was irreparably damaged in France. This disillusionment reflected negatively on German claims of remarkable sanatorium cure rates. A member of the Academy of Medicine, Dr. Raoul Brunon, scoffed at the republic's proclivity for imitating its eastern neighbor. "A great number of doctors dream of a France covered with sanatoria," and to every objection they respond: "Look at what the Germans have done." But the limited curative value of sanatorium treatment, Brunon contended, was hardly worth the "colossal effort," the prohibitive expense, and the social regimentation. Creating centers for home treatment, he suggested, would be preferable to construction of distant asylums.[33] These reservations, ever more frequently repeated in the Academy, were compounded by fresh doubts about the theory of contagion. Heredity, it seemed, was back in vogue, and with it questions about the prophylactic value of sanatorium treatment. As for contagion, said the eminent pathologist Étienne Lancereaux, "I do not hesitate to state that its importance has been greatly exaggerated."[34] Such rumbles within the medical community raised concern among reformers that the republic might regress. Paul Strauss worried that more negativism might lead to "the condemnation of the entire German system." And he admonished: "This is not the time to discredit German organization without having the certainty of replacing it by a better and more secure procedure."[35] Strauss thereby raised the obvious issue that would now have to be addressed. If France refused to copy German methods of combatting tuberculosis, what options would be available?

Clarity was wanting but activity was not. A national antituberculosis congress in Paris in March 1892 drew 350 delegates from thirty-seven French cities. They heard Paul Brouardel announce that a "national struggle" was underway that could become a "crusade."[36] Later that year, in October, a convention of mutualists gathered at Saint-Étienne and pledged support. This time the keynote speaker was Léon Bourgeois, who frankly deplored the lack of adequate care for tuberculosis patients and urged that mutualism participate more actively in prevention of the disease.[37] Meanwhile the government mounted a drive to encourage the construction of inexpensive public housing (*habitations à bon marché* or HBMs) and to enforce the disinfection of existing dwellings. This accorded with a report by Édouard Fuster, recently sent to Germany on a mission by the French cabinet to evaluate the effect of similar initiatives there. Fuster found the housing shortage in German cities to be even more acute than in France, a result of more rapid urbanization there, but he noted the exemplary collaboration of Germany's private and public sectors in meeting the crisis. He hinted, moreover, that there was "nothing so idiosyncratically German that it cannot inspire legislators and administrators in other countries."[38]

Yet these positive notes were offset by the loud volume of negative strains. Dr. Camille Savoire, for example, had also been dispatched on a mission to Germany by the Ministry of Commerce with a special assignment to investigate the popular sanatoria. Typically, Savoire admired the methodical character of Teutonic medical treatment, but he charged that the Germans were unduly concerned to impose their supremacy on French visitors and that they were "attempting to crush us under the weight of their grandiose achievements." Praiseworthy as the German model might be, Savoire reported, it was attainable only through an authoritarian structure that rested on an autocratic government and a "military spirit" among the people. France had valuable lessons to learn from Germany's example, Savoire was convinced, but he doubted that "it is completely applicable to our country or compatible with our spirit and our customs."[39]

This critical message was replayed by Dr. Albert Robin in a series of polemical articles in nonprofessional journals that attacked Brouardel and other advocates of the sanatorium movement. "Upon their return from Berlin," Robin wrote, "certain personalities envisaged the German system as a revelation; and full of the ardor of neophytes, [they] saw in the sanatorium the most powerful instrument to halt the advance of tuberculosis." Robin argued that French fatalities from the disease were not so elevated as alleged: no more than 90,000 annually, he estimated, rather than the 150,000 supposed by Brouardel. Nor were the German rates of cure as impressive as claimed. "It must be said, and said quite frankly, that the sanatorium does not heal; the sanatorium does not fulfill any of the promises that have been dangled before our eyes."[40] Forceful as this thrust was, a still unkinder cut was administered by Joseph Grancher, who had once again revised his position. Frustrated by his own unsuccessful attempts to discover a tuberculosis vaccine, he had withdrawn to a "temporary retirement" in Spain, whence he disclosed his current advice in the Delphic phrase: "I am *for* the English sanatorium and *against* the German sanatorium." Grancher did not wish to dismiss the therapeutic value of sanatorium treatment altogether, but he thought that it should be regarded merely as a complement to a variety of other medical and sanitary measures, rather than assigned a pivotal role as in Germany.[41]

These conflicting opinions were brought into direct confrontation by the government of Émile Combes in the autumn of 1903, when the new premier attempted to resuscitate the extraparliamentary committee on tuberculosis formed by his predecessor Waldeck-Rousseau. The leadership of this body was programmatically reformist—that is, prosanatorium—but in actuality cautious. The tone was set in an inaugural statement by the committee's new president Léon Bourgeois, who defined the fundamental ideological contest, once again, between liberty and obligation. Everyone could agree about the "national peril" of a tuberculosis epidemic, Bourgeois said, but at issue was the degree of state intervention. He favored the introduction of some (still unspecified) mandatory measures. Yet "in all these questions we must seek the boundary of individual liberty and public authority."[42]

Flanking Bourgeois at the podium were the committee's four prominent vice-presidents, moderates all: Alexandre Millerand, Paul Strauss, Professor Georges Debove (chosen to succeed Paul Brouardel as dean of the Paris medical faculty), and Joseph Grancher. Of these, it was Grancher who proved to be the most outspoken in his role as chairman of a subcommittee that had to consider the complex question of compulsory legislation. On two basic issues Grancher refused to recommend mandatory provisions: neither did he support obligatory reporting of the names of tuberculous patients to public health officials, nor did he favor required fumigation of all dwellings occupied by known victims. "Unfortunately, public opinion regards this malady as a sort of original sin," he commented, "which is true or false according to one's standpoint." He believed that only voluntary provisions were feasible, although he speculated that the day would arrive when French families would demand a compulsory system. Still, it followed for the time being that the sanatorium movement could not hope to overcome popular resistance against its strict enforcement. "You recall," Grancher told his colleagues, "all the magnificent progress claimed by the tuberculosis sanatoria in Germany. Unfortunately, the initial hopes have been deceived. . . . It is a mode of treatment that offers only mediocre medical results." Given this dubious record and "the current state of our *moeurs*," Grancher now advocated that the sanatorium in France should remain a relatively minor and purely voluntary institution.[43]

The evidence presented here is ample to illustrate the impasse reached before 1905 and to explain why that was so. The sanatorium debate, as Paul Strauss summed it up in the *Revue philanthropique*, had polarized opinion into two hostile camps whose mutual enmity tended to leave the republic in suspended animation. As a result, the French were unable to transcend what Strauss referred to as the "platonic" phase of reform. The intransigeance of the "rival and virtually enemy schools" had effectively paralyzed the sanatorium movement.[44] To this analysis by Strauss, which was surely accurate, it is appropriate to add one further observation: the difference between the two sides could best be understood in terms of their acceptance or rejection of the German example.

Devoted Reformers and Imposing Obstacles

If the antituberculosis campaign hoped to maintain any momentum, it was up to the paladins of reform to rescue it. Publicity was no longer lacking; progress was. To move ahead would require a redefinition of objectives and some willingness to compromise. Realistic steps, not leaps and bounds, were in order. Such was the evident conclusion among five representative figures of reformism whose names were well known to every politically informed person: Monod, Brouardel, Strauss, Bertillon, and Bourgeois. As if on cue, each in his fashion commented on the deadlock.

Henri Monod had served as the chief welfare officer of the French republic since the inception of his Bureau of Public Health and Hygiene in 1886. No bloodless bureaucrat, he often argued with flair and conviction for reformist legislation and identified himself closely with the cause of solidarism. He also did not hide his admiration for the vigorous welfare measures adopted in other countries, especially Germany, to cope with their health problems. "Sanitary solidarity," as he said, "knows no frontiers." Approaching retirement after nearly two decades in office, Monod remained a proponent of stronger state intervention, necessitated by France's prolonged demographic slump. In the decade of the 1890s, he pointed out, the German rate of population growth was 138.6 per 1,000, whereas that of France was 6.5. To turn things about, he believed, France must shed inhibitions about mandatory legislation, as it had finally done so in 1902 by requiring a smallpox vaccination of every resident. Monod claimed to respect personal and local interests, but he was insistent on the need to enforce a national code of public health. This message was at the heart of his long valedictory statement published in 1904, in which he concluded: "Legal coercion, in the limits where it is demonstrably necessary to protect the health of the majority, is not only legitimate but is one of the essential duties inherent to society."[45] No more cogent expression of reformist philosophy in France was ever formulated.

Paul Brouardel was a close and frequent collaborator of Monod. As a member of the Academy of Medicine since 1880 and long-time dean of the Sorbonne medical faculty, he was at the top of his profession. But it was the many administrative activities that distinguished his career, particularly as president of the Comité Consultatif d'Hygiène Publique, on which he labored for many years to promote and enforce progressive legislation. Recently he had become a leader of the antituberculosis campaign and, as such, a staunch advocate of popular sanatoria. Like other reformers, he acknowledged that the movement had bogged down after 1900. Yet he remained unflinching in his support for the adoption of a German style of therapy in France, with its clearly implicit mandate of isolation for the afflicted. "It is thus necessary," Brouardel wrote, "to have asylums ready to receive tuberculosis patients; whether they bear the name of sanatorium or that of hospital is without importance."[46] Unfortunately for Brouardel, a stately man in his early sixties, his personal health was already breaking and, like Monod, he was soon to pass from the scene.

Paul Strauss was the most ubiquitous of French reformers. Not only editor of the influential *Revue philanthropique*, he was to be seen and heard at various times on the Municipal Council of Paris, the Conseil Supérieur de l'Assistance Publique, the Academy of Medicine, the French Senate, and innumerable reform committees. Before 1900 Strauss had tended to chafe at the inertia of French liberals and to argue vociferously against the ethic of voluntarism. But his experience as a senator acquainted him with the political realities and forced him to tolerate mutualism, despite his continued distrust of it. If he remained as committed in principle as Monod or Brouardel to increased state regulation of public health, he acknowledged a need for a gradual transition. He deplored the deep split over public sanatoria, which he ascribed to a "legitimate divergence of doctrines and opinions among the French medical corps." But he condemned the "mediocrity of results" heretofore obtained by the antituberculosis campaign and demanded "a more positive action, a more effective effort."[47] Temporarily stymied, Strauss was still far from resigned.

Jacques Bertillon enjoyed a reputation as France's premier statistician. Undoubtedly his career also profited from his literary ability to dramatize data and to draw out their political significance. In a thorough report on French mortality in 1904, he allowed the numbers to speak largely for themselves. But he did not neglect an opportunity to stress a point: "One is immediately struck by the enormous preponderance of pulmonary tuberculosis (*phtisie*) . . . , which alone causes more than a fifth of all deaths." Still more shocking were statistics about the global mortality rate, which suggested that sanitary conditions were perhaps even worse in other French cities than in Paris. In fact, Lyon was the only urban center whose level (excluding the very aged) was consistently lower. As for consumption alone, the official Paris mortality rate was exceeded only by the two Norman municipalities of Rouen and Le Havre. In general Bertillon detected a slight diminution in tuberculosis mortality in France, but he documented three caveats: that the decline was not evident in crowded urban quarters, that the poorer populace was suffering far more severely than others (at a rate in Paris nearly double that of Berlin), and that the scant amelioration in the tuberculosis rate was "less than that of most other causes of fatality."[48] If the major conclusions that might be drawn from Bertillon's survey were not without ambiguity, they hardly argued for a relaxation of efforts to combat tuberculosis on the assumption that improvement would be automatic.

Léon Bourgeois had emerged as a chief advocate of solidarism and the principal political figure in the antituberculosis campaign. It was his task in one public oration after another to articulate the issues, which he did with admirable lucidity. But he had an inclination, shared with many a republican politician, to equate rhetoric with action. Thus he may legitimately be credited for encouraging the extraparliamentary committee, which he chaired, to draft a strong resolution favoring the creation of isolation wards in French hospitals. Yet immediately after that proposal was accepted by an administrative council (Conseil de Surveillance), Bourgeois boasted to the committee that "we have won a great battle!" That was in the spring of 1904. As he was forced to admit in the following autumn, however, the policy met with resistance from physicians and its implementation was "still far from being realized." Consequently, as a disabused Bourgeois conceded, "everything has been placed back into question."[49]

If, in spite of this formidable array of reformist leaders, the antituberculosis campaign was in danger of stalling, what impediments were to blame? In reply one cannot neglect to note how typical the tuberculosis question was of France's health and welfare needs in general. For that reason, the salient factors were not unfamiliar.

We need only underscore here the striking differences between the French pattern and the German model.

Lack of funding was first. The French nation was rich but the French state was not. Most wealth remained in private hands, without an effective means—other than charity or excise taxes—for the state to transfer additional funds to the public sector and to deploy them for welfare. The German social security laws had created just such a mechanism, the financial imperatives of which induced most of the Reich's member states to adopt an income tax. Not so in France. There, instead, such devices as revenue from alcoholic beverages and pari-mutuel betting remained crucial items in the national budget, generating endless controversies about their distribution. Given the divisions within the French medical profession about the etiology and treatment of tuberculosis, it was irresistibly tempting to curtail subsidies for sanatorium construction. In Germany, where the state-supported insurance agencies were obliged in principle to cover every tuberculous employee, the popular sanatoria provided a relatively cheap mode of therapy and received massive infusions of public money. Meanwhile, the French mutual aid societies routinely continued to exclude applicants discovered to have a chronic lung ailment, because their presence in a small privately funded insurance scheme would become intolerably expensive.[50] The inevitable consequences were apparent to all those who wrestled with the tuberculosis problem. In 1905 André Mesureur attempted to explain the budgetary shortfalls and delays in expansion of treatment facilities. Recommendations by the extraparliamentary antituberculosis committee had been refused for lack of funding, he complained, so that the effort to provide adequate care for patients remained "definitively blocked by the decayed and ruined state of our hospital equipment" and by "the lamentable condition of our old buildings."[51]

A shortage of specialized facilities therefore persisted. Dozens of reports from hospital inspectors and physicians commented on the chronic overcrowding, the constantly high number of stretcher cases for whom no beds were available, and the common practice of admitting tuberculosis victims to unsegregated wards. Louis Landouzy estimated, moreover, that half of the hospital personnel themselves were consumptive.[52] Little wonder that a third of Paris hospital fatalities were attributed to the disease. One can well imagine the terror of someone suffering from another ailment, or from a fracture, who woke up in the night next to a patient coughing and spitting blood. The corrective to these deplorable conditions was easy enough to envisage: a vast system of neighborhood medical dispensaries, hospital isolation wards, and popular fresh-air sanatoria. This was the "rational and scientific path," as Paul Strauss called it, that had been pioneered in Germany and toward which he and other reformers hoped France would turn.[53] But this solution remained beyond the reach of the early Third Republic, whose citizens continued to suffer the dismaying consequences of their government's impotence.

The inadequacy of enforcement was another seemingly insuperable obstacle. Even when sanitary regulations existed, Léon Bourgeois remarked, "it is their application that is delicate."[54] Not only did budgetary considerations restrict the number of state inspectors; there was a limit to what they could accomplish by irregular visits to factories, ateliers, schools, and hospitals. Nor did they have access to private dwellings, even in the worst city slums where the danger of tuberculosis was unquestionably greatest. Without the direction and coordination of an effective national campaign, as a Parisian city councillor correctly observed, French efforts to combat tuberculosis consisted of "little packages." Accordingly, most attempts to reduce tubercle infection by enforcing fumigation procedures foundered both on a lack of equipment and on the disinclination of citizens to be singled out by the authorities, lest their property be devalued and their families disgraced.[55]

Reluctance of the populace to cooperate was confounding. The Municipal Council of Paris, for instance, was repeatedly besieged by petitions and individual protests about plans to locate a sanatorium or any other facility for infectious disease in the suburbs. Property owners adjacent to prospective sites joined in "violent opposition" to such new construction, and of course parents were alarmed over the potential hazard for their children.[56] Yet alternative proposals to locate sanatoria far from the city encountered the objection that patients would refuse to be removed at a distance from relatives and friends. Another problem was spitting in public, still a common practice among men despite repeated admonitions against it. The refusal to abstain was revealed in a survey conducted by the Academy of Medicine at a major Paris railway terminal, the Gare du Nord, where very few passengers bothered to use spittoons strategically placed on the platforms. Most of them preferred to spit at random. Police agents and government inspectors were helpless to counteract such expressions of personal liberty that were not unambiguously illegal, albeit possibly lethal.[57]

Finally, in matters large and small, the antituberculosis campaign failed to receive vigorous government support. The formation of extraparliamentary committees by the Waldeck-Rousseau and Combes cabinets, although assuring that public attention was drawn to the epidemic, was a virtual admission that the normal legislative process was malfunctioning. Allocations, for reasons we have examined, were never forthcoming in amounts adequate to the need. Briefly it appeared that a new impetus would be provided by Georges Clemenceau, who became premier and interior minister in 1907 and who called the lack of effective preventive measures "criminal." But he, too, found that limited means and incorrigible prejudices made it extremely difficult for his regime to gain compliance for sanitation laws, which, as Clemenceau complained, "everyone conspires to paralyze."[58] While stalemated on so many other essential issues, the Third Republic found insufficient reason to make an exception for tuberculosis.

Ill Effects and Profound Sorrow

Certain statistical indications are that tuberculosis mortality was declining in France during the immediate prewar period. Available data do not offer definitive proof of that assumption, however, and it may in any case obfuscate the more telling fact: relative to Britain and Germany, France was failing to make significant improvement. Neither the strong local initiatives of the English nor the state-sponsored social insurance agencies of the Germans marked the French antituberculosis campaign.[59]

Indicative of conditions in France was a survey, conducted by the Ministry of the Interior in 1909, of 150 hospitals throughout the nation. Two-thirds of them had completely disregarded ministerial instructions (issued five years earlier) to provide isolation quarters for tuberculosis victims; and of the 50 that complied, most had simply designated a few separate rooms that lacked any special air, light, or equipment for consumptives. The report added unappetizing details about the neglect, particularly in provincial facilities, to provide the prescribed metal spittoons containing phenic acid. Instead, one often found wooden boxes filled with sawdust in which flies swarmed about, "seeking the sputum of lung patients, which they spread to the food and drink."[60]

As for popular sanatoria, after the addition at Brévannes, new construction was at a standstill. Dr. Georges Petit explained why. Earlier there had been much enthusiasm in France for having sanatoria "à l'allemande," he wrote, but it was discovered that "this was to assume considerable expense for minimal results." Instead, an attempt was made to devise "a more French method," which comprised a mixture of antitubercular institutions such as dispensaries, fresh-air camps for children, and cheaper public housing. Unfortunately, these efforts had too seldom received support from local and departmental officials, who appeared "uninterested in the great social question that is tuberculosis."[61] The same could certainly not be said of Léon Bourgeois, who exploited his position as chairman of the antituberculosis campaign to urge that an interlocking network of treatment facilities be created, so that patients would be carefully moved along a medical track in accordance with the nature and severity of their infection. Thus the special tuberculosis dispensary at the Laennec Hospital in Paris separated consumptives and then offered them access either to the sanatorium at Angicourt (for the curable) or to the one at Brévannes (for the incurable). Unfortunately, this arrangement was but one of a kind in France, and it was available only to a small percentage of Parisians. Most urban hospitals remained crowded and unsegregated. Consequently, admitted the director of public health in Paris, Dr. Auguste-Louis Navarre, "we are not equipped like the Germans." Despite years of agitation for better hospital care, he later added, "we are still disarmed against contagion."[62]

The quantitative evidence, because of the notorious practice of underreporting, is difficult to assess. Data on mortality, charged Paul Brouardel, frequently originated with "incompetent persons" who provided "incomplete information" that left his state committee on public health "unable to render a decision."[63] The unreliability of numbers was suggested by a dispute over the annual toll of tuberculosis fatalities in Paris. Estimates around the turn of the century ranged from a maximum of 25,000 to a minimum of 12,000. Hence, even in the capital, where the data were presumably most reliable, the reality was murky.[64] As for the countryside, one could only conjecture. French statistics were based largely on tabulations from fewer than 700 of the larger urban zones; about life and death in the other 35,570 provincial communes, nothing was certain. There was some reason to believe that, whereas some cities might be marginally reducing their mortality rates, the provinces were being touched by "the expansion of tuberculosis in the small rural villages."[65] In the absence of indisputable facts, we must rely on the judgment of the medical person most qualified to offer one: Dr. Georges Guilhaud, secretary-general of the recently formed Conseil Supérieur de l'Hygiène Publique, who drafted a series of annual reports from 1908 to 1911 on the mortality rates of rural France. Like Brouardel, Guilhaud complained that "no precise indications" existed for many areas; and what was known presented a confusing portrait. In Rennes mortality from tuberculosis rose, in Marseille it was stable, and in Lyon it had declined. Guilhaud's general conclusion was nevertheless categorical. He found that "constant increases" were occurring in provincial France and producing a "critical situation." Offsetting some urban improvement, "the number of deaths is increasingly high in the villages and in the countryside."[66]

Among the many attempts during the prewar years to analyze these data, one deserves commendation for its comparative slant. Henri Lasvignes's comprehensive study of the French and German systems of public health was published in 1911. It described imperial Germany as the "classical land of legal obligation" and contrasted it with France's inveterate voluntarism. Other European countries had been drawn toward the German model, Lasvignes observed, but the French republic had stubbornly resisted that trend and suffered the ill effects, notably in its elevated tuberculosis rate. With their Kulturkampf well behind them, the Germans had meanwhile integrated state welfare with private philanthropy, whereas France still harbored powerful charities that "possessed an importance at least triple that of public assistance." National differences were painfully evident in the struggle against tuberculosis, in which "Germany has furnished us a remarkable example." It had done so, Lasvignes continued, because Germany alone had applied a system of obligatory social insurance that the French—"a people of such different idiosyncracy"—were unwilling to implement despite their adoption of the universal principle of free medical care in the law of 1893. Although it would be "chimerical" to transpose the "magnificent organization" of German social security to France, Lasvignes concluded, "the voluntary system appears . . . to be definitively condemned."[67]

In actuality that conclusion was left unclear. Still open, for example, was the basic question whether notifying public health officials of all tubercular illness would be mandatory, without which disinfection procedures could not be thoroughly implemented. On the first day of July 1913 the Academy of Medicine finally adopted a resolution to that effect, but it did so by the narrowest of margins: 45 to 43.[68] Such patent indecision was not likely to sway a parliament already divided, or to persuade a government accustomed to gridlock. If reformers greeted the Academy's vote as another victory, their mood was hardly jubilant. Paul Strauss made the weary comment: "How much time has been lost . . . in vain discussions about the methods of treatment."[69] But the final word belonged to Léon Bourgeois as he reflected in 1913 on the entire history of the French antituberculosis campaign that he had led for a decade. He made no attempt to embellish the uncomfortable reality that Great Britain and Germany had succeeded in substantially reducing their rate of tuberculosis fatalities. "To the contrary," Bourgeois lamented, "in France the work remains fragmentary, incoherent, incomplete, and in certain respects barely commenced." Reviewing the performance of his own country, therefore, he could only express "profound sorrow."[70]

The First World War provided a sobering postscript. At its outset isolation wards and sanatorium space were immediately confiscated to care for military casualties. France's fragile infrastructure of tuberculosis facilities thereupon collapsed. Hospitals were more than ever crowded with beds and stretchers containing consumptives side by side with other patients. The inevitably disastrous result was not long to appear. Aggravated outbreaks of tubercular infection after 1914, as Louis Landouzy said, were "equal to the worst epidemics of the Middle Ages." Public health officials were shocked but helpless. They could only attempt to associate consumptives with the war effort by referring to them as the "wounded by tuberculosis," and some construction of temporary barracks for them was hastily arranged.[71] During the final months of the war, on the home front as in the field, help began to arrive from the United States. Funds from the Rockefeller Foundation were forthcoming to assist in the effort of reconstituting special tuberculosis sanatoria. In January 1919 Premier

Georges Clemenceau lent his support for a revived movement in the Academy of Medicine to obtain a law of mandatory notification. Recalling hesitations in the prewar years, he declared that the war had opened a new era and had "profoundly modified the hearts and minds" of the French.[72] So it seemed when the so-called Loi Honnorat was adopted by the parliament in the autumn of 1919 and France thereby launched a program to build popular sanatoria in every department. Although it is impossible to ascertain the precise impact of these measures on the slowly declining rate of tuberculosis fatalities during the interwar years, we may at least recognize the irony that it required a long and bitter war against Germany before France moved decisively to adopt the German model.

Chapter 12

The Embarrassment of Choice

Competition with Germany had long been one of the primary motives of French social reform. That fact became especially obvious in the final years before 1914. Although those who lived at the time were without our informed hindsight, there is nothing distorting or anachronistic about describing their mentality as "prewar." Arguably ever since the first Moroccan crisis of 1905, and certainly after the second in 1911, the threat of a conflict with Germany came home again to France.[1] If it would be hyperbolic to speak of panic, one can at least detect a foreboding that affected the conduct of public life. Just as the earliest social legislation of the Third Republic—such as the Loi Roussel in 1874—should be evaluated as the aftermath of a war with Germany, so the last enactments before the battle of the Marne may be viewed in anticipation of another.

The durable epithet that republican France had become a "stalemate society" has a manifest element of truth about it.[2] Yet that cliché deserves to be questioned both for its vagueness and its inflexibility. We should not, in the first place, accept a general hypothesis without identifying its major components. What were the specific issues that remained unresolved? What form did the deadlock take? And for what reasons? These are essential questions that merit more precise answers. Second, we might well boggle at the notion that France was utterly static. Although enfeebled, the French economy continued to grow erratically after 1870 and showed definite signs of revival at the turn of the century. True, in certain matters of social reform the French lagged behind some of their neighbors, particularly Germany; yet the communal, departmental, and national expenditures for public health notably increased before 1914, as did enrollments in savings banks and mutual societies. Moreover, despite repeated parliamentary delays and practical frustrations, a corpus of social legislation was taking form.

Overarching all these details was social theory. Our most authoritative guide to that subject has commented about the prewar era that "without doubt the great question of principle was the problem of obligation."[3] To some that word meant merely the sensible enforcement of measures necessary to ensure the implementation of public sanitation and welfare. But to others it connoted the unwarranted coercion of an unwilling populace by interventionist governments bent on imposing state socialism. We have witnessed how these two positions became defined and hardened across the decades since 1870. Yet here, too, important qualitative changes were occurring as the ideology of classical liberalism began to flag. Historians love to find turning points, and perhaps that temptation should be resisted now. But we cannot overlook how the nature of the social question was being altered at the brink of the First World War.

The Ideological Options

During the first four decades after 1870, French public opinion about social reform—insofar as we can judge it by the utterances of elected representatives and administrative officials—wavered between the imaginary poles of Great Britain and Germany. Despite a host of complexities and contradictions, these two nations remained immutably cast in their respective roles as the exponents of liberalism and etatism. Never mind that England encouraged municipal governments to execute programs of slum clearance through drastic confiscations and demolitions; and ignore the fact that the Kaiserreich was in important regards a federal system that allowed states' rights to an extent unknown in France. The two poles nonetheless remained fixed.

Immediately after 1870 the image of a progressive Germany had been troubling for all true French patriots, and politicians naturally hesitated to identify themselves with it. But already before 1900, as we saw, it became common for social reformers to invoke the German example, which was indelibly marked in French public discourse as "a vast intervention by the state through the principle of obligatory insurance."[4] French delegations frequently returned from congresses or missions of inquiry in Germany to extol German techniques in combatting disease, constructing hospitals and sanatoria, improving municipal sanitation, providing workers' compensation or maternal care, and so on. Some Frenchmen were persuaded, others were not. The resulting polarization became particularly evident during the prolonged debate over a national pension plan. The idea of creating an extensive and costly system of welfare entitlement for the elderly was something that one might be decisively for or against. Few were neutral. Final passage of the 1910 reform bill appeared to be a victory for the principle of obligation and thus, in a sense, for the German model over the English model.

The foregoing scenario, however, did not survive the prewar years. As the fissure widened between supporters and opponents of mandatory health insurance, inevitably perhaps, another theoretical option appeared. Its origins were lodged in an often expressed desire to devise a means of reconciling liberty and obligation.[5] Many analysts continued to regard those terms as oxymoronic and to argue that France must either reject compulsory measures altogether as a matter of principle or adopt them in a sweeping package of reform. Then, suddenly it seemed, a third possibility arrived in the form of a Belgian model.

Before 1910 references to Belgium in reformist discussions were scattered and incoherent. The first noteworthy mention of recent Belgian social legislation, which became operative in 1899, was made in a motion authored by an obscure French deputy, Achille Adam, in December 1902. After surveying other pension schemes in Europe, Adam pontificated that "of all the states [Belgium] is the one that seems to have found the best solution," which he described as "quite prudent" in its provisions for state intervention as well as "judicious" in its reliance on mutual aid societies. The Belgian plan, he said, was both "intelligent and liberal."[6] But Adam's suggestion had no immediate political resonance in parliament, and it was soon shuffled back into a large pack of other ignored bills. Five years later, in 1907, a brief discussion of factory inspection in the Commission d'Assurance et Prévoyance Sociales involved specific comparisons among the German, Belgian, and English systems. But again no firm conclusions were reached.[7] In the years following it became more common to cite this triad of models and to contend or imply that France would be well served to pursue the middling alternative offered by Belgium. In 1909, for example, when Senator Paul Cuvinot conducted his inquiry about retirement pensions, he concluded that most workers favored an obligatory scheme as in Germany but that employers would prefer a Belgian plan of state-subsidized mutualism. He also observed that, while a majority of the French (including those in agriculture, who tended to side with employers) favored the voluntarist character of welfare laws, opposition to some mandatory legislation had diminished.[8]

The simplistic polarization of the past, in sum, had become inappropriate. Scarcely known though it was, the Belgian model provided a convenient theoretical outlet for those who found the laissez-faire tenets of British liberalism no longer acceptable but who were still unprepared to embrace a German style of social insurance. The attractiveness of a third option was further enhanced by news that the English themselves were contemplating adoption of an obligatory pension program much like Germany's. For the first time the names of David Lloyd George and Winston Churchill became known in France, and liberal ideology suddenly appeared to be standing on its head.[9] Given this confusion, it made all the more sense in the French perspective to identify Belgium as the true alternative to Germany. Émile Cheysson provided an illustration. In a discussion of extending pensions to widows, he wrote: "On this point, as on many others, Germany has taken the lead." Yet such benefits for unemployed women were only possible in Germany within the framework of a mandatory social insurance system. "Elsewhere, for example in Belgium, it would be optional like the pensions themselves." Cheysson omitted any mention of England at all, stating only that the solution to this problem would finally depend on "the social armament of each country."[10]

Passage of the French pension bill on 5 April 1910 released a covey of theoretical analyses. Although diverse in their conclusions, these writings displayed a remarkable consistency in defining the ideological options available to the republic. We may briefly survey five examples, each of which posited a tripartite spectrum of welfare models.

1. *Léon Mirman*, as the successor of Henri Monod, was centrally placed but thoroughly perplexed. All the nations of western Europe faced similar social problems without agreeing on how to attack

them. Germany imposed a compulsory withholding plan on workers and employers, to which the state was obligated to add a subsidy. Belgium was attempting, without mandatory participation of the labor force, to encourage social insurance through mutual aid societies that received heavy state funding. England and Denmark required no direct personal contribution by individual workers or their employers. "Such are the three great routes among which the nations must choose," Mirman wrote, adding how "remarkable" it was that France had simultaneously begun to set foot on all of them. The 1905 law on public assistance corresponded to the English-Danish model; a recent allocation of 700,000 francs of state funds to the *mutualité* suggested the Belgian model; and the 1910 pension system with its principle of obligation followed the German model. Although Mirman made clear that he favored more state intervention in matters of health and welfare, he hesitated to specify the proper path.[11]

2. *Louis Puech*, deputy and sometime minister, made an identical analysis of the alternatives, except that he extended somewhat Mirman's list of examples. Along with Belgium he categorized Italy and the Swiss cantons of Vaud and Neuchâtel, and to Germany he appended Austria. Puech agreed that France's 1905 legislation resembled the English-Danish model of public assistance without compulsory contributions by individual citizens. But he also regarded the 1910 law as a step toward the German model. Although that bill was admittedly imperfect—the age limit of sixty-five was too high and the compensation too low—he favored its implementation.[12]

3. *Henri Vermont* was well known as a champion of mutualism. He dismissed the English and Danish examples (to which he added Australia and New Zealand) as "rudimentary," whereas he thought the German and Austrian schemes were unduly "feudal." Thus his own choice was clear: "In ten years, without new taxes [and] without new functionaries, Belgium has accomplished more than we did in fifty years." Unlike Puech, Vermont was totally hostile to the 1910 law. Movement toward the German model, he said, meant the destruction of mutualism: "That is what we must recognize and what true mutualists will never condone." If left to Vermont, then, the selection of a model would be categorical: "From the standpoint of pensions, Belgium has succeeded as much as Germany has failed."[13]

4. *Claude Lucas*, a Parisian barrister, contributed some arresting

observations. He noted that all three models were rejected by those at the poles of French political theory: Paul Leroy-Beaulieu for the orthodox liberals and Jules Guesde among the doctrinaire Marxists. Otherwise each of the models had its supporters and, just as Mirman had stated, elements of all three had already been adopted in France. He agreed that the German solution manifestly posed a "serious threat" to the mutual societies, whereas the Belgian legislation was "largely favorable." Yet Lucas pointed out that French tradition was not in fact inclined to an exclusive reliance on mutualism and that there was a centralizing tendency to administer public health programs through prefects and mayors. If so, perhaps none of the existing models was appropriate.[14]

5. *Gabriel Cros-Mayrevieille* traced the triagonal paradigm almost precisely. He confirmed that the examples of England and Denmark were consonant with France's 1905 law, and he adopted the phrase "subsidized liberty" to describe Belgium and Italy. But he stressed that the most recent French enactment of 1910 had "borrowed greatly from Germany" and that France's present welfare status was thus "altogether analogous to the German law." If fully implemented, he implied, the new pension scheme would commit the republic definitively to this course, presumably to the exclusion of others.[15]

These informed opinions helped to outline the possibilities and contradictions of French welfare reform. Their most striking feature was the erosion of support for a liberal model associated with England. One observer was reminded of Charles Gide's remark in 1883 that France was sure to see a "great thaw" of classical liberalism.[16] In reality it would be more accurate to speak of a slow meltdown in the heat of ideological debates generated by the social question. The residual issue was no longer whether the state should intervene in matters of public health but to what degree and in what form. Thus recast, the resulting choice was a Belgian model or a German model, that is, either massive state subsidies for voluntarist mutual aid societies or a mandatory national insurance program under strict government regulation.

Old Business and New

No matter what theoretical option was chosen or what new legislation was adopted, the problems of implementation remained. We have seen that these practical difficulties continued to plague the republic, and that the 1910 pension act was no deviation from the rule. Likewise, sanitation measures adopted in 1902 were still irregularly applied, despite Georges Clemenceau's pointed reminder to French prefects about the "obligatory character" of the law.[17] As always, one must distinguish carefully between what was intended by reformers and what actually became part of French mores. Perhaps the record would have been less cluttered had there been a prior decision, on a host of specific issues, whether regulations were to be optional or strictly compulsory. Failing that, *faute de mieux*, the French republic muddled on.

It is well, therefore, to descend from the elevated plateau of ideological models to the rather less tidy reality of social issues. These were integrated in such an elaborate fashion as to render their disaggregation dubious. Yet for purposes of diagnosis we may locate three distinct clusters of social problems in the prewar years: poverty, public health, and labor practice. Each was to remain unresolved.

Poverty had never been the first concern of French politicians. It was the demographic crisis, not the spread of pauperism in the nineteenth century, that provided the chief motive for social reform. Private charity and public assistance were left to cope with the truly poor as best they could, while maternal care, workers' compensation, and public housing became the more urgent issues of the Belle Epoque. Lamentations about the demise of liberalism were thus, as a practical matter, premature. Because the prevailing public ethic was still one of self-help, vagabonds and beggars remained an embarrassing annoyance. Furthermore, what many saw as the major vehicle of social amelioration, the system of mutual aid societies, did not address this problem at all. Poverty was thus far down on the national agenda. If anything, it was unpatriotic to be poor.

A ninety-six-page parliamentary report in 1910 outlined the dimensions of pauperism, which, it alleged, had expanded in the previous two decades. Charitable institutions and state-sponsored *dépôts de mendicité*, rather than eradicating destitution, had actually encouraged "social parasitism." Approximately 400,000 individuals constituted the hard core of unemployed who were thought guilty of theft, arson, and physical violence. Among those spreading such "terror" in the provinces, the report specified, were bands of nomads—such as gypsies and "even some French"—who were "particularly feared because their passage is always accompanied by depredations of all sorts." In French cities the situation was somewhat less menacing, yet a common denominator was evident: the disinclination of both rural vagabonds and urban beggars to seek honest work. The French welfare system still offered no solution to this problem. The report cited Germany and the Lowlands as examples of efforts to cope with it, and urged that France soon do likewise.[18]

After several months of committee deliberations, a proposal was submitted by the conservative Catholic deputy Georges Berry to declare vagabondage and mendicity illegal. This repressive measure, explained Berry, was necessary to protect the citizenry against those "who terrorize our cities and countryside." In a second bill Berry went on to move that the law expressly forbid the exploitation of children by professional paupers who "invent a thousand ways to circumvent welfare."[19] These bills raised two fundamental questions. The first, obviously, was whether the French literally wished to treat all mendicants as criminals. Should the police use physical force to rid society of nearly half a million undesirables? The second was more subtle but no less crucial. Paradoxically, Berry's supplementary motion against abuses of child labor recalled earlier anticlerical measures aimed at Roman Catholic orphanages. When this resemblance was pointed out, the deputies fell once more to bickering about the possible excesses of state interference with private charities. The theoretical clarity of the separation between church and state thereby became further clouded in reality, and the French Kulturkampf continued. Poverty, meanwhile, remained ineradicable.[20]

Public health was a second insoluble problem. One of its most debated aspects was the mandatory disinfection of private lodgings by sanitation officials. Not all obligatory rules met with the same resistance. Compulsory vaccination, for instance, had been generally accepted even before its enactment in 1902. Not so disinfection procedures. Municipal councils remained wary of allocating funds for equipment, physicians often objected to singling out their clients for fumigation, and public opinion deplored intrusions by state inspectors.[21] A proposal by André Honnorat would have required the dwellings of all government employees to be disinfected during every change of residence. The state, he argued, might thereby set an example to the public. But half measures were irregularly applied, and it appeared certain that France must either adopt strict rules applicable to everyone or perpetuate the ineffectuality of optional guide-lines.[22] Behind this issue was the perennial question of mandatory notification of tuberculosis cases to public health officers. A motion in favor of that measure, we recall, had been passed by such a narrow margin in the Academy of Medicine that the parliament felt no com-pulsion to ratify it. This reluctance was reinforced by reports hinting that most rural doctors were hostile to the Academy's resolution. When the government offered a legislative bill to enforce more strin-gent measures of disinfection, a poll was conducted of fifty medical syndicates throughout the nation. Twenty of them favored the mo-tion, while thirty opposed it. Hence, as a member of the Chamber's committee on public health dryly observed, opinion remained "very divided."[23]

Another divisive problem of public health was related: whether patients should always be allowed free choice of their doctors. Inevi-tably, as accident and illness insurance became more commonplace, incidents of noncompliance occurred and aroused controversy. At-tempts to regulate abuses by creating a scale of medical fees (the so-called *Tarif Dubief*) produced complaints about gouging and kick-backs. Such malfeasance, it was alleged, thrived on pressure exerted by employers or mutual aid societies to impose their own choice of a physician who was often more concerned with profit than with public health.[24] The hybrid character of French health care was thereby exposed. The state intervened, but without an unambiguous man-date of compulsory legislation. The mutual societies were active, but without a carefully defined status vis-à-vis local officials and medical practitioners. And the physicians plied their profession, but without a sense of unity or a clear delimitation of their responsibility to all the other parties concerned. These competing interests were bound to engender conflicts and hard feelings, which they did.[25]

No health problem seemed more inscrutable than hospital care. Even when procedural questions could be settled, the republic was still a long way from realizing the ideal of free medical treatment for every indigent citizen. Chronic overcrowding, especially in Paris, was unabated. "Despite all of its efforts," admitted the director of the capital's health services in 1912, public assistance "currently finds itself unable to assure . . . the hospitalization of mandatory patients." Most families with adequate housing and financial means preferred home care. But many cases (two-thirds of them women) were referred to hospitals, only to be turned back at the door. Municipal councillor Ambroise Rendu pointed out that barely a third of rejected patients were born in Paris, and he argued that the elderly without adequate family support should be sent back to the department of their origin. This suggestion foundered, however, on the refusal of individuals to be forced into deportation.[26] On other occasions the difficulty was that persons ordered to undergo hospital treatment would demur and demand to be left at home. Should insurance funds or state welfare agencies then cut off their financial aid (as might happen in Germany to tuberculosis victims who resisted transfer to a sanatorium)? During debates on this matter in the Chamber's welfare committee, concern was expressed about the proper limitation of personal choice. Laurent Bonnevay reiterated the principle that "individual liberty should always be respected unless it clashes with a manifest social interest."[27] Yet, precisely, manifest social interests were now under scrutiny, and politicians were presumably charged with finding a means to meet them. Symptomatic of the quandary was a ballot in the Municipal Council of Paris in December 1913. In view of the city's chronic undercapacity of hospital beds, a motion was introduced to increase subsidies for home care under the auspices of public assistance. The choice, in other words, lay between modest appropriations to be distributed to patients directly through *bureaux de bienfaisance* or major new allocations for hospital construction. The vote of the CMP was 41 to 35 in favor of the former. For a host of reasons by now quite familiar—political, financial, and ideological—this inconclusive outcome was altogether appropriate for a divided and uncertain nation.[28]

Like the foregoing questions of public health, labor practices in France were nationally regulated only in a few specific matters such as the employment of children. Issues like hours, wages, and working conditions were still ordinarily left to negotiation between employers and individual employees or, on occasion, their trade union representatives. French capitalism was thus largely unfettered, and in the marketplace a liberal work ethic continued to prevail. In the prewar years, however, pressure mounted for the state to intercede. Although the most elemental explanation for such increasing involvement was usually left unspoken, it was not difficult to discern: in case the republic were soon to face an armed conflict with Germany, it must secure the cooperation and compliance of its labor force.

Two problems predominated, neither of which was entirely new. The first was reintroduced in July 1910 by a motion from Minister of Labor René Viviani that France adopt a uniform ten-hour day, thereby standardizing the still-irregular conditions of industry. Thrown into the parliament that autumn, Viviani's proposal was rapidly adopted by the Senate with one variation: a sixty-hour week might be acquitted by a worker either in six ten-hour days or through a "semaine anglaise" that required a shortened Saturday after permitting a daily maximum of eleven hours of labor during the week. But in the Chamber of Deputies this version was opposed by a coalition of solidarists and Socialists, albeit for somewhat different reasons. The latter rejected the bill as altogether excessive and wanted the maximum working day reduced to nine or, preferably, eight hours. Such a limitation was no longer unthinkable, but neither did it as yet appear to be politically feasible. The motion for a forty-eight-hour week presented by Jules Guesde to the Chamber's labor committee was defeated by a ballot of 12 to 5.[29] As for the solidarists, they regarded any admission of an eleven-hour day as a relapse and wished to hold the line strictly at ten. Eventually a solution was devised by Albert de Mun, who suggested a "semaine anglaise" of five ten-hour working days plus Saturdays on which all labor would cease by 4:00 P.M. This arrangement, which in effect meant a fifty-eight-hour week for most workers, finally received the committee's unanimous endorsement. Yet the French government nonetheless balked at what it considered to be "a new principle difficult to apply" (even though de Mun's scheme was known to be operative in Germany), presumably because it would prove too inflexible to meet the various needs of French industry.[30] From 1910 to 1914, consequently, no definitive action was forthcoming. We may wonder at this impasse, considering that the only actual difference in maximum working hours was between sixty (proposed by the government and the Senate) and fifty-eight (favored by the Chamber). This apparent absurdity is lessened by recognizing how practical arrangements embodied general axioms that mattered. By adopting a ten-hour maximum, and thus outlawing eleven hours of consecutive labor for all workers, the state would be curtailing the flexibility of management by imposing binding labor regulations. Here was the real issue, a precedent on whose slopes the republican political process now stalled.

The second major labor problem of the prewar era was compul-

sory arbitration. Industrial strikes had become a common feature of
the social landscape, so much so that they threatened to paralyze the
national economy. Yet a nation at peril could not afford to have such
stoppages and disorders beyond control. Regulation was the obvious
answer. But how? Several different legislative bills in 1910 proposed
to limit strikes and lockouts, advocating a variety of means to do so.
Basic to most of them was a motion to create arbitration boards that
would head off disputes between labor and management before they
reached a rupture. There the questions began. Would workers always
be required to seek arbitration before declaring a strike; or managers, a lockout? Would the decision of the board be binding on both
parties? Who would choose the board? Would its rulings be enforced
in all branches of enterprise, public and private, or only a few? Minutes of the Chamber's labor committee recorded that such issues
were debated heatedly and at length. For once it was the Socialists
who adamantly opposed state intervention, because they considered
it to be nothing more than a facade for prohibiting the right to
strike. Most of the bills, charged Jules Guesde, would only unite the
army with employers against the workers.[31] The pivotal figure in
this instance proved to be Joseph Paul-Boncour, who served for a
year in 1911–12 as minister of labor and otherwise (before and after
his cabinet stint) as legislative reporter for the arbitration bill in the
Chamber. He was, in short, entrusted with drafting a compromise
that would pass through parliament. It was an unenviable and perhaps insoluble task. In essence, Paul-Boncour's position was that arbitration should be binding only in the public sector, whereas in private industry moral sanctions would suffice. Under ordinary circumstances this resolution might have been sensible. But it was touched
at its most vulnerable spot by Albert de Mun, who asked: what of
railway workers? Advocates of arbitration manifestly wanted neither
to forbid them to strike nor, in case of a national emergency, to allow
them to do so. Behind this dilemma, in other words, was the problem
that railway companies were private and yet essential to the prosperity and security of France. Their strict regulation—or indeed na-
tionalization—would bring the most fundamental aspects of state intervention to the surface. The French republic could not hope to face
Germany economically or militarily without total reliance on its trans-
port system. Yet if the labor force retained the right to organize, it
was doubtful that recalcitrant railway workers could be denied the

right to strike. As the summer of 1914 approached, these were troubling questions without clear answers.[32]

The Housing Issue

Another illustration of French indecision was the debate over construction of inexpensive public housing. Theoretical concern about this question can be traced well back into the nineteenth century, but like most aspects of welfare it did not become concrete until the late 1880s. The first new block of workers' dwellings broke ground in 1888, and in the year following the Société Française des Habitations à Bon Marché was founded under the presidency of Jules Siegfried. At the same time the first international congress on "cheap housing" convened in connection with the Paris Exposition of 1889. The national census of 1891 produced the first statistics on how the French were housed, which provided some momentum for the initial housing reform act, the Loi Siegfried, in 1894.[33]

These bare data suggest a story of rising expectations; they do not explain the nature of the problem or the reasons for disappointment. Altercations over the 1894 legislation were more indicative. Siegfried's intention was to secure public aid for housing construction, but he was met by opposition, centered in the Senate, against state intervention into an economic sector heretofore reserved for private enterprise. His bill consequently proved to be no more than a further encouragement for privately financed housing societies to join, with government approval, in a program of erecting HBMs. Accordingly, a boom in such private societies—in effect joint-stock construction companies—followed into the new century. A series of legal measures adopted before 1910 was designed to strengthen the Loi Siegfried but not to alter its basic orientation. The public sanitation act of 1902 allowed health officials to intercede if landlords attempted to block improvements in water supplies and sewers. A second bill drafted by Siegfried in 1904 aimed to hasten the expropriation of insalubrious dwellings that were declared a public nuisance. And a third law sponsored by Alexandre Ribot in 1906 favored the extension of housing credits to rural as well as to urban construction through the creation of regional societies.[34]

All of these steps notwithstanding, the prewar years were marked by a *crise de logement* in Paris and in some of the other major French cities. Jacques Bertillon estimated that fully half of Parisians at the turn of the century were forced to live in "overpopulated" or "insufficient" dwellings. By 1911 that percentage dropped to 43.26, but because of the capital's population growth, the absolute number actually increased.[35] Still worse was the fact that these masses were huddled in certain lower-class districts that were infamous for their extraordinarily high incidence of disease and mortality, especially related to tuberculosis. Already in 1906 Paris authorities identified six "dark spots" (*îlots noirs*) that together accounted for nearly half of the city's death rate. Municipal councillor Ambroise Rendu undertook to lead a movement to clean out those areas. He estimated that a fund of 50 million francs would be necessary to begin. But this fabulous sum, for reasons we have examined, was not soon to materialize.[36]

Inadequate financing was by no means the sole explanation for inertia. Among the other reasons, first, one must as always take into account the highly centralized structure of French administration. The monopoly of Paris over political initiative meant that most municipalities were not prepared to conceive land reform or to control urban development. Reformers came to see this effort as a solution to the social problem of insalubrious housing, all the more so as they observed the success of Germany in this regard. One expert has commented that "the French became increasingly aware of the achievements of German towns in the field of land reform. . . . In the 1900s French reformers began to urge cities to implement a municipal land policy of their own, based on foreign examples."[37] These pleas went mostly unheeded, however, and the real estate market was left to the mercy of private speculators whose first priority was assuredly not inexpensive housing for the poor.

Second, in those instances when a serious attempt was made to generate a coherent policy, sharp disagreements arose about the role of the municipality. In Paris the champion of a tough civic program to attack the housing issue was a Socialist councillor named Henri Turot. Armed with Bertillon's statistics and invoking the national leadership of Jules Siegfried and Paul Strauss, in the Chamber and the Senate respectively, Turot advocated "rigorous measures" to punish slumlords who impeded expropriation of condemned urban housing.[38] But that was only the beginning. Turot wanted the city not only to execute the demolition of blighted areas but also to carry out construction of new dwellings. Yet this step would require municipal governments to formulate land policy, to develop a clear planning strategy, and in effect to enter the real estate business. Here Turot's opponents drew the line: slum clearance yes, but municipally financed construction no. Ambroise Rendu was among those to denounce "this very dangerous Socialist proposal."[39] We may once again make note of the paradox that measures commonly practiced in imperial Germany could be condemned in republican France as too radically socialistic.

The third cause of inertia was an irreconcilable difference of priorities when it came to funding. In spite of early warnings about duplication of effort, an open competition developed between municipalities and private societies. Complaints against the societies were that they failed to attract enough private capital and that they preferred to invest in more expensive dwellings rather than in HBMs with rents low enough to meet the social problem. A delegation of members from the Municipal Council of Paris consequently visited parliament in 1912 to demand the right and the subsidy to deal with the housing crisis directly. But there they were confronted by a Senate majority that favored private modes of finance, just as it also backed mutual aid societies. Léon Bourgeois thereupon stepped forward in his accustomed role of peacemaker, which is to say that he took a stand squarely on both sides of the issue by supporting the municipalities and yet "respecting" the societies.[40] Back in the CMP this pronouncement was correctly translated by Gustave Poirier de Narçay: between the two conceptions, in reality, "profound differences" continued to exist. And in a public commentary on the outcome Gabriel Cros-Mayrevieille drew a contrast with Germany, where state insurance agencies promoted administrative cooperation and public morality restrained private speculation: "the rules are rarely violated." Meanwhile in France, he added, the atmosphere was charged with mutual suspicion and behavior was marred by indiscipline.[41]

The conclusion is inescapable, all in all, that the profit motive prevailed and that the housing problem remained virtually untouched. A joint statement in November 1911 from the French ministries of labor and finance conceded that the attempt to encourage regional HBM societies had wilted and that greater local initiatives were necessary instead. Yet these efforts, too, were obstructed. Paris municipal councillor Frédéric Brunet cited figures in 1912 showing that more apartments with annual rents under 500 francs were actually being destroyed than constructed, and matters were growing "constantly worse." Even if the situation was in fact more complex than Brunet indicated, the determinant fact persisted that inexpensive housing was not nearly sufficient to the need. As a consequence, the *îlots noirs* remained and tuberculosis continued to ravage the urban poor. Private investors hesitated to place their money in HBMs, yet municipal authorities lacked the means to do so. The reform movement was meanwhile divided, favoring both and significantly aiding neither.[42]

Women and Children First

In an issue of the *Revue hebdomadaire* in 1909 Professor Charles Gide told of a penny postcard that was circulating with a projected map of Europe in the year 1950. At its center was a huge red blotch extending from the North Sea to the Adriatic and from the Rhine to the Black Sea, an immense German empire with 250 million inhabitants. Next to it, dwarfed by comparison, was a tiny speck, republican France, containing barely 40 million, half of them foreigners. In presenting a bill to the Chamber of Deputies favoring special social welfare subsidies for parents of large families, the deputy Jean-Baptiste Argeliès reminded his auditors that Gide's futuristic postcard did not portray pure fantasy. About 1870 the population of the two nations had stood in equilibrium. But thereafter the balance tipped precipitously to the Germans. In the four years from 1906 through 1909, Argeliès claimed, the German nation increased by 3.5 million, the French by 35,000. "Within ten years," he said, "Germany will count a population double that of France. . . . Suppose a conflict were to occur between the two nations. What a prospect!"[43]

In this evocation of the demographic crisis, of course, there was nothing new. But a clearer sense of urgency was creeping into such admonitions in the prewar years. One dramatic example was a speech by Ambroise Rendu before the Municipal Council of Paris in July 1910. Rendu began by citing Jacques Bertillon's "cry of alarm" about France's declining birth rate, which was costing the republic nearly a quarter of a million "little Frenchmen" every year. As the population leveled off and began to age, taxation tended to rise. But, in terms of demography, the tax increase was counterproductive because it only constrained growth all the more. To break this vicious cycle, Rendu argued, the French must revise their welfare priorities: "Let us not fear to say it, for it is the truth. A nation should above all protect the productive elements of its population. It has the duty, in order to live and to develop, to think first of those who are the future rather than those who represent the past." Hence, he went on, the orientation of social policy ought to be "exactly the contrary" of current French legislation. Instead of lavishing funds on the mentally retarded, the aged, and the incurable, parliament should "completely transform" the system by granting major allocations to promote larger families. By putting fecundity first, France might yet survive. To be sure, this action would be "brutal," Rendu conceded, but "it is born of patriotic necessity."[44]

For such a thoroughgoing realignment of public health and welfare policy, it was very late in the day. Rendu's rhetoric could easily be dismissed as tardy and too cruel. Yet a rising pitch of concern was evident both in parliament and in public. An incident in the streets of Paris drew further attention to the population question. In April 1911 a demonstration at the Invalides by the Ligue des Familles Nombreuses was forcibly dispersed by mounted and armed troops. When the president of this group, a father of nine, was roughly apprehended, rioting ensued that had to be suppressed. Called to account in the Municipal Council, the prefect of police blamed anarchist elements waving red flags: "It is the way that leads to revolution." This remark drew an indignant reply from one Socialist councillor: "Your words are an insult to the working class." But the apparent moral of the episode was best stated by Poirier de Narçay: France's basic problem remained the demographic imbalance with Germany. "Bourgeois egoism" had infected all strata of French society, he said, "and the consequence is that the birth rate in France has declined to the point that we are obliged to call in black troops to offset the incessant increase of German forces." Another disturbing symptom of crisis was the extremely high rate of abortions, recently estimated by a medical authority at seventy for every one hundred births. In a shocked voice Poirier added that "some high functionaries even contend that a woman should have free disposal of her body." He concluded that what was required, after all, was not the suppression of demonstrations but the passage of legislation to assuage the penury of large families.[45]

These details fit snugly into the general pattern of a renewed prewar campaign to deal with the depopulation problem. Specifically, the government decided to create another extraparliamentary committee and to reconsider the question afresh. A previous initiative of this sort, attempted a decade earlier by the Waldeck-Rousseau cabinet, "remained sterile," admitted Minister of Finance L.-L. Klotz, who now took charge of the movement. Klotz spoke of a "veritable social and national danger" facing the republic, and he urged that a coordinated scheme of family assistance be considered an element of the national defense "on the same basis as programs of military or naval armament." Five subcommittees were appointed to study such issues as the simplification of marriage and naturalization procedures; the repression of infanticide, abortion, and "neo-Malthusian" propaganda; infant mortality and maternity aid to expectant mothers; financial assistance to large families and special bonuses for childbearing; and the damaging effects of alcoholism, tuberculosis, and the "general lack of hygiene."[46]

All of this official activity had a certain air of compensating for lost time and wasted opportunity. Despite Klotz's booster spirit, it was not long before deep differences over policy options began to appear. In March 1912 Henri Chéron (soon to enter the cabinet) used the forum of the Chamber's welfare committee to express support for family subsidies, but only if they were administered through mutual societies. He was frank to say that he considered mutualism to be a "guarantee of moral quality." He did not, in other words, favor an increase of state allocations to encourage all poor families to produce more children. Not just the quantity but the quality of French progeny mattered, in his view, so that a proper selection was imperative to enhance the nation's well-being. Some other members of the committee vehemently denounced this proposal as inadmissible. When brought to a ballot in CAPS, Chéron's motion narrowly passed by 9 to 7.[47]

Another dispute hinged on the amount of funds to be awarded for fecundity. A bill by Adolphe Massimy would have allocated 500 francs annually to parents for every child after the third. He hoped thereby to halt "the constant decline of our race"; and, alluding to Gide's disturbing postcard of a future Germany's hegemony over Europe, Massimy called his motion "a question of life and death." But in committee Henri Chéron advocated only 120 francs for each child after the third (under thirteen years of age), plus 60 francs to widows for all children after the second. Even though this scale represented less than a quarter of Massimy's proposal, Chéron insisted in addition that *prévoyance*—a code word for mutualism—be given preference over indiscriminate aid to the poor.[48] To both these legislative drafts the objection arose that they would be futile if family assistance were withheld until the birth of a fourth child. Some financial inducement must become available much sooner. In the summer of 1912 the welfare committee grudgingly settled on a scale of aid beginning with the birth of a third child. A year later, on Bastille Day of 1913, the bill was signed into law.[49]

Meanwhile, a related piece of legislation found its way through the parliamentary labyrinth: financial aid to mothers during four months before and four months after delivery. We need not follow that course, except to record that this bill was a special project of the veteran reformer Paul Strauss, who had campaigned unstintingly for it throughout the previous decade. By 1912, as Strauss editorialized in his *Revue philanthropique*, France still stood with the two most backward states of Europe, Turkey and Russia, in failing to provide adequately for pregnant women and recent mothers. Other nations had followed "the remarkable example" of Germany and Austria, he wrote, and it was time that France join them.[50] When this second bill was passed in mid-June 1913, a brief moment of celebration was surely justified. But to reverse the demographic decline of many decades, the twin laws of 1913 were at best a feeble and belated palliative. Looking back, we know now what the French could then only intuit: that the republic's salvation in case of an imminent conflict with the German Reich would depend more on military preparation and luck than on social policy and legislation.

Painful Conclusions

As France moved into the twentieth century, public health was becoming an increasingly major factor in the governance and daily life of the nation. By any standard, the social question had assumed in 1914 an importance unimagined before 1870. The Third Republic had been hesitant to accept this responsibility, so that welfare reform actually began in the Belle Epoque after 1890. Yet perceptions and policies were being demonstrably altered well before the First World

War. The precision of official numbers may be dubious, but they afford an approximate picture of growth in what the French called public assistance. In the course of two decades, appropriations to the Ministry of the Interior barely doubled, whereas the expenditures for public health increased tenfold (see Table 10). A clear upward trend was created by the 1893 law on free medical care for the indigent, but the greatest jump was induced by the reform act of 1905. Passage of this bill affected welfare outlays at all levels of administration, especially those directly provided by the central regime (see Table 11). Even allowing for the vagaries of French bookkeeping, it is evident that the contribution of funding for public health measures had shifted sharply to the state. Allocations everywhere increased, and all were interrelated. Yet the transparent tendency was toward creation of a centralized social welfare system of ever greater proportions.

Just how great, all told, is impossible to calculate. By some official reckoning—once all expenditures for hospitals, hospices, and *bureaux de bienfaisance* were included—the aggregate national outlay for public health and welfare reached 400 million francs by 1910, thus doubling the total since 1890. These estimates were accepted by an independent expert of note, Anatole Weber, who went on to speculate that private charity accounted for an additional annual sum of 600 million francs. If so, the grand total of expenditures for French health services on the eve of the Great War stood at 1 billion francs a year.[51]

So much for the good tidings. The bad began with the fact that, for a nation of nearly 40 million, the average allocation (accepting the optimistic estimates just noted) for each French citizen was twenty-five francs annually. Thus everything depended on the distribution of health and welfare funds, and here the Third Republic continued to have its problems. We have witnessed, for example, the unpopularity of the 1910 pension act, the many proposals to alter it, and the failure to implement it fully before 1914. This disability was compounded by court decisions that forbade employers to enforce withholding from the wages of workers without their consent. Meanwhile, the income tax issue remained in purgatory as politicians searched for some way to allay fears of inquisitorial inspection of private fortunes.[52] This inertia, in turn, stirred concern that rising health costs could not be met at any level of administration. The

Table 10 / French Government Appropriations (in Francs) for Public Health, 1890–1910

Year	Total Budget of the Ministry of the Interior	Portion Designated for Public Assistance
1890	73,368,784.49	6,726,803.57
1895	74,308,074.90	9,001,746.21
1900	80,145,087.25	11,501,097.94
1905	86,505,474.13	14,296,288.23
1909	132,459,122.07	58,279,288.23
1910	165,032.298.38	67,019,000.00

Source: Raphaël Milliès-Lacroix, "Le budget national de l'assistance publique," Revue philanthropique 29 (1911): 129–38.

Table 11 / Total Allocations (in Francs) for Public Assistance in France, 1890–1909

Year	Communes	Departments	State	Total
1890	10,503,216	28,120,652	3,981,479	42,605,347
1895	15,402,686	31,389,837	8,043,671	54,836,194
1900	22,329,780	37,268,830	9,047,449	68,646,059
1905	24,368,498	33,086,615	16,527,346	73,982,459
1909	57,964,200	51,717,615	67,377,050	177,058,865

Source: Raphaël Milliès-Lacroix, "Le budget national de l'assistance publique," Revue philanthropique 29 (1911): 129–38.

parliament, which was simultaneously alarmed about shortfalls of the military budget, had reason to worry that the state was living beyond its means. Pressure mounted on already beleaguered municipalities to raise their own revenues by local taxation, which they were reluctant to do. As the year 1914 began, consequently, the current president of the Municipal Council of Paris had to announce that the capital city faced a "hideous deficit."[53]

Prewar France was thus in a phase of social transition, with rising costs and meager results. If the nation was at last turning a corner toward public welfare, the major impediments to reform in the past were not yet overcome: women were still covered inadequately or not

at all by existing social insurance laws; physicians remained em-
broiled in disputes with state officials or mutual aid societies about
the disposition of patients and fees; health and sanitation measures
were enforced erratically in the cities and hardly at all in the countryside; and many workers continued to evince cynicism about pension
programs and withholding procedures, thereby perpetuating both
clashes with management and dissension in the labor movement.
Documentation of the period is replete with these palpable if immea-
surable facts of public life.

No society has a single standard by which it may be judged. But
one of the most salient criteria was once more cited in 1913 by Minister of Labor Klotz, the man in charge of the government's extraparliamentary campaign to combat the depopulation crisis. Compared
with other major states of western Europe, he repeated, France was
last in efforts to reduce tuberculosis mortality.[54] The real problem
was not that the nation was poor or lacked economic resources in the
public and private sectors. Rather, as we have so often witnessed, it
had failed to establish firm priorities. Many committed reformers,
such as Ernest Lairolle, kept pointing toward the pioneering efforts
of imperial Germany. There, he claimed, the 1899 revision of social
security legislation was functioning without difficulty; the only fault
of France's 1910 pension act was not to have copied that model exactly enough.[55] Traditionalists meanwhile drew the opposite conclusion: that France had gone too far. The liberal Henri Rousselle accused Lairolle of advocating the "absolute Germanization" of French
public health, and he argued instead for a return to unconstrained
voluntarism.[56] Frozen in his pose as the great compromiser, Léon
Bourgeois pleaded tirelessly for a national reconciliation beneath the
tattered rhetorical banners of solidarism.[57] To all of which a sole
comment seems appropriate: *plus ça change, plus ça reste la même chose.*

How should the republic proceed? One means was for the government to bear down on the enforcement of programs already enacted. A single instance, superbly illustrative, may suffice. At the
outset of 1914 the Ministry of Labor renewed attempts to implement
the requirement that workers regularly purchase pension stamps
(thus withholding from their wages) and attach them to cards kept by
employers. Whenever this procedure was not observed, the ministry
warned, management would be held responsible and was liable to
punishment. A formal protest against this fiat was forthcoming from

the French Retail Merchants' Association, whose president blamed noncompliance on the recalcitrance of labor. Furthermore, he condemned "the interference of the state in the organization of commercial enterprises, which can only hinder their proper functioning and consequently their normal development." To this blistering critique the new minister of labor, Albert Métin, responded with still more stringent instructions to the prefects. He added a historical commentary on the association's stance, which displayed a "simplistic form of the ancient quarrel between the liberal school and the interventionist school."[58]

Another possibility was to promote supplementary legislation like that proposed by Henri Chéron in November 1913 to extend invalidity insurance through the mutual aid societies. Discussions in the Chamber's social insurance committee (CAPS), however, produced sharp disagreement. A young deputy from the Vosges, Henri Schmidt, contested Chéron's intention to limit coverage only to the mutualists. "In matters of social legislation," he said, "we are at a decisive juncture." The state needed to attack vigorously "all the causes of the degeneration of our race"—of which he specified alcoholism, tuberculosis, and slums—but legislation would not be effective unless the truly poor were also included in health and welfare reform. "In this regard Germany provides an admirable example through the creation of an ensemble of institutions."[59] During subsequent sessions of CAPS Schmidt received strong support from such noted reformers as Ernest Lairolle and André Honnorat. Meanwhile, in a cabinet shuffle, Albert Métin replaced Henri Chéron in the Ministry of Labor, while Schmidt was named committee reporter for the new insurance bill. Without entering further into these complex maneuvers, we may summarize the outcome succinctly as a clear political victory for Schmidt. His version of the bill, which included but was not restricted to the mutual societies, was approved on the last day of March 1914.[60]

This action pointed the French parliament toward a path already indicated by the 1910 pension law—a path, if pursued, that might have led the republic toward a German model of welfare reform. But other events intervened, and we shall never know whether a gradual progression in that direction would have ensued. It was indicative that the final session of CAPS on 31 March 1914 was prolonged by deliberations about insurance for accidents resulting from military service. The prophetic closing words of the minutes of that last pre-war meeting recorded the committee's decision that "the law shall be applicable in peacetime . . . and wartime."[61]

Perhaps the most appropriate epitaph was that presented to the Senate in late 1913 by a group of republican notables including Léon Bourgeois, Alexandre Ribot, and Paul Strauss. It was an admission of failure: "The situation of public health in our country is altogether disquieting. We are far from being placed, in this respect, at the station we should occupy through our intellectual development, our financial capacity, and the totality of our moral and social theories." Hitherto, the report read, French social legislation had produced "completely insufficient results." It was statistically verifiable, for instance, that the French mortality rate from consumption continued to exceed by far that of neighboring states. "These conclusions are painful," the report confessed. Yet they must be faced if the French people expected to "resume the ascending path necessary for the future of our race." A crusade had begun, but it would have to march in full awareness of "a peril, at home as well as abroad, menacing the existence of France."[62]

There is little that the historian need add to these words. They eloquently expressed the hopes and fears of the French nation as it stood on the precipice of another war. Moreover, they testified to the fact that imperial Germany preoccupied the thinking of the Third Republic not only in the guise of an armed foreign enemy but also as a disturbing challenge in French domestic affairs. Development of public health and welfare reform, no less than construction of military fortifications, had long been conceived in the shadow of an imposing German presence. If the French shied from adopting the German model, they could not remain oblivious to it. Throughout history France had always been a country of choices, torn between being a land power and a sea power, between the Mediterranean world and the European continent, between authority and democracy, between agriculture and industry. These many options were both a blessing and a curse, and the French had consequently learned to be ambiguous, subtle, and often quarrelsome. So it was with the social question of the nineteenth century. Before 1914 the French republic went its own way, not by virtue of firm decisions but through a failure to reach them.

Conclusion

Republic and Reich, 1870–1914

To recount the interaction between two great nations necessarily requires a history that is long and complex. But in the end it may be useful to summarize as succinctly as possible the principal themes of such a broad subject, even at the risk of undue simplification. The synopsis that follows is an attempt to trace the main contours of the relationship between republican France and imperial Germany from 1870 to the First World War. Throughout that time the Kaiserreich exerted a powerful influence over the French nation. The significance of that phenomenon, essential to a full understanding of the Third Republic, is not to be grasped solely in terms of formal treaties, diplomatic contacts, and international affairs. The German factor became part of the internal composition of France, affecting in one fashion or another every major aspect of public life.

This is to suggest that the German influence was not of a single kind. Over the course of the half century in question, after allowances are made for the simultaneity and ambiguity of historical occurrence, one may observe three fairly distinctive phases of reform. Accordingly, this analysis can be clarified by dividing the notion of influence into three components—manipulation, competition, and imitation—and by applying them in turn to those successive phases. The utility of this procedure is enhanced by accounting thereby for various degrees of directness, starting with the most immediate and deliberate forms of influence and then moving down the scale to those that were indirect and often involuntary.

Manipulation

The most direct form of political and economic influence is warfare. Napoleon Bonaparte proved that proposition before 1815 and Otto von Bismarck demonstrated it again in 1870. *L'année terrible* left France more helpless and humiliated than at any time heretofore in its modern history. It was therefore fitting that Adolphe Thiers emerged as the first president of the nascent republic, because he possessed both of two indispensable qualifications: not only was he a popular choice in France, he was also acceptable to Germany. Thiers promptly did what was necessary by signing France's name to the treaty of Frankfurt, dictated by Bismarck, which committed the republic to the forfeit of Alsace-Lorraine, the payment of 5 billion francs in reparations, and the fulfillment of a most-favored-nation commercial agreement with the conqueror. Such concessions were all the easier for Bismarck to obtain once Thiers was confronted with the Paris Commune and was obliged to seek German cooperation in crushing it. From the day of its inception, then, the new French republic was subject to German blackmail.

The German occupation of northeastern France lasted for three years, a time of ugly incidents and shameless threats. French statesmen were repeatedly drenched with a "cold shower," as Bismarck forcefully reminded them of their vulnerability. Diplomatically isolated, politically troubled, economically weakened, morally confused, the French nation found itself reduced to the status of a compliant satellite in the sphere of German domination.

It was no coincidence that a muffled coup d'état immediately followed final negotiations for the evacuation of French territory. His aura of indispensability removed, Thiers fell when his pretensions to personal autocracy became exposed at their true value. His opponents did not hesitate to substitute a caretaker president in the person of Marshal MacMahon, thereby assuring the primacy of parliament—unless the monarchy were restored. But a royalist alternative was unacceptable to Bismarck, who preferred to keep France internally divided and externally isolated from the other kingdoms of Europe. France did not become a parliamentary republic merely because the German chancellor wished it so, but a restoration of the monarchy failed partially because he discouraged it. The collapse of fusionism between Legitimists and Orleanists was largely a story of self-destruction after Bismarck's peremptory action to hinder the Kaiser from responding to overtures from the Comte de Chambord. German disapproval of French monarchism was further reinforced by ominous troop movements and a hint of renewed hostilities should the moderate republic be replaced. The same strictures fell on the Bonapartists, who had no access to power after the death of Napoleon III except through the kind of serious domestic crisis in France that it was Bismarck's policy to preclude. After 1873, therefore, German political influence was exercised not to achieve change but to prevent it. Once a centrist republicanism was established within a defeated and exhausted French nation, Germany needed only to abet a natural inertia. The remarkable ineptitude of royalist and Bonapartist leaders thus made them Bismarck's unwitting partners.

Such a posture was not without its problems. Two developments in France were watched from Berlin with special concern: military rearmament and Catholic revivalism. In the German perspective they were closely related. Hence the volatile combination of revanche and religion became a target of German propaganda and of direct pressure, best illustrated by the harsh attacks on French bishops who dared to express solidarity with the faithful in the lost provinces and to offer public prayers for their return to France. The constant hectoring from Germany and the unsubtle admonitions of military reprisal if republican officials lagged in silencing dissidents reached a peak in the so-called war scare of 1875. In actuality France was in no condition for a fight, and the incident was bloated out of all proportion. But it was typical of German bullying, and it unquestionably stirred emotions of fear among the French. The depth of this popular reaction should not be underestimated, for it helps to explain the outcome of a far more significant crisis of the republic in 1877. As usual, the major German objectives were to maintain the political status quo in France, to serve warning against religious pilgrimages and military augmentations, and in general to sustain a suitably high level of French anxiety. These purposes ran contrary to the high-handed attempt by President MacMahon and his conservative supporters to throttle the republican majority through a tightly managed and selectively rigged electoral campaign. In the wake of the recent war scare, both sides sought to establish themselves as guarantors of European peace. Yet only the republicans behind Thiers and

Léon Gambetta could effectively sustain that claim once they received overt encouragement from Germany. With little regard for diplomatic proprieties, Bismarck deliberately intervened to impress upon French voters that a victory for MacMahon would be considered by Berlin as tantamount to a declaration of war. If an exact count of the electoral impact of these maneuvers is impossible, evidence nonetheless suggests that the German menace should be considered among the salient factors of republican success.

After opportunist republicanism was secure, following MacMahon's resignation in early 1879, a period of Franco-German détente could begin. The relaxation of Bismarck's grasp carried one condition, however, of which the Gambettists and other moderates were constantly reminded: the republic must not fall prey to leftist radicalism. Henceforth successive French cabinets—before and after Gambetta's premature death in the early 1880s—were subjected to German complaints about the restless ambition of Georges Clemenceau and his allegedly unreliable allies. But these innuendos, as we now know, were mostly gratuitous. The truth was that the French republic had assumed a political structure that conformed closely to the German ideal of it.

Meanwhile, the relative lassitude of France's economic performance was related from the beginning to the horrendous cost of the war against Germany in 1870. Although precise sums are literally incalculable, the total may probably be placed in the vicinity of 20 billion francs. Allowance must be made not only for the period of combat itself but also for the burden of reparations, the bill for defraying German expenses during the occupation, the payment of interest on two major public bond issues, and the extensive material damage to agriculture, industry, and commerce. The edifice of the Third Republic was thereby heavily mortgaged from the outset. In the first years of its existence, consequently, at least half of the French national budget was absorbed by the amortization of public debts.

These early financial difficulties served all the better, from the viewpoint of Berlin, to keep the French from launching a vast program of military rearmament. Presumably the only means for France to recover quickly would have been either to introduce an income tax or to impose high tariffs. Thiers would not allow the former and could not obtain the latter. A progressive tax on personal revenue would encroach both on business interests and private wealth and was thus unacceptable to the president and his bourgeois backers. As for a shift to protectionism, the way was blocked by a reluctant Assembly and by restrictions imposed through the treaty of Frankfurt. In the absence of such bold initiatives, the financial shock of the defeat in 1870 was slow to dissipate.

Symptomatic of an altered Franco-German economic symbiosis, and contributing importantly to it, was a dramatic shift in the bilateral balance of trade. Throughout most of the 1870s France was able to maintain a surplus in its commerce with Germany. But after the Reich's conversion to protectionism, that tilt was decisively reversed. With their own markets protected, German entrepreneurs were able to penetrate the comparatively free commercial field of France. German imports declined, whereas exports westward across the Rhine began to soar. In this direct and deliberate fashion, Germany took advantage of France's economic weakness during the postwar era. The enduring implications are well known and may be briefly suggested here. Germany's economic boom brought the Reich hurtling into the Second Industrial Revolution. Not only did German coal and steel production reach unprecedented levels, its industry also gained the lead in chemicals and dyes, electrical products, tools and machines. By 1914 France had dropped far to the rear in all of these crucial sectors. As a consequence, the early Third Republic was unprepared to compete equally with imperial Germany in the European market for finished products and found itself increasingly dependent on colonial outlets. Comparatively unevolved in its economic structure, France tended to remain a dealer in raw materials, agricultural produce, semifinished goods, and luxury items. Measured against Germany, the republic experienced a slower pace of urbanization and a persistence of small enterprise.

These developments have blended indistinguishably into the dynamic economic pattern of the twentieth century. They permit the simple observation that the period from 1870 to 1914 proved to be an unconscious preparation for the present European Common Market. Out of this distant background of conflict came an inadvertent economic cooperation and, one may even say, a certain complementarity. Largely through shortsighted calculations and manipulations, the two nations were in fact planting the seeds of their own prosperity.

Competition

After the swift Prussian victory over Habsburg troops in 1866, an armed confrontation between France and Germany became likely, if not quite inevitable. The immediate prize was the still-independent cluster of south German states. Beyond that, of course, it was a matter of national prestige and pride. To prepare his realm for a contest with Prussia, Napoleon III proposed to adopt a system of universal conscription. This reform was not realized in time, however, and Bonapartist France entered the war of 1870 with a professional army that was quickly stunned and trounced. Further resistance by the hastily organized militia forces of Léon Gambetta fared no better and soon ended in capitulation. With these two options—a hired army and a popular militia—effectively eliminated as suitable models, French reformers were left after 1870 to define the military question in terms of a stark alternative: to copy the German example or not.

The elaborate pattern of this long debate can be reduced to the proposition that, except for the critical matter of recruitment, the republic chose to create a military organization closely analogous to that of Germany. Because Adolphe Thiers opposed such a fundamental shift, his removal from the presidency in May 1873 brought an immediate rejection of his military policy. He, for example, wished the French army to comprise twelve corps with three divisions each. But his chief military antagonist, Marshal MacMahon, countered that such a system would be slow, unstable, and ineffective; hence France must have eighteen corps with two divisions each, just as Germany. By agreeing to replace Thiers as president of the republic, MacMahon assured that his own conception would prevail. Thereafter, in deciding what was modern in military affairs, France gravitated toward the German model. The extent to which the prospect of a future conflict with Germany guided French military planning can be charted in minute detail. The placement of fortifications, deployment of troops, adoption of artillery and infantry weapons, inauguration of a new officers' training school like the Prussian *Kriegsakademie*, development of strategy, augmentation of the military budget—all were predicated on achieving parity with Germany. That alone served as a criterion to measure the success or failure of French reorganization.

Before 1890, one must conclude, such ambition remained far from realized. If the artillery was France's stoutest and proudest arm, it was so widely dispersed in static positions along the eastern and northern frontiers that only a fraction of its firepower could be deployed against a German invasion. Infantry units were perpetually undermanned, compared with units in Germany, and they were handicapped by the inadequate training and sparse equipment of their regional reserves. Likewise, the cavalry suffered from a chronic shortage of healthy steeds and skilled horsemen. All three combat branches complained of a deficiency of experienced noncommissioned officers, in contrast to the remarkable retention rate of NCOs in the German army. Drilled primarily to endure the rigors of Parisian bureaucracy, senior staff officers of the French État-Major usually lacked the field experience of their German counterparts. Furthermore, the French military budget was, despite appearances of parity created by national differences in accounting procedures, significantly inferior to that of Germany. All in all, France was unable to close the military gap before the 1890s, a deficit readily conceded by ranking officers in sequestered sessions of the Conseil Supérieur de la Guerre.

Actual planning for the French army that went to the Marne in 1914 should properly be credited to the five-year tenure of Charles de Freycinet as minister of war, starting in 1888. Above all, it was Freycinet who finally presided over the passage of a three-year recruitment bill that began to justify the heretofore hollow rhetoric of a French nation-in-arms. At the same time, technological advances in munitions and weapons caused the French to recast their defensive system, refurbishing fortresses on their eastern frontier from Verdun southward and abandoning or declassifying those on the entire northern border with Belgium. In doing so, French strategists in effect conspired with German commanders to mold the Schlieffen Plan, the probability of which became evident to all in the decade prior to the war. From beginning to end, in sum, the military question of the early Third Republic pivoted on rivalry with Germany.

The religious question was perhaps less obvious. Still, especially concerning public education, it can best be viewed in the context of international competition. At the outset it was by no means self-evident that Roman Catholicism and French republicanism would blend.

But the circumstances of the war in 1870 and the ensuing German occupation dictated a cooperation of church and state in France. Disregarding simmering quarrels over the investiture of bishops, the French hierarchy hastened to the defense of the country and readily, albeit provisionally, accepted its republicanization. Since both Versailles and the Vatican were threatened with total isolation, they embraced one another in commiseration. Despite the church's scarcely disguised preference for royalism, a cordial relationship developed with the Thierist regime. This marriage of convenience acquired some passion through mutual opposition to the Paris Commune, and harmony was further enhanced by the German occupation of eastern France, during which the church turned to republican officials for protection against encroachment on Catholic rights and altars. Thereafter the German attacks on French prelates and the charges of collusion between religiosity and revanchism in France provided ample reason for church and civil authorities to join in national self-defense.

Yet these accommodations, temporarily imposed by Germany's military incursion, could not long camouflage the inherent conflict between ultramontane Catholic revivalism and the secularizing aspirations of French radicalism. Given the virulence of anticlerical sentiment detectable beneath the surface of public life, and expressed notably in the secrecy of masonic lodges, it was actually a wonder that open hostility did not sooner erupt. One demonstrable reason for a delay was the triangular configuration of the religious question in Europe's heartland. Uncomfortably locked in a struggle with the Roman papacy in the early 1870s, Bismarck actively sought to draw France into the fray. As long as the German Kulturkampf endured, however, any republican assault on the church in France was bound to be castigated as a national betrayal—that is, as an act of obeisance to the German chancellor. But once Berlin and Rome began an elaborate ritual of reconciliation after the death of Pius IX in 1878, French anticlericals were relieved of that onus and were free to pursue their campaign of secularization in the 1880s. A complete reversal of fronts thus came about: while imperial Germany cultivated an ostentatious amicability in religious affairs, the French Kulturkampf was unleashed with a ferocity that eventually carried the republic to a complete rupture with the church in 1905. Documentation of the period leaves no doubt that the rhythm as well as the content of the religious question were substantially influenced by Franco-German rivalry.

Within France no facet of this story was more crucial than public education, beginning with the application of the Ferry laws in the 1880s. Mandatory primary schooling was a natural complement to universal military training. Both had their origins in the rankling defeat at the hands of Germany. The logic of reform was impeccable: if the republic were to raise a modern popular army, then French citizens would need to be sufficiently instructed to make it function. But the church understandably worried about losing its grip on primary education. In the republic's very early years the Catholic hierarchy therefore balked and the reform movement stalled in the Conseil Supérieur de l'Instruction Publique. But once the Gambettists triumphed in 1877 and the international religious scene began to change, Jules Ferry was able to proceed with new legislation. In secondary education the basic problems took longer to resolve. The prestige of the classical *lycée* proved insurmountable, and only with misgivings and disclaimers were the French finally disposed in the early 1890s to add an alternative track, called *enseignement secondaire modern*, which was intended to match the German *Realgymnasium* or *Oberrealschule*. As for higher education, despite a considerable admiration among reformers for the variety and quality of German provincial universities, which they wanted to emulate, no government was willing to compromise the *grandes écoles* that were the essence of French elitism. Thus, at every pedagogical level, France moved only hesitantly to meet the German challenge.

Fundamental to all French reform initiatives in education was the fear of losing scientific leadership to Germany. That sense of competition was plainly evident in the demands for more intensive instruction of natural science, geography, history, and modern languages. The war had exposed these deficiencies, among others, and reformers urged a reorientation in order to keep France competitive. This plea was particularly apparent in regard to medical training, in which Germany's international prestige loomed over France. The pressure to keep pace motivated republican reformers to demand more laboratories, seminars, libraries, fellowships, and ancillary academic positions (*maîtres de conférence* resembling the German *Privatdozenten*). Actually to obtain and to integrate such improvements was another matter, and the observation is inescapable that scientific equality with Germany remained as much a mirage as military parity. Yet one should by no means overlook the French determination after 1870 to retain a leading role in the European scientific community or underestimate the persistence of national pride as a spur to intellectual excellence. Even though the record shows that the Third Republic was outdistanced by imperial Germany, the very fact that the French performance was perceived by that standard was in itself significant. Rivalry saved France from resignation.

Imitation

A conspicuous feature of the French republic after 1870 was that it possessed neither the ideological premises nor the public institutions to deal with widespread poverty. As long as the liberal tenets of self-help and laissez faire were left intact, the new regime would be impotent to meet the urgent needs of its citizens who were indigent, ill, injured, invalid, or aged. For the social question liberalism had no adequate response. The republican reformers were thus constrained to look elsewhere for a potential solution to France's mounting problems of public health and hygiene. With mixed emotions of apprehension and admiration, they turned to imperial Germany.

Through a series of bold enactments in the 1880s, the German Reich took a lead in social legislation and thereby issued a challenge that the other states of Europe could not ignore. In measuring itself against Germany, the French republic was exceptional only insofar as its demographic performance was far below the European average. Passage of the Loi Roussel in 1874 was an early indication that French reformers recognized a need to redress the balance of population. But a steady accumulation of statistics by 1890 revealed the alarming reality that France was continuing to lose ground. The greatest obstacle to social reform was identifiable: because of its prevailing liberal ethos, the French nation retained a framework of voluntarism. Shorn of such inhibitions, imperial Germany was meanwhile moving down a separate path of state interventionism. Was France to follow? Was, in other words, the German model to be emulated, modified, or rejected? It was in these terms that the social question was habitually framed by French reformers in the Belle Epoque and that it can best be understood in retrospect.

Although French evaluations of Germany's welfare system varied, there was agreement about its general characteristics. To praise the German example was to advocate the principle of obligatory social security and the practice of increased governmental regulation. Statistical evidence and eyewitness reports by French investigators appeared to confirm the growing success of German legislation and sanitation. Yet opponents of similar reforms in France could always raise two formidable objections: that the advantages of the German model would be offset by unwarranted interference of the state with the private sphere of business firms, charitable institutions, and individual families; and that the rigid enforcement of mandatory measures would require a discipline quite inappropriate for the French people, whose national character and public morals made them ill-suited for Teutonic regimentation. If so, France must pursue its own course.

This blanket of generalities covered a swarm of political issues. The multiplicity and complexity of France's social problems seemed bewildering, but they could be conveniently located on a spectrum between the poles of liberty and obligation—or, as it was often expressed at the time, between the English and German models. This simplistic conception was particularly appealing to the advocates of solidarism, like Léon Bourgeois, who wished to distinguish themselves from both liberalism and socialism and who attempted to articulate a social compromise that would set the nation on a uniquely French way between the extremes. The solidarists can best be understood as heirs of Gambettist opportunism and hence as guardians of republican continuity since the electoral victory of 1877. Meanwhile, withered by its inadaptability to social conditions of the late nineteenth century, traditional liberalism could only watch over a waning past, whereas socialism now sought to outflank the solidarists by openly espousing the German model. In ideological terms, the essential paradox of the social question in prewar France was that the more progressive reformers hoped as nearly as possible to imitate imperial Germany.

These propositions may be measured against the transcripts of dozens of policy debates, of which only a few representative instances can be recalled here. One of the recurrent concerns of French reformers, for example, was the fate of women. This solicitude, however, stemmed not from a revulsion against the gross inequities of gender relationships but from an alarm over the republic's growing demographic deficit with Germany. If the nation were ever again to play a major role in Europe, it must first restore a healthy rate of reproduction. The post-1870 period was distinguished by impassioned discussions about abandoned children, unwed mothers, illegitimacy, abortion, infanticide, wet-nursing, prostitution, and female labor practices. The underlying theme of all this talk was a need to encourage parenthood and therewith an increment of "little Frenchmen." By the end of the century, however, France was more in arrears than ever and its demographic growth was completely stagnant. In order to promote a rise in population, it became necessary to envisage new measures that would allow paid maternity leave for working women and mandate state subsidies for mothers of large families. These bills, finally adopted in 1913, underscored the fact that French social legislation had previously made insufficient provision for women.

The introduction of an extensive welfare program was certain to cause serious repercussions within the medical profession. Admission to hospitals and hospices, allocation of patients, distribution of fees, free choice of physicians—these were a few of the customary practices thrown into question. Beyond such specific issues, the conservative and elitist character of French medicine was challenged by a new movement of syndicalization among provincial doctors. This protest was but one symptom of a pervasive sense that the profession was failing to modernize. Not only was the physical plant for medical care too often antiquated, but training and organization were inadequately specialized. In these respects, once more, Germany set the standard. Sorting out mental as well as physical maladies and sending them to special hospital wards or separate medical facilities were much more frequently practiced in Germany. French missions sent across the Rhine to study these impressive developments returned with glowing praise for the progress they had observed there. German supremacy in science seemed evident not only in a stronger emphasis on medical research but also in a willingness to attack with greater vigor the practical problems of poverty and disease. The so-called Elberfeld system of health care was much vaunted by French officials, for instance, although it could be replicated only in a single arrondissement of Paris. Clearly, gaps existed between recognizing viable solutions and implementing them. The most glaring illustration of that truism was the failure in France to legislate an obligatory program of smallpox vaccination until 1902, even though the virtually total success of that measure in Germany after 1874 left no ambiguity about its efficacy. In public medicine, as in public education, the republic was often a reluctant imitator.

The confounding difficulties of extending health care and welfare regulations to remote villages and rural areas were not unique to France. But they were compounded in the French case by the high degree of state centralism and the hesitancy or incapacity of the national regime to impose mandatory regulations throughout the land. Thus social and sanitary legislation, even when intended by its drafters to approximate the German precedent, sometimes lacked enough impetus to penetrate the provinces. The 1893 law on free medical aid to the indigent did not have a major impact in practice. Its extension through a supplementary bill in 1905 raised somewhat the level of public assistance but without altering its patchwork enforcement. Nor did these enactments move much beyond traditional modes of poor relief. Before 1910, again and again, French reformers came to the brink of a German-style national pension plan, only to turn back. Those who urged such a daring new approach, notably Socialists like Jean Jaurès and Édouard Vaillant, were left to extol the German model, for which they wished in vain to create a French analogy.

The labor movement in France after 1870 shared many of the same problems as that of Germany, among them indecent wages, industrial accidents, and inadequate housing. Moreover, both had to contend with a political combination of repression and reform perpetrated by their respective governments. Yet the rhythm was again different. As in the Kulturkampf, republic and Reich traded positions during the two decades after 1870. With regard to socialism France passed from persecution to toleration; Germany did the opposite. Contemporaries were well aware of these juxtapositions, which unquestionably affected the tenor of French politics. After a rabid anti-Socialist campaign was opened by Bismarck in the late 1870s, moderate republicans in France moved to permit a total amnesty for the communards and to authorize trade unionism. In contrast to the German Social Democrats, French Socialists thereby secured a niche within the ruling consensus under a relatively indulgent political regime. Later, however, this latitude found its limits when Alexandre Millerand was forced to forgo a cabinet post and his ministerialism stood condemned by the Second International, which was dominated by German Social Democracy.

These political changes bore on the social question after 1890 because leftist deputies and trade unionists in France were henceforth able to exert added pressure for labor reforms. They did so with growing confidence and frankness in advocating the German model. One striking example was an effort to convert French law to no-fault accident insurance, which had been incorporated into German legislation in the 1880s. France adopted such a measure in 1898, thereby mitigating one of the most serious legal inequities of the modern factory system. Although the Socialist demand for a universal pension plan remained unrequited in practice before 1914, it is proper to assess the reform bill adopted in 1910 as an adaptation of the German principles of social security. Even granted the stubborn opposition from some quarters (including, not least, the workers themselves) to the pension plan in its prewar form, the question of whether Germany's example importantly influenced the course of French labor reforms can be unhesitatingly answered in the affirmative.

If the full extent of French welfare was still uncertain, the necessity of meeting greater costs to implement it was not. No matter how the state's contributions were to be calculated, a growing strain on the national budget was inexorable. Earlier welfare costs had been offset largely by such devices as an excise tax on alcoholic beverages, a percentage of pari-mutuel wagering, or a direct levy on doors and windows. But after 1905 reformers looked covetously at income tax schemes that had already been adopted by other European states. When Prussia was cited as a pertinent example, however, objections rebounded against the inquisitorial nature of inspection and collection procedures that seemed more suitable for a Germanic than a Latin populace. This type of nineteenth-century racism was deeply embedded in the public discourse of the Belle Epoque, and no analysis of French recalcitrance in matters of taxation should neglect to take note of it. Apart from presumed differences of national character, of course, there were structural reasons why the funding of reform was more problematical in France than in Germany. Perhaps the most significant of these was the long duration of the French Kulturkampf, which vastly complicated any effective integration of private charity and public assistance. In this regard, too, Germany presented an enviable but apparently unattainable profile to the French.

A quintessential French institution of the prewar years, and the one that best defined the difference between republic and Reich, was the mutualist movement. Mutual aid societies basically represented a scheme of voluntary illness and accident insurance. If amply supported and subsidized by the state, without the imposition of excessive bureaucratic controls, they offered a possible compromise between the indifference of classical laissez-faire liberalism and the intrusion of obligatory social insurance. This middle course, which might preserve the precepts of self-help and individual foresight, while yet alleviating the worst effects of poverty and disease, was altogether compatible with the centrist political philosophy of solidarism. Yet it also betrayed the congenital flaw of all French social legislation: a limited applicability. Precisely those who most needed aid could hardly hope to obtain it through mutualism, which ministered to a working-class elite rather than to the truly indigent. Accordingly, reservations by French reformers about mutual societies were invariably couched in comparisons with Germany's more comprehensive coverage. Many of them made their peace with the mutualist movement only in the expectation that it represented a transition to a broader mandatory social insurance system. The more widely the mutual societies became established, however, the less motivation remained for thoroughgoing reform.

No single aspect of public health and welfare more clearly revealed the frustrations of French reformers than the tuberculosis question. Public alarm over the continuing high rate of mortality due to tuberculosis in France coincided in the 1890s with Germany's apparent rise to leadership in therapeutic technique. French delegations that visited German sanatoria in those years returned with reports of remarkable curative success achieved by treatments of rest, diet, and fresh air. Yet for a number of reasons, this enthusiasm waned after 1900. Disillusionment with Robert Koch's failure to produce an antitubercular vaccine was reinforced by spreading insinuations that German claims to improved rates of cure were inflated and that the sanatorium movement was a sort of medical imperialism. These doubts, in turn, stirred existing ambiguities among French physicians about the relative etiological importance of heredity and contagion. Beyond these explanations was another: given its lack of mandatory social legislation and its limitations of available funding, the republic simply could not afford to emulate the German example, no matter how compelling the case for doing so. The outcome, in any event, was a stalemate in French efforts to contain the disease. While extraparliamentary committees and republican officials continued to debate the merits of sanatorium treatment, thousands of French citizens died of tuberculosis at a rate nearly double that of Germany. The reasons for such a discrepancy were doubtless complex, but among them must surely be counted the pusillanimity of the French state. The republic remained unwilling to promote medical specialization or to provide adequate institutional facilities that might have assisted in controlling the epidemic.

Social history should not depend on dubious analogies with military engagements or sporting events. The evolution of an entire people is not to be measured by body counts or points on a scoreboard. In the end, there is no absolute standard of a society's victory or defeat. But the early Third Republic cannot, even by the relative standards of its own time, be considered successful in most matters of public health and welfare. That the French nation did not lack options is demonstrated by the simultaneous conversion of liberal England to a German style of social insurance. In France no such volte-face occurred. Consequently, the decades between the wars of 1870 and 1914 were characterized instead by a gradual erosion of liberal principles without a clear sense of charting a new course in social policy. The republic drifted onto a separate path of political expediency and legislative inertia. Not until the French nation had suffered the shock of two world wars in the early twentieth century would it finally make a decisive choice for a system of social security like that of Germany.

Notes

Abbreviations

UNPUBLISHED SOURCES

AA   Auswärtiges Amt, Bonn
AAM   Archives de l'Académie de Médecine, Paris
AN   Archives Nationales, Paris
AP   Archives de Paris (formerly Archives de la Seine)
APP   Archives de la Préfecture de Police, Paris
BN   Bibliothèque Nationale, Paris
MAE   Ministère des Affaires Étrangères, Paris

ADMINISTRATIVE ORGANIZATIONS

CAPS   Commission d'Assurance et Prévoyance Sociales
CCHP   Comité Consultatif de l'Hygiène Publique
CMP   Conseil Municipal de Paris
CPPCT   Commission Permanente de Préservation Contre la Tuberculose
CSAP   Conseil Supérieur de l'Assistance Publique
CSHP   Conseil Supérieur de l'Hygiène Publique
CSIP   Conseil Supérieur de l'Instruction Publique

Introduction

1. See Mitchell, *German Influence.*
2. See Mitchell, *Victors and Vanquished.*
3. Rémond, *XIXe siècle.*
4. Ibid., p. 105.

5. Ibid., pp. 86–95.

6. Hatzfeld, *Du paupérisme à la sécurité sociale*. A second edition of this work, with a new introduction, has been published at Nancy in 1989.

7. Flora and Heidenheimer, *Development of Welfare States*.

8. Ibid., pp. 60–63. A similar thought has been more recently expressed by Gerhard A. Ritter: "The level of research does not permit an estimation of what *influence by the German model of social insurance* . . . was extended to other countries. . . . Not only the more or less exact adoption of the German example but also the conscious development of alternative solutions could be traced back to a confrontation with German social insurance. Its importance as a starting point for public discussion and for legislative initiatives can only become clarified through concrete investigations of the origins of modern systems of social security in individual countries." Ritter, *Sozialstaat*, pp. 98–99. On the question of "diffusion," also see Alber, *Vom Armenhaus zum Wohlfahrtstaat*, pp. 134–46.

Chapter 1

1. General overviews of liberal thought may be found in Ruggiero, *European Liberalism*; Girvetz, *From Wealth to Welfare*; Bullock and Shock, *Liberal Tradition*; Sidorsky, *European Thought*; and more recently Arblaster, *Rise and Decline*.

2. A contrast between the "Anglo-Saxon" and "Continental" types of liberalism is suggested by Gall, *Liberalismus*, p. 10. "If it makes any sense at all to talk about a national Sonderweg in the nineteenth century, surely liberal England is the case to which the term can most readily be applied," writes Sheehan, "Reflections," p. 52. Also see Kocka, *Arbeiter und Bürger*, p. 337.

3. For some examples, see Sell, *Tragödie des deutschen Liberalismus*; Winkler, *Preussischer Liberalismus und deutscher Nationalstaat*; Gall, "Liberalismus und 'bürgerliche Gesellschaft,'" pp. 324–56; Sheehan, *German Liberalism*; and Langewiesche, *Liberalismus in Deutschland*. This discussion of liberalism has extended into the so-called *Sonderweg* debate, in which one side has attributed the unique course of Germany's history to a failure there to realize a successful bourgeois revolution, as in Britain and France. A principal advocate of that view has been Wehler, *Das deutsche Kaiserreich*, now available in English as *The German Empire 1871–1918* (Leamington Spa, 1985). Highly critical of Wehler's thesis are Blackbourn and Eley, *Mythen deutscher Geschichtsschreibung*, revised and expanded in an English edition as *The Peculiarities of*

German History: Bourgeois Society and Politics in Nineteenth-Century Germany (Oxford, 1984).

4. Representative of French historiography on liberalism are Droz, *Histoire des doctrines politiques*; Burdeau, *Le libéralisme*; Jardin, *Histoire du libéralisme politique*; Girard, *Les libéraux français*; and Daumard, *Les bourgeois et la bourgeoisie*. For a critique of this scholarship, see Krumeich, "Der politische Liberalismus," pp. 353–66.

5. These central postulates are spelled out by Mitchell, "Bürgerlicher Liberalismus und Volksgesundheit," pp. 395–417.

6. See Goubert, *Cent mille provinciaux*, pp. 386–92; and Hufton, *The Poor of Eighteenth Century France*, pp. 1–7.

7. See Forrest, *The French Revolution and the Poor*. Several regional monographs fill out the background: Gutton, *La société et les pauvres*; Kaplow, *The Name of Kings*; Fairchilds, *Poverty and Charity*; Jones, *Charity and Bienfaisance*; and Norberg, *Rich and Poor*.

8. See Pautreau, "La survivance du système du renfermement des pauvres," pp. 205–11.

9. See Laporte, *L'assistance publique et privée*, p. 5; and Hatzfeld, *Du paupérisme à la sécurité sociale*, pp. 7–12.

10. See Ferdinand-Dreyfus, *L'assistance*, pp. 9–11.

11. See Baudot, "La situation des monts-de-piété durant le second empire," pp. 185–93. The innovative importance of the July Monarchy is stressed by Sewell, *Work and Revolution*, pp. 194–218.

12. Cunin-Gridaine (minister of agriculture and commerce) to Molé, 28 Dec. 1844, AN Paris, F^{12} 4814.

13. Delessert (prefect of police) to Duchatel (minister of the interior), 29 Nov. 1845, ibid.

14. "Mémoire adressé à M. le Ministre de l'Agriculture et du Commerce par les délégués de la Caisse de Retraites pour les classes laborieuses des deux sexes," [?] April 1846, ibid.

15. See Sewell, *Work and Revolution*, pp. 251–55. Further background is available in such works as Price, *The French Second Republic*; Agulhon, *1848 ou l'apprentissage de la république*; and Merriman, *The Agony of the Republic*.

16. Jean-Baptiste Dumas, "Projet de loi relatif aux caisses de retraites pour la vieillesse," 26 Nov. 1849, AP Paris, D.2 X^2 4. See Price, "Poor Relief and Social Crisis," pp. 423–54.

17. There is still no satisfactory biography of Thiers. Three older accounts were unduly laudatory: Malo, *Thiers, 1797–1877*; Pomaret, *Monsieur*

Thiers et son siècle; and Roux, *Thiers*. Two recent works are more critical but far too brief to do justice: Guiral, *Adolphe Thiers*; and Bury and Tombs, *Thiers, 1797–1877: A Political Life*.

18. Adolphe Thiers, *Rapport*, pp. 1–16.

19. Ibid., pp. 17–139.

20. Ibid., p. 153. See Ferdinand-Dreyfus, *L'assistance*, pp. 198–207.

21. Girard, *Les libéraux français*, p. 171. Also see Margadant, *French Peasants in Revolt*.

22. See Mitchell, "Mutual Aid Societies."

23. See Mitchell, *Bismarck and the French Nation*, pp. 37–53.

24. The quotations are, respectively, from Charles de Mazade, "Chronique de la quinzaine," *Revue des deux mondes* 86 (1870): 752–64; and Paul Leroy-Beaulieu, "La question ouvrière au dix-neuvième siècle: le radicalisme et les grèves," ibid., pp. 88–116. See Perrot, *Les ouvriers en grève*, 1:74–80; Tilly, *Rebellious Century*, pp. 19–21 and passim; and Mitchell, "Subversion and Repression," pp. 409–11.

25. Ministry of the Interior to prefects, 12 Jan. 1870, AN Paris, F^{1a} 2125.

26. See Serman, *La commune de Paris*, pp. 494–540.

27. To name but three: Ligou, *Histoire du socialisme en France*; Moss, *Origins of the French Labor Movement*; and Judt, *Socialism in Provence*. Also see the comment by Hudemann, "Politische Reform und gesellschaftlicher Status quo," pp. 332–52.

28. Inexplicably, Paul Leroy-Beaulieu is neglected in the otherwise perspicacious survey of liberal theory by Logue, *From Philosophy to Sociology*.

29. Paul Leroy-Beaulieu, *Essai sur la répartition des richesses*, pp. 7–9.

30. Ibid., pp. 409–25.

31. Ibid., pp. 465–76.

32. Ibid., pp. 586–97.

33. Ibid., p. 587. The comment by Léon Say appeared in the article "Budget de 1895: libéraux et socialistes," *Revue des deux mondes* 125 (1894): 518–19.

34. Haussonville, *Misères et remèdes*, pp. 253–76, 327–28. Both Leroy-Beaulieu and Haussonville were frequent contributors to the *Revue des deux mondes*, where they continued their polemic throughout the 1880s.

35. See the chapter entitled "Interkatholische Kontroversen in Hinblick auf den Liberalismus," in Jedin, *Handbuch der Kirchengeschichte*, 6:738–60. For further background, also see Reardon, *Liberalism and Tradition*, pp. 86–

112; Duroselle, *Les débuts du catholicisme social en France*, pp. 36–59; Girard, *Les libéraux français*, pp. 213–23; and Motzkin, "Säkularisierung," pp. 141–71.

36. Quoted from Kohn, *The Modern World*, pp. 153–56.

37. Anatole Leroy-Beaulieu, "La paupté, le socialisme et la démocratie: l'église, l'intervention de l'état et la législation sociale," *Revue des deux mondes* 109 (1892): 356–88.

38. Tocqueville, *Old Regime*, pp. 57–60.

39. See Mitchell, *German Influence*, pp. 150–59. On the failure to reverse this tendency, see Riemenschneider, *Dezentralisation*.

40. Suleiman, *Private Power and Centralization*, p. 17.

41. See Rosanvallon, *La crise de l'état-providence*, pp. 25–28, 45–48, 59–106; and the theoretical work of Ewald, *L'état providence*, pp. 85–107.

42. "The rhetoric of decentralization becomes an indispensable tool of administrations that nonetheless continue to concentrate their activity at the center . . . : surveillance and decision making [are] the growing specialties of Paris and its region," writes Tilly, *The Contentious French*, p. 67.

43. See Crozier, *The Bureaucratic Phenomenon*, pp. 224–27. These stark terms of the Crozier model may be nuanced by a study of the revival of civic traditions in the early Third Republic. See Agulhon, "Les citadins et la politique," in Duby, *Histoire*, 4:601–22. Agulhon properly warns that we should not overdraw the contrast between "urban dynamism" and "rural inertia" (ibid., p. 639). His point is well taken, yet it does not alter the contemporary observation of late nineteenth-century social reformers that rural France—and indeed much of urban France—generally failed to respond to the welfare and sanitation needs of its populace.

44. See Sachsse and Tennstedt, *Geschichte der Armenfürsorge*, pp. 23–41.

45. Suleiman, *Private Power and Centralization*, p. 302.

46. "Commission relative aux heures de travail dans les usines et les manufactures," 23 March and 25 May 1887, AN Paris, C 5429. Charles Ferry, "Rapport fait au nom de la commission chargée d'examiner le projet de loi . . . sur le travail des enfants, des filles mineures et des femmes dans les établissements industriels," 20 June 1889, ibid., F²² 333.

47. Fernand de Ramel et al., "Proposition de loi sur l'organisation d'une caisse de retraites de travailleurs et des invalides de travail, et d'une caisse de capitalisation," 8 July 1890, ibid., C 5452.

48. Commission . . . Dujardin-Verkinden, *procès-verbaux*, 12 July 1890, ibid., C 5437. See the chapter entitled "L'objection libérale et le problème de

l'obligation," in Hatzfeld, *Du paupérisme à la sécurité sociale*, pp. 33–101.

49. Commission du travail, *procès-verbaux*, 30 Oct. and 7 Nov. 1890, AN Paris, C 5433.

50. Ibid., 11 Nov. 1890.

51. Lockroy, "Proposition de loi à l'organisation des services de l'hygiène publique," 19 Nov. 1889, ibid., C 5486.

52. CSAP, *procès-verbaux*, 29 June 1892 (morning), fasc. 39. See Hatzfeld, *Du paupérisme à la sécurité sociale*, pp. 65–79.

Chapter 2

1. See Kleinert, *Die frühen Modejounale in Frankreich*, pp. 226–49, and Bellanger et al., *Histoire générale de la presse*, 2:149–61.

2. For the background, see Chevalier, *La formation de la population parisienne*; Pouthas, *La population française*; and Armengaud, *La population française au XIXe siècle*. On the sources and problems of gathering statistics about public health in the nineteenth century, see Coleman, *Death*, pp. 137–48; and Vallin and Meslé, *Causes de décès*, pp. 7–20.

3. From the vast literature, see especially Crouzet, "Essai de construction d'un indice annuel," pp. 56–99; Lévy-Leboyer, "La décélération de l'économie française," pp. 485–507; and the pair of useful surveys by Kemp, *Economic Forces in French History* and *The French Economy*.

4. Administration générale de l'assistance publique à Paris (service de secours à domicile), *Répartition entre les bureaux de bienfaisance des vingt arrondissements des fonds de secours pour l'exercice 1865* (Paris, 1865), p. 12.

5. "Mouvement de la population de la France pendant l'année 1864," *Moniteur Universel*, 16 April 1867. See Haupt, *Sozialgeschichte Frankreichs*, pp. 92–104.

6. *Bulletin de l'Académie de Médecine*, 28 Oct. 1890.

7. Léon Lefort, "Du mouvement de la population en France," *Revue des deux mondes* 69 (1867): 462–81.

8. See Mitchell, *Victors and Vanquished*, pp. 3–15.

9. For the background, see Challener, *Nation in Arms*; Ralston, *Army of the Republic*; and Porch, *March to the Marne*.

10. See Monteilhet, *Les institutions militaires*; Schnapper, *Le remplacement militaire*; and Mitchell, *Victors and Vanquished*, pp. 29–32.

11. *Journal Officiel*, 26–27 July 1874.

12. Ibid., 14 Sept. 1876.

13. The classic account by Spengler, *France Faces Depopulation*, has been

reviewed by Nye, *Crime, Madness, and Politics*, pp. 132–44. Also see the useful survey in the third volume of Dupâquier et al., *Histoire de la population française*.

14. See Digeon, *La crise allemande*; Swart, *Decadence*; and Weber, *France: Fin de siècle*, pp. 9–26, 147–58.

15. Gustave Lagneau, "Situation démographique de la France: décroissance de la population de certains départements," *Bulletin de l'Académie de Médicine*, 20 Jan. 1885.

16. Ibid., 27 Jan. 1885.

17. Ibid., 3 Feb. 1885.

18. Ibid., 10 Feb. 1885.

19. Ibid., 17 Feb. 1885.

20. Lefort, "Du mouvement de la population en France," *Revue des deux mondes* 69 (1867): 465–67.

21. See Mitchell, *German Influence*, pp. 27–34, 43–46.

22. *Journal Officiel*, 14 Sept. 1876. News of the flap created by Léonce de Lavergne, accompanied by details of the new French census, was reported back to Berlin by the German ambassador: Hohenlohe to Bismarck, 30 Aug. and 23 Sept. 1876, AA Bonn, I.A.B.c 79, Bde. 10–11.

23. Cheysson, *La question de la population*, pp. 1–28.

24. Lagneau, "Situation démographique de la France," *Bulletin de l'Académie de Médecine*, 20 Jan. 1885. Lagneau drew on the writings of two other population experts: Émile Levasseur, "Note sur la situation faite à la France parmi les grandes puissances par les événements politiques et par le progrès de la population depuis le XVIIIe siècle," *Annales de démographie internationale* 3 (1879): 309–14; and Charles Grad, "La population de l'empire allemand," *Revue des deux mondes* 67 (1885): 78–112.

25. *Bulletin de l'Académie de Médecine*, 27 Jan. 1885.

26. Ibid., 10 Feb. 1885.

27. Ibid., 10 March 1885.

28. Quoted by Michel, *Les habitants*, pp. 70–71. Bertillon's statistics and opinions were also highly regarded by French liberals such as Paul Leroy-Beaulieu, *La question de la population*, pp. 346–51, 414–19. See Vallin and Meslé, *Causes de décès*, pp. 26–28.

29. *Bulletin de l'Académie de Médecine*, 28 Oct. 1890. It is patent nonsense to assert that "the bitterness of the French defeat in the war of 1870–71 generally meant that any experience coming from the other side of the Rhine was of little interest to the French," as does Yves Saint-Jours, "France," in Köhler and Zacher, *The Evolution of Social Insurance*, p. 95.

30. See Mitchell, "The Xenophobic Style," pp. 414–25.

31. E.g., Lefort, "Du mouvement de la population en France," *Revue des deux mondes* 69 (1867): 479.

32. *Bulletin de l'Académie de Médecine*, 27 Jan. 1885.

33. Ibid., 7 Oct. 1890. See Wahl, *Alsatiens-Lorrains*.

34. Cheysson was quoted by Rochard, *Bulletin de l'Académie de Médecine*, 27 Jan. 1885. On Cheysson's reformism, see Elwitt, *Third Republic Defended*, pp. 51–84.

35. *Bulletin de l'Académie de Médecine*, 27 Jan. 1885.

36. Ibid., 10 Feb. and 3 March 1885.

37. Ibid., 15 July 1890. See Barrows, *Distorting Mirrors*, pp. 93–113; and Mitchell, "The Unsung Villain," pp. 447–71.

38. *Bulletin de l'Académie de Médecine*, 15 July 1890.

39. Ibid., 7 Oct. 1890 and 10 March 1891.

40. Albert de Broglie (minister of the interior) to Jules Béclard (permanent secretary of the Academy of Medicine), 31 Jan. 1874, AAM Paris, liasse 140.

41. CCHP, *Recueil* 18 (1888): i–vii.

42. Martin Nadaud, "Proposition de loi tendant à modifier la loi du 13 avril 1850 sur l'assainissement des logements insalubres," 3 Dec. 1881, AN Paris, F^8 212; and "Rapport sommaire fait au nom de la 2e commission . . . sur l'assainissement des logements insalubres," 19 Jan. 1882, ibid. For background, see Bullock and Read, *The Movement for Housing*; and Shapiro, *Housing the Poor*.

43. Hippolyte Maze, "Rapport fait au nom de la commission chargée d'examiner la proposition de loi de M. Martin Nadaud," 21 April 1883, AN Paris, F^8 212. See Guerrand, *Propriétaires et locataires*, pp. 183–204.

44. Ernest Deligny, "Rapport, au nom de la 6e commission, sur le projet de règlement relatif à l'assainissement de Paris," 1883, AP Paris, V.D.^{6} 719.

45. *Bulletin de l'Académie de Médecine*, 5 Jan. 1886.

46. Édouard Lockroy, "Projet de loi relatif à l'assainissement des logements et habitations insalubres," 13 Jan. 1887, AN Paris, F^8 212. Lockroy's tough attitude was later reflected in his "Proposition de loi ayant pour objet d'assurer la répression des contraventions aux règlements sur les établissements dangereux, insalubres ou incommodes," 19 Nov. 1889, ibid., C 5486.

47. For further consideration of the housing question, see Chapter 12.

48. *Bulletin de l'Académie de Médecine*, 24 June and 15 July 1890.

49. Ibid., 30 Sept. and 21 Oct. 1890.

50. Ibid., 10 March 1891.

Chapter 3

1. For further background and bibliography, see Price, *Social History*, pp. 45–91; and Mitchell, *German Influence*, pp. 21–27, 113–23.

2. For an overview of the German development, see Born, *Wirtschafts- und Sozialgeschichte*, pp. 77–84.

3. See Huber, *Deutsche Verfassungsgeschichte*, 4:1130–31; and Ritter, *Sozialversicherung*, p. 36.

4. Ibid., pp. 38–39.

5. That said, the thesis by Rauh, *Parlamentarisierung*, is too curtly dismissed as merely a "pious legend" by Wehler, "Wie 'bürgerlich' war das Deutsche Kaiserreich?" p. 263.

6. See Huerkamp, "Smallpox Vaccination in Germany," pp. 617–35; and Mitchell, "Bürgerlicher Liberalismus und Volksgesundheit," pp. 408–10.

7. See Tennstedt, *Vom Proleten zum Industriearbeiter*, pp. 305–35; Frevert, *Krankheit als politisches Problem*, pp. 151–84; Huerkamp, *Aufstieg der Ärzte*, pp. 87–118, 245–54; and Mitchell, "Bürgerlicher Liberalismus und Volksgesundheit," pp. 404–8.

8. "Soll Revolution sein, so werden wir sie lieber machen als erleiden." Cited by Rein, *Die Revolution in der Politik Bismarcks*, p. 158.

9. A typical example is Hentschel, *Geschichte der deutschen Sozialpolitik*, pp. 9–10 and passim. Also see Detlev Zöllner, "Germany," in Köhler and Zacher, *Evolution of Social Insurance*, pp. 1–92.

10. Cited and analyzed in the classic 1928 account by Kleeis, *Geschichte der sozialen Versicherung*, pp. 95–101.

11. See Mitchell, "Subversion and Repression," pp. 411–13.

12. A cross section of recent writings is represented by Wehler, *Das deutsche Kaiserreich*, pp. 80–83; Gall, *Bismarck*, pp. 526–91; and Stürmer, *Das ruhelose Reich*, pp. 193–248. See Mitchell, "Bonapartism," pp. 189–95.

13. See Nipperdey, "Interessenverbände und Parteien," pp. 369–88; and Sachsse and Tennstedt, *Geschichte der Armenfürsorge*, pp. 27–38.

14. See Gladen, *Geschichte der Sozialpolitik*, p. 56; and Ritter, *Sozialversicherung*, p. 39.

15. Cited by Kleeis, *Geschichte der sozialen Versicherung*, p. 102.

16. See Huber, *Deutsche Verfassungsgeschichte*, 4:1192–1206. On Ger-

many's innovative role, see Flora and Heidenheimer, *Development of Welfare States*, pp. 17–18; Alber, *Vom Armenhaus zum Wohlfahrtsstaat*, pp. 43–44; and Ritter, *Sozialstaat*, pp. 60–101. Unfortunately, the recently completed work of Otto Pflanze, *Bismarck and the Development of Germany*, 3 vols. (Princeton, 1990), appeared too late to be incorporated here.

17. See Kleeis, *Geschichte der sozialen Versicherung*, pp. 104–7. The same conclusion is more critically seen by Hentschel, *Geschichte der deutschen Sozialpolitik*, pp. 11–13. A balanced summary is offered by Baron, "Die Entwicklung der Armenpflege," pp. 11–71.

18. See Tennstedt, *Geschichte der Selbstverwaltung*, pp. 24–38.

19. Tennstedt, *Sozialgeschichte der Sozialpolitik*, p. 166.

20. See Gladen, *Geschichte der Sozialpolitik*, pp. 61–63.

21. See Huerkamp, *Aufstieg der Ärzte*, pp. 216–21.

22. See Gladen, *Geschichte der Sozialpolitik*, p. 58; and Tennstedt, *Vom Proleten zum Industriearbeiter*, pp. 335–40.

23. See Tennstedt, *Sozialgeschichte der Sozialpolitik*, pp. 174–81.

24. See Huber, *Deutsche Verfassungsgeschichte*, 4:1202–4; Gladen, *Geschichte der Sozialpolitik*, pp. 67–70; and Tennstedt, *Sozialgeschichte der Sozialpolitik*, pp. 186–87.

25. See Hentschel, *Geschichte der deutschen Sozialpolitik*, p. 24; and Tennstedt, *Sozialgeschichte der Sozialpolitik*, pp. 181–84.

26. For an overview of the available German statistical sources, see Spree, *Soziale Ungleichheit*, pp. 22–30.

27. Ibid., pp. 30–36.

28. Ibid., pp. 19, 39, 47. Curiously, Spree himself does not bring these numbers into conjunction.

29. See Huerkamp, *Aufstieg der Ärzte*, pp. 250–51.

30. See Spree, *Soziale Ungleichheit*, p. 101; and Göckenjan, *Kurieren und Staat machen*, pp. 230–31.

31. See Tennstedt, *Sozialgeschichte der Sozialpolitik*, p. 211.

32. "Well over half of the population" was insured before 1914, concludes Huerkamp, *Aufstieg der Ärzte*, p. 225. "About half," says Tennstedt, *Sozialgeschichte der Sozialpolitik*, p. 170, thereby revising an earlier estimate of 35.3 percent in his "Sozialgeschichte der Sozialversicherung," 3:387. The lower figure, however, is maintained by Göckenjan, *Kurieren und Staat machen*, p. 338.

33. See Tennstedt, *Geschichte der Selbstverwaltung*, p. 35.

34. See Hentschel, *Geschichte der deutschen Sozialpolitik*, p. 23.

35. See Kleeis, *Geschichte der sozialen Versicherung*, pp. 107–11.

36. See Gladen, *Geschichte der Sozialpolitik*, p. 78.

37. See Hentschel, *Geschichte der deutschen Sozialpolitik*, p. 23.

38. See Spree, *Soziale Ungleichheit*, pp. 105–6. The curative value of sanatorium treatment nonetheless remains in doubt. See, for example, Göckenjan, *Kurieren und Staat machen*, pp. 19, 49–58.

39. See Spree, *Soziale Ungleichheit*, pp. 101–3. "The victory of Prussianism over liberalism" and "the triumph of state intervention over *laissez faire*" after 1870 are also observed by Evans, *Death in Hamburg*, p. viii.

40. See Huber, *Deutsche Verfassungsgeschichte*, 4:1204–5; Tennstedt, *Sozialgeschichte der Sozialpolitik*, pp. 194–97; and Faust, *Arbeitsmarktpolitik*, pp. 29–45.

41. See Sachsse, *Mütterlichkeit als Beruf*, pp. 36–48.

42. That the state often "pursued its own purpose . . . even against local resistance" in implementing welfare measures is illustrated by Frevert, *Krankheit als politisches Problem*, pp. 167–72.

43. See Spree, *Soziale Ungleichheit*, pp. 34–36.

44. The correlation between relative economic retardation and resistance to progressive welfare measures is well stated by Hatzfeld, *Du paupérisme à la sécurité sociale*, pp. 263–67.

45. Cited by Hentschel, *Geschichte der deutschen Sozialpolitik*, p. 19. Also see Huber, *Deutsche Verfassungsgeschichte*, 4:1237–49.

46. This thesis was first suggested by Roth, *Social Democrats in Imperial Germany*. It was later explored in greater depth by Groh, *Negative Integration*; and it was adopted by Wehler, *Das Deutsche Kaiserreich*, pp. 96–100. But it has been called "a gross exaggeration and distortion" by Born, *Wirtschafts- und Sozialgeschichte*, p. 91; and it is considered dubious by Ritter, "Entstehung und Entwicklung," pp. 34–38.

47. The quotations are, respectively, from Conze, "Sozialgeschichte," p. 638; Ritter, *Sozialversicherung*, p. 35; and Gladen, *Geschichte der Sozialpolitik*, pp. 78–79. Fundamental improvements in the standard of living of the lower classes are also posited by Stearns, *Lives of Labour*, pp. 229–35.

48. Hentschel, *Geschichte der deutschen Sozialpolitik*, pp. 21–24.

49. Spree, *Soziale Ungleichheit*, p. 46.

50. Göckenjan, *Kurieren und Staat machen*, p. 53.

51. Spree, *Soziale Ungleichheit*, pp. 150–62; and Göckenjan, *Kurieren und Staat machen*, pp. 214–37. More balanced is Huerkamp, *Aufstieg der Ärzte*, pp. 153–66.

52. Spree, *Soziale Ungleichheit*, pp. 115–18; and Göckenjan, *Kurieren und Staat machen*, pp. 50–53.

53. A flagrant example is the presentation of tuberculosis mortality. In the wake of a notable statistical improvement in Prussia between 1870 and 1914—at least 30 percent—the somewhat higher death rate of men was reduced by a fraction more than that of women; that is, the gender difference became slightly less. This result is grotesquely summarized as a "relative degradation in the health of women" by Spree, *Soziale Ungleichheit*, pp. 47–48.

54. A cryptic overview of the European pattern is presented by Ritter, *Sozialversicherung*, pp. 9–17. He states that the German model was largely accepted by Austria, Hungary, and Luxembourg, but that France demurred: "As in England, the strength of political and economic liberalism, among other things, long delayed the development of an obligatory state system of social insurance." Ibid., p. 15.

55. In this regard, the German deficit compared with England's rate in 1905 is estimated—doubtless with some exaggeration—as high as 60 percent by Göckenjan, *Kurieren und Staat machen*, p. 50. Yet Germany's prewar efforts to found sanatoria and finance public housing "undoubtedly had prophylactic effects," says Tennstedt, *Sozialgeschichte der Sozialpolitik*, p. 187. An admiring French historian writes this in reference to the year 1905: "At this date only Germany, through its system of social insurance, had found the solution of the problem." Guillaume, *Du désespoir au salut*, p. 259.

56. See Mitchell, "An Inexact Science," pp. 387–403.

57. See Huerkamp, *Aufstieg der Ärzte*, pp. 87–97, 177–85.

58. Ibid., p. 163.

59. The fact that a French citizen was nearly twice as likely as "other Europeans" to die from tuberculosis during the 1930s is noted by Zeldin, *France*, 2:970. One must wonder why this was so. See Mitchell, "Obsessive Questions and Faint Answers," pp. 215–35.

60. In reality the German system continued to allow the proliferation and differentiation of small local groups, especially in scattered rural locales. See Sachsse and Tennstedt, *Geschichte der Armenfürsorge*, pp. 27–38.

61. Again, the German reality was somewhat different and far more complex. Despite the collapse of the National Liberal party, an educated liberal urban bourgeoisie continued to play an important role in community health and welfare programs. Ibid., pp. 44–45.

62. The same generalization held true for Great Britain. Hence one expert speaks of the principles adopted by English reformers: "They were consciously borrowed from Germany and put forward on the basis of statistics generated by the administration of the German insurance system. Thus the Workmen's Compensation Act of 1897 clearly showed the influence of Ger-

man social insurance on British legislation. . . . By opting for compulsion and wider coverage and turning to German social insurance as their model for achieving it, the architects of National Insurance were embarking on a reinterpretation of the role of the State in a liberal society and indeed of the fundamental nature of liberalism." Hennock, *British Social Reform and German Precedents*, pp. 2–10.

63. See Chapter 10.

64. It has been argued that the greater degree of state intervention in Germany was actually a source of social dissonance there. See Kaelble, "Französisches und deutsches Bürgertum," pp. 127–32.

Chapter 4

1. The proceedings were published in two volumes as *Congrès international d'assistance* (Paris, 1889). They were cited by David Raynal (minister of the interior) to prefects, 18 May 1894, CSAP, fasc. 46. This document was signed in Reynal's stead by Henri Monod.

2. See the essay by Peter Flora and Jens Alber, "Modernization, Democratization, and the Development of Welfare in Western Europe," in Flora and Heidenheimer, *Development of Welfare States*, pp. 37–80.

3. CSAP, "Séance d'ouverture," *procès-verbaux*, 13 June 1888, fasc. 16; Monod to Floquet, 26 Jan. 1889, ibid., fasc. 32. See Weiss, "Origins," pp. 58–60.

4. CSAP, *procès-verbaux*, 1 Feb. 1889 (morning), fasc. 25.

5. See Mitchell, *Victors and Vanquished*, pp. 32–41, 154–58.

6. Raynal (minister of the interior) to Sadi Carnot (president of the republic), 14 Jan. 1894, CSAP, fasc. 43.

7. "Arrêté instituant les sections du Conseil Supérieur," 25 May 1888, ibid., fasc. 1.

8. Ibid., *procès-verbaux*, 13 June 1888, fasc. 16.

9. "Rapport au Conseil Supérieur de l'Assistance Publique au nom de la IIe section . . . sur l'assistance médicale dans les campagnes," 1889, ibid., fasc. 21. It is noteworthy that Lucien Dreyfus-Brisac's brother Édmond was an outspoken advocate of educational reforms based on the German model. See Mitchell, *Victors and Vanquished*, pp. 202–10.

10. CSAP, *procès-verbaux*, 1 Feb. 1889 (morning), fasc. 25.

11. Monod to Dupuy, 26 June 1893, ibid., fasc. 42. For the text of the Loi Roussel, see the *Journal Officiel*, 9 June 1874.

12. See Hildreth, *Doctors*, pp. 107–52.

13. Details in the annual *Recueil des travaux du comité consultatif d'hygiène publique de France et des actes officiels de l'administration sanitaire* (hereafter cited as CCHP, *Recueil*).

14. Ibid. 11 (1884): v–xii.

15. Ibid. The same point was emphasized by A.-J. Martin, "Installation et fonctionnement dans la ville de Berlin d'un service d'étuves . . . ," 28 March 1887, ibid. 17 (1887): 177–88.

16. Brouardel to Jean Constans (minister of the interior), ibid. 19 (1889): i–viii.

17. Brouardel, "Rapport," ibid. 28 (1898): vii–xi.

18. Brouardel to Lockroy (minister of commerce and industry), ibid. 17 (1887): i–xi

19. For the background, see Léonard, *Archives du corps*, pp. 53–148.

20. Henri Monod, "Étuves à désinfection de 1889 à 1892," CCHP, *Recueil* 22 (1892): 63–74.

21. For an overview, see Dupeux, *La société française*, pp. 10–53.

22. In addition to Coleman, *Death*, pp. 171–80, for the background see Delaporte, *Disease and Civilization*; and Bourdelais and Raulot, *Une peur bleue*. Recent research is deftly analyzed by Kearns, "Death," pp. 425–32.

23. See Pinkney, *Napoleon III and the Rebuilding of Paris*, pp. 49–74, 105–50.

24. "Rapport du Citoyen Treillard . . . sur la suppression des bureaux de bienfaisance et l'organisation des bureaux d'assistance dans les vingt arrondissements de Paris," [1871], AP Paris, V.D.^{6} 721.

25. See Watson, *Georges Clemenceau*, p. 63; Ellis, *Early Life of Georges Clemenceau*, pp. 59–70; and Mitchell, "Crucible of French Anticlericalism," pp. 395–98.

26. Émile de Marcère to Ferdinand Herold (prefect of the Seine), 8 Feb. 1879, AP Paris, V.Q.^{3}; Michel Möring (director of public assistance in Paris) to Herold, 25 Feb. 1879, ibid.; Möring to Herold, [?] May 1879, ibid., V.Q.^{1}. Records of the Conseil de Surveillance and the Conseil Municipal de Paris are housed in AP Paris (formerly known as the "Archives de la Seine").

27. See Mitchell, "Municipal Council of Paris," pp. 435–50.

28. CMP, *procès-verbaux*, 10 and 13 June 1887.

29. Ibid., 26 Dec. 1887.

30. Ibid., 11 March 1888.

31. Ibid., 15 Nov. 1889.

32. Ibid., 18 July 1890.

33. Ibid., 11 July 1891.

34. Ibid., 13 June 1892.

35. Ibid., 8 July 1892 and 28 Dec. 1893.

36. Ibid., 17 June 1892.

37. Ibid., 8 July 1892.

38. Conseil de Surveillance, *procès-verbaux*, 18 Jan. 1894, AP Paris, D.1 X¹ 15.

39. "Rapport sur un projet de création d'une faculté de médecine et de pharmacie dans la ville de Marseille," CSIP (section permanente), 14 May 1890, AN Paris, F¹⁷ 12983. See Mitchell, *Victors and Vanquished*, pp. 215–19.

40. Brouardel, *La profession médicale*, p. 40. See Hildreth, "Les syndicats médicaux," pp. 4–5.

41. A brief sketch of the Academy's history and structure is contained in the *Index biographique des membres et des associés et des correspondants de l'Académie de Médecine 1820–1984* (Paris, 1985), pp. vii–xii.

42. Statement by Jules Rochard, *Bulletin de l'Académie de Médecine*, 15 April 1890.

43. On smallpox, see Chapter 6; and on tuberculosis, Chapter 11.

44. See Chapter 10.

45. See Hildreth, *Doctors*, pp. 164–214 and passim.

46. Hatzfeld, *Du paupérisme à la sécurité sociale*, p. 34.

47. Minutes of the individual committees of the Chamber of Deputies are to be found in the so-called C-Series, AN Paris. Unfortunately, these records are dispersed alphabetically in dossiers for each legislative period, and the classifications are not always constant over time. The intricacy of piecing together this evidence may explain why these documents have heretofore been employed little or, as in the case of Hatzfeld, not at all.

48. These problems were particularly evident in efforts to obtain tax reform. See Chapter 9.

49. "Projet de loi," signed by President Jules Grévy, 26 Feb. 1887, AN Paris, C 5407. Commission des finances, *procès-verbaux*, 28 March 1887, ibid.

50. "Proposition de loi sur l'organisation d'une caisse d'épargne-retraite," 30 Dec. 1891, ibid., C 5452.

51. "Enquête parlementaire sur les conditions du travail en France," [1872–75], ibid., C 3018–20.

52. "Rapport de la commission chargée d'examiner les propositions de loi . . . ," 10 March 1884, ibid., F²² 333.

53. Ramel et al., "Proposition de loi sur l'organisation d'une caisse de

retraites . . . ," 8 July 1890, ibid., C 5452.

54. Commission . . . Dujardin-Verkinden, *procès-verbaux*, 12 July 1890, ibid., C 5437.

55. The objective and functions of this key legislative body were discussed by Léon Bourgeois and others at the committee's opening session. CAPS, *procès-verbaux*, 19 Jan. 1894, AN Paris, C 5545.

56. See Mitchell, *German Influence*, p. 143.

57. See, for example, Seager, *Boulanger Affair*; and Sternhell, *La droite révolutionnaire*, pp. 77–145.

58. See Auspitz, *Radical Bourgeoisie*; and Mitchell, *Victors and Vanquished*, pp. 196–97.

59. See Mitchell, "The Unsung Villain," pp. 463–66.

60. Among the most important of such organizations was the Musée Social, founded in Paris in 1895. From its inception, however, the Musée Social was closely identified with mutualism, and its role in promoting reform was therefore problematical. See Dreyfus, *La mutualité*, pp. 31–42; Stone, *Search for Social Peace*, pp. 52–54; and Elwitt, "Social Reform," pp. 431–51.

61. Paul Strauss, "Notre programme," *Revue philanthropique* 1 (1897): 1–8.

62. Strauss, "Bulletin," ibid. 1 (1897): 155–60; and for example A. Cambillard, "La protection de l'enfance au Congrès de Rouen," ibid. 2 (1897–98): 224–43.

Chapter 5

1. For background, see McMillan, *Housewife or Harlot*; Sowerwine, *Sisters or Citizens*; McLaren, *Sexuality and Social Order*; and House and Kenney, *Women's Suffrage and Social Politics*.

2. See Zeldin, *France*, 1:347–50; Bidelman, *Pariahs Stand Up!*; Moses, *French Feminism*; and Offen, "Depopulation, Nationalism, and Feminism," pp. 648–76. The importance of the feminist struggle in France is stressed by Offen, "Defining Feminism," pp. 142–50. Yet there is little evidence that social reformers were highly sensitive to it or that social legislation before 1914 was in direct response to it. In fact, it is more plausible that most male reformers were "indifferent to working women's discontent." Stewart, *Women*, p. 4.

3. *Renseignements statistiques recueillis au cours de l'année 1899 sur la popula-*

tion indigente de Paris à secourir en 1900 (Montvérain, 1899), pp. 4–9.

4. Isabelle Bogelot and Madame Pérouse (president of the Union des Femmes de France) were introduced as new members by chairman Paul Strauss, CSAP, *procès-verbaux*, 18 Dec. 1906 (morning), fasc. 106.

5. Ibid., 23 March 1893 (morning), fasc. 41. *Rapport général sur le fonctionnement des vingt bureaux de bienfaisance pendant les années 1896 et 1897* (Paris, 1898), pp. 3–5. According to a 1904 law, female admission officers were to be assigned to *maisons maternelles* in each French department. See Fuchs, *Abandoned Children*, p. 58.

6. An example was the debate on breast-feeding, CSAP, *procès-verbaux*, 30 Jan. 1891 (morning), fasc. 34. See Boxer, "Protective Legislation and Home Industry," pp. 45–65.

7. Statement by Dr. Louis Hardy, *Bulletin de l'Académie de Médecine*, 19 Nov. 1890. See McLaren, *Sexuality and Social Order*, pp. 44–64; and Nye, "Honor," pp. 48–71.

8. Statement by Dr. Henri-Alfred Henrot, CSAP, *procès-verbaux*, 29 June 1892 (afternoon), fasc. 39.

9. Statement by Loys Brueyre, ibid., 21 March 1905 (morning), fasc. 97. The Municipal Council of Paris favored having so-called *dames visiteuses* in each of the city's twenty *bureaux de bienfaisance*, but only on the condition that welfare expenses not be increased. Report by Jules Auffray, CMP, *procès-verbaux*, 5 July 1901.

10. See Watson, "The Politics of Educational Reform," pp. 81–99; and Mayeur, *L'enseignement secondaire*, pp. 9–84, and *L'éducation des filles*, pp. 139–47, 167–80.

11. CSIP (section permanente), *procès-verbaux*, 5 July 1893, AN Paris, F[17] 12971. See Zeldin, *France*, 1:260–64.

12. Hufton, *The Poor of Eighteenth Century France*, p. 318.

13. See Badinter, *Mother Love*, pp. 58–114; Sussman, *Selling Mother's Milk*, pp. 19–35; and Fuchs, *Abandoned Children*, pp. 13–16, 163–77, 184–89. As the Germans say: "Vater werden ist nicht schwer, Vater sein dagegen sehr."

14. Reports by Dr. Charles Porak, *Bulletin de l'Académie de Médecine*, 20 Nov. 1900, 10 Dec. 1901, and 1 Dec. 1903. See Fuchs, *Abandoned Children*, pp. 21–23, 151–54.

15. "Mémoire au Conseil de surveillance sur la suppression de la direction des nourrices," 31 March 1875, AP Paris, V.Q.[43]. See Sussman, "The End of the Wet-Nursing Business," pp. 237–58.

16. "Projet de loi [Roussel]," *Journal Officiel*, 9 June 1874. The first article of this law prescribed that every infant under the age of two who was placed with a wet nurse should be subject to inspection by public authorities; but the second article allowed that local committees of regulation were to be instituted only when deemed necessary by their departments.

17. Louis Buffet (minister of the interior) to the Academy of Medicine, 7 June 1875, AAM Paris, liasse 140; Drouineau, *De l'assistance*, p. 65.

18. Statement by Lunier, *Bulletin de l'Académie de Médecine*, 3 Feb. 1885. On the practice of birth control in the countryside, see Weber, *Peasants into Frenchmen*, pp. 177–86.

19. Statement by Gaston Gerville-Réache, 15 July 1886, AN Paris, C 5396. France's retardation, compared with the "Germanic" countries, in the matter of morally abandoned children was also stressed by Loys Brueyre, "Rapport au Conseil de l'Assistance Publique au nom de la 1re section (service d'enfance) sur le projet présénté par le gouvernement," CSAP, 1888, fasc. 17.

20. "Rapport au Conseil Supérieur de l'Assistance Publique … sur l'extension des attributions des inspecteurs des enfants assistés," ibid., 1888, fasc. 21.

21. CSAP, *procès-verbaux*, 1 Feb. 1889 (afternoon), fasc. 25. See Mitchell, *Victors and Vanquished*, pp. 202–3.

22. CSAP, *procès-verbaux*, 1 Feb. 1889 (morning), fasc. 25.

23. Monod to Bourgeois, 28 Jan. 1889, CSAP, fasc. 23.

24. Bertillon was cited by the deputy Jean-Baptiste Duchasseint in "Rapport fait au nom de la commission chargée d'examiner la proposition de loi de M. Henri de Lacretelle pour la création d'asiles d'enfants nouveaux-nés," 26 May 1891, AN Paris, C 5473.

25. Henri de Lacretelle, "Proposition de loi ayant pour objet la création d'asiles des enfants nouveaux-nés," 26 May 1891, ibid.

26. "Révision de la loi Roussel. Rapport présenté par M. le docteur Thulié," *Congrès national d'assistance*, 1:21–78. Monod to Émile Loubet (minister of the interior), 25 June 1892, CSAP, fasc. 53.

27. Statement by Lefort, *Bulletin de l'Académie de Médecine*, 3 Feb. 1885.

28. E.g., statement by Hardy, ibid., 18 Nov. 1890.

29. CSAP, *procès-verbaux*, 28 Jan. 1892 (afternoon), fasc. 37.

30. Émile Rey, "Rapport sur l'assistance aux enfants des familles indigentes présenté au nom de la première section," 1898, ibid., fasc. 78.

31. See Segalen, *Mari et femme*, pp. 87–121.

32. Nadaud, "Proposition de loi concernant la durée des heures de tra-

vail dans les usines et les manufactures," 10 Dec. 1885, AN Paris, F²² 333. See Stewart, *Women*, pp. 19–40.

33. Commission du travail, *procès-verbaux*, 9 March 1887, ibid., C 5429.

34. Ibid.

35. Ibid., 23 March 1887.

36. Ibid.

37. Ibid., 25 May 1887.

38. Ibid., 21 Nov. 1888. See Stewart, *Women*, pp. 130–33.

39. Commission du travail, *procès-verbaux*, 30 Nov. 1888, AN Paris, C 5429.

40. *Bulletin de l'Académie de Médicine*, 15 April 1890.

41. Commission du travail, *procès-verbaux*, 7 March 1894, AN Paris, C 5613².

42. Ibid.

43. Ibid., 14 Feb. 1896.

44. Ibid., 22 Nov. 1899, AN Paris, C 5673. For a monographic study of these issues in the Lille-Roubaix area, see Hilden, *Working Women*.

45. Some historians have argued, however, that French reforms ultimately increased gender distinctions. See Guilbert, *Les fonctions des femmes*, pp. 202–17; McDougall, "The Meaning of Reform," pp. 404–17; and Boxer, "Protective Legislation," pp. 55–56.

46. Commission de la prostitution, *procès-verbaux*, 20 Jan. 1892, AN Paris, C 5513. See Corbin, *Les filles de noces*, pp. 55–83; and Harsin, *Policing Prostitution*, pp. 242–52. In the Academy of Medicine, Léon Lefort estimated the number of *insoumises* much higher: "At the moment in Paris there are forty, fifty, sixty thousand girls engaging in prostitution, maybe more; but there are barely two thousand registered and submitted to sanitary inspection." *Bulletin de l'Académie de Médecine*, 28 Feb. 1888.

47. Simon, *L'ouvrière*, pp. 145–54, 295–300.

48. "Rapport général sur les travaux de la commission d'hygiène du 4me arrondissement pendant l'année 1872," 7 May 1874, AP Paris, V.D.⁶ 370. See Marrus, "Social Drinking," pp. 115–41; Barrows, "After the Commune," pp. 205–18; and Mitchell, "The Unsung Villain," pp. 448–50.

49. Report by Alfred Le Roy de Méricourt, *Bulletin de l'Académie de Médecine*, 27 May 1890. Harsin recognizes that "abolitionism" (of regulations on prostitution) was "in decline for a number of years," but she offers no explanation. Harsin, *Policing Prostitution*, pp. 331, 335–47.

50. The two statements on pimps (*souteneurs*) were made, respectively, by Labrousse and Vallé in the "Commission chargée de l'examen du projet de

loi concernant les logeurs, débitants de boissons et autres individus qui facilitent la prostitution des femmes et filles de débauche," *procès-verbaux*, 27 Nov. 1891, AN Paris, C 5513.

51. Ibid., 20 Jan. and 23 March 1892.

52. See Harsin, "Syphilis," pp. 72–95.

53. CSAP, *procès-verbaux*, 29 Jan. 1892 (afternoon), fasc. 37.

54. E.g., Monod to Loubet, 25 June 1892, ibid., fasc. 53.

55. Report on *crèches* by Dr. Louis Charpentier, *Bulletin de l'Académie de Médecine*, 24 Nov. 1896. Monod's opinion that state regulation of the *crèches* had become "absolutely urgent" was repeated by Henri Napias, CCHP, *procès-verbaux*, 21 Dec. 1896.

56. CAPS, *procès-verbaux*, 19 Jan. 1894, AN Paris, C 5545.

57. Harsin, *Policing Prostitution*, pp. 325, 334.

58. Ministry of Labor (First Bureau) to prefects of the Côtes du Nord et al., [23 May] 1912, AN Paris, F^{22} 307. See Corbin, *Les filles de noces*, pp. 507–10.

59. See Fuchs, *Abandoned Children*, p. 58; and Stone, *Search for Social Peace*, p. 139.

60. Fernand Engerand, "Proposition de loi sur la protection avant et après l'accouchement," 5 July 1906, AN Paris, C 7398. The connection with Jules Simon and the Berlin congress was claimed by Paul Strauss, "La lutte contre la mortalité infantile," *Revue philanthropique* 15 (1904): 255–57, and again in his "Bulletin," ibid. 24 (1908–9): 143–44. The continuity from Simon to Strauss was emphasized by E. Bonnaire, "La mutualité maternelle," ibid. 27 (1910): 245–77.

61. CSAP, *procès-verbaux*, 29 June 1892 (morning), fasc. 39.

62. Ibid., 29 May 1900 (morning), fascs. 77, 78.

63. Constant Dulau, "Proposition de loi sur la protection de la mère et de l'enfant nouveau-né," 7 March 1899, AN Paris, C 5654. For the culmination of this story, see Chapter 12.

Chapter 6

1. See Sussman, "The Glut of Doctors," pp. 287–304. A wide variance in the density of French medical personnel before 1870 is illustrated by Ramsey, *Professional and Popular Medicine*, pp. 302–5.

2. For background, see the various works of Léonard, *La vie quotidienne du médecin*; *Les médecins de l'ouest*; *La France médicale*; *La médecine entre les*

savoirs et les pouvoirs; and *Archives du corps*. A useful guide to Léonard's labyrinthine writings is provided by Ramsey, "History of a Profession," pp. 319–38.

3. The three principal medical faculties were designated in 1808; in addition there were twenty-two "preparatory" schools that offered the equivalent of the first two years of medical training. See Weisz, *Emergence*, p. 20; and Mitchell, *Victors and Vanquished*, pp. 214–15.

4. "Mémoire au Conseil de Surveillance sur le projet de budget des recettes et des dépenses pour l'exercice 1879," 1879, AP Paris, V.Q.^{31}.

5. Lockroy, "Projet de loi relatif à l'assainissement des logements insalubres," 13 Jan. 1887, AN Paris, F^8 212. "Whatever the causes of the peasants' ill health or their reservations about modern healing techniques, one thing is clear: physically, the rural folk lagged behind the city dwellers," writes Weber, *Peasants into Frenchmen*, p. 154.

6. Brouardel and A.-J. Martin, "Exercice de la médecine. Projet de révision . . . relative à l'exercice de la médecine," 15 Feb. 1886, CCHP, *Recueil* 16 (1886): 95.

7. E.g., CMP, *procès-verbaux*, 22 July 1885. See Mitchell, "The Municipal Council of Paris," pp. 435–50.

8. For background, see Hildreth, *Doctors*; Zeldin, *France*, 1:23–42; and Weisz, *Emergence*, pp. 48–51.

9. René Goblet, "Remarques sur la 'Proposition de loi concernant l'organisation de l'administration de la santé publique,'" 16 May 1887, AN Paris, C 5407; statement by August-Louis Navarre, CMP, *procès-verbaux*, 26 Dec. 1887; Monod to Floquet, 10 June 1888, CSAP, fasc. 26.

10. CMP, *procès-verbaux*, 27 Dec. 1889 and 17 March 1890.

11. Ibid., 26 Dec. 1888. The national administration's "unjustifiable negligence" was also attacked by Ernest Dumas, reporting for the municipal welfare committee (*5e commission*), ibid., 15 Nov. 1889.

12. Report by Alexandre Patenne, ibid., 27 Feb. 1889.

13. Report by François Cattiaux for the welfare committee, ibid., 27 Nov. 1889.

14. *Bulletin de l'Académie de Médecine*, 3 March 1891.

15. CMP, *procès-verbaux*, 8 July 1892.

16. CSAP, *procès-verbaux*, 24 March 1893 (afternoon), fasc. 41. The importance of the often disputed German example in the ideology of reform is emphasized by Weisz, *Emergence*, pp. 69–81.

17. Pronounced in the Senate on 11 July 1893, Dupuy's statement was

cited by Henri Napias and Georges Rondel, "La loi du 15 juillet 1893 sur l'assistance médicale gratuite et ses conséquences administratives," *Congrès national de l'assistance*, 1:137.

18. Statement by Dr. Louis Charpentier, *Bulletin de l'Académie de Médecine*, 4 Sept. 1894.

19. CMP, *procès-verbaux*, 31 Dec. 1895.

20. André Mesureur in the introduction to proceedings of the Congrès international de la tuberculose, pp. i–xxxi.

21. Conseil de Surveillance, *procès-verbaux*, 18 March 1897, AP Paris, D.1 X[1] 18.

22. Statement by Dreyfus-Brisac, CSAP, *procès-verbaux*, 16 May 1899 (afternoon), fasc. 68.

23. The first two statements, respectively, were made by Eugène-Marie Faillet and André Lefèvre. CMP, *procès-verbaux*, 6 April 1900.

24. *Bulletin de l'Académie de Médecine*, 20 Nov. 1900. Porak added a second report, ibid., 10 Dec. 1901.

25. See Darmon, *Variole*.

26. Ibid., pp. 358–66.

27. See Huerkamp, "Smallpox Vaccination," pp. 626–30; and Mitchell, "Bürgerlicher Liberalismus und Volksgesundheit," pp. 408–10.

28. Camescasse (prefect of police) to Floquet (prefect of the Seine), 13 March 1882, AP Paris, V.Q.[3]; "Rapport à Monsieur le préfet de la Seine," 8 May 1882, ibid.

29. Goblet, "Remarques sur la 'Proposition de loi concernant l'organisation de la santé publique,'" 16 May 1887, AN Paris, C 5407.

30. Report by Émile Chautemps, CMP, *procès-verbaux*, 13 June 1887.

31. CCHP, *Recueil* 18 (1888): i–vii.

32. Monod to Floquet, 5 Nov. 1888, AAM Paris, liasse 140; Adrien Proust, "Rapport sur la vaccine," CCHP, *Recueil* 19 (1889): 175–268.

33. *Bulletin de l'Académie de Médecine*, 11 Nov. 1890.

34. Ibid., 13 Jan. 1891.

35. Ibid.

36. Ibid., 17 Feb. 1891.

37. See Darmon, *Variole*, pp. 366–71.

38. Statement by Lagneau, *Bulletin de l'Académie de Médecine*, 10 Feb. 1891.

39. Statements by Drs. Hyacinthe Vincent and André Chantemesse, ibid., 21 Dec. 1909 and 8 Feb. 1910. As noted, French impressions of Germany were sometimes inaccurate insofar as they overlooked local variations.

For example, Hamburg, with a more liberal regime, had a far poorer record in fighting infectious diseases than did interventionist Bremen. See Evans, *Death*, pp. 301–4.

40. Statements by Drs. Louis Vaillard and Émile Vallin, *Bulletin de l'Académie de Médecine*, 26 Oct. and 30 Nov. 1909.

41. Conseil de Surveillance, *procès-verbaux*, 6 June 1901, AP Paris, D.1 X¹ 22.

42. Statement by Dr. Ulysse Trélat, *Bulletin de l'Académie de Médecine*, 7 Jan. 1890.

43. Statements by Émile Dubois and Raoul Bompard, CMP, *procès-verbaux*, 12 March and 2 May 1894.

44. Statements by Drs. Léon Lereboullet and Albert Josias, *Bulletin de l'Académie de Médecine*, 7 March 1900 and 13 Jan. 1903. Émile Loubet, "Désignation des maladies . . . ," 10 Feb. 1903, AN Paris, F²² 520.

45. Statements by Drs. Arnold Netter and Charles Fernet, *Bulletin de l'Académie de Médecine*, 3 Jan. 1905.

46. Ibid.

47. Ibid., 20 June 1905.

48. Statement by Dr. Jules Bucquoy, ibid., 5 Jan. 1909.

49. Henri Doizy, "Proposition de loi tendant à modifier les articles 4 et 5 de la loi du 15 février 1902 sur la protection de la santé publique . . . ," 8 Nov. 1912, AN Paris, C 7470; statement by Édouard Lachaud in the Commission de l'hygiène publique, *procès-verbaux*, 22 Nov. 1912, ibid.

50. Ibid., 26 Feb., 12 and 19 March 1913.

51. "Rapport sur le service des aliénés," 1872, AP Paris, D.2 X³ 25; Du Camp, *Paris*, 4:319–92. For the background, see Castel, *L'ordre psychiatrique*; Nye, *Crime, Madness, and Politics*, pp. 31–34, 227–64; and Goldstein, *Console and Classify*, pp. 339–77. Despite its comprehensive subtitle, Goldstein's account extends only to 1876. A sequel is suggested by Micale, "Salpêtrière," pp. 703–31.

52. Victor de Bled, "Les aliénés à l'étranger et en France," *Revue des deux mondes* 77 (1886): 896–933; and ibid. 78 (1886): 122–67. Monod to Floquet, 4 Jan. 1889, CSAP, fasc. 35.

53. Joseph Reinach, "Proposition de loi sur le régime des aliénés," 3 Dec. 1890, AN Paris, C 5434. Some recent studies, however, suggest that French science in general may not have been quite so retarded, compared with that of Germany, as many contemporaries thought. See Paul, *From Knowledge to Power*; and Nye, *Science in the Provinces*.

54. Commission des aliénés, *procès-verbaux*, 12 Jan. 1894, AN Paris, C

5540; *Bulletin de l'Académie de Médecine*, 5 March 1895.

55. Statement by Paul Brouardel, Commission des aliénés, *procès-verbaux*, 1 July 1891, AN Paris, C 5434; Monod to Waldeck-Rousseau, 22 Feb. 1901, CSAP, fasc. 83; "Rapport sur la création d'asiles spéciaux pour les aliénés criminels au nom de la IVe section par M. le Dr. Regnard," ibid.

56. Dr. Bondet, "De l'organisation hospitalière il y a un siècle et de l'organisation actuelle," *Congrès national d'assistance*, 1:285–374.

57. Sérieux, *L'assistance des aliénés*, pp. 30–49, 974–77.

58. CSAP, *procès-verbaux*, 11 June 1902 (morning), fasc. 87; ibid., 22 March 1905 (afternoon), fasc. 98; ibid., 23 March 1905 (morning), fasc. 99.

59. Dr. Paul-Maurice Legrain, "Rapport introductif présenté à la IVe section du Conseil Supérieur de l'Assistance Publique," 1912, ibid., fasc. 111. Statements by Paul Strauss and Maurice Dide, *Bulletin de l'Académie de Médecine*, 17 Feb. and 21 July 1914.

60. See Weisz, *Emergence*, pp. 359–68; and Hildreth, "Medical Rivalries," pp. 5–29, and "Les syndicats médicaux," pp. 7–21.

61. See Hildreth, *Doctors*, pp. 164–214.

62. "In 1893 French medical care was at a crossroads. The nation had two long-standing official medical traditions, one institutional and bureaucratic, and the other based on private practice and home care." Hildreth, "Medical Rivalries," p. 28.

63. Statement by Dreyfus-Brisac, 12 June 1902 (morning), CSAP, *procès-verbaux*, fasc. 89. See Mitchell, "Mutual Aid Societies."

64. Dr. Jean Jules Gairal, "Du libre choix du médecin dans les sociétés de secours mutuels," *Congrès des praticiens*, 1:301–3.

65. CAPS, *procès-verbaux*, 10 June 1904, AN Paris, C 7278.

66. Henri Huchard, "Agrégation et privat docentisme," *Congrès des praticiens*, 2:5–21.

67. "Compte rendu des séances," 12 April 1907 (morning), ibid., 3:9–18, 39. The latter statement was by Dr. Lafontaine.

68. Étienne Bazot, "Le ministère de la médecine en Allemagne," 14 April 1907 (morning), ibid., pp. 208–16.

69. See Hildreth, "Medical Rivalries," pp. 27–29, and *Doctors*, pp. 270–312.

Chapter 7

1. Tocqueville, *Old Regime*, p. 72.

2. The most explicit example is Gravier, *Paris et le désert français*.

3. See Sorlin, *La société française*, 1:45–73.

4. The background was reviewed by Floquet, "Projet de loi sur les syndicats de communes," 1888, CSAP, fasc. 15.

5. Nadaud, "Proposition de loi tendant à modifier la loi du 13 avril 1850 sur l'assainissement des logements insalubres," 3 Dec. 1881, AN Paris, F^8 212; Hippolyte Maze, "Rapport fait au nom de la Commission chargée d'examiner la proposition de loi de M. Martin Nadaud . . . ," 21 April 1883, ibid. See Weber, *Peasants into Frenchmen*, pp. 156–66.

6. Monod, "Statistique des dépenses publiques d'assistance en France pendant l'année 1885," 1885, CSAP, fasc. 24.

7. Statement by Thulié, CSAP, *procès-verbaux*, 1 Feb. 1889 (morning), fasc. 25.

8. Monod to Floquet, 26 Jan. 1889, ibid., fasc. 32.

9. CSAP, 1 and 2 Feb. 1889, ibid., fasc. 25.

10. Cited by Lallemand, *De l'assistance des classes rurales*, p. 34.

11. Statement by Jules Simon, CSAP, *procès-verbaux*, 3 March 1890 (afternoon), fasc. 31.

12. Statement by Jules Crisenoy, 30 Jan. 1889, ibid., fasc. 25; "Rapport au Conseil Supérieur de l'Assistance Publique au nom de la IIIe section sur la question de la réunion des commissions administratives des bureaux de bienfaisance et des établissements hospitaliers," 1889, ibid., fasc. 26.

13. Statement by Dr. Antoine Gailleton (mayor of Lyon), 28 Feb. 1890 (afternoon), ibid., fasc. 31.

14. Commission . . . Dujardin-Verkinden, *procès-verbaux*, 28 Nov. 1890, AN Paris, C 5437.

15. Statements by Monod and Dreyfus-Brisac, CSAP, *procès-verbaux*, 26 Feb. 1890, fasc. 31. A theoretical model of the dual "gap" (*écart*) between enunciated and adopted policy, and then between adopted and applied policy, has been designed (with the example of welfare legislation in Québec) in the collaborative work of Lajoie, Molinari, et al., *Pour une approche critique du droit de la santé*.

16. Brouardel, "Rapport sur la déliverance des médicaments aux indigents," [1891?], AN Paris, C 5437.

17. Monod, "Étuves à désinfection de 1889 à 1892," 25 April 1892, CCHP, *Recueil* 22 (1892): 63–74.

18. Commission . . . Dujardin-Verkinden, *procès-verbaux*, AN Paris, C 5437; CSAP, *procès-verbaux*, 10 June 1891 (morning), fasc. 36.

19. Commission du travail, *procès-verbaux*, 11 Dec. 1890, AN Paris, C 5433.

20. Statement by Félix Voisin in the Conseil de Surveillance, *procès-verbaux*, 28 April 1892, AP Paris, D.1 X¹ 13.

21. Commission du travail, *procès-verbaux*, 16 Feb. 1894, AN Paris, C 5613².

22. CAPS, *procès-verbaux*, 6 June 1894, ibid., C 5544.

23. "Rapport sur l'assistance des vieillards et des incurables présenté par M. Sabran," 26 Jan. 1891, CSAP, fasc. 32.

24. Émile Chautemps, "Proposition de loi relative aux pensions de retraite de la vieillesse et des invalides du travail," 17 June 1893, AN Paris, C 5559. See Hatzfeld, *Du paupérisme à la sécurité sociale*, pp. 57–58.

25. See Mitchell, "Crucible of French Anticlericalism," pp. 403–5, and "Municipal Council of Paris," pp. 435–40.

26. CMP, *procès-verbaux*, 3 June 1887.

27. "Commune de Créteil: Pétition," 27 June 1887, AP Paris, V.Q.⁴².

28. "Ville de Neuilly, Conseil Municipal: Extrait du registre des délibera-tions," 19 July 1889, ibid.

29. CMP, *procès-verbaux*, 27 Feb. and 27 Nov. 1889.

30. Ibid., 15 Nov. 1912.

31. Conseil de Surveillance, *procès-verbaux*, 9 Jan. 1890 and 19 March 1891, AP Paris, D.1 X¹ 11–12.

32. Report by Ambroise Rendu, CMP, *procès-verbaux*, 31 Dec. 1902.

33. "Rapport sur les secours à domicile à Paris par M. Fleury-Ravarin," [1892], CSAP, fasc. 40.

34. Statement by Paul Strauss, 1 Feb. 1894 (afternoon), *procès-verbaux*, ibid., fasc. 45.

35. "Rapport présenté au nom des deuxième et troisième sections par M. le Dr. Drouineau," [1897], ibid., fasc. 63.

36. CMP, *procès-verbaux*, 1 July 1898 and 6 April 1900. The statement quoted was by Eugène-Marie Faillet.

37. Ibid., 30 Dec. 1904, 17 Dec. 1906, and 31 Dec. 1907. See Mitchell, "Municipal Council of Paris," pp. 445–46.

38. Justin de Selves (prefect of the Seine) to René Waldeck-Rousseau (prime minister), 27 July 1900, AP Paris, D.2 X¹ 1; Émile Combes (prime minister) to prefects, 1 Aug. 1902, ibid. See Watson, "The Nationalist Move-ment," pp. 49–84.

39. CMP, *procès-verbaux*, 10 March 1902.

40. Émile Rey and Albert Lachièze, "Proposition de loi relative à l'assis-tance des vieillards et des infirmes," 22 Feb. 1895, AN Paris, C 5543.

41. *Bulletin de l'Académie de Médecine*, 5 March 1895.

42. CSAP, *procès-verbaux*, 6 March 1895 (morning), fasc. 51.

43. CAPS, *procès-verbaux*, 5 Dec. 1899, AN Paris, C 5622.

44. Ibid., 27 Nov. 1901.

45. Respectively, statements by Hermann Sabran, CSAP, *procès-verbaux*, 5 March 1895 (afternoon), fasc. 51; Georges Rondel, ibid., 30 Jan. 1896 (morning), fasc. 54; Paul Van Cauwenberghe, ibid., 18 March 1898 and 17 May 1899 (afternoon), fasc. 70; and Gustave Dron, ibid.

46. Statement by Albert Bluzet, 7 June 1901 (morning), ibid., fasc. 84.

47. Monod to Louis Barthou, "Rapport à monsieur le ministre de l'intérieur concernant l'exécution pendant l'année 1895 de la loi du 15 juillet 1893 sur l'assistance médicale gratuite," 29 Dec. 1896, ibid., fasc. 55.

48. Ibid., 30 Jan. 1896 (afternoon), fasc. 59.

49. Ibid., 11 March 1897 (morning), fasc. 58.

50. CAPS, *procès-verbaux*, 10 March 1898, AN Paris, C 5544.

51. Jean Cruppi, "Proposition de loi relative aux moyens d'assistance à prévenir ou à réprimer le vagabondage et la mendicité," 25 Jan. 1899, AN Paris, C 5622; "Rapport sur les dépôts de mendicité présenté au nom de la IVe section par M. Jean Cruppi, député," [1899], CSAP, fasc. 73; statement by Cruppi, CSAP, *procès-verbaux*, 19 May 1899 (morning), ibid.

52. Alfred Lambert, "Un étrange délit: le vagabondage," *Revue philanthropique* 4 (1899): 453–63.

53. Conseil de Surveillance, *procès-verbaux*, 26 Oct. 1899, AP Paris, D.1 X¹ 21.

54. Brouardel, "Taux de la mortalité générale d'après la statistique du ministère de l'intérieur de 1893 à 1898," CCHP, *Recueil* (1900): 85–119.

55. Monod, "Statistique des dépenses publiques d'assistance en 1896," 19 March 1900, CSAP, fasc. 76.

56. Statements by Monod and Brueyre, CSAP, *procès-verbaux*, 30 May 1900 (morning), fasc. 78.

57. Monod, "Application de la loi du 15 février 1902 sur la santé publique," CCHP, *Recueil* 33 (1903): 24–32.

58. *Bulletin de l'Académie de Médecine*, 7 Jan. 1908.

59. CSAP, *procès-verbaux*, 10 Dec. 1912 (morning), fasc. 111.

60. CAPS, *procès-verbaux*, 4 June 1903, AN Paris, C 7278.

61. CCHP, *Recueil* 31 (1901): vii–ix.

62. CPPCT, *procès-verbaux*, 12 Dec. 1903.

63. Report by Dr. E. Mosny in "Services d'hygiène dans les arrondissements: organisation et fonctionnement," CCHP, *Recueil* 35 (1905): 507–625. This investigation included the following departments: Basses-Alpes,

Hautes-Alpes, Alpes-Maritimes, Bouches du Rhône, Corse, Drôme, Gard, Hérault, Isère, Var, and Vaucluse.

64. Report by Dr. Eugène Deschamps, ibid. [CCHP became designated as CSHP] 36 (1906): 643–724. This report included these departments: Allier, Ardèche, Aveyron, Cantal, Corrèze, Creuse, Loire, Haute-Loire, Lot, Lozère, Puy-de-Dôme, Rhône, and Haute-Vienne.

65. Clemenceau, "Application de la loi du 15 février 1902 sur la santé publique: constitution des bureaux municipaux d'hygiène," 20 Nov. 1906, ibid. 36 (1906): 59.

66. Clemenceau, "Organisation de l'hygiène publique en France: bureaux d'hygiène, services publiques de désinfection," 27 April 1907, ibid. 37 (1907): 28–33.

67. Albert Bluzet, "Loi du 15 février 1902 sur la santé publique: application," 20 Dec. 1907, ibid. 39 (1909): 251–315.

68. "Discours prononcé par M. Maujan, sous-secrétaire d'état au ministère de l'intérieur," 20 Jan. 1908, ibid. 38 (1908): 306–12; Dr. Georges Guilhaud, "Rapport général sur les travaux des conseils départementaux d'hygiène et des commissions sanitaires pendant l'année 1907," 20 Dec. 1909, ibid. 39 (1909): 547–730; and Bluzet, "Loi de 15 février 1902 sur la santé publique: application [par les] services départementaux de vaccination et de désinfection," [date?], ibid. 40 (1910): 220–75.

69. Guilhaud, "Travaux des conseils départementaux d'hygiène pendant l'année 1909," [date?], ibid. 41 (1911): 631–798. See Mitchell, "An Inexact Science," pp. 392–93.

Chapter 8

1. See Perrot, *Les ouvriers en grève*, 1:74–80; Tilly et al., *Rebellious Century*, pp. 19–21; and Mitchell, "Subversion and Repression," pp. 409–11.

2. Louis Reybaud, "Les agitations ouvrières et l'association internationale," *Revue des deux mondes* 81 (1869): 871–902.

3. Charles de Mazade, "Chronique de la quinzaine," ibid., 86 (1870): 752–64.

4. Paul Leroy-Beaulieu, "La question ouvrière au dix-neuvième siècle: le radicalisme et les grèves," ibid., pp. 88–116.

5. "Situation du Service de la Justice et résultats qu'on peut apercevoir," 15 Jan. 1872, AN Paris, BB^{30} 487. See Rougerie, *Procès des communards*, pp. 17–24.

6. Police reports, 29 Nov. and 22 Dec. 1871, APP Paris, B A/86. For background, see Berlanstein, *Working People*.

7. Rémusat to Gabriac, 7 Sept. 1871, MAE Paris, Allemagne 1.

8. Gabriac to Rémusat, 1 Oct. 1871, ibid., 2.

9. *Journal Officiel*, 13–15 March 1872. See Bourgin, "La lutte contre la première Internationale," pp. 39–138; and Mitchell, "Subversion and Repression," pp. 411–13.

10. Court records indicated 23,288 cases dismissed (*non lieu*), 12,082 convictions, 2,275 acquittals, and 8,940 refusals to testify—for a total of 46,585 judicial proceedings. Weekly police report, 30 June 1873, AN Paris, BB^{30} 487.

11. "Enquête parlementaire sur les conditions du travail en France, 1872–75," AN Paris, C 3018–20.

12. See Hatzfeld, *Du paupérisme à la sécurité sociale*, pp. 263–67; and Haupt, "Les petits commerçants," pp. 7–34.

13. Schneider to Thiers, 2 Sept. 1872, BN Paris, Papiers Thiers, NAF 20625; Thiers to Schneider, 19 Sept. 1872, ibid., 20626.

14. Police report, 3 April 1876, APP Paris, B A/87.

15. Ibid., 20 and 25 March 1876.

16. Ibid., 13 April 1876.

17. Ibid., 29 July–1 Oct. 1876. On Chabert's role, see Kelso, "Inception," pp. 173–93.

18. Police reports, 4–5 Aug. 1876, APP Paris, B A/87.

19. Ibid., 12–19 Aug. 1876.

20. Ibid., 1–20 Oct. 1876; *Séances du congrès ouvrier de France: session de 1876* [microfiche] (Paris, 1975).

21. "La commission spéciale à M. le directeur de la Sûreté générale," 2 Nov. 1876, AN Paris, F^7 12488. See Ligou, *Histoire du socialisme*, pp. 20–21.

22. These police reports were forwarded from Prefect of Police Félix Voisin to the French cabinet during November 1876; they are to be found in AN Paris, F^7 12488.

23. Reports by police agents, [?] May and 11 June 1878, APP Paris, B A/962.

24. Wesdehlen to Dufaure, 2 July 1878, AN Paris, F^7 12488. Wesdehlen's message was sent by Dufaure to the Ministry of Justice, 4 July 1878, ibid.

25. Prefecture of Police to the Ministry of the Interior (*Sûreté générale*), 17 July 1878, ibid., 12504; Ministry of the Interior to the Prefecture of Po-

lice, 30 July 1878, ibid. The state's efforts of surveillance and repression were summarized in a "Note pour Monsieur le Ministre: congrès ouvrier," 1 Sept. 1879, ibid., 12522. See Willard, *Le mouvement socialiste*, pp. 11–15; Moss, *Origins*, pp. 82–88; and Mitchell, "Subversion and Repression," pp. 418–26.

26. Hohenlohe to the Auswärtiges Amt, 20 Aug. 1878, AA Bonn, I.A.B.c 79, Bd. 25; Hohenlohe to Bülow, 5 Sept. 1878, ibid., 73, Bd. 2. Hohenlohe's speculations were largely unfounded. See Rothney, *Bonapartism after Sedan*, pp. 230–69.

27. Maurice Rouvier to prefects, 6 Feb. 1885, AN Paris, F^8 211.

28. Richard Waddington, "Rapport de la commission chargée d'examiner les propositions de loi . . . ," 10 March 1884, ibid., F^{22} 333. See Cross, *Quest for Time*, pp. 45–51.

29. Charles Ferry, "Rapport fait au nom de la Commission chargée d'examiner le projet de loi . . . sur le travail des enfants, des filles mineures et des femmes dans les établissements industriels," 20 June 1889, AN Paris, F^{22} 333.

30. Charles de Freycinet, "Déclaration lue à la Chambre des Députés au nom du Conseil des Ministres," 18 March 1890, ibid., C 5493.

31. Commission du travail, *procès-verbaux*, 4–5 Nov. 1890, ibid., C 5433.

32. Ibid., 7 Nov. 1890.

33. Ibid., 21 Jan. 1891.

34. Paplier, "Proposition de loi sur l'organisation d'une caisse d'épargne-retraite," 30 Dec. 1891, ibid., C 5452.

35. CAPS, *procès-verbaux*, 23 May 1894, ibid., C 5544.

36. E.g., Rogé (president of the Nancy *chambre de commerce*), "Conséquences de la limitation de la durée du travail et de sa réduction à onze heures par jour pour l'industrie métallurgique," 18 May 1894, ibid., F^{22} 333.

37. Guesde et al., "Proposition de loi tendant à interdire aux employeurs tant collectifs qu'individuels de faire travailler plus de 8 heures par jour . . . ," 22 May 1894, ibid., C 5613; Vaillant et al., "Proposition de loi pour l'établissement de la journée de huit heures et d'un salaire minimum," 27 Oct. 1894, ibid. On the campaign for an eight-hour day, see Cross, *Quest for Time*, pp. 52–78.

38. Commission du travail, *procès-verbaux*, 15 March 1895, AN Paris, C 5613^2.

39. Ibid.

40. Statement by Charles Ferry, 11 Nov. 1896, ibid.

41. Ibid., 16 Feb. 1894; CAPS, *procès-verbaux*, 1 and 6 June 1894, ibid., C 5544.

42. Commission du travail, *procès-verbaux*, 5 and 7 Feb. 1896, ibid., C 5613².

43. Ibid., 12 Feb. and 20 March 1896. The other dissenter was Aimé Lavy.

44. Commission du travail, *procès-verbaux*, 23 Nov. 1898, ibid., C 5673.

45. Ibid., 31 [*sic*] Nov. 1898.

46. Lagard (inspector in the tenth circumscription of Marseille) to Millerand (minister of commerce and industry), 3 May 1901, ibid., F²² 438; Dupont (inspector in the second circumscription of Limoges) to Millerand, 24 May 1901, ibid.

47. Congy, "Proposition de loi tendant à abroger l'article 2 de la loi du 30 mars 1900 sur la durée du travail dans l'industrie," 20 Oct. 1903, ibid., C 7338.

48. E. Duval (president of the Union des industries métallurgiques et minières) to Fernand Dubief (president of the Commission du travail), 18 Nov. 1901, ibid., C 5673.

49. For background see Mitchell, *German Influence*, pp. 185–93.

50. Georges Graux, "Proposition de loi ayant pour objet de modifier la loi du 9 avril 1898 sur les accidents du travail," 2 May 1899, AN Paris, C 5615.

51. Albert Poulain et al., "Proposition de loi tendant à modifier la loi du 9 avril 1898 sur les accidents du travail," 7 Feb. 1901, ibid.

52. Mirman, "Proposition de loi réglant les conditions de compétence et de délais pour la fixation des indemnités journalières . . . ," 15 Feb. 1901, ibid.

53. Mirman, "Proposition de loi ayant pour objet d'étendre à toutes les exploitations commerciales les dispositions de la loi du 9 avril 1898 sur les accidents du travail," 10 June 1902, ibid., C 7255. The importance of the 1898 law, although not the German precedent for it, is stressed by Ewald, *L'état providence*, pp. 231–380.

54. On Millerand's career, see Sorlin, *Waldeck-Rousseau*, pp. 399–404, 460–80; and Derfler, *Alexandre Millerand*.

55. Vaillant et al., "Proposition de loi tendant à l'établissement de la journée de huit heures et d'un salaire minimum . . . ," 13 Jan. 1905, AN Paris, C 7338; "Proposition de loi ayant pour objet l'institution de la journée de huit heures et du salaire minimum . . . ," 27 Nov. 1905, ibid.

56. *Bulletin de la Chambre de Commerce de Paris* (Paris, 1907), p. 267.

57. *Assemblée des présidents des chambres de commerce de France: compte rendu in extenso* (Paris, 1912), pp. 147–49.

58. Commission du travail, *procès-verbaux*, 31 Jan. 1912, AN Paris, C 7486.

59. Jules Coutant, "Proposition de loi relative aux salaires des ouvriers étrangers et ayant pour but de prévenir la dépression de la main-d'oeuvre ouvrière," 8 Nov. 1910, ibid.

60. Paul Pugliesi-Conti, "Proposition de loi sur la protection du travail national," 7 Nov. 1911, ibid.

61. Michel, *Les habitants*, pp. 154–55. See Shorter and Tilly, *Strikes in France*, pp. 46–51, 112–22, 360–62. Contemporary statistics compiled by the Commission du Travail are generally corroborated by Shorter and Tilly. One discrepancy occurs in the number of strikers in 1905 (was it ca. 75,000 or 175,000?), but the general trend is clearly upward.

62. Michel, *Les habitants*, p. 148.

63. Commission du travail, *procès-verbaux*, 29 Jan. and 3 Feb. 1904, AN Paris, C 7338.

64. See Tenfelde and Volkmann, *Streik*, pp. 295–96. As in the case of French strikes, the contemporary statistics before 1914 have been, with slight discrepancies, confirmed by scholarly research.

65. Pierre Colliard, "Rapport fait . . . au nom de la Commission du Travail sur les propositions de loi relatives aux différends relatifs aux conditions du travail et arbitrage obligatoire," 16 June 1910, ibid., C 7486.

66. Ibid.

Chapter 9

1. The four principal direct taxes were on land (*impôt foncier*), property (*contribution personnelle-mobilière*), residence (*portes-et-fenêtres*), and business activities (*patentes*). See the superb summary by Jean Bouvier, "Le système fiscal français du XIXe siècle," in Bouvier et al., *Deux siècles*, pp. 226–62.

2. Ibid., pp. 236–41.

3. Arnim to the Auswärtiges Amt, 1 Dec. 1872, AA Bonn, I.A.B.c 75, Bd. 3. Thiers, *Notes et souvenirs*, pp. 238–49. Also see Pomaret, *Monsieur Thiers*, pp. 148–54; Robert Schnerb, "La politique fiscale de Thiers," in Bouvier et al., *Deux siècles*, pp. 158–220; and Ardant, *Histoire de l'impôt*, 2:404–10.

4. See Bouvier, "Le système fiscal français du XIXe siècle," in Bouvier et al., *Deux siècles*, pp. 246–54.

5. For background, see Mitchell, *German Influence*, pp. 190–93.

6. Pierre Mathieu-Bodet, "La réforme des impôts," *Revue des deux mondes* 39 (1880): 627–61.

7. Mazade, "Chronique de la quinzaine," ibid. 42 (1880): 945–58; and ibid. 54 (1882): 945–55.

8. Commission relative à la réforme de la contribution personnelle mobilière, *procès-verbaux*, 28 March 1887, AN Paris, C 5407.

9. Paul Peytral, "Projet de loi portant établissement d'un impôt général sur le revenu," 30 Oct. 1888, ibid.

10. Commission relative à la réforme de la contribution personnelle mobilière, *procès-verbaux*, 12 Dec. 1888, AN Paris, C 5407.

11. Ibid., 11 Jan. 1889.

12. CAPS, *procès-verbaux*, 11 Dec. 1891, ibid., C 5452.

13. CSAP, *procès-verbaux*, 28 Jan. 1892 (morning), fasc. 37.

14. Michel, *Les habitants*, pp. 76–79. For background, see Barrows, *Distorting Mirrors*, pp. 61–63; Marrus, "Social Drinking," pp. 115–41; Mitchell, "The Unsung Villain," pp. 448–50; and Prestwich, *Drink*, pp. 6–36.

15. *Bulletin de l'Académie de Médecine*, 17 Nov. 1885.

16. Ibid., 23 March 1886.

17. Report by Dr. Jules Rochard, ibid., 6 July 1886; Peytral, "Projet de loi portant établissement d'un impôt général sur le revenu," 30 Oct. 1888, AN Paris, C 5407. See Ardant, *Histoire de l'impôt*, 2:404–5.

18. Guillemet et al., "Proposition de loi ayant pour objet la réforme générale de l'impôt," 10 Feb. 1894, AN Paris, C 5597.

19. Fleury-Ravarin et al., "Proposition de loi tendant à rendre obligatoire, sous le contrôle hygiènique de l'État, l'épuration des alcools destinés à la consommation . . . ," 18 Dec. 1894, ibid., C 5534.

20. Cavaignac et al., "Proposition de loi tendant à modifier la répartition de la contribution personnelle et mobilière . . . ," 10 March 1894, ibid., C 5597.

21. Commission de l'impôt, *procès-verbaux*, 8, 9, 16, and 21 Nov. 1894, ibid.

22. Ibid., 28 Nov. and 5 Dec. 1894, 3 April and 12 June 1895.

23. Ribot, "Projet de loi portant suppression de la contribution des portes et fenêtres et transformation de la contribution personnelle-mobilière," 22 Oct. 1895, ibid.

24. Doumer, "Exposé des motifs du projet de loi portant fixation du budget général des dépenses et des recettes de l'exercice 1897," ibid., C 5550; Cochery, "Projet de loi portant fixation des impôts directs sur les

revenus et des taxes y assimilées de l'exercice 1897," 4 June 1896, ibid., C 5552.

25. Peytral, "Projet de loi portant établissement d'un impôt général sur le revenu," 25 Oct. 1898, ibid., C 5661; Klotz, "Proposition de loi établissant un impôt sur le revenu," 12 Dec. 1898, ibid.

26. Cochery, "Projet de loi relatif au contrôle hygiénique et fiscal de l'alcool," 31 Oct. 1896, ibid., C 5534.

27. Chambre de Commerce de Paris, "Rapport sur le monopole de l'alcool," 9 June 1897, ibid.

28. Commission d'hygiène publique, *procès-verbaux*, 29 March, 5 April, and 1 Dec. 1911, ibid., C 7470.

29. Félix Chautemps, "Proposition de loi tendant à interdire la vente, la circulation et la fumerie de l'opium . . . et de toutes substances analogues," 6 May 1913, ibid.; Jean Colly, "Proposition de loi tendant à réglementer la vente des toxiques . . . ," 14 May 1913, ibid. See Kudlick, "Alcoholism," pp. 129–58; and Prestwich, *Drink*, pp. 128–40.

30. Commission d'hygiène publique, *procès-verbaux*, 21 Nov. 1913, AN Paris, C 7470. See Mitchell, "The Unsung Villain," pp. 461–68.

31. For background, see the classic articles by Mead, "Study of National Character," pp. 70–85; and Inkeles and Levinson, "National Character," pp. 418–506. On the "national identity" of the French, see Zeldin, *France*, 2:3–28.

32. *Bismarcks Briefe*, p. 86.

33. But it is well to cite this word of caution: "The fact is, the French fuss so much about the nation because it is a living problem, became one when they set the nation up as an ideal, remained one because they found they could not realize the ideal. The more abstractly the concept of France-as-nation is presented, the less one notes discrepancies between theory and practice. When one gets down to facts, things become awkward." Weber, *Peasants into Frenchmen*, p. 112.

34. See Harsin, "Syphilis," pp. 72–75.

35. Statement by Léon Lefort, *Bulletin de l'Académie de Médecine*, 28 Oct. 1890. See Chapter 5.

36. Statement by Gustave Drouineau, CSAP, *procès-verbaux*, 25 March 1893 (morning), fasc. 41.

37. Paul Strauss, "La lutte contre la tuberculose," *Revue philanthropique* 6 (1899–1900): 385–89; and "Contre l'alcoolisme," ibid., pp. 627–28. See Barrows, "After the Commune," pp. 205–18.

38. E.g., statement by Loys Brueyre, CSAP, *procès-verbaux*, 29 May 1900 (morning), fasc. 78.

39. See Wylie, *Village in the Vaucluse*, pp. 206–39; and Weber, *Peasants into Frenchmen*, pp. 41–49.

40. See Mitchell, "The Unsung Villain," pp. 453–57.

41. These questions were raised by the "Rapport sur les dépôts de mendicité présenté . . . par M. Jean Cruppi," [1899], CSAP, fasc. 73. A debate ensued: CSAP, *procès-verbaux*, 19–20 May 1899, ibid.

42. E.g., Monod to Floquet, CSAP, 26 Jan. 1889, fasc. 32.

43. CSAP, *procès-verbaux*, 27 Jan. 1892 (morning), fasc. 37.

44. Ibid., 1 Feb. 1889 (morning), fasc. 25.

45. E.g., Paplier, "Proposition de loi sur l'organisation d'une caisse d'épargne-retraite," 30 Dec. 1891, AN Paris, C 5452.

46. See Mitchell, "The Xenophobic Style," pp. 414–25.

47. For an anecdotal attempt to comprehend this elusive subject, see Zeldin, *The French*.

48. CMP, *procès-verbaux*, 29 Nov. 1875. See Mitchell, "Crucible of French Anticlericalism," pp. 396–97.

49. See Mitchell, *Victors and Vanquished*, pp. 220–43.

50. CMP, *procès-verbaux*, 26 Jan. 1885.

51. Ibid., 28 Jan. 1885.

52. Statement by Louis Monteil, ibid., 6 Nov. 1885. See Mitchell, "Municipal Council of Paris," pp. 435–36.

53. Conseil de Surveillance, *procès-verbaux*, 8 Dec. 1887, 26 July 1888 and 3 April 1890, AP Paris, D.1 X¹ 9, 11.

54. CMP, *procès-verbaux*, 11 Feb. and 10 June 1887.

55. Ibid., 26 Dec. 1887.

56. Conseil de Surveillance, *procès-verbaux*, 21 and 28 July 1892, AP Paris, D.1 X¹ 13.

57. Poubelle, "Projet de mémoire au Conseil Municipal," 24 May 1893, ibid., D.2 X¹ 1.

58. Risler, "Les dépenses de la laïcisation des hôpitaux," 24 Nov. 1892, ibid., D.1 X¹ 14.

59. Statement by A.-J. Martin, CSAP, *procès-verbaux*, 27 Jan. 1892 (morning), fasc. 37.

60. Émile Loubet, "Déclaration lue à la Chambre des Députés au nom du Conseil des Ministres," 8 March 1892, AN Paris, C 5493.

61. Monod to Loubet, 25 June 1892, CSAP, fasc. 53.

62. CSAP, *procès-verbaux*, 24 March 1893 (morning), fasc. 41.

63. Haussonville, "L'assistance par le travail?" *Revue des deux mondes* 122 (1894): 40–71; and ibid. 123 (1894): 383–413.

64. Statements by Rochard and Strauss, 29 Jan. 1896 (morning), CSAP, *procès-verbaux*, fasc. 53; and by Monod, 31 Jan. 1896 (morning), ibid.

65. Strauss, "Bulletin," *Revue philanthropique* 6 (1899–1900): 126–28.

66. Strauss, "Le congrès d'assistance," ibid. 7 (1900): 385–87; Münsterberg, "L'assistance en France: opinion d'un étranger," ibid. 11 (1902): 129–41.

67. Rivière, "La science de l'assistance," ibid. 11 (1902): 251–53.

68. Loys Brueyre, "Observations sur le projet de loi relatif à la surveillance des établissements de bienfaisance privés," ibid. 9 (1901): 529–58.

69. CAPS, *procès-verbaux*, 25 Jan. 1901, AN Paris, C 5623; Émile Combes, "Projet de loi sur la surveillance des établissements de bienfaisance privés," 21 Oct. 1902, ibid., C 7323.

70. CAPS, *procès-verbaux*, 17 March 1903, ibid.; and later on 27 March and 4 June 1903, ibid., C 7278.

71. Émile Flourens, "Proposition de loi tendant à affecter les immeubles, couvents et monastères saisis . . . á l'usage d'hôpitaux et de sanatoria pour les malades tuberculeux," 26 Oct. 1903, ibid., C 7337.

72. Statement by Émile Magniaudé, Commission de la législation fiscale, *procès-verbaux*, 1 March 1905, ibid., C 7324.

73. Statement by Magloire Bourneville, CSAP, *procès-verbaux*, 23 March 1905 (morning), fasc. 99.

74. Monod, "Oeuvres privées laïques," *Revue philanthropique* 19 (1906): 330–34.

75. Statement by Victor Augagneur, CSAP, *procès-verbaux*, 4 June 1901 (afternoon), fasc. 82.

76. Statement by Émile Cheysson, ibid.

77. Monod to Combes, "Conséquences financières de l'application de la loi sur l'assistance aux vieillards, infirmes et incurables," ibid., fasc. 94. See Hatzfeld, *Du paupérisme à la sécurité sociale*, pp. 70–72.

78. Jaurès et al., "Proposition de loi ayant pour objet l'organisation générale et immédiate des retraites et des soins de maladie pour les travailleurs," 4 Nov. 1897, AN Paris, C 5559.

79. Joseph Caillaux, "Projet de loi portant réforme des contributions directes," 12 April 1900, ibid., C 5662. On Caillaux's financial policy, see Bouvier, "Le système fiscal français du XIXe siècle," in Bouvier et al., *Deux siècles*, p. 252; Maurice Flamant, "Remarques sur l'évolution de la composi-

tion du prélèvement fiscal en France depuis cinquante ans," ibid., pp. 284–307; and Stone, "Radicals," pp. 173–86. In Germany, actually, only the member states had access to direct taxation whereas the central government was forced to rely on indirect levies. The best treatment of that complex matter is Witt, *Finanzpolitik*.

80. Paul Guieysse, "3e rapport," 31 Jan. 1902, AN Paris, C 5623.

81. Commission de la législation fiscale, *procès-verbaux*, 3 July 1906, ibid., C 7399. See Hatzfeld, *Du paupérisme à la sécurité sociale*, pp. 73–74.

82. Commission de la législation fiscale, *procès-verbaux*, 14 and 28 Feb. 1907, AN Paris, C 7399.

83. Ibid., 12 March 1907. For the sequel, see Frajerman and Winock, *Le vote de l'impôt général sur le revenu*.

Chapter 10

1. This lack was pointed out by Zeldin, *France* 1:660–65. For background, see Gibaud, *De la mutualité à la sécurité sociale*; Dreyfus, *La mutualité*; Gueslin, *L'invention*, pp. 167–212; and Mitchell, "Mutual Aid Societies."

2. See Bennet, *La mutualité française*; and Sewell, *Work and Revolution*, pp. 169–71, 184–87.

3. "Note de MM. les délégués de la Caisse de Retraites pour les classes laborieuses," 9 Jan. 1846, AN Paris, F^{12} 4814; "Mémoire adressé à M. le Ministre de l'Agriculture et du Commerce par les délégués de la Caisse de Retraites pour les classes laborieuses des deux sexes," [?] April 1846, ibid. See Dreyfus, *La mutualité*, pp. 16–19.

4. Dumas, "Projet de loi relatif aux caisses de retraites pour la vieillesse," 26 Nov. 1849, AP Paris, D.2 X^2 4.

5. Persigny, "Instruction générale pour l'exécution du décret relatif aux sociétés de secours mutuels," 29 May 1852, AP Paris, V.D.[6] 690; Persigny to Roger (mayor of the tenth arrondissement of Paris), 17 June 1852, ibid.; Roger to the Prefecture of Police, 1 Dec. 1852, ibid., 563. See Gueslin, *L'invention*, pp. 167–76.

6. *Rapport à l'Empereur sur la situation des sociétés de secours mutuels . . . année 1852* (Paris, 1853); "Assemblée générale des sociétés municipales de secours mutuels de l'arrondissement," 18 Feb. 1861, AP Paris, V.D.[6] 690.

7. Vicomte de la Guéronnière, "Discours prononcé à l'assemblée générale de La Vraie Humanité," 3 April 1859, ibid.

8. Forcade to prefects, 3 Oct. 1868, in *Caisses d'assurances en cas de décès et en cas d'accidents instituées sous la garantie de l'état par la loi du 11 juillet 1868* (Paris, 1869), pp. 18–25. This brochure is to be found in AP Paris, D.2 X² 4.

9. Prefect of the Seine to the mayor of the fifth arrondissement of Paris, 22 Feb. 1872, ibid., V.D.⁶ 690; *Rapport sur les opérations des sociétés de secours mutuels pendant l'année 1874* (Paris, 1876), pp. 7–9.

10. "Rapport de la Commission supérieure des caisses d'assurances en cas de décès et en cas d'accidents à M. le Président de la République, sur les opérations et la situation de ces deux caisses . . . ," 1875, AP Paris, V.Q.⁴⁴.

11. Waldeck-Rousseau, "Rapport sur les opérations des sociétés de secours mutuels pendant l'année 1882," 31 Dec. 1882, ibid., D.2 X² 4.

12. Fallières, "Rapport sur les opérations des sociétés de secours mutuels pendant l'année 1885," 1887, AN Paris, C 5427.

13. Lockroy, "Proposition de loi tendant à la constitution du crédit populaire par les caisses d'épargne," 2 June 1887, ibid., C 5384. Millerand, "Rapport au Président de la République sur les opérations des caisses d'épargne en 1899," 7 June 1901, ibid., C 5633.

14. Statements by deputies Balsan, Lemercier, and Dron in the Commission du travail, *procès-verbaux*, 30 Oct. and 11 Nov. 1890, ibid., C 5433.

15. Statements by deputies Ricard, Jamais, and Mercier, 4, 7, and 11 Nov. 1890, ibid.

16. Statements by Albert de Mun, 11 and 20 Nov. 1890, ibid.

17. Ibid.

18. Richard, "Proposition de loi ayant pour objet l'assurance obligatoire . . . ," 27 Jan. 1891, ibid.

19. Commission du travail, *procès-verbaux*, 27 Feb. 1891, ibid.

20. Ibid., 5 May 1891.

21. See Hayward, "Solidarity," pp. 261–84, and "Léon Bourgeois and Solidarism," pp. 19–48. Also see Zeldin, *France*, 1:640–82; Weiss, "Origins," pp. 56–59; and Elwitt, *Third Republic Defended*, pp. 170–216.

22. CAPS, *procès-verbaux*, 19 Jan. 1894, AN Paris, C 5545.

23. Ibid., 24 Jan. 1894, C 5544.

24. Ibid., 14 Feb. and 23 May 1894.

25. Ibid., 14 March 1894.

26. Ibid., 30 Nov. 1894.

27. Ibid., 30 May and 1 June 1894.

28. Ibid., 5 and 9 April 1895.

29. Ibid., 4 Dec. 1895; "Mémoire à messieurs les membres de la commission parlementaire du projet de loi sur les sociétés de secours mutuels et de

prévoyance," [1896], ibid., C 5612; Paul Leroy-Beaulieu, *Essai sur la répartition des richesses*, pp. 465, 475–76.

30. Escuyer, *Proposition de loi*; and "Projet de loi Escuyer sur les retraites ouvrières avec soins gratuits en cas de maladies," 7 Aug. 1896, AN Paris, C 5559.

31. Barthou, "Rapport sur les opérations des sociétés de secours mutuels pendant l'année 1894," 1 Nov. 1896, ibid., C 5612; Jaurès et al., "Proposition de loi ayant pour objet l'organisation générale et immédiate des retraites et des soins de maladie pour les travailleurs," 4 Nov. 1897, ibid., C 5559.

32. Strauss, "Bulletin," *Revue philanthropique* 2 (1897–98): 745–800; CAPS, *procès-verbaux*, 10 Feb. 1898, AN Paris, C 5544.

33. Ibid., 10 March 1898.

34. The relevant parliamentary debates are summarized by Gobin, *L'idée de l'obligation*, pp. 202–12. On the 1898 "charter" of mutualism, see Gueslin, *L'invention*, pp. 183–86.

35. E.g., Mirman, "Proposition de loi tendant à modifier l'article 3 de la loi du 9 avril 1898 sur les accidents du travail," 27 June 1898, AN Paris, C 5615; Dufontaine et al., "Proposition de loi ayant pour but de séparer les dommages causés aux victimes d'accidents du travail et à leurs ayant droit par l'application de la loi du 9 avril 1898," 8 July 1898, ibid., C 7339.

36. CAPS, *procès-verbaux*, 7 July 1898, ibid., C 5623.

37. Gervais, "Proposition de loi relative à l'organisation des retraites et la création des services de prévoyance sociale," 12 July 1898, ibid., C 5633.

38. Vaillant et al., "Proposition de loi pour assurer une retraite aux travailleurs des deux sexes âgés de soixante ans," 4 March 1899, ibid.

39. E.g., statement by M. Chatelus (president of the mutual aid society Prévoyants de l'Avenir), CAPS, *procès-verbaux*, 19 May 1899, ibid., C 5623.

40. Ricard, "Proposition de loi sur les retraites ouvrières, l'invalidité et l'assurance au décès au profit des travailleurs," 30 March 1899, ibid., C 5633. See Delorme and André, *L'état et l'économie*, pp. 384–85.

41. Vaillant et al., "Proposition de loi ayant pour objet l'institution d'une assurance sociale," 13 Nov. 1900, AN Paris, C 5623.

42. Mirman, "Proposition de loi étendant le bénéfice de la loi sur les accidents de travail à tous les salariés," 13 Dec. 1900, ibid., C 5615; and "Proposition de loi relative aux accidents de travail survenus dans les exploitations agricoles," 13 Dec. 1900, ibid.

43. Vaillant et al., "Proposition de loi ayant pour objet d'assurer contre l'indigence les vieillards, infirmes et incurables . . . ," 17 Jan. 1902, ibid., C 5623.

44. Resolution of the Conseil Supérieur de Secours Mutuels sent from Waldeck-Rousseau to the Chamber of Deputies, 21 June 1901, ibid., C 5672.

45. Strauss, "Bulletin," *Revue philanthropique* 6 (1899–1900): 762–64.

46. Strauss, "Bulletin," ibid. 8 (1901): 382–84.

47. Strauss, "Bulletin," ibid. 12 (1902–3): 254–56; and "Bulletin," ibid. 15 (1904): 283–84.

48. Strauss, "Bulletin," ibid. 17 (1905): 399–400.

49. See Haupt, *Sozialgeschichte Frankreichs*, pp. 271–82.

50. See Lenoir, "Sécurité sociale et rapports sociaux," pp. 259–74.

51. CAPS, *procès-verbaux*, 7 Feb. 1905, AN Paris, C 7278.

52. Ibid., 10 Feb. 1905.

53. Drs. Bolliet and Albertin, "Le libre choix du médecin dans la mutualité," *Congrès des praticiens*, 1:305–44. Proceedings of the congress, 12 April 1907 (afternoon), ibid., 3:43–74.

54. Bourgeois, "La mutualité et la lutte contre la tuberculose," *Congrès international de la tuberculose*, 3:22–56.

55. E.g., Vincent Carlier et al., "Proposition de loi tendant à constituer au profit de l'État le monopole des assurances," 27 Feb. 1908, AN Paris, C 7343; Jean-Baptiste Couderc, "Proposition de loi sur le monopole des assurances par l'État," 12 July 1909, ibid.

56. Conseil Supérieur des Sociétés de Secours Mutuels, *procès-verbaux*, 3–7 April 1907.

57. Cuvinot, "Rapport fait au nom de la commission chargée d'examiner la proposition de loi, adoptée par la Chambre des Députés, sur les retraites ouvrières," 2 April 1909, AN Paris, F^{22} 1.

58. Cuvinot, "Compte rendu de la situation," 13 Nov. 1907, ibid.; Cuvinot to Clemenceau, 12 Feb. 1908, ibid.

59. "M. René Viviani écrit à M. Cuvinot," in *La Petite République*, 12 Dec. 1908, ibid., F^7 12535. See Hatzfeld, *Du paupérisme à la sécurité sociale*, pp. 58–64; and Saint-Jours, "France," in Köhler and Zacher, *Evolution of Social Insurance*, p. 91. All evidence to the contrary, the 1910 law is termed "a major advance" by Stone, *Search for Social Peace*, p. 122.

60. CAPS, *procès-verbaux*, 15 Nov. 1890, AN Paris, C 7422.

61. Ferdinand Buisson, "Rapport . . . sur le monopole des assurances par l'État," 1 July 1910, ibid., C 7423; statements by mutualist officials Barbant and Ducreaux, CAPS, *procès-verbaux*, 6 Dec. 1910, ibid., C 7422. Statistics are from Anatole Weber, *L'assistance aux miséreux*, 1:9. See Gueslin, *L'invention*, pp. 195–212.

62. See Hatzfeld, *Du paupérisme à la sécurité sociale*, pp. 288–94.

63. Syndicat Générale des Oculistes Français to the Groupe Parlementaire Médical, 26 March 1911, AN Paris, C 7422.

64. CAPS, *procès-verbaux*, 4 July 1911 and 27 Feb. 1912, ibid.

65. Guesde et al., "Proposition de loi tendant à modifier la loi du 5 avril 1910 sur les retraites ouvrières et paysannes," 23 Jan. 1911, ibid., C 7486; and Charles-Louis Goniaux et al., "Proposition de loi tendant à modifier l'article 2 de la loi du 31 mars 1910 sur les retraites ouvrières et paysannes," 14 April 1911, ibid., C 7484.

66. Honnorat et al., "Proposition de loi tendant à compléter la loi du 5 avril 1910 sur les retraites ouvrières et paysannes," 10 July 1911, ibid.; CAPS, *procès-verbaux*, 22–23 Nov. 1911, ibid., C 7422.

67. Michel, *Les habitants*, p. 286.

68. Strauss, "Bulletin," *Revue philanthropique* 26 (1909–10): 263–64; and "Les causes de la mortalité," ibid. 31 (1912): 97–128.

69. Bourgeois, "Alliance d'hygiène sociale," ibid. 35 (1914): 112–15.

70. Gauthier, "Rapport fait au nom de la commission des finances . . . ," 9 Feb. 1911, AN Paris, F^{22} 306; Ministry of Labor to the prefects, [?] 1911, ibid., F^{22} 436.

71. Reports to the Ministry of Labor from divisional inspectors in Limoges (27 Sept. 1911), Lyon (8 Oct. 1911), Toulouse (9 Oct. 1911), and Dijon (18 Oct. 1911), ibid.

72. Fallières et al., "Projet de loi portant modification de la loi du 5 avril 1910 sur les retraites ouvrières et paysannes," 7 Nov. 1911, ibid., F^{22} 5; René Renoult (minister of labor) to divisional inspectors, 4 Dec. 1911, ibid., F^{22} 436.

73. Cuvinot, "Rapport fait au nom de la commission chargée d'examiner les articles 72 à 81 . . . relatifs aux retraites ouvrières et paysannes," 15 Feb. 1912, ibid., F^{22} 4.

74. Details of the amended law were discussed by Bourgeois, "Retraites ouvrières et paysannes," 28 March 1912, ibid., F^{22} 436.

Chapter 11

1. For background, see Grellet and Kruse, *Histoires de la tuberculose*; Guillaume, *Du désespoir au salut*; Dessertine and Faure, *Combattre la tuberculose*; Smith, *Retreat of Tuberculosis*; and Mitchell, "Obsessive Questions and Faint Answers," pp. 215–35.

2. See Szreter, "Importance of Social Intervention," pp. 1–37; and Mitchell, "An Inexact Science," pp. 401–3.

3. For the period before 1870, see Coleman, *Death Is a Social Disease*; Delaporte, *Disease and Civilization*; and Bourdelais and Raulot, *Une peur bleue*.

4. "Logements insalubres (Enquête sur l'application de la loi du 13 avril 1850)," 11 March 1879, AN Paris, F⁸ 211.

5. Nadaud, "Proposition de loi tendant à modifier la loi du 13 avril 1850 sur l'assainissement des logements insalubres," 3 Dec. 1881, ibid., F⁸ 212.

6. Bertillon, *La statistique humaine*, pp. 18, 109.

7. Maze, "Rapport fait au nom de la commission chargée d'examiner la proposition de loi de M. Martin Nadaud . . . ," 21 April 1883, AN Paris, F⁸ 212; Maurice Rouvrier (minister of commerce) to the prefects, 6 Feb. 1885, ibid., F⁸ 211.

8. Lockroy, "Projet de loi relatif à l'assainissement des logements insalubres," 13 Jan. 1887, ibid., F⁸ 212.

9. Richard, "Office sanitaire impérial d'Allemagne (das kaiserliche Gesundheitsamt)," CCHP, *Recueil* 17 (1887): 412–26.

10. CMP, *procès-verbaux*, 20 March 1889. See Mitchell, *Victors and Vanquished*, pp. 208–19.

11. *Bulletin de l'Académie de Médecine*, 30 July 1889.

12. Ibid., 7 and 14 Jan. 1890.

13. Ibid., 28 Jan. 1890.

14. Ibid., 25 Feb. 1890. See Guillaume, *Du désespoir au salut*, p. 51.

15. E.g., report by Dr. Georges Daremberg, "De la cur à l'air et au repos appliqués aux tuberculeux," *Bulletin de l'Académie de Médecine*, 3 June 1890; statement by Brouardel, ibid., 3 March 1891.

16. Statement by Auguste-Louis Navarre in CMP, *procès-verbaux*, 30 Dec. 1890.

17. E.g., statement by Dr. Eugène Moutard-Martin, *Bulletin de l'Académie de Médecine*, 6 Jan. 1891.

18. "Rapport sur les travaux de la commission d'hygiène et de salubrité du 1er arrondissement pour l'année 1893," [1893], AP Paris, V bis 1-I⁵ 1.

19. CMP, *procès-verbaux*, 30 March 1893 and 12 July 1894; Conseil de Surveillance, *procès-verbaux*, 18 May 1893 and 10 May 1894, AP Paris, D.1 X¹ 14–15.

20. Statement by Dr. Victor Cornil, *Bulletin de l'Académie de Médecine*, 27 Feb. 1894.

21. Statement by Jaccoud, ibid., 28 Jan. 1896; Bourgeois to Justin de Selves (prefect of the Seine), 27 March 1896, AP Paris, D.1 X¹ 17.

22. CMP, *procès-verbaux*, 7 Dec. 1896. See Mitchell, "Obsessive Questions and Faint Answers," pp. 220–22.

23. CMP, *procès-verbaux*, 31 March 1891; Strauss, "Notre programme," *Revue philanthropique* 1 (1897): 1–8.

24. *Bulletin de l'Académie de Médecine*, 3 May 1898; Grancher, *Prophylaxie*, pp. 11–14.

25. *Bulletin de l'Académie de Médecine*, 4 July 1899.

26. Ibid., 20 March 1900. Germany's "incontestable leadership" at this time is noted by Guillaume, *Du désespoir au salut*, p. 144.

27. "Contre la tuberculose: une lettre de M. Raoul Bompard," *Revue philanthropique* 6 (1899–1900): 106–7; "Commission de la tuberculose," ibid., pp. 354–55.

28. Strauss, "La lutte contre la tuberculose," ibid. 6 (1899–1900): 385–89; "La lutte contre la tuberculose," ibid. 7 (1900): 130–38; "Bulletin," ibid. 8 (1900–1901): 126–28; "Bulletin," ibid., pp. 382–84.

29. *Bulletin de l'Académie de Médecine*, 12 Feb. 1901. See Mitchell, "An Inexact Science," pp. 395–401.

30. Conseil de Surveillance, *procès-verbaux*, 6 June 1901, AP Paris, D.1 X¹ 22.

31. Cheysson, "Les rapports des lois d'assurances ouvrières et de la santé publique," *Revue philanthropique* 8 (1900–1901): 521–30.

32. Sous-commission de la tuberculose, *procès-verbaux*, 12 Feb. 1901, AN Paris, C 5660.

33. *Bulletin de l'Académie de Médecine*, 2 April 1901.

34. Ibid.

35. Strauss, "Bulletin," *Revue philanthropique* 9 (1901): 124–28.

36. "Fédération des oeuvres anti-tuberculeuses françaises," ibid. 10 (1901–2): 736–54.

37. Report on the Saint-Étienne congress by Navarre in CMP, *procès-verbaux*, 14 Nov. 1902.

38. Fuster, *Recueil*, p. 25.

39. Savoire, *La lutte antituberculeuse*, pp. 3–11.

40. "La tuberculose. L'opinion du Dr. Albert Robin sur les sanatoria," *Éclair*, 15 Jan. 1903; and Robin, *La lutte contre la tuberculose*, reprinted from the *Revue de Paris*, 15 July 1903.

41. Grancher, *Tuberculose pulmonaire*, p. 28. See Mitchell, "Obsessive Questions and Faint Answers," pp. 220–22.

42. CPPCT, *procès-verbaux*, 24 Oct. 1903.

43. Ibid., 14 Nov. 1903.

44. Strauss, "Bulletin," *Revue philanthropique* 13 (1903): 282–84; and "Bulletin," ibid. 14 (1903–4): 379–80.

45. Monod, *La santé publique*, pp. 1–8.

46. Brouardel, "La lutte contre la tuberculose," *Revue philanthropique* 15 (1904): 252–55.

47. Strauss, "Bulletin," ibid. 13 (1903): 282–84.

48. Bertillon, *De la fréquence des principales causes de décès*, pp. 125–29, 176–94.

49. Statements by Bourgeois in CPPCT, *procès-verbaux*, 5 March and 29 Oct. 1904; and Conseil de Surveillance, *procès-verbaux*, 3 Nov. 1904, AP Paris, D.1 X¹ 26.

50. See Mitchell, "Mutual Aid Societies."

51. Conseil de Surveillance, *procès-verbaux*, 9 Feb. 1905, AP Paris, D.1 X¹ 26. André Mesureur, introduction to *L'oeuvre de l'assistance publique*, pp. i–xxxi.

52. Landouzy's study was cited by Anatole Ranson in CMP, *procès-verbaux*, 24 March 1902. See Mitchell, "Obsessive Questions and Faint Answers," pp. 228–30.

53. Strauss, "Bulletin," *Revue philanthropique* 18 (1905–6): 255–56.

54. CPPCT, *procès-verbaux*, 19 March 1904.

55. Statement by Ambroise Rendu in CMP, *procès-verbaux*, 13 July 1906. See Bullock and Read, *Housing Reform*, pp. 505–11.

56. Statement by Léonce Mossot in CMP, *procès-verbaux*, 14 Feb. 1910.

57. Statement by Dr. Charles Périer, *Bulletin de l'Académie de Médecine*, 12 Nov. 1901. See Mitchell, "Obsessive Questions and Faint Answers," pp. 224–25.

58. CSHP, *Recueil* 37 (1907): 28–33; "Commission permanente de la tuberculose: discours de M. Clemenceau," *Revue philanthropique* 21 (1907): 743–47.

59. See Mitchell, "An Inexact Science," pp. 387–89.

60. "Les rapports d'ensemble de l'inspection générale," *Revue philanthropique* 28 (1910–11): 309–64.

61. Petit, "La lutte sociale antituberculeuse," ibid. 26 (1909–10): 293–97.

62. CMP, *procès-verbaux*, 23 March 1908 and 29 Dec. 1911. The same issue was still being debated at the outbreak of war: Conseil de Surveillance, *procès-verbaux*, 2 April 1914, AP Paris, D.1 X¹ 35.

63. Brouardel, "Rapport," 15 Dec. 1899, in CCHP, *Recueil* 28 (1898): vii–xi.

64. An estimate of 25,000 annual fatalities from tuberculosis in Paris was made by Rendu in CMP, *procès-verbaux*, 16 March 1900; whereas the number was set at 12,000 to 14,000 by Ranson, ibid., 24 March 1902.

65. Maurel and Arnaud, "Morbidité de la tuberculose dans la population rurale de la région toulousaine," *Congrès international de la tuberculose* (1905), 3:528–34.

66. Dr. Georges Guilhaud, "Rapport général sur les travaux des conseils départementaux d'hygiène et des commissions sanitaires," for the year 1906 in CSHP, *Recueil* 38 (1908): 587–707; for the year 1907, ibid. 39 (1909): 547–730; for the year 1908, ibid. 40 (1910): 513–638; and for the year 1909, ibid. 41 (1911): 631–798.

67. Lasvignes, *Essai*, pp. 40–45, 222, 234–35, 382.

68. *Bulletin de l'Académie de Médecine*, 1 July 1913.

69. Strauss, "Bulletin," *Revue philanthropique* 33 (1913): 383–84.

70. Bourgeois, "L'alliance d'hygiène sociale," ibid., pp. 513–25.

71. Landouzy to Mesureur, 22 Dec. 1915, letter printed in Conseil de Surveillance, *procès-verbaux*, 3 Feb. 1916, AP Paris, D.1 X¹ 37.

72. Clemenceau et al., "Projet de loi relatif à la déclaration obligatoire des cas de tuberculose pulmonaire ouverte . . . ," 14 Jan. 1919, AAM Paris, liasse 226. See Rist, *La tuberculose*, pp. 265–73; Guillaume, *Du désespoir au salut*, pp. 194–215; Mitchell, "Obsessive Questions and Faint Answers," pp. 234–35; and Vallin and Meslé, *Causes de décès*, pp. 156–57.

Chapter 12

1. For background, see Weber, *Nationalist Revival*; and Becker, *1914*.

2. The phrase originated with Stanley Hoffmann, "Paradoxes of the French Political Community," in Hoffmann et al., *In Search of France*, pp. 3–21.

3. Hatzfeld, *Du paupérisme à la sécurité sociale*, p. 56.

4. Statement by Louis Puech in CAPS, *procès-verbaux*, 7 July 1898, AN Paris, C 5623.

5. E.g., statement by Henri Michel in the Conseil Supérieur des Sociétés de Secours Mutuels, *procès-verbaux*, 7 April 1905, ibid., C 7279.

6. Achille Adam et al., "Proposition de loi sur les retraites ouvrières," 6 Dec. 1902, ibid., C 7291.

7. CAPS, *procès-verbaux*, 14 March 1907, ibid., C 7343.

8. Cuvinot, "Rapport fait au nom de la commission chargée d'examiner la proposition de loi . . . sur les retraites ouvrières," 2 April 1909, ibid., F²² 1.

9. E.g., Albert de Mun, "Proposition de loi relative à l'institution de comités professionels chargés d'établir des salaires minima pour les travailleurs à domicile," 10 June 1910, ibid., C 7486. The "remarkable volte-face"

by Britain's liberal government, which "clearly showed the influence of German social insurance on British legislation," is well analyzed by Hennock, *British Social Reform*, pp. 2–4 and passim.

10. Cheysson, "La situation des veuves et des orphelins," *Revue philanthropique* 26 (1909–10): 137–51. Social welfare in Belgium during the late nineteenth century has been studied by Defourny, "Histoire sociale," 2:329–64; and Chlepner, *Cent ans*, pp. 109–234. Also, a monograph worth citing is Bayer-Lothe, *Paupérisme et bienfaisance*. Yet the topic is scarcely mentioned by Kossmann, *The Low Countries*, pp. 500–501.

11. Mirman, "Incurabilité, vieillesse," *Revue philanthropique* 28 (1910–11): 5–26.

12. Puech, "Rapport fait au nom de la commission d'assurance et de prévoyance sociales . . . sur les retraites ouvrières et paysannes," 23 March 1910, AN Paris, F²² 436.

13. Vermont, *Le problème de la vieillesse*, pp. 20–34, 56–57. See Marec, "Henri Vermont," pp. 18–26.

14. Lucas, *La mutualité et les retraites*, pp. 18–20, 87–112.

15. Cros-Mayrevieille, "L'assistance publique et les retraites ouvrières," *Revue philanthropique* 29 (1911): 497–528.

16. Cited by Delprat, *La crise du libéralisme*, p. 27.

17. Clemenceau, "Application de la loi du 15 février 1902 sur la santé publique: constitution des bureaux municipaux d'hygiène," CSHP, *Recueil* 36 (1906): 59.

18. Marc Réville, "Rapports faits . . . au nom de la commission relative à la répression du vagabondage et de la mendicité," 13 June 1910, AN Paris, C 7487.

19. Berry, "Proposition de loi tendant à la suppression du vagabondage et de la mendicité," 9 Nov. 1910, ibid.; and "Proposition de loi tendant à la répression de l'exploitation de l'enfance," 5 Dec. 1910, ibid., C 7450.

20. CAPS, *procès-verbaux*, 17 Jan. 1911, ibid., C 7422.

21. Albert Bluzet, "Loi du 15 février 1902 sur la santé publique: application [par les] services départementaux de vaccination et de désinfection," CSHP, *Recueil* 40 (1910): 220–75.

22. Honnorat et al., "Proposition de résolution tendant à rendre obligatoire, à chaque changement d'occupant, la désinfection . . . ," 17 June 1912, AN Paris, C 7470.

23. "Voeu de la Société de médecine et de chirurgie de Bordeaux," ibid., 18 Dec. 1912; statement by Édouard Lachaud, ibid., 19 March 1913.

24. CAPS, *procès-verbaux*, 24 June 1913, ibid., C 7422.

25. Ibid., 8 July 1913.

26. CMP, *procès-verbaux*, 15 Nov. 1912.

27. CAPS, *procès-verbaux*, 11 Nov. 1913, AN Paris, C 7422.

28. CMP, *procès-verbaux*, 8 Dec. 1913.

29. Viviani, "Projet de loi tendant à réduire à dix heures la durée normale de travail des ouvriers adultes dans les établissements industriels," 7 July 1910, AN Paris, F^{22} 335; Commission du travail, *procès-verbaux*, 23 Nov. 1910, ibid., C 7486.

30. Ibid., 7 and 21 Dec. 1910.

31. Ibid., 25 Jan. 1911.

32. Ibid., 5 April 1911.

33. Allowance should be made here for previous pilot projects, such as that in Mulhouse thirty years earlier, and for housing cooperatives founded under Napoleon III in the late 1860s. See Bullock and Read, *Housing Reform*, pp. 318–24, 454–58, 478–87; Shapiro, *Housing the Poor*, pp. 101–2; Elwitt, *Third Republic Defended*, pp. 129–43; and Guerrand, *Propriétaires et locataires*, pp. 98–120, 253–300.

34. Ribot et al., "Proposition de loi relative à la petite propriété et aux maisons à bon marché," 19 Nov. 1906, AN Paris, C 7398.

35. See Bullock and Read, *Housing Reform*, p. 307; and Price, *Social History*, pp. 54–58.

36. CMP, *procès-verbaux*, 14 March, 11 June, and 19 Nov. 1906.

37. James Read in Bullock and Read, *Housing Reform*, p. 362.

38. CMP, *procès-verbaux*, 24 June 1907.

39. Ibid., 19 June 1905. See Bullock and Read, *Housing Reform*, pp. 488–94.

40. CAPS, *procès-verbaux*, 29 Feb. and 21 March 1912, AN Paris, C 7422.

41. Statement by Poirier de Narçay in CMP, *procès-verbaux*, 1 April 1912; Cros-Mayrevieille, "La crise du logement ouvrier à l'étranger et les moyens mis en oeuvre pour combattre cette crise," *Revue philanthropique* 32 (1912–13): 529–44.

42. René Renoult (minister of labor) and L.-L. Klotz (minister of finance), "Projet de loi tendant à modifier diverses dispositions de la loi du 10 avril 1908 relative à la petite propriété et aux maisons à bon marché," 20 Nov. 1911, AN Paris, C 7470; statement by Brunet in CMP, *procès-verbaux*, 30 March 1912. The impasse is well described by Read, who finds that "the housing society movement had a negligible impact on the housing market,"

but also that "municipal action comparable to that in England or Germany was out of the question." Bullock and Read, *Housing Reform*, pp. 487, 511. For the sequel, see Sutcliffe, *Autumn*, pp. 258–62.

43. Charles Gide, "Le dépeuplement de la France," *Revue hebdomadaire* 19 (8 May 1909): 141–48; Argeliès, "Proposition de loi tendant à instituer l'assistance aux familles nombreuses et nécessiteuses," 2 April 1909, AN Paris, C 7398.

44. CMP, *procès-verbaux*, 25 July 1910.

45. Ibid., 12 April 1911.

46. Klotz, "La nouvelle commission de la dépopulation," *Revue philan-thropique* 32 (1912–13): 81–83; and "Commission de la dépopulation," ibid., pp. 184–92, 223–32.

47. CAPS, *procès-verbaux*, 12 March 1912, AN Paris, C 7422. This entry is incorrectly dated 1911.

48. Massimy et al., "Proposition de loi ayant pour but l'attribution d'une allocation immédiate ou d'une pension viagère ultérieure aux mères de familles françaises . . . ," 28 May 1912, ibid.; CAPS, *procès-verbaux*, 6 June 1912, ibid.

49. Ibid., 18 and 26 June, 9 and 10 July 1912.

50. Strauss, "Bulletin," *Revue philanthropique* 32 (1912–13): 255–56; and "Bulletin," ibid. 33 (1913): 511–12. On Strauss and the campaign for maternity leave, see Stewart, *Women*, pp. 169–90.

51. Raphaël Milliès-Lacroix, "Le budget national de l'assistance publique," *Revue philanthropique* 29 (1911): 129–38; Anatole Weber, *L'assistance aux miséreux*, 1:59–62.

52. Massimy et al., "Proposition de loi à introduire en France l'inventaire obligatoire après décès . . . ," 20 March 1914, AN Paris, C 7471.

53. Statement by Paul Chassaigne-Goyen in CMP, *procès-verbaux*, 31 Dec. 1913.

54. "Discours . . . par M. Klotz . . . à l'occasion de l'assemblée générale de la Société de préservation contre la tuberculose," *Revue philanthropique* 33 (1913): 53–56.

55. Lairolle, "Proposition de loi tendant à la modification . . . de la loi du 5 avril 1910 sur les retraites ouvrières et paysannes," 30 Jan. 1913, AN Paris, F²² 306.

56. Société des Agriculteurs de France, *procès-verbaux*, 19 Feb. 1913, ibid., C 7422.

57. See the collected speeches of Bourgeois, *La politique et la prévoyance sociale*.

58. Georges Maus (president of the Fédération des Commerçants de France) to Albert Métin (minister of labor), 23 Jan. 1914, AN Paris, F²² 302; Métin, "Réglementation de la durée du travail dans le commerce," 6 June 1914, ibid.

59. CAPS, *procès-verbaux*, 25 Nov. 1913, ibid., C 7422.

60. Ibid., 23 Dec. 1913, 24 Feb., 6 and 31 March 1914.

61. Ibid.

62. "Dispensaires d'hygiène sociale et de préservation antituberculeuse," *Revue philanthropique* 34 (1913–14): 578–600.

Bibliography

Manuscript Sources

Archives de l'Académie de Médecine, Paris
    Liasse 140–145 Commission de la tuberculose
    Liasse 226   Correspondance: Ministère de l'Intérieur
Archives de la Préfecture de Police, Paris
    B A/86–87 Rapports quotidiens
    B A/962   Bismarck
Archives de Paris (formerly Archives de la Seine, Paris)
    D.1 X^1 Assistance publique. Affaires générales (registres)
    D.2 X^1 Assistance publique. Affaires générales (cartons)
    D.2 X^2 Bienfaisance (cartons)
    D.2 X^3 Aliénés (cartons)
    V.D.   Administration générale
    V.Q.   Assistance publique
Archives Nationales, Paris
    C   Procès-verbaux des assemblées nationales
    F^1 Administration générale
    F^7 Police générale
    F^8 Police sanitaire
    F^{12} Commerce et industrie
    F^{17} Instruction publique
    F^{22} Travail et prévoyance sociale
    BB^{30} Versements de 1904 et 1905
Auswärtiges Amt, Bonn
    I.A.B.c 70–87   Frankreich

Bibliothèque Nationale, Paris
    NAF 20601–84   Papiers Thiers
Ministère des affaires étrangères, Paris
    Allemagne 1–2   Correspondance politique

Published Documents and Journals

Assemblée des présidents des chambres de commerce de France: compte rendu in extenso
    (1912)
Bulletin de l'Académie de Médecine
Bulletin de la Chambre de Commerce de Paris
Congrès des praticiens: réforme de l'enseignement médical en France (1907). 3 vols.
Congrès international d'assistance (1889). 2 vols.
Congrès international de la tuberculose (1905). 4 vols.
Congrès national d'assistance tenu du 26 juin au 3 juillet 1894. 2 vols.
Conseil Municipal de Paris: Procès-verbaux.
Conseil Supérieur de l'Assistance Publique: Recueil
Conseil Supérieur de l'Hygiène Publique: Recueil
Conseil Supérieur des Sociétés de Secours Mutuels: Procès-verbaux
Journal Officiel
Le Moniteur Universel
Rapport à l'Empereur sur la situation des sociétés de secours mutuels (1852)
Rapport général sur le fonctionnement des vingt bureaux de bienfaisance pendant les
    années 1896 et 1897
Rapport sur les opérations des sociétés de secours mutuels pendant l'année 1874
Recueil des travaux de la commission permanente de préservation contre la tuberculose
Recueil des travaux du comité consultatif d'hygiène publique de France et des actes
    officiels de l'administration sanitaire
Renseignements statistiques recueillis au cours de l'année 1899 sur la population
    indigente de Paris à secourir en 1900
Répartition entre les bureaux de bienfaisance des vingt arrondissements des fonds de
    secours pour l'exercice 1865
Revue des deux mondes
Revue philanthropique
Séance du congrès ouvrier de France: session de 1876

Contemporary Essays, Letters, and Speeches

Bertillon, Jacques. *De la fréquence des principales causes de décès à Paris pendant la seconde moitié du XIXe siècle et notamment pendant la période 1886–1905.* Paris, 1906.

————. *La statistique humaine de la France (naissance, mariage, mort).* Paris, 1880.

Bismarck, Otto von. *Bismarcks Briefe an seine Gattin aus dem Kriege 1870/71.* Stuttgart, 1903.

Bourgeois, Léon. *La politique et la prévoyance sociale.* 2 vols. Paris, 1914–19.

Brouardel, Paul. *La profession médicale au commencement du XXe siècle.* Paris, 1903.

Cheysson, Émile. *La question de la population en France et à l'étranger.* Paris, n.d.

Delprat, Georges. *La crise du libéralisme en matière d'assistance.* Paris, 1912.

Drouineau, Gustave. *De l'assistance aux filles-mères et aux enfants abandonnés.* Paris, 1878.

Du Camp, Maxime. *Paris, ses organes, ses fonctions et sa vie dans la seconde moitié du XIXe siècle.* 6 vols. Paris, 1898.

Escuyer, Jacques. *Proposition de loi relative à la création d'une caisse nationale de prévoyance.* Paris, 1896.

Ferdinand-Dreyfus, Camille. *L'assistance sous la seconde république (1848–1851).* Paris, 1907.

Fuster, Édouard. *Recueil de documents sur la prévoyance sociale: l'habitation ouvrière et les pouvoirs publics en Allemagne.* Paris, 1903.

Gobin, Maurice. *L'idée d'obligation au groupement.* Paris, 1908.

Grancher, Joseph. *Prophylaxie de la tuberculose.* Paris, 1898.

————. *Tuberculose pulmonaire et sanatoriums.* Paris, 1903.

Guilhaud, Georges. *Du pouvoir des maires en matière d'hygiène publique.* Paris, 1909.

Haussonville, Othenin d'. *Misères et remèdes.* Paris, 1886.

Lallemand, Léon. *De l'assistance des classes rurales au XIXe siècle.* Paris, 1889.

Lasvignes, Henri. *Essai d'assistance comparée.* Paris, 1911.

Leroy-Beaulieu, Paul. *Essai sur la répartition des richesses et sur la tendance à une moindre inégalité des conditions.* 4th ed. Paris, 1896.

————. *La question de la population.* 2d ed. Paris, 1913.

Lucas, Claude. *La mutualité et les retraites ouvrières et paysannes. Étude de droit comparé (France, Allemagne, Belgique).* Paris, 1911.

Mesureur, André. *L'oeuvre de l'assistance publique à Paris contre la tuberculose (1896–1905).* Paris, 1905.

Michel, Édmond. *Les habitants.* Paris and Nancy, 1910.

Monod, Henri. *La santé publique (législation sanitaire de la France)*. Paris, 1904.

Robin, Albert. *La lutte contre la tuberculose*. Paris, 1903.

Savoire, Camille. *La lutte antituberculeuse en Allemagne*. Paris, 1903.

Sérieux, Paul. *L'assistance des aliénés en France, en Allemagne, en Italie et en Suède*. Paris, 1903.

Simon, Jules. *L'ouvrière*. 7th ed. Paris, 1871.

Thiers, Adolphe. *Notes et souvenirs de M. Thiers 1870–1873*. Paris, 1904.

――――. *Rapport général présenté par M. Thiers au nom de la commission de l'assistance et de la prévoyance publique*. Paris, 1850.

Tocqueville, Alexis de. *The Old Regime and the French Revolution*. New York, 1955.

Vermont, Henri. *Le problème de la vieillesse. Les retraites et la mutualité*. Paris, 1911.

Weber, Anatole. *A travers la mutualité. Étude critique sur les sociétés de secours mutuels*. Paris, 1908.

――――. *L'assistance aux miséreux en France*. 2 vols. Paris, 1914.

――――. *Les errements des sociétés de secours mutuels*. Paris, 1913.

Books and Articles

Agulhon, Maurice. *1848 ou l'apprentissage de la république*. Paris, 1973.

Alber, Jens. *Vom Armenhaus zum Wohlfahrtsstaat. Analysen zur Entwicklung der Sozialversicherung in Westeuropa*. Frankfurt, 1982.

Arblaster, Anthony. *The Rise and Decline of Western Liberalism*. London, 1984.

Ardant, Gabriel. *Histoire de l'impôt*. 2 vols. Paris, 1971–72.

Armengaud, André. *La population française au XIXe siècle*. Paris, 1965.

Auspitz, Katherine. *The Radical Bourgeoisie: The Ligue de l'Enseignement and the Origins of the Third Republic, 1866–1885*. New York, 1982.

Badinter, Elizabeth. *Mother Love: Myth and Reality. Motherhood in Modern History*. New York, 1981.

Baron, Rüdeger. "Die Entwicklung der Armenpflege in Deutschland vom Beginn des 19. Jahrhunderts bis zum Ersten Weltkrieg." In *Geschichte der Sozialarbeit. Hauptlinien ihrer Entwicklung im 19. und 20. Jahrhundert*, edited by Rolf Landwehr and Rüdeger Baron, pp. 11–71. Weinheim, 1983.

Barrows, Susanna. "After the Commune: Alcoholism, Temperance, and Literature in the Early Third Republic." In *Consciousness and Class Experience in Nineteenth-Century Europe*, edited by John M. Merriman, pp. 205–18. New York, 1979.

———. *Distorting Mirrors: Visions of the Crowd in Late Nineteenth-Century France.* New Haven, 1981.

Baudot, Marcel. "La situation des monts-de-piété durant le second empire." In *Assistance et assistés de 1610 à nos jours,* pp. 185–93. Paris, 1977.

Bayer-Lothe, Jeannine. *Paupérisme et bienfaisance à Namur au XIXe siècle, 1815–1914.* Brussels, 1978.

Becchia, Alain. "Les milieux parlementaires et la dépopulation de 1900 à 1914." *Communications* 44 (1986): 201–46.

Becker, Jean-Jacques. *1914: comment les Français sont entrés dans la guerre.* Paris, 1977.

Bellanger, Claude, et al. *Histoire générale de la presse française.* 3 vols. Paris, 1969–72.

Bennet, Jean. *La mutualité française des origines à la révolution de 1789.* Paris, 1983.

Berlanstein, Lenard R. *The Working People of Paris, 1871–1914.* Baltimore, 1984.

Bidelman, Patrick Kay. *Pariahs Stand Up! The Founding of the Liberal Feminist Movement in France, 1858–1889.* Westport, Conn., 1982.

Blackbourn, David, and Geoff Eley. *Mythen deutscher Geschichtsschreibung.* Frankfurt, 1980. Revised English version: *The Peculiarities of German History: Bourgeois Society and Politics in Nineteenth-Century Germany.* Oxford, 1984.

Born, Karl Erich. *Wirtschafts- und Sozialgeschichte des Deutschen Kaiserreichs (1867/71–1914).* Stuttgart, 1985.

Bourdelais, Patrice, and Jean-Yves Raulot. *Une peur bleue. Histoire de choléra en France.* Paris, 1987.

Bourgin, Georges. "La lutte contre la première Internationale." *International Review for Social History* 4 (1939): 39–138.

Bouvier, Jean, et al. *Deux siècles de fiscalité française, XIXe et XXe siècles: histoire, économie et politique.* Paris, 1973.

Boxer, Marilyn J. "Protective Legislation and Home Industry: The Marginalization of Women Workers in Late Nineteenth-Early Twentieth Century France." *Journal of Social History* 20 (1986): 45–65.

Boxer, Marilyn J., and Jean H. Quataert, eds. *Connecting Spheres: Women in the Western World, 1500 to the Present.* New York, 1987.

Bullock, Alan, and Maurice Shock, eds. *The Liberal Tradition from Fox to Keynes.* 2d ed. London, 1966.

Bullock, Nicholas, and James Read. *The Movement for Housing Reform in Germany and France, 1840–1914.* Cambridge, 1985.

Burdeau, Georges. *Le libéralisme*. Paris, 1979.

Bury, J. P. T., and R. P. Tombs. *Thiers, 1797–1877: A Political Life*. London, 1986.

Castel, Robert. *L'ordre psychiatrique. L'âge d'or de l'aliénisme*. Paris, 1976.

Challener, Richard D. *The French Theory of the Nation in Arms, 1866–1939*. New York, 1955.

Chevalier, Louis. *La formation de la population parisienne au XIXe siècle*. Paris, 1950.

Chlepner, B.-S. *Cent ans d'histoire sociale en Belgique*. Brussels, 1972.

Coleman, William. *Death Is a Social Disease: Public Health and Political Economy in Early Industrial France*. Madison, Wis., 1982.

Conze, Werner. "Sozialgeschichte 1850–1918." In *Handbuch der deutschen Wirtschafts- und Sozialgeschichte*, 2 vols., edited by Wolfgang Zorn, 2:602–84. Stuttgart, 1976.

Corbin, Alain. *Les filles de noces*. 2d ed. Paris, 1982.

Cross, Gary. *A Quest for Time:. The Reduction of Work in Britain and France, 1840–1940*. Berkeley, 1989.

Crouzet, François. "Essai de construction d'un indice annuel de la production française au XIXe siècle." *Annales* 25 (1970): 56–99.

Crozier, Michel. *The Bureaucratic Phenomenon*. Chicago, 1964.

Darmon, Pierre. *La longue traque de la variole. Les pionniers de la médecine préventive*. Paris, 1986.

Daumard, Adeline. *Les bourgeois et la bourgeoisie en France depuis 1815*. Paris, 1987.

Defourny, M. "Histoire sociale: les faits, les idées, la législation." In *Histoire de la Belgique contemporaine, 1830–1914*, 2 vols., 2:329–64. Brussels, 1928–29.

Delaporte, François. *Disease and Civilization: The Cholera in Paris, 1832*. Cambridge, Mass., 1986.

Delorme, Robert, and Christine André. *L'état et l'économie. Un essai d'explication de l'évolution des dépenses publiques en France (1870–1980)*. Paris, 1983.

Derfler, Leslie. *Alexandre Millerand: The Socialist Years*. The Hague, 1977.

Dessertine, Dominique, and Olivier Faure. *Combattre la tuberculose, 1900–1940*. Lyon, 1985.

Digeon, Claude. *La crise allemande de la pensée française 1870–1914*. Paris, 1959.

Dreyfus, Michel. *La mutualité. Une histoire maintenant accessible*. Paris, 1988.

Droz, Jacques. *Histoire des doctrines politiques en France*. Paris, 1963.

Duby, Georges, et al. *Histoire de la France urbaine*. 5 vols. Paris, 1980–85.

Dupâquier, Jacques, et al. *Histoire de la population française*. 4 vols. Paris, 1988.

Dupeux, Georges. *La société française 1789–1970*. Paris, 1972.

Duroselle, Jean-Baptiste. *Les débuts du catholicisme social en France (1822–1870)*. Paris, 1951.

Ellis, Jack D. *The Early Life of Georges Clemenceau, 1841–1893*. Lawrence, Kans., 1980.

Elwitt, Sanford. "Social Reform and Social Order in Late Nineteenth-Century France: The Musée Social and Its Friends." *French Historical Studies* 11 (1980): 431–51.

––––––. *The Third Republic Defended: Bourgeois Reform in France, 1880–1914*. Baton Rouge, La., 1986.

Evans, Richard J. *Death in Hamburg: Society and Politics in the Cholera Years 1830–1910*. Oxford, 1987.

Ewald, François. *L'état providence*. Paris, 1986.

Fairchilds, Cissie C. *Poverty and Charity in Aix-en-Provence, 1640–1789*. Baltimore, 1976.

Faust, Anselm. *Arbeitsmarktpolitik im deutschen Kaiserreich. Arbeitsvermittlung, Arbeitsbeschaffung und Arbeitslosenunterstützung 1890–1918*. Stuttgart, 1986.

Flora, Peter, and Arnold J. Heidenheimer, eds. *The Development of Welfare States in Europe and America*. New Brunswick, N.J., 1981.

Forrest, Alan. *The French Revolution and the Poor*. Oxford, 1981.

Frajerman, Myriam, and Dominique Winock. *Le vote de l'impôt général sur le revenu 1907–1914*. Paris, 1972.

Frevert, Ute. *Krankheit als politisches Problem 1770–1880*. Göttingen, 1984.

Fuchs, Rachel Ginnis. *Abandoned Children: Foundlings and Child Welfare in Nineteenth-Century France*. Albany, N.Y., 1984.

Gall, Lothar. *Bismarck. Der weisse Revolutionär*. Frankfurt, 1980.

––––––. "Liberalismus und 'bürgerliche Gesellschaft.' Zu Character und Entwicklung der liberalen Bewegung in Deutschland." *Historische Zeitschrift* 220 (1975): 324–56.

––––––, ed. *Liberalismus*. 2d ed. Königstein, 1980.

Gibaud, Bernard. *De la mutualité à la sécurité sociale*. Paris, 1986.

Girard, Louis. *Les libéraux français 1814–1875*. Paris, 1984.

Girvetz, Harry K. *From Wealth to Welfare: The Evolution of Liberalism*. Stanford, 1950.

Gladen, Albin. *Geschichte der Sozialpolitik in Deutschland*. Wiesbaden, 1974.

Göckenjan, Gerd. *Kurieren und Staat machen. Gesundheit und Medizin in der bürgerlichen Welt.* Frankfurt, 1985.

Goldstein, Jan. *Console and Classify: The French Psychiatric Profession in the Nineteenth Century.* Cambridge, 1987.

Goubert, Pierre. *Cent mille provinciaux au XVIIe siècle. Beauvais et le Beauvaisis de 1600 à 1730.* 2d ed. Paris, 1968.

Gravier, Jean-François. *Paris et le désert français.* Paris, 1947.

Grellet, Isabelle, and Caroline Kruse. *Histoires de la tuberculose. Les fièvres de l'âme, 1800–1940.* Paris, 1983.

Groh, Dieter. *Negative Integration und revolutionärer Attentismus.* Berlin, 1973.

Guerrand, Roger-Henri. *Propriétaires et locataires. Les origines du logement social en France 1850–1914.* Paris, 1987.

Gueslin, André. *L'invention de l'économie sociale. Le XIXe siècle français.* Paris, 1987.

Guilbert, Madeleine. *Les fonctions des femmes dans l'industrie.* Paris, 1966.

Guillaume, Pierre. *Du désespoir au salut: les tuberculeux aux 19e et 20e siècles.* Paris, 1986.

Guiral, Pierre. *Adolphe Thiers, ou de la nécessité en politique.* Paris, 1986.

Gutton, Jean-Pierre. *La société et les pauvres: l'exemple de la généralité de Lyon, 1534–1789.* Lyon, 1971.

Harsin, Jill. *Policing Prostitution in Nineteenth-Century Paris.* Princeton, 1985.

————. "Syphilis, Wives, and Physicians: Medical Ethics and the Family in Late Nineteenth-Century France." *French Historical Studies* 16 (1989): 72–95.

Hatzfeld, Henri. *Du paupérisme à la sécurité sociale 1850–1940.* Paris, 1971.

Haupt, Heinz-Gerhard. "Les petits commerçants et la politique sociale: l'exemple de la loi sur le repos hebdomadaire." *Bulletin du Centre d'Histoire de la France Contemporaine* 8 (1987): 7–34.

————. *Sozialgeschichte Frankreichs seit 1789.* Frankfurt, 1989.

Hayward, J. E. S. "The Official Social Philosophy of the French Third Republic: Léon Bourgeois and Solidarism." *International Review of Social History* 6 (1961): 19–48.

————. "Solidarity: The Social History of an Idea in Nineteenth-Century France." *International Review of Social History* 4 (1959): 261–84.

Hennock, E. P. *British Social Reform and German Precedents: The Case of Social Insurance, 1880–1914.* Oxford, 1987.

Hentschel, Volker. *Geschichte der deutschen Sozialpolitik 1880–1980.* Frankfurt, 1983.

Hilden, Patricia. *Working Women and Socialist Politics in France, 1880–1914: A Regional Study.* Oxford, 1986.

Hildreth, Martha Lee. *Doctors, Bureaucrats, and Public Health in France, 1888–1902.* New York, 1987.

———. "The French National Public Health Bureaucracy and the Bacteriological Revolution." *Proceedings of the Western Society for French History* 11 (1983): 316–26.

———. "Medical Rivalries and Medical Politics in France: The Physicians Union Movement and the Medical Assistance Law of 1893." *Journal of the History of Medicine and Allied Sciences* 42 (1987): 5–29.

———. "Les syndicats médicaux et la mutualité: le début du conflit au commencement du XXe siècle et l'exemple du syndicat toulousain." *Revue de l'économie sociale* 10 (1987): 7–21.

Hoffmann, Stanley. "Paradoxes of the French Political Community." In *In Search of France: The Economy, Society, and Political System in the Twentieth Century,* edited by Stanley Hoffmann et al., pp. 1–117. New York, 1963.

House, Steven C., and Anne R. Kenney. *Women's Suffrage and Social Politics in the French Third Republic.* Princeton, 1984.

Huber, Ernst Rudolf. *Deutsche Verfassungsgeschichte seit 1789.* 7 vols. Stuttgart, 1957–69.

Hudemann, Rainer. "Politische Reform und gesellschaftlicher Status quo. Thesen zum französischen Liberalismus im 19. Jahrhundert." In *Liberalismus im 19. Jahrhundert. Deutschland im europäischen Vergleich,* edited by Dieter Langewiesche, pp. 332–52. Göttingen, 1988.

Huerkamp, Claudia. *Der Aufstieg der Ärzte im 19. Jahrhundert.* Göttingen, 1985.

———. "The History of Smallpox Vaccination in Germany: A First Step in the Medicalization of the General Public." *Journal of Contemporary History* 20 (1985): 617–35.

Hufton, Olwen. *The Poor of Eighteenth Century France.* Oxford, 1974.

Inkeles, Alex, and Daniel J. Levinson. "National Character: The Study of Model Personality and Sociocultural Systems." In *Handbook of Social Psychology,* edited by Gardner Lindzey, pp. 418–506. Cambridge, Mass., 1954.

Jardin, André. *Histoire du libéralisme politique de la crise de l'absolutisme à la constitution de 1875.* Paris, 1984.

Jedin, Hubert, ed. *Handbuch der Kirchengeschichte.* 7 vols. Freiburg, 1962–79.

Jones, Colin. *Charity and Bienfaisance: The Treatment of the Poor in the Mont-*

pellier Region, 1740–1815. New York, 1982.

Judt, Tony. *Socialism in Provence, 1871–1914: A Study in the Origins of the French Left.* Cambridge, 1979.

Kaelble, Hartmut. "Französisches und deutsches Bürgertum 1870–1914." In *Bürgertum im 19. Jahrhundert. Deutschland im europäischen Vergleich,* edited by Jürgen Kocka, 3 vols., 1:107–40. Munich, 1988.

Kaplow, Jeffrey. *The Name of Kings: The Parisian Laboring Poor in the Eighteenth Century.* New York, 1972.

Kearns, Gerry. "Death in the Time of Cholera." *Journal of Historical Geography* 15 (1989): 425–32.

Kelso, Maxwell R. "The Inception of the Modern French Labor Movement (1871–79): A Reappraisal." *Journal of Modern History* 8 (1936): 173–93.

Kemp, Tom. *Economic Forces in French History.* London, 1971.

———. *The French Economy, 1913–1939: The History of a Decline.* New York, 1972.

Kleeis, Friedrich. *Die Geschichte der sozialen Versicherung in Deutschland.* 2d ed. Bonn, 1981.

Kleinert, Annemarie. *Die frühen Modejournale in Frankreich. Studien zur Literatur der Mode von den Anfängen bis 1848.* Berlin, 1980.

Kocka, Jürgen, ed. *Arbeiter und Bürger im 19. Jahrhundert. Varianten ihres Verhältnisses im europäischen Vergleich.* Munich, 1986.

Köhler, Peter A., and Hans F. Zacher, eds. *The Evolution of Social Insurance, 1881–1981: Studies of Germany, France, Great Britain, Austria, and Switzerland.* London, 1982.

Kohn, Hans, ed. *The Modern World: 1848 to the Present.* New York, 1963.

Kossman, E. H. *The Low Countries 1780–1940.* Oxford, 1978.

Krumeich, Gerd. "Der politische Liberalismus im parlamentarischen System Frankreichs vor dem Ersten Weltkrieg." In *Liberalismus im 19. Jahrhundert. Deutschland im europäischen Vergleich,* edited by Dieter Langewiesche, pp. 353–66. Göttingen, 1988.

Kudlick, Catherine. "Fighting the Internal and External Enemies: Alcoholism in World War I France." *Contemporary Drug Problems* 12 (1985): 129–58.

Lajoie, Andrée, Patrick A. Molinari, et al. *Pour une approche critique du droit de la santé. Droit et matérialisation des politiques sociales.* Montreal, 1987.

Langewiesche, Dieter. *Liberalismus in Deutschland.* Frankfurt, 1988.

Laporte, André. *L'assistance publique et privée en France.* Paris, 1952.

Lenoir, Remi. "Sécurité sociale et rapports sociaux: l'apparation et le développement des systèmes de retraite en France." In *Bedingungen für die*

Entstehung und Entwicklung von Sozialversicherung, edited by Hans F. Zacher, pp. 259–93. Berlin, 1979.

Léonard, Jacques. *Archives du corps. La santé au XIXe siècle*. Rennes, 1986.

———. *La France médicale: médecins et malades au XIXe siècle*. Paris, 1978.

———. *La médecine entre les savoirs et les pouvoirs: histoire intellectuelle et politique de la médecine française au XIXe siècle*. Paris, 1981.

———. *Les médecins de l'ouest au XIXe siècle*. Paris, 1978.

———. *La vie quotidienne du médecin de province au XIXe siècle*. Paris, 1977.

Lévy-Leboyer, Maurice. "La décélération de l'économie française dans la seconde moitié du XIXe siècle." *Revue d'histoire économique et sociale* 49 (1971): 485–507.

Ligou, Daniel. *Histoire du socialisme en France, 1871–1961*. Paris, 1962.

Logue, William. *From Philosophy to Sociology: The Evolution of French Liberalism, 1870–1914*. Dekalb, Ill., 1983.

McDougall, Mary Lynn. "The Meaning of Reform: The Ban on Women's Night Work, 1892–1914." *Proceedings of the Western Society for French History* 12 (1984): 404–17.

McLaren, Angus. *Sexuality and Social Order: The Debate over the Fertility of Women and Workers in France, 1770–1920*. New York, 1983.

McMillan, James F. *Housewife or Harlot: The Place of Women in French Society, 1870–1914*. London, 1981.

Malo, Henri. *Thiers, 1797–1877*. Paris, 1932.

Marec, Yannick. "L'apôtre de la Mutualité: Henri Vermont (1836–1928)." *L'économie sociale* 10 (1987): 3–39.

Margadant, Ted W. *French Peasants in Revolt: The Insurrection of 1851*. Princeton, 1979.

Marrus, Michael R. "Social Drinking in the Belle Epoque." *Journal of Social History* 7 (1974): 115–41.

Mayeur, Françoise. *L'éducation des filles en France au XIXe siècle*. Paris, 1979.

———. *L'enseignement secondaire des jeunes filles sous la troisième république*. Paris, 1977.

Mead, Margaret. "The Study of National Character." In *The Policy Sciences*, edited by Daniel Lerner and Harold D. Lasswell, pp. 70–85. Stanford, 1951.

Merriman, John M. *The Agony of the Republic: The Repression of the Left in Revolutionary France, 1848–1851*. New Haven, 1978.

Micale, Mark S. "The Salpêtrière in the Age of Charcot: An Institutional Perspective on Medical History in the Late Nineteenth Century." *Journal of Contemporary History* 20 (1985): 703–31.

Mitchell, Allan. *Bismarck and the French Nation, 1848–1890.* New York, 1971.

———. "Bonapartism as a Model for Bismarckian Politics." *Journal of Modern History* 49 (1977): 181–209.

———. "Bürgerlicher Liberalismus und Volksgesundheit im deutsch-französischen Vergleich 1870–1914." In *Bürgertum im 19. Jahrhundert. Deutschland im europäischen Vergleich,* edited by Jürgen Kocka, 3 vols., 3:395–417. Munich, 1988.

———. "Crucible of French Anticlericalism: The Conseil Municipal de Paris, 1871–1885." *Francia* 8 (1980): 395–405.

———. "The Function and Malfunction of Mutual Aid Societies in Nineteenth-Century France." In *Medicine and Charity before the Welfare State,* edited by Jonathan Barry and Colin Jones. London, forthcoming.

———. *The German Influence in France after 1870: The Formation of the French Republic.* Chapel Hill, 1979.

———. "The German Influence on Subversion and Repression in France during the Early Third Republic." *Francia* 13 (1986): 409–33.

———. "An Inexact Science: The Statistics of Tuberculosis in Late Nineteenth-Century France." *Social History of Medicine* 3 (1990): 387–403.

———. "The Municipal Council of Paris and the Problems of Public Welfare in France (1885–1914)." *Francia* 14 (1987): 435–50.

———. "Obsessive Questions and Faint Answers: The French Response to Tuberculosis in the Belle Epoque." *Bulletin of the History of Medicine* 62 (1988): 215–35.

———. "The Unsung Villain: Alcoholism and the Emergence of Public Welfare in France, 1870–1914." *Contemporary Drug Problems* 13 (1986): 447–71.

———. *Victors and Vanquished: The German Influence on Army and Church in France after 1870.* Chapel Hill, 1984.

———. "The Xenophobic Style: French Counterespionage and the Emergence of the Dreyfus Affair." *Journal of Modern History* 52 (1980): 414–25.

Monteilhet, Joseph. *Les institutions militaires de la France, 1814–1924.* Paris, 1926.

Moses, Claire Goldberg. *French Feminism in the 19th Century.* Albany, N.Y., 1984.

Moss, Bernard H. *The Origins of the French Labor Movement 1830–1914.* Berkeley, 1976.

Motzkin, Gabriel. "Säkularisierung, Bürgertum und Intellektuelle in Frankreich und Deutschland während des 19. Jahrhunderts." In *Bürgertum im*

19. Jahrhundrt. Deutschland im europäischen Vergleich, edited by Jürgen Kocka, 3 vols., 3:141–71. Munich, 1988.

Nipperdey, Thomas. "Interessenverbände und Parteien in Deutschland vor dem Ersten Weltkrieg." In *Moderne Deutsche Sozialgeschichte*, edited by Hans-Ulrich Wehler, pp. 369–88. 5th ed. Cologne, 1975.

Norberg, Kathryn. *Rich and Poor in Grenoble, 1600–1814*. Berkeley, 1985.

Nye, Mary Jo. *Science in the Provinces: Scientific Communities and Provincial Leadership in France, 1860–1930*. Berkeley, 1986.

Nye, Robert A. *Crime, Madness, and Politics in Modern France*. Princeton, 1984.

―――. "Honor, Impotence, and Male Sexuality in Nineteenth-Century French Medicine." *French Historical Studies* 16 (1989): 48–71.

Offen, Karen. "Defining Feminism: A Comparative Historical Approach." *Signs: Journal of Women in Culture and Society* 14 (1988): 119–57.

―――. "Depopulation, Nationalism, and Feminism in Fin-de-Siècle France." *American Historical Review* 89 (1984): 648–76.

Paul, Harry W. *From Knowledge to Power: The Rise of the Science Empire in France, 1860–1939*. Cambridge, 1985.

Pautreau, Roberte. "La survivance du système du renfermement des pauvres au XIXe siecle: le dépôt de mendicité de Saint-Maixent." In *Assistance et Assistés de 1610 à nos jours*, pp. 205–11. Paris, 1977.

Perrot, Michelle. *Les ouvriers en grève: France, 1871–1890*. 2 vols. Paris, 1974.

Pinkney, David H. *Napoleon III and the Rebuilding of Paris*. Princeton, 1958.

Pomaret, Charles. *Monsieur Thiers et son siècle*. Paris, 1948.

Porch, Douglas. *The March to the Marne: The French Army, 1871–1914*. Cambridge, 1981.

Pouthas, Charles. *La population française pendant la première moitié du XIXe siècle*. Paris, 1956.

Prestwich, Patricia E. *Drink and the Politics of Social Reform: Antialcoholism in France since 1870*. Palo Alto, Calif., 1988.

Price, Roger. *The French Second Republic: A Social History*. London, 1972.

―――. "Poor Relief and Social Crisis in Mid-Nineteenth-Century France." *European Studies Review* 13 (1983): 423–54.

―――. *A Social History of Nineteenth-Century France*. London, 1987.

Ralston, David B. *The Army of the Republic: The Place of the Military in the Political Evolution of France, 1871–1914*. Cambridge, Mass., 1967:

Ramsey, Matthew. "History of a Profession, *Annales* Style: The Work of Jacques Léonard." *Journal of Social History* 17 (1983–84): 319–38.

―――. *Professional and Popular Medicine in France, 1770–1830*. Cambridge, 1988.

Rauh, Manfred. *Die Parlamentarisierung des Deutschen Reiches.* Düsseldorf, 1977.

Reardon, Bernard. *Liberalism and Tradition: Aspects of Catholic Thought in Nineteenth-Century France.* Cambridge, 1975.

Rein, Gustav Adolf. *Die Revolution in der Politik Bismarcks.* Göttingen, 1957.

Rémond, René. *Le XIXe siècle, 1815–1914.* Paris, 1974.

Riemenschneider, Rainer. *Dezentralisation und Regionalismus in Frankreich um die Mitte des 19. Jahrhunderts.* Bonn, 1985.

Rist, Édouard. *La tuberculose.* 3d ed. Paris, 1954.

Ritter, Gerhard A. "Entstehung und Entwicklung des Sozialstaates in vergleichender Perspektive." *Historische Zeitschrift* 243 (1986): 1–90.

———. *Der Sozialstaat. Entstehung und Entwicklung im internationalen Vergleich.* Munich, 1989.

———. *Sozialversicherung in Deutschland und England. Entstehung und Grundzüge im Vergleich.* Munich, 1983.

Rosanvallon, Pierre. *La crise de l'état-providence.* Paris, 1981.

Roth, Guenther. *The Social Democrats in Imperial Germany: A Study in Working-Class Isolation and National Integration.* Totowa, N.J., 1963.

Rothney, John. *Bonapartism after Sedan.* Ithaca, N.Y., 1969.

Rougerie, Jacques. *Procès des communards.* Paris, 1964.

Roux, Georges. *Thiers.* Paris, 1948.

Ruggiero, Guido de. *The History of European Liberalism.* Cambridge, Mass., 1948.

Sachsse, Christoph. *Mütterlichkeit als Beruf. Sozialarbeit, Sozialreform und Frauenbewegung 1871–1929.* Frankfurt, 1986.

Sachsse, Christoph, and Florian Tennstedt. *Geschichte der Armenfürsorge in Deutschland. Bd. 2: Fürsorge und Wohlfahrtspflege 1871–1929.* Stuttgart, 1988.

Schnapper, Bernard. *Le remplacement militaire en France: Quelques aspects politiques, économiques et sociaux du recrutement au XIXe siècle.* Paris, 1968.

Seager, Frederic H. *The Boulanger Affair: Political Crossroads of France, 1886–1889.* Ithaca, N.Y., 1969.

Segalen, Martine. *Mari et femme dans la société paysanne.* Paris, 1980.

Sell, Friedrich. *Die Tragödie des deutschen Liberalismus.* Stuttgart, 1953.

Serman, William. *La commune de Paris.* Paris, 1986.

Sewell, William H., Jr. *Work and Revolution in France: The Language of Labor from the Old Regime to 1848.* Cambridge, 1980.

Shapiro, Ann Louise. *Housing the Poor of Paris.* Madison, Wis., 1985.

Sheehan, James J. *German Liberalism in the Nineteenth Century.* Chicago, 1978.

_____. "Some Reflections on Liberalism in Comparative Perspective." In *Deutschland und der Westen*, edited by Henning Köhler, pp. 44–58. Berlin, 1984.

Shorter, Edward, and Charles Tilly. *Strikes in France, 1830–1968*. Cambridge, 1974.

Sidorsky, David, ed. *The Liberal Tradition in European Thought*. New York, 1970.

Smith, F. B. *The Retreat of Tuberculosis, 1850–1950*. London, 1988.

Sorlin, Pierre. *La société française*. 2 vols. Paris, 1971.

_____. *Waldeck-Rousseau*. Paris, 1966.

Sowerwine, Charles. *Sisters or Citizens: Women and Socialism in France since 1876*. Cambridge, 1982.

Spengler, Joseph J. *France Faces Depopulation*. 3d ed. Durham, N.C., 1979.

Spree, Reinhard. *Soziale Ungleichheit vor Krankheit und Tod. Zur Sozialgeschichte des Gesundheitsbereichs im Deutschen Kaiserreich*. Göttingen, 1981.

Stearns, Peter N. *Lives of Labour: Working in a Maturing Industrial Society*. London, 1975.

_____. *Paths to Authority: The Middle Class and the Industrial Labor Force in France 1820–48*. Urbana, Ill., 1978.

Sternhell, Zeev. *La droite révolutionnaire, 1885–1914. Les origines française du fascisme*. Paris, 1978.

Stewart, Mary Lynn. *Women, Work, and the French State: Labour Protection and Social Patriarchy, 1879–1919*. Kingston, Ont., 1989.

Stone, Judith F. "The Radicals and the Interventionist State: Attitudes, Ambiguities and Transformations, 1880–1910." *French History* 2 (1988): 173–86.

_____. *The Search for Social Peace: Reform Legislation in France 1890–1914*. Albany, N.Y., 1985.

Stürmer, Michael. *Das ruhelose Reich. Deutschland 1866–1918*. Berlin, 1983.

Suleiman, Ezra N. *Private Power and Centralization in France: The Notaries and the State*. Princeton, 1987.

Sussman, George D. "The End of the Wet-Nursing Business in France, 1874–1914." *Journal of Family History* 2 (1977): 237–58.

_____. "The Glut of Doctors in Mid-Nineteenth Century France." *Comparative Studies in Society and History* 19 (1977): 287–304.

_____. *Selling Mother's Milk: The Wet-Nursing Business in France, 1715–1914*. Urbana, Ill., 1982.

Sutcliffe, Anthony. *The Autumn of Central Paris: The Defeat of Town Planning*. London, 1970.

Swart, K. W. *The Sense of Decadence in Nineteenth-Century France*. The Hague, 1964.

Szreter, Simon. "The Importance of Social Intervention in Britain's Mortality Decline *c*. 1850–1919: A Reinterpretation of the Role of Public Health." *Social History of Medicine* 1 (1988): 1–37.

Tenfelde, Klaus, and Heinrich Volkmann, eds. *Streik. Zur Geschichte des Arbeitskampfes in Deutschland während der Industrialisierung*. Munich, 1981.

Tennstedt, Florian. *Geschichte der Selbstverwaltung in der Krankenversicherung*. Bonn, 1977.

———. *Sozialgeschichte der Sozialpolitik in Deutschland*. Göttingen, 1981.

———. "Sozialgeschichte der Sozialversicherung." In *Handbuch der Sozialmedizin*, edited by M. Blohmke et al., 3 vols., 3:385–492. Stuttgart, 1975–77.

———. *Vom Proleten zum Industriearbeiter. Arbeiterbewegung und Sozialpolitik in Deutschland 1800 bis 1914*. Cologne, 1983.

Tilly, Charles. *The Contentious French*. Cambridge, Mass., 1986.

Tilly, Charles, et al. *The Rebellious Century, 1830–1930*. Cambridge, Mass., 1975.

Vallin, Jacques, and France Meslé. *Les causes de décès en France de 1925 à 1978*. Paris, 1988.

Van de Welle, Etienne. *The Female Population of France in the Nineteenth Century*. Princeton, 1974.

Wahl, Alfred. *L'option et l'émigration des Alsatiens-Lorrains (1871–1872)*. Paris, 1974.

Watson, David R. *Georges Clemenceau: A Political Biography*. London, 1974.

———. "The Nationalist Movement in Paris, 1900–6." In *The Right in France, 1890–1919: Three Studies*, edited by David Shapiro, pp. 49–84. Carbondale, Ill., 1962.

———. "The Politics of Educational Reform in France during the Third Republic, 1900–1940." *Past and Present* 34 (1966): 81–99.

Weber, Eugen. *France: Fin de Siècle*. Cambridge, Mass., 1986.

———. *The Nationalist Revival in France, 1905–1914*. Berkeley, 1959.

———. *Peasants into Frenchmen: The Modernization of Rural France, 1870–1914*. Stanford, 1976.

Wehler, Hans-Ulrich. *Das deutsche Kaiserreich 1871–1918*. 5th ed. Göttingen, 1983.

———. "Wie 'bürgerlich' war das Deutsche Kaiserreich?" In *Bürgertum und Bürgerlichkeit im 19. Jahrhundert*, edited by Jürgen Kocka, pp. 243–80. Göttingen, 1987.

Weiss, John H. "Origins of the French Welfare State: Poor Relief in the Third Republic, 1871–1914." *French Historical Studies* 13 (1983): 47–78.

Weisz, George. *The Emergence of Modern Universities in France, 1863–1914.* Princeton, 1983.

Willard, Claude. *Le mouvement socialiste en France, 1893–1905: les guesdistes.* Paris, 1965.

Winkler, Heinrich August. *Preussischer Liberalismus und deutscher Nationalstaat.* Tübingen, 1964.

Witt, Peter-Christian. *Die Finanzpolitik des Deutschen Reiches von 1903 bis 1913. Eine Studie zur Innenpolitik des Wilhelminischen Deutschlands.* Lübeck, 1970.

Wylie, Laurence. *Village in the Vaucluse.* 3d ed. Cambridge, Mass., 1974.

Zeldin, Theodore. *France 1848–1945.* 2 vols. Oxford, 1973–77.

———. *The French.* New York, 1982.

Index